Researching and Understanding Educational Networks

Books are +

The idea of networks is ubiquitous. The images and metaphors of electronic networks in particular permeate our thinking, including that in education.

Researching and Understanding Educational Networks extends the discussion of educational networks in a unique and novel way by relating it to teacher learning. Following an investigation of teacher and school networks in the United Kingdom, the authors found that theoretical perspectives taken from existing work on such networks were not adequate to provide an understanding of their potential, or to provide the basis for researching them in ways that reflected the variety of teacher experience.

This book presents analyses of the problems with existing theories of teacher learning, which for example draw on ideas of 'communities of practice', and explores what network theories can be brought to the problem of how teachers and schools create and share new knowledge about practice. Innovative networking theories discussed include:

* social network analysis;
* social capital theories;
* actor-network theory;
* investigations of electronic networks, including computer-mediated conferencing;
* how people learn at events such as conferences.

Researching and Understanding Educational Networks explores a new application of network theories derived from quite different fields of work, and extends it by being concerned about networks beyond organisations, and specifically about educational networks. Their application to educational networks, and to teacher learning in particular, is a unique contribution of the book. This enables it to be of interest to both researchers and those studying for higher degrees, including students who are professionals working in schools.

Robert McCormick is Professor of Education at the Department of Education, The Open University.

Alison Fox is at the Department of Education, University of Cambridge.

Patrick Carmichael is Professor of Educational Research at the Faculty of Education, Community and Leisure, Liverpool John Moores University.

Richard Procter is a research student at the Institute of Education, London.

LIVERPOOL JMU LIBRARY

3 1111 01333 7017

New Perspectives on Learning and Instruction

Editor in Chief – Mien Segers (Leiden University and Maastricht University – The Netherlands)
Assistant Editor – Isabel Raemdonck (Leiden University – The Netherlands)

Editorial Board Members
David Gijbels (University of Antwerp – Belgium)
Sanna Järvelä (University of Oulu – Finland)
Margareta Limon (Autonoma University of Madrid – Spain)
Karen Littleton (The Open University – UK)
Wolff-Michael Roth (University of Victoria – Canada)

Advisory Board Members
Costas Constantinou (University of Cyprus – Cyprus)
Veléria Csépe (Hungarian Academy of Sciences – Hungary)
Sibel Erduran (University of Bristol – UK)
Sylvia Rojas-Drummond (UNAM – Mexico)
Martin Valcke (Ghent University – Belgium)
Lieven Verschaffel (Katholieke Universiteit Leuven – Belgium)
Kate Wall (Newcastle University – UK)
Marold Wosnitza (Murdoch University – Australia)

New Perspectives on Learning and Instruction is published by Routledge in conjunction with EARLI (European Association for Research on Learning and Instruction). This series publishes cutting-edge international research focusing on all aspects of learning and instruction in both traditional and non-traditional educational settings. Titles published within the series take a broad and innovative approach to topical areas of research, are written by leading international researchers and are aimed at a research and postgraduate student audience.

Also available:

Transformation of Knowledge through Classroom Interaction
Edited by Baruch Schwarz, Tommy Dreyfus and Rina Hershkowitz

Contemporary Perspectives on Reading and Spelling
Edited by Clare Wood and Vincent Connelly

Forthcoming titles:

Use of Representations in Reasoning and Problem Solving
Edited by Lieven Verschaffel, Erik De Corte, Ton de Jong and Jan Elen

Learning across Sites: New Tools, Infrastructures and Practices
Edited by Sten Ludvigsen, Andreas Lund, Ingvill Rasmussen and Roger Säljö

Researching and Understanding Educational Networks

Robert McCormick,
Alison Fox, Patrick Carmichael
and Richard Procter

Routledge
Taylor & Francis Group

LONDON AND NEW YORK

First published 2011
by Routledge
2 Park Square, Milton Park, Abingdon, Oxon, OX14 4RN

Simultaneously published in the USA and Canada
by Routledge
270 Madison Avenue, New York, NY 10016

Routledge is an imprint of the Taylor & Francis Group, an informa business

© 2011 Robert McCormick, Alison Fox, Patrick Carmichael and Richard Procter

Typeset in Galliard
by Keystroke, Tettenhall, Wolverhampton
Printed and bound in Great Britain
by CPI Antony Rowe, Chippenham, Wiltshire

All rights reserved. No part of this book may be reprinted or reproduced or
utilised in any form or by any electronic, mechanical, or other means, now
known or hereafter invented, including photocopying and recording, or in any
information storage or retrieval system, without permission in writing from the
publishers.

British Library Cataloguing in Publication Data
A catalogue record for this book is available from the British Library

Library of Congress Cataloging-in-Publication Data
Researching and understanding educational networks / by Robert McCormick
... [et al.] – 1st ed.
p. cm.
1. Teachers–In-service training. 2. Educational change. 3. Effective teaching.
I. McCormick, Robert.
LB1731.R465 2011
370–dc22
2009053352

ISBN13: 978–0–415–49482–3 (hbk)
ISBN13: 978–0–415–49483–0 (pbk)
ISBN13: 978–0–203–84917–0 (ebk)

Contents

Figures

Tables

Preface

In the twenty-first century, what could be more important than networks? Our society is awash with technology that enables us to communicate, to join all kinds of networks and, in the contemporary phrase, to engage in 'social networking'. Such is the power of this technological influence that it is unsurprising that our thinking about networks is permeated with images and metaphors from electronic networks. This orientation may equally influence thinking about education, whether done by students or by teachers. Our concern is with teacher education, in particular their learning of new practices. Ideas of collaboration of teachers in improving classroom practice have a long history, and to this has been brought 'network thinking'. Thus, images of software developers spread across the globe, sharing computer program construction in electronic networks, is an inviting one to bring to thinking about how teachers could work together and share practice. As researchers, we were influenced by these ideas and had in our various ways been working with groups of teachers in what had become known as 'electronic communities', particularly in computer-mediated conferencing. We had seen the power of teachers being able to exchange ideas and practices through this means. But this book is not about such networks, though we do discuss them.

Our interest in networks took shape in work on the Learning How to Learn (LHTL) project (2001–5), which was concerned with how schools learn about and develop classroom and school practices associated with assessment for learning (AfL). We were responsible for part of this large project that investigated how schools shared knowledge about, and the practices of, AfL. Other parts of the project looked *inside* the schools; our concern was with what happened *between* schools. (We will give details about the project later.) Our previous interest in electronic networks, and those of our colleagues in the project, led us to frame research questions focused on these networks. We felt well qualified to investigate them. However, as we conducted our initial fieldwork with those in schools, we realised that such electronic networks were unlikely to be very significant to teachers and schools. We therefore needed different ways of thinking about links across schools. So, we investigated more traditional 'community of practice' ideas. At that time, Hakkarainen *et al.* (2004) were finalising their book and we were privileged to have sight of the manuscript. This opened up a whole area of work that we thought could be used not just in commercial innovative knowledge communities but in education, and in particular with teachers.[1] It prompted and enabled a rethinking of our understanding of networks. As our fieldwork evolved, so did our understanding of the potential of network theory, and with it our analysis of the data we collected.

Teacher learning was the driving force for all our concerns, and this was the lens through which we interpreted network theory.

This book examines the way our thinking developed and the use of network theory to make sense of how AfL practices were, or could be, shared by schools involved in the LHTL project. We will present data from this project on the educational networks involved. But we will also explore different kinds of theory, network and otherwise, that give different perspectives on such data. Subsequent to the LHTL project we have all conducted projects that enabled us to investigate networks in other ways, and we will also use these.

The book is aimed at helping those who would like to conduct research on educational networks, particularly networks associated with schools. Where we were not able to conduct specific kinds of apparently productive approaches, we give some ideas on them, in an effort to help those who will extend work in this field. It has been a rewarding journey, one which we hope you will share.

Inevitably, there is much we have to learn, particularly in a field that has in recent years expanded and developed in relation to education.

Acknowledgements

We would particularly like to acknowledge the Learning How to Learn project, which gave birth to so many of our ideas, and the people who were part of the research team, with whom it was such a privilege to work. They did much to help us develop ideas and ways of working. The 'Learning How to Learn – in classrooms, schools and networks' project was funded by the UK Economic and Social Research Council as part of the Teaching and Learning Research Programme (see www.tlrp.org). The project (ref.: L139 25 1020) was directed by Mary James (then at the Institute of Education, London) and co-directed by Robert McCormick (The Open University). Other members of the team were Patrick Carmichael, Mary-Jane Drummond, John MacBeath, David Pedder, Richard Procter and Sue Swaffield (all then at the University of Cambridge), Paul Black and Bethan Marshall (King's College London), Leslie Honour (University of Reading) and Alison Fox (then at The Open University). Past members of the team were Geoff Southworth, Colin Conner, David Frost, Dylan Wiliam and Joanna Swann. Further details are available at www.learntolearn.ac.uk.

Among the many people who worked on the project we would like to pick out Dave Ebbutt, who, as part of the work for LHTL, collected some of our network data.

Although the LHTL project team has already thanked the many schools and teachers who were our 'respondents' in its publications, we feel it is important to reiterate the acknowledgement. So, we thank the forty project schools and ten trials schools with which we worked, and the hundreds of teachers and pupils who have contributed in some way. Without them there would have been no study. We were constantly amazed at how willing they were to give of their time and expertise at a pressured period in educational history, including putting up with our requests to draw and elaborate maps of their professional relationships. We cannot name them for confidentiality reasons, but we are indebted to them and have learned so much from them. There is a sense in which we have not 'discovered' new knowledge but have been privileged to find out about, interpret and communicate the knowledge that teachers themselves create.

Like all researchers, we drew upon the 'unseen' services of those who staff the libraries of the institutions where we have worked: the University of Cambridge and The Open University. We are appreciative of those in The Open University library document delivery section, particularly Debbie Snook, who not only processed so many requests but also searched for those not available from conventional library sources.

We would also like to thank Martyn Hammersley, Alan Daly and Cheri Logan for reading specific chapters to help us express our ideas comprehensibly and accurately. We also express our particular gratitude to Mary James and Tuire Palonen for reading the whole manuscript, and for doing so with such helpful comments and grace. Any failings in the book are in spite of all these colleagues' best efforts and are entirely our responsibility.

Thanks are appropriate to the National College for Leadership of Schools and Children's Services (formerly the National College for School Leadership, the name we use throughout) for Figure 8.2 (the image is taken from the 'Leading from Practice – Learning about Leading' Research Associates event held at the National College for School Leadership on 16 March 2007). Thanks also to etc.venues for Figure 8.3.

Finally, we would like to thank all our families, who put up with so much during the time writing the book. Without their support we would not have completed this task.

Abbreviations

AAIA	Association of Achievement and Improvement through Assessment
AfL	assessment for learning
AIDS	acquired immune deficiency syndrome
AM	acquisition metaphor
ANT	actor-network theory
AST	advanced skills teacher
AT	activity theory
Becta	British Educational Communications and Technology Agency
CARN	Classroom Action Research Network
CPD	continuing professional development
DCSF	Department for Children, Schools and Families
DfES	Department for Education and Skills
DHT	deputy headteacher
FCL	fostering communities of learning
HEI	higher education institution
HT	headteacher
ICT	information and communications technology
INSET	in-service training
IU	Innovation Unit (within the Department for Education and Skills)
KMOFAP	King's Medway and Oxfordshire Formative Assessment Project
LA	local authority
LEA	local education authority (the original name for the part of a local authority concerned with education)
LHTL	Learning How to Learn
NAHT	National Association of Head Teachers
NCSL	National College for School Leadership (now the National College for Leadership of Schools and Children's Services)
NLC	networked learning community
NWP	National Writing Project
OECD	Organisation for Economic Co-operation and Development
PLC	professional learning community
PM	participation metaphor
QCA	Qualifications and Curriculum Authority
SATs	Standard Assessment Tests
SEN	special educational needs

SENCO	special educational needs co-ordinator
SMT	senior management team
SNA	social network analysis
SSAT	Specialist Schools and Academies Trust
TDA	Training and Development Agency for Schools
TLRP	Teaching and Learning Research Programme
TN	teacher network
VEAZ	virtual education action zone

Chapter 1

Educational policy and technological contexts

Introduction

The Learning How to Learn project sought to understand how teachers and their students could develop 'learning how to learn' practices (James *et al.* 2007). This was set in a world where 'knowledge economies' require lifelong learning and the need to respond to social and economic change. For those in schools, it asks that they focus students' attention on their learning, and hence the popular term 'learning to learn'. For teachers and those who support them, this orientation requires a new focus on their pedagogy. They too have to learn. But in the Learning How to Learn (LHTL) project we went one step further and wanted them too 'to learn how to learn'. This was not a research project taking a passive view of its subjects, but had an agenda both to change practice and to investigate the issues that this raised. Any such undertaking brings with it a legacy of attempts to deal with teacher learning, on both intellectual and policy fronts. In this chapter we will attempt to explore these contextual factors.

First we will look at the specific change we wanted to bring about, namely 'assessment for learning', an idea that at its core tries to focus students and their teachers on learning. As our concern is with teacher learning, we will explore some of the antecedents for our particular interest within the project in networks within education, some of which use different conceptions, most notably 'professional communities'. Some of these antecedents have had ambitious visions of the role of networks of schools and teachers, and we will explore one in particular that saw them leading as it were to an 'epidemic' in education, such could be the impact of these networks. Whatever academics do in universities or through policy think tanks, in the end the education system needs to find ways of enabling *all* institutions to engage in the visions or theoretical models of how networks can improve what is done in schools and colleges. We explore some of these, not with a view to seeing if they were effective, but to understand just what constituted networks and their processes.

All of these are the starting point of the LHTL project's interest in networks. But we brought one more, the role of technology. Although few of the antecedents of educational networks had any concern for technologies, in our contemporary society they are ubiquitous. Our personal interests and skills drew on an understanding of electronic networks, and this was reflected in the research questions the project set itself. All these considerations set the scene for the rest of the book, and in particular for the need to understand the nature of networks and of the teaching learning they seek to enable. First, we return to the specifics of the project and what we were trying to investigate.

Background

The LHTL project started from the base provided by assessment for learning practices with which many of the research team had been involved: research on specific aspects of assessment for learning (AfL) (reviewed by Black and Wiliam 1998a), or projects that worked intensively with teachers (e.g. the King's Medway and Oxfordshire Formative Assessment Project [KMOFAP]; Black *et al.* 2003). In the KMOFAP, secondary school teachers and university academics developed new practices of AfL (also referred to as formative assessment) over a long period of time and involving some twenty days of support through group meetings. The LHTL project wanted to see how ordinary schools could build on this previous work and develop it into methods of learning how to learn, without the kind of intensive support provided in KMOFAP. The teachers had to learn new classroom methods in situations for which no such methods existed for their specific teaching situation. Thus, a technique such as questioning used by secondary science teachers had to be developed by those in the early years of schooling for, say, literacy work.

The LHTL project was therefore concerned with some basic questions about professional knowledge creation, and took as its starting points these key research aims (among several):

- to investigate what characterises the school in which teachers successfully create and manage the knowledge and skills of learning how to learn;
- to investigate how educational networks can support the creation, management and transfer of knowledge and skills of learning how to learn.

The project built upon a wealth of evidence about the importance of teachers and schools taking more responsibility for their professional development and their practice, and about how development should take place. Such an approach has a long history with school-based curriculum development in the 1960s and 1970s (Skilbeck 1976) and, perhaps more profoundly, the 'teacher as researcher' ideas of the 1970s (Stenhouse 1975). Stenhouse, in particular, saw the creation of professional knowledge as the fundamental task of the teacher, who would investigate his or her classroom and build a professional understanding of practice. These early approaches took classroom-based inquiry as an essential element of the development of professional practice.[1] This approach was updated in the 1990s as a view of the teaching profession where a 'new professionalism' was moving away from individual teacher development to institutional development, and a collaborative culture was developing (Hargreaves 1994). Another strand included critiques of educational research, and here David Hargreaves (1996) saw teachers taking more control over the research agenda and with less of a division between researchers and teachers in the production of evidence as the basis for professional practice. Hargreaves (1999) developed this further through his concept of the 'knowledge-creating school', where he outlined four elements of such schools: audits of professional working knowledge, management of the process of creating new knowledge, validating the professional knowledge created and dissemination of the created professional knowledge. The first (audit), second (management) and fourth (dissemination) are of particular interest to the focus of this book and we will examine them later in the chapter.

Although these initiatives appeared to be the views of academics, they have found their way into policy. In England, school-based continuing professional development (CPD) was advocated by the government in 2000, with a key principle being that 'effective teachers should take ownership and give high priority to professional development, and schools and teachers should share responsibility and commitment for development supported by Government' (DfEE 2000: 3).

This policy document also talks of work-based learning, where teachers are to see their development as part of their work in school.[2] This was taken up by the Teacher Training Agency (later to be renamed the Training and Development Agency for Schools [TDA]) in its policy statement when it took on responsibility for CPD (TTA 2005). More recently, it commissioned research to ascertain the 'state of the nation' (England), premised on the idea that schools should be at the centre of determining their own professional development (Pedder et al. 2008).

The above are all based in the United Kingdom, but internationally the professional development literature also reflects this tradition, as is evident in the review by Wilson and Berne (1999). They identified a number of central features of such professional development: teacher education situated in the classroom (school based and embedded in work); collaboration among teachers; focused on student learning; teachers in control of their professional development. However, they concluded that many of these features (and others they identified from the literature) were based on beliefs, unsupported by empirical evidence. In considering in detail a number of initiatives where the focus was on subject matter, student learning and teaching practices, Wilson and Berne concluded that common themes were ideas of communities of learners (teachers as learners) and teachers' interaction with one another. Indeed, all the examples involved communities of teachers being set up to discuss their classroom practice. (Some of the examples they considered included teacher networks and we will consider these in the next section, 'Antecedents'.) Since this early review there has been an accumulation of empirical evidence about what is effective CPD, though not all of it can be related strongly to student learning outcomes. (For example, Cordingley et al. [2005a, b] show the effectiveness of teachers' collaboration in terms of student outcomes; see also Borko [2004] for more general US evidence on CPD.) Looking at a number of major studies concentrating on England, some of which drew on an international literature, McCormick et al. (2008) indicated that there is strong evidence for the effectiveness of the following CPD activities: coaching and mentoring, networks, observation and inquiry.[3] Some of these activities are central to the collaboration that forms the strongest strand in professional development and learning.

In a recent international text on CPD, similar themes come through, but with a recognition of a performance orientation being required of teachers from governments (Day and Sachs 2004). In the same volume as the contribution by Day and Sachs, Bolam and McMahon (2004: 41) characterise worldwide changes in CPD policy and practice that affects teacher learning as being based on a model that included 'self-developing, reflective teachers, in self-managed schools with devolved funding . . . [with] professional development programmes aimed at meeting an appropriate balance of individual teacher, school and national needs and priorities'. However, they recognise that there is a tendency for the agenda for professional development to be set nationally. They also say that 'a new form of professionalism is emerging in which teachers work more closely and collaboratively with colleagues, students and parents, linking teacher and school development' (ibid.: 47). In concluding and looking forward to what is needed by way of research, they acknowledge that there is little evidence of the impact of research on CPD's policy and practice. State-of-the-nation research for England (Pedder *et al.* 2008) indicates that many of the features of CPD discussed above and by Bolam and McMahon (2004) are still absent from schools: teachers mainly experience passive forms of CPD, rather than active ones, and most teachers' approaches to CPD tend not to be collaborative, nor clearly contextualised in classroom practice (even though they and their school leaders value these features).

Day and Sachs (2004) draw out school-based CPD, partnerships and teacher and school networks as the strategies for CPD that they see as contributing to improving teacher performance and student learning. We will consider later some of the 'current' networks that are in the international handbook (edited by Day and Sachs), but first let us trace some of the earlier work on this. Wilson and Berne (1999) consider a number of teacher networks, in particular drawing on the earlier work of Lieberman and Grolnick (1996), which have a strong theme of community at their heart. We shall shortly argue that in many of these approaches to networks, the focus is actually on communities, and that, although these are important for knowledge creation, they often fail to address the wider network aspects and in particular the sharing of knowledge with those who are not involved in creating it. Wilson and Berne note that there is a tension in balancing insider and outsider (to the community) knowledge and expertise and, focusing on networks as an organisational entity, they tend to see a network as a means of the service delivery of CPD rather than as a *form* of CPD. Others see the formation and use of networks as important in themselves. We first want to examine the antecedents to our concern for networks, as they indicate to us both the strengths and the limitations of what is an almost exclusive concern in the literature with teacher communities. These communities are a powerful and necessary part of the creation and sharing of teacher knowledge, but we shall argue that this exclusive concern has prevented researchers from examining what networks more broadly conceived have to offer; indeed, they have simply redefined networks as communities.

Antecedents

In this section we will examine a number of initiatives that are labelled as 'networks', or are related to them, and indicate how these have been perceived and implemented. These initiatives have also formed the way networks have been interpreted in both academic research and policy. In particular, we will consider the UK Classroom Action Research Network (CARN),[4] US networks (for example, as indicated by Lieberman and Grolnick 1996), professional learning communities and an initiative that advocated networks of schools in the United Kingdom (Hargreaves 2003a). All of these, apart from the last-named initiative, are based on universities working with teachers and/or schools. In the next section we will look at how some of these found their way into policy through the initiative of government (or its agencies).

The Classroom Action Research Network

Stenhouse (1975) advocated that teachers should be researchers and render problematic their own classroom practice so that inquiry into it can reveal new professional knowledge about that practice, and lead to improvement. This started a whole genre of work with the 'teacher-as-researcher' that also incorporated action research.[5] These ideas led John Elliott to his work in 1975 on the Ford Teaching Project, which in turn led to the establishment of the Classroom Action Research Network (CARN). This network was founded to bring together teachers who had been carrying out research in their own classrooms, often as a result of their work on higher degree programmes, initially centred at the University of East Anglia and Cambridge Institute of Education; others have carried on this work. In the early 1990s the network changed its name to the Collaborative Action Research Network and has continued to hold annual conferences, which have become international in their venues.[6] It regularly published the work of teachers in their classrooms through CARN Bulletins and in 1993 it established an international journal, *Educational Action Research*. This extended the range of work reported, which in any case had always included writings about theory and research methods by teacher educators and educationists. The network is international with regional groups in a number of countries, and a co-ordinating group. There can be no doubt that the work produced was an effective form of knowledge creation, and that the network enabled some element of sharing, though this latter aspect was not itself subject to investigation.[7] This network started a strong tradition of action research, which seems to be the thrust of the continuing discussion in the journal, and indeed is how Somekh and Zeichner (2009) reflect on the origins of this work in a recent issue. Somekh (2009) has written a history of CARN using activity theory as a basis for analysis, rather than a network analysis, although she describes it as a network, not an organisation. Its role as a collaborative community is a strong element of Somekh's account and it has extended the community to include not just those in education but practitioners in other fields, along with students, parents and their communities. The CARN website lists 'networking' as taking place:

- through the sharing of accounts of action research, in bulletins, on the CARN website, in *Educational Action Research* and through other CARN publications;
- through attentive personal encouragement and critical feedback;
- through engaging with CARN colleagues at steering group meetings, regional events and at the CARN annual conference.

Somekh's focus is on the form of educational inquiry (action research), rather than how the network operates to enable sharing of knowledge.[8]

US networks

Networks have a long history in the United States, according to Lieberman and Grolnick (1996), starting with work by Parker in 1977, who considered the following features of networks:

- a strong sense of commitment to the innovation;
- a sense of shared purpose;
- a mixture of information sharing and psychological support;
- an effect facilitator;
- voluntary participation and equal treatment (Parker 1977: 25; cited in Lieberman and Grolnick 1996: 9).

Parker thought that members should 'have a sense of being part of a special group or movement' (Lieberman and Grolnick 1996: 9). Lieberman and Grolnick reviewed sixteen networks and found five organisational themes, one of which was 'building collaboration, consensus and commitment'. Lieberman and Grolnick use the idea of the network as a professional community, which implies that teachers form strong links with each other, which they build up over time as trust develops. They also had a theme of 'activities and relationships as important building blocks', and in discussing this they cite Granovetter (1973). He argues that links between people in a network should not just be strong ones, born out of collaborative relationships, but should also include weak links that enable knowledge outside the strongly linked group to be included.[9] Lieberman and Grolnick, on the other hand, use Granovetter's work as support for collaboration. (The significance of this will become evident shortly.) In a later article, Lieberman (2000: 43) indicates that networks provide an *organisational structure* (independent of, yet attached to, schools or universities).[10] Indeed, she refers to a network as an entity: 'networks have their own . . .' (ibid.: 43). Lieberman and Grolnick also had an interest in seeing these networks as a reform movement for the whole education system, through teacher development. Thus, the two strong features of this view of networks is that they are based on collaboration and have a particular organisational form across schools: they even talk of them as 'coalitions or partnerships' (Lieberman and Grolnick 1996: 41), which could be seen to detract from the idea of labelling them as networks.

Elsewhere, Lieberman and colleagues refer to the local and national networks of the National Writing Project (NWP), a particular network organisation (Lieberman and Wood 2004), although, as we shall see in the next section, they talk of this NWP in terms of a community (Lieberman and Miller 2008a). Evidently they see 'network' as some kind of metaphor, but it is not clear that it is one that would be associated with its metaphorical use elsewhere, as will become clear in this and the next chapter. We will return to Lieberman's influence on networked learning communities in England, but it appears that her interest in the community element of networks has developed as a more potent metaphor. In an account of NWP, in a book devoted to networks across a number of domains of life (McCarthy *et al.* 2004), Lieberman and Wood (2004) set out to untangle the links between networks, professional communities and teacher learning, which would help to clarify the confusions that seem to exist, certainly between networks and communities; this clarification is not forthcoming. David Hargreaves (2004) examines this account and takes them to task, first for not being able to provide hard evidence of the effectiveness of the NWP in terms of student learning (e.g. from outcome data such as tests), but second, and more importantly for our discussion, in terms of the structure and culture of networks. He questions what structures the NWP has and, if there are networks organised locally and linked nationally, what the local networks are like and how they vary across different types of localities. Hargreaves argues that the account given by Lieberman and Wood (2004) does not answer these types of questions, echoing our questions about the role of weak ties in the national networks and the strong ones in the local network. He concludes that the structures of the networks are unclear, though their culture is more visible, which he sees in terms of the social capital that they create, which leads to trust. Hargreaves asks, however, what different ways might exist for producing this social capital, besides those established for 'writing' (e.g. in other subject areas).

Similarly, he wonders if peer-to-peer approaches (the NWP model) are better than expert-to-novice approaches (as advocated by Lave and Wenger 1991). He goes on to question too whether Lieberman and Wood could have benefited from the growth in understanding of knowledge creation and transfer that has come about over the period of reporting on the NWP, and how networks relate to this. Finally, he wonders whether information and communications technology (ICT) has a role in such networks. In many of these questions and this critique he has in mind his own ideas on these subjects, which he had outlined a year earlier (Hargreaves 2003a). We will come to these shortly.

We are left wondering about just what view of networks and networking activity Lieberman and her various colleagues have when they give accounts of these US networks; this view is not helped by their use of 'community' in relation to them, to the extent that they are also found making similar arguments when discussing professional learning communities (e.g. Lieberman and Miller 2008a; Lieberman 2007), our next topic.

Professional learning communities

Work on professional learning communities (PLCs) has had its strongest development in the United States, although Stoll *et al.* (2006) trace early developments from Dewey, Stenhouse and the 1970s school-based curriculum development movement, and extends these into ideas of the problem-solving and creative school in the late 1970s and to ideas of the self-reviewing and self-evaluating school in the 1980s.[11] In the United States the advocacy of PLCs has a strong concern for school reform and it has become part of the school improvement and effectiveness movement, with an international following. This can be seen in Stoll and Louis (2007a), as this work is a product of the International Congress of School Effectiveness and Improvement. Stoll *et al.* (2006: 223) draw on one of their sources to provide a definition of a PLC:

> [A PLC is one] in which the teachers in a school and its administrators continuously seek and share learning, and act on their learning. The goal of their actions is to enhance their effectiveness as professionals for the students' benefit; thus, this arrangement may also be termed communities of continuous inquiry and improvement.

It is clearly seen as focused on a school, as Bolam *et al.* (2005: iii)[12] make clear: 'An effective professional learning community has the capacity to promote and sustain the learning of all professionals in the school community with the collective purpose of enhancing pupil learning.' The concept of a PLC is of a community of learners based on the idea of collective learning with shared beliefs and understanding, interaction and participation, interdependence, concern for individual and minority interests, and meaningful relationships (Stoll *et al.* 2006: 225). The characteristics that are seen to make it effective include shared values and vision, collective responsibility, reflective professional inquiry (e.g. mutual observation), collaboration and the promotion of group, as well as individual, learning (ibid.: 227). In elaborating on collaboration, they say that it 'go[es] beyond superficial exchanges of help, support or assistance' (ibid.)

and thus, as we have seen already with regard to the US networks, focuses on strong links to others. Reflective inquiry is seen as 'tacit knowledge constantly [being] converted into shared knowledge through interaction' (ibid.), an important model that we will examine in Chapter 7.

Although there is an evident focus on the school as the learning community, views of PLCs also recognise the need to look beyond the school for sources of learning and ideas, and this is stressed through a consideration of the importance of interacting and drawing on external agents. The three features of this are the need for external support (e.g. for help with inquiry or reflection, critical friendship, or to develop collaborative processes); partnerships (e.g. with parents, district agencies or higher education institutions); and networks. The last-named category includes networks of schools that can encourage learning between as well as within schools, but also the use of new technologies related to the ideas of the networked society. Again reference is made to networked learning communities (NLCs), which Stoll *et al.* (2006) explicitly link to PLCs, saying they 'rest on similar assumptions about how teachers learn and change their practice' (ibid.: 242). In reviewing the literature on networks in relation to PLCs, they cite work that says that they are the same or share the same assumptions, in a way that implies they agree with their sources. Stoll *et al.* (2006) also refer to the early work of Lieberman and Grolnick (1996), but none of the latter's more recent work that informed NLCs (of which more later). In this whole discussion of networks, it is difficult to see just what the unique elements are of their external links or ways of working.

This idea of PLCs has apparently had a strong influence in England through the recent large research project Creating and Sustaining Effective Professional Learning Communities (Bolam *et al.* 2005), to which we have referred. The evidence from this project led to the adoption of PLCs by the Department for Children, Schools and Families (the current name for the government department responsible for education in England) in its Innovation Unit website.[13] (As we will argue later, it appears that PLCs have replaced the networks that were 'current' a few years earlier.) Andy Hargreaves (2007), in reviewing international evidence on the rise of PLCs, notes that they are spreading rapidly through the English-speaking world.

In an edited collection that takes stock of PLCs, with contributions by leading researchers, Stoll and Louis (2007a) reinforce the similar features of networks and PLCs. But they recognise a major challenge of the need to balance the cohesive internal ties in such a community with links to those outside the school, citing Granovetter (1973).[14] The collection does not contain an analysis of how other kinds of links work within the school or external to it and to the whole system. One contribution in Stoll and Louis (2007a) on NLCs argues that these communities need to extend to include other schools (Jackson and Temperley 2007), and another advocates the value of an international community of schools linked across England, Australia, New Zealand and Canada (Stoll *et al.* 2007). At the same time, it is recognised that PLCs, in the likes of secondary schools, may be at only the department level, with links across the school being more difficult (Stoll and Louis 2007b). There is almost a dismissal of 'networking' ties, including both weak and strong ties, by Jackson and Temperley (2006, 2007), which they contrast with 'networked learning'. This will be taken up in a later section entitled 'Educational policy and networks' (p. 16), where we deal with NLCs.

Indeed, we come almost full circle in combining the two conceptions (PLC and network) in such texts as Veugelers and O'Hair (2005a). In this text the series editors, in discussing network learning in their preface, argue that, building on evidence from PLCs, the enhancement of teacher learning through collaboration in PLCs leads to improved student learning:

> The same principles apply to professional learning communities in themselves – they grow stronger and become more vibrant when they are connected to other learning communities, rather than when they operate entirely alone. The best way to bring this about is through networks.
>
> (ibid.: ix)

Such networks are in effect networked PLCs, hence the term used in England, namely networked learning communities. As we will show later, the uniqueness of ideas on networks is continually conflated with that of communities of teachers, thus reducing the potential of NLCs to exhibit different aspects of their contribution to knowledge creation and sharing.

Besides this conflation, it is evident that there are a number of problems that are part of the idea of PLCs – in particular, when they are to be created in ordinary schools that are not in the privileged position of having extra resources or working in partnership with a higher education institution (HEI), as is the case in many of the initiatives discussed above. We have already discussed the stress on 'community' and the implied strong links that are required for the collaborative activities that are at the heart of any community. These are essential as part of knowledge creation, as we will show in Chapters 3 and 7. However, they are necessarily a difficult form to scale up to all schools and to sustain in any particular school.

PLCs: 'scaling up' and sustainability

'Scaling up' is not a straightforward concept, as there are a number of possible dimensions to it. First, scaling up can be *within* the school to involve all teachers (and other staff), and there is some discussion of this in the literature. For example, Stoll *et al.* 2006: 225, 227) consider the inclusion of support staff, and whether all departments in a secondary school might be equally strong communities. It appears that there is very little discussion in this PLC literature on the extent to which a school PLC is indeed school-wide, and the way in which this comes about. There is more discussion on scaling up *across* schools, and Lieberman and Miller (2008d) discuss this as a challenge that communities face; they show how scaling up occurs in two of the five studies they feature. In one study there is an expansion from six districts where PLCs exist, to thirty, with an issue of preserving a regional nature bounded geographically. But we get no feel for how these PLCs were operating; Lieberman and Miller say that at one point seventeen school–university learning communities met regularly, implying that though there may have been thirty, they were not all functioning. At no point are we given information on just how many teachers were involved, including the actual versus the potential number. They report that the introduction of a funded project reduced the amount of school–university collaboration and hence the communities reduced.

The second example of scaling up, the National Writing Project (NWP) (which in other sources has been described as 'arguably the single most successful professional development *network* in the USA' [Lieberman and Wood 2004: 66; emphasis added]), started in one site in 1974 and successfully spread to 195 sites in fifty US states, involving more than 2 million teachers and administrators (Lieberman and Miller 2008d: 36).[15] A site is based at a university and links schools in a particular area (Lieberman and Wood 2004), and, given the figures from Lieberman and Miller (2008d), would have on average 1,000 individuals involved. Just how many schools, or the number of teachers in each school that are involved, is unclear, as is what constitutes a particular PLC. However, most other accounts (e.g. Stoll and Louis 2007a; Lieberman and Miller 2008a) indicate that in only a few cases are all teachers involved in a school, or indeed in a district. We should of course have no expectation that all teachers or school staff could be involved, at least at any particular time, and it would seem reasonable and desirable, given the workloads of teachers, that they might be involved for only a period of time and perhaps on particular problems or pedagogic issues.

There is thus always a concern for sharing any insights produced by those involved to the larger population of staff, both within a school and beyond – exactly what forming *networks* of such communities involves. In their discussion of the model of formation and maturity, Lieberman and Miller (2008b: 13) say nothing about scaling up, inclusiveness or activity *outside* of the community. There is a discussion of how individuals and indeed communities have to 'go public'. Most of this is within the community. Where it does go outside, it is via publishing on the web, disseminating written texts and the involvement of community members in initial teacher training. While these are all useful and important elements of sharing the knowledge created by the PLCs, they are not apparently examined as part of the research, which has different interests. In particular, Lieberman and Miller bring to bear no 'network insights' to analyse the sharing process. It seems to us that there is more focus on knowledge creation than on knowledge sharing. Although models of making implicit knowledge explicit are acknowledged in PLCs (Stoll *et al.* 2006), this is not, for example, the only possible way of considering knowledge creation; in Chapter 7 we will examine views of 'creation' and 'sharing' and look at what processes are involved.

None of this is to say that those involved with PLCs are not concerned about external issues, as we have indicated, but there is an apparent inward-looking preoccupation even when considering these issues. For example, Lieberman and Miller (2008c: 22) recognise that 'inside teacher knowledge is not enough, even the best learning communities become stale when they are closed to outside knowledge'. They go on to indicate the importance of library and internet use, the reading of articles and outside sources. There are limited examples of moving outside of the immediate community: a project in which teachers in a group generated text for use by other communities (Lieberman and Miller 2008c: 23); two teachers who put video recordings of their classrooms on their personal websites (Mace 2008). These are related to some of the issues that concern us, namely how knowledge 'moves' from one site to another, but were not the central subject of the research on PLCs.

Sustainability is addressed by Stoll *et al.* (2006), although they say that there is insufficient empirical research on this, and cite evidence (unconnected with the PLCs as such) on changes in schools that led to a decline in the communities. They discuss the issue of funding, with the requirement to use existing resources rather than relying on special projects – just the situation we sought to address in LHTL. There is also an implication in much of the work that the role of universities is important in working with schools, again a mode that makes sustainability across all schools impractical. Stoll *et al.* (2006) argue that outside support is a factor of importance in creating, developing and sustaining PLCs. The issue is the extent to which this can be scaled up to all schools, especially when resources are tight and, as is the case currently, focused on the school (that is, not directly available to external agencies that might support schools). Lieberman and Wood (2003b) also address sustainability of the NWP networks, but apparently attribute this to the general conditions of the networks, as it is these conditions that they discuss. In their introduction they identify the creation of a 'third space' for teachers, where they can 'engage in genuine collaboration about serious classroom issues' (ibid.: 478). The nature of this 'third space' and the democratic principles of NWP 'rally teachers around a shared vision' (ibid.: 479). The site director is an important element, but this is seen mainly in terms of maintaining the principles of NWP, rather than specifically sustaining the sites. The challenges they examine do not include sustainability as such, though when they discuss them they acknowledge in passing the resources that universities bring (site directors have a fundraising role, again mentioned only in passing).

In summary, then, the PLCs and networks that we have examined seem to be difficult to distinguish. Both focus on community and its cohesion to support knowledge creation. Although the literature acknowledges external links, there is insufficient examination of their role in the community or in how sharing should take place. The next antecedent steps beyond this with a vision of networks that was encapsulated in a document entitled *Education Epidemic*.

Education Epidemic

Education Epidemic was a policy document by David Hargreaves (2003a), building on his earlier ideas of the role of the school and his view of the new professional and of how he saw educational research serving and being controlled by teachers. In particular, he draws upon his ideas on 'the knowledge-creating school' (Hargreaves 1999), where he saw knowledge creation as including many of the aspects we have discussed so far in the chapter in relation to schools as communities, including reflection, dialogue and inquiry, but he also started to hint at some of his later ideas on networks. The first element of the knowledge-creating school, auditing professional knowledge, is conducted through mapping, such that a 'system is devised to promote and support the school's internal networks' (ibid.: 125). This knowledge management Hargreaves relates to the realisation of the intellectual capital of teachers, which goes beyond that of individuals and groups but also includes the organisational capital embedded in the school's structures and culture.[16] In the knowledge-creation element of such schools he advocates that there should be a strong awareness of the external environment and a capacity to recognise, assimilate and exploit external knowledge, and to engage in partnerships, alliances and networks to further such work. Part of the knowledge-creation process involves the changing of tacit knowledge of teachers into explicit knowledge. Hargreaves draws on the work of Nonaka and Takeuchi (1995), who investigated industrial companies using a cyclic model of making tacit knowledge explicit at a variety of levels, an approach we will examine in Chapter 3. His third element of the knowledge-creating school is unique among the approaches we have examined so far in that Hargreaves is concerned with dissemination of professional knowledge. He draws upon ideas on networks that for him offer new models, including local and virtual networks for knowledge sharing. Indeed, he argued that '[n]etworks are the key to this different model of dissemination in which *all* schools can now be linked through ICT and so *all* can take part in the activities of professional knowledge creation, application and dissemination' (Hargreaves 1999: 139; emphasis in the original). Interestingly, and in contrast to the literature on PLCs, he emphasises 'all' schools. His view of networks rejects a centre–periphery model of dissemination, and he uses the metaphor of a 'web of inter-linked knowledge-creating schools' (ibid.: 140), although, as we shall see in Chapter 2, there are different interpretations of the web metaphor.

These ideas are developed more fully in *Education Epidemic* (Hargreaves 2003a), where he takes a systemic view and gives key ingredients for the reform of the education system. One such ingredient is the mobilisation of capital, something he had written on previously (Hargreaves 1999, 2001). In addition to the capacity to mobilise intellectual capital, he is concerned with social capital, which has cultural and structural elements:

> Culturally, social capital consists in the trust that exists between the school's members and its various stakeholders; structurally, social capital is the extent and quality of the networks among its members – between head and staff, staff and students, staff and parents – as well as the school's networks with external partners.
> (Hargreaves 2003a: 25)

Although he goes on to talk about the school as a community, he is clearly aware of additional ideas on networks that are evident in network theory (as we shall see in Chapter 2) – additional, that is, to those of the authors we examined in the previous sections. Further, he sees that organisational capital is required to make use of the intellectual and social capital of the school.

Hargreaves argues that innovation requires transformation, and he details five transformations: creating the right climate, disciplining innovation, devising and implementing a lateral strategy, using ICT laterally and making a learning system. Here we will examine the elements of the transformations that relate to our concern with networks and related theories. (We will outline them here as Hargreaves uses them, but explore the underlying ideas in Chapter 2, and in some cases in later chapters.) The first transformation involves creating the right climate for innovation, a climate in which risk taking and allowing failure are supported, but in the second transformation the need is to create knowledge in a disciplined way. This second transformation recognises that not all schools will be involved at the same level of engagement, and that there will need to be leading-edge schools that take a lead in knowledge creation. This is accompanied by a 'levelling up' of other schools through transferred innovation using collaborative relationships or by their being embedded in networks, as explored in the third trans-formation, 'devising and implementing a lateral strategy'. Hargreaves argues that trans-ferring innovation is difficult and that we know little about sharing and disseminating good practice. The use of print, the web and video are common methods that he sees as weak because they are disembodied and decontextualised. Transfer he sees happening through networks, using champions that are well connected and that can bridge into established networks run by local authorities or central agencies such as Becta (originally known as the British Educational Communications and Technology Agency)[17] and the networked learning communities. Hargreaves points to early internet models and to the more recent hackers and network wizards who co-operate freely and have a culture of sharing and exchange. He also sees the public creation of software, citing Linux (an operating system for computers that has been created as open-source software that can be used and modified without paying any copyright costs). These cultures act as a guide for what he would like to see for education, with a professionally self-governed system of knowledge creation and sharing for education, one that would therefore be decentralised, without central control.

This is explored more fully in the fourth transformation, 'using ICT laterally'. Hargreaves develops these ideas of a sharing culture by drawing on examples of how readers can review and rate books on commercial sites such as Amazon.com,[18] and how such sites tell would-be purchasers of a particular book that other purchasers of the book have also purchased. Similarly, he points to sites dedicated to reviewing products, such as Epinions.com.[19] But then he draws on a different kind of electronic network, computer-supported co-operative work. He sees this as locating and giving access to those with expertise, though it has a number of manifestations, even in the educational world. Some such networks are no more than discussion forums, others question-and-answer areas, and yet others are workspaces where problems or tasks can be worked on together (i.e. knowledge creation environments).[20] He extends this sharing culture to peer-to-peer file-sharing sites such as Napster.com, which, even by the time Hargreaves was writing about it, had been changed from its peer-to-peer *free* sharing culture by court action.[21] Nevertheless, it did spawn a range of file-sharing software to support such cultures. In this account of using ICT laterally, Hargreaves moved through many different ideas on networks – ideas such as 'the network as a self-organising system' (his earlier work used the decentralised 'web' metaphor). But then he moves on to other ideas on networks, for example seeing schools as 'nodes' that have 'six degrees of separation' from other useful nodes, drawing on what is termed the 'small-world' view of networks. He also appears to counter the decentralised metaphor of earlier work with schools as hubs to feed a network, and hubs with satellites, implying a hierarchy. (In the fifth transformation, 'making a learning system', he goes on to talk of local authorities as hubs in networks of schools that can act as brokers for networks to co-ordinate disciplined innovation and knowledge transfer.) In the fourth transformation he combines these two ideas of networks (decentralised systems and small-world networks), returning to his champions (a small number of super-connected individuals who can spread the 'infection' of innovation) with Gladwell's (2002) idea of 'tipping points' created by well-connected people. He stretches this medical part of the network metaphor by referring to a 'climate of contagion'. But it is not clear with respect to contagion whether he means the same as the social network analysis idea on this (where embedded networks of, say, friends may be used to pass on ideas and practices), an idea we will consider in Chapter 2 and later chapters.

He finishes *Education Epidemic* with a flourish: 'Once the system, rich in intellectual and social capital, has thereby acquired a stronger and more resilient capacity for improvement through innovation and peer-to-peer transfer of best practice, then transformation is within our collective grasp' (Hargreaves 2003a: 74).

This work is a whirlwind of ideas on networks, and its use of network metaphors is arresting and invigorating. However, it makes numerous assumptions about the appropriateness for education of, for example, the transfer of ideas from the ICT world (such as open-source software development), or social capital as seen in social network theory, or indeed ideas on the person-to-person networked society. We will return to many of these ideas in Chapter 2 and examine some of them in this light, as we were left wondering how all these ideas are to be put together, and how such a systemic view could ever come about.[22] Hargreaves' ideas are more ambitious than those of the reformers advocating PLCs. In particular, he is trying to move beyond the confines of community views of knowledge creation and sharing (without denying its central features). Hargreaves employs a collection of metaphors on networks, some of which go beyond the work of those who think they are also concerned with networks, for example Veugelers and O'Hair (2005a) in their book *Network Learning for Educational Change* (from which we draw in what follows).

Educational policy and networks

We have already noted that networks and PLCs are internationally influential, and here we will examine some examples to show how they have been encapsulated in educational policy in a number of contexts.

The Netherlands

The Ministry of Education formed a working group in 1988 and institutionalised the network a year later (Veugelers and Zijlstra 2005, from which all the details here are taken). The network's purpose was to interpret government policy, to learn from and use teachers' experience and expertise and to create new approaches and knowledge. Initially, twenty schools with two teachers from each school formed the network, which set up subject groups (eight teachers from different schools). The groups were chaired by University of Amsterdam staff and met six times a year. A group activity would include a presentation by a teacher and collective reflection, and perhaps the compiling of a book of experiences. The government funded up to thirty secondary school networks, and participation changed over time. For example, if teachers had to travel to a centre for the group meeting and the focus did not meet their needs, they might leave the group because the school would not continue to support their participation. The networks changed as their relationship to policy changed. At their inception these networks were a tool for implementing government educational policy, and in the 1990s there was a climate of experimentation and feeling of empowerment within the networks. In particular, work was done on critical-democratic citizenship, co-operative learning and student research projects. Later, when government policy changed, the networks dwindled somewhat, and became a defence against centralising tendencies of the new policy, including a national curriculum and centralised assessment. In contrast to their earlier interpretation and implementation of government policy, the networks found themselves defending earlier achievements. Veugelers and Zijlstra (2005) conclude that networks flourish in a climate that is open, but when the climate becomes 'top down', then the networks become defensive. They also acknowledge that there was an issue of how other teachers in a school, not in the network, could be involved, recognising that other methods of school and professional development are required for such networking.

Singapore: teacher networks

Singapore's teacher networks were established by the Ministry of Education in 1997 to develop interactive professionalism, with a teacher network (TN) as a learning organisation. The network employed professional development activities such as action research in learning circles to make explicit tacit knowledge to be shared through teacher-to-teacher workshops and conferences, along with a website acting as a repository (Tripp 2004). The TN clearly shares some features with PLCs, although in this case there appears to be some effort to enable the showcasing of teacher research projects with those not involved in the activity, through conferences, symposia and in-service courses (Salleh 2006). Tripp (2004: 195) notes the role of knowledge management through its articulation, archiving and dissemination, but his account is too general to provide an analysis of how this is achieved. Salleh (2006) reports on the formation of learning circles with an analysis of the nature of the groups that make up each TN, though his concern is with the action research and how it fits in with the Singapore context. Like Tripp (2004), he argues that a TN is a form of PLC, and he cites the features noted by Bolam *et al.* (2005) to indicate this. In considering the problems and paradoxes of their implementation, he notes that classroom teachers may be losing ownership (to school leaders). Unsurprisingly, teachers report that they are short of time for the collaborative activities that are at the heart of the learning circles. In looking at sustainability, Salleh wonders whether the lack of time will mean that teachers become users of knowledge rather than creators of it.

The website[23] and TN conferences are still active and e-resources are available, which include teachers sharing their work (workshops are also given by teachers and advertised on the website). It is evident that the focus of reporting and research work on these TNs has treated them as PLCs, rather than the network activities that might lead to a wider sharing of knowledge. An evaluation of their functioning was apparently under way in 2006 (Salleh 2006). At an earlier time, Tripp (2004) reported the evaluation of the satisfaction of the teachers involved.

The United Kingdom: networked learning communities and primary strategy learning networks

Networked learning communities were established by a programme funded by the National College for School Leadership (NCSL)[24] that resulted in 137 networks involving 1,500 schools between 2002 and 2006 (Jackson and Temperley 2006). Each network, or NLC, was funded with £50,000 annually for three years and was expected to show sustainability by operating in the fourth year without NCSL funding (Earl and Katz 2005: 14). The NCSL supported these networks through its Networked Learning Group, which reached a staff of fifty. The size of networks varied from six to sixty schools, though the average was ten schools in a network. As noted earlier, effectively an NLC is a PLC, but across schools. It involves joint work and collaboration between schools; Jackson and Temperley (2006: 10) themselves refer to an NLC as an 'expanded professional learning community'.[25] All this lifts the unit of community from the school to the locality, although we have not found any details of how many active teachers might be involved in collaborative activity. As we will see in Chapter 9, when we discuss an example of such an NLC, most teachers are not involved, except in some large 'set-piece' conferences or staff days. Drawing on Church *et al.* (2002), Jackson and Temperley (2006: 8) give a conceptualisation of a network of schools connected by threads, which represent 'relationships, communication and trust'. Between schools will be 'knots', which represent what participants do together.[26] Examples of knots are joint work groups (e.g. project groups), collective planning (e.g. steering groups), mutual problem-solving teams (focus groups), collaborative inquiry groups and shared professional development activities such as a joint staff day.[27] These are all quite different activities and not all may be collaborative; a collaborative inquiry group will involve quite different processes from a joint staff day. Jackson and Temperley argue that strong threads (with trust and high levels of communication) are needed for good knots, enabling joint work and openness. The focus is on collaboration across schools, leading to the idea of 'networked learning', which has four 'learning processes':

- learning from one another (sharing knowledge, etc.);
- learning with one another (co-constructing learning);
- learning on behalf of (other individuals within their school);
- meta-learning (individuals learning about their own processes of learning).

There is little attempt to say how those not involved in the collaborative work benefit from the 'learning on behalf of'. (Indeed, none of the processes involved in the types of learning is detailed, except where it refers to the familiar collaborative activities of PLCs.) Jackson and Temperley (2006: 9) do mention 'shared professional development activities (learning forums/joint staff days)' but give no details. The discussion of 'network learning' contrasts it with 'networking':

> Within schools and between schools, adults are involved in multiple random 'networking' relationships, some with strong ties, others arising from weak ties (Granovetter 1973; Watts 2003). These connections offer rich opportunities for learning and make up an unpredictable tapestry of interpersonal connections. They are not, though, 'networked learning' – they are 'networking'.
>
> (Jackson and Temperley 2006: 6)

This seems to us to be simply a confusion about the nature of network relationships, which can, as we will show in later chapters, involve learning. However, it may be that there is an attempt to say something about networks as structures. Kerr *et al.*, in a literature review commissioned by the NCSL for its NLC programme, make the distinction 'between the terms *network* [which is about *structure*] and *networking* [which concerns *process, action and activity*]' (2003: 46; emphasis in the original). Hadfield (2005), a member of the NCSL Networked Learning Group, is unhappy with this distinction and, like us, thinks that it ignores the work of sociologists and others who use the analysis of social relationships to reveal social structure, as we will see in the next chapter.[28] Many of those connected to the NLC programme seem, however, to see a network only as an organisational entity, a view that could be seen as undervaluing individual personal networks.

Jackson and Temperley (2006: 6) consider that it is only in the joint working that learning takes place:

> [W]hen individuals from different schools in a network come together in groups to engage in purposeful and sustained developmental activity informed by the public knowledge base, utilising their own know-how and co-constructing knowledge together, as in the above model. In doing so, they learn with one another, from one another, and on behalf of others.

Not all of the types of 'knots', mentioned earlier, seem to qualify as network learning under this definition, and we are left with the puzzle about those teachers not involved in collaborative work but who could nevertheless benefit from what is found.

The reference to PLCs by Jackson and Temperley (ibid.: 10) reflects the influence on NLCs of the US networks we considered earlier, and in particular of Lieberman's work.[29] The NLC programme was also supported by a literature review from the National Foundation for Educational Research (Kerr *et al.* 2003), which focused on networks as a form of organisation. This also stressed partnership and collaboration:

> [I]t was agreed to focus the review on partnerships where there appeared to be a genuine collaboration and where information knowledge was circulated to all participants involved within the network. The emphasis was on *inter* as opposed to *intra* partnerships. References concerning one-to-one partnerships, or partnerships that appeared to be one-directional in the way in which they worked were excluded.
>
> (ibid.: 4; emphasis in the original)

The definition (by Church *et al.* 2002) of a network that Kerr *et al.* (2003) favoured focused on voluntary relationships, autonomous participants and mutual and joint activities. There is one short discussion of dissemination (despite the reference to 'where information knowledge was circulated to all participants involved within the network' in the above quotation), but it lists only meetings, forums and training activities (ibid.: 38). There is no mention of sharing knowledge in the challenges that networks face, and the nearest we get to it is in a recommendation for further research on electronic networking for co-ordination, communication, dissemination and evaluation.[30] Similarly, when a review of research on the impact of networks was carried out, there is an emphasis on collaborative work, and indeed the synonyms for 'networks' they quote are 'partnerships, consortia, collaboration, alliance' (NLG/CUREE 2005: 79). They do discuss the transfer of knowledge from one context to another and the role of experts and events (e.g. conferences) in this, but as the focus of the review is on outcomes, their discussion is necessarily limited.

Although we are not concerned with how effective the NLC programme was, an evaluation by Earl *et al.* (2006) throws further light on how networks are conceived. This consisted of a survey covering some 1,200 teachers in 365 schools, with up to five teachers in any one school responding on behalf of their colleagues. The authors acknowledge a poor response rate, but there are some interesting insights of relevance to this discussion.[31] When the teachers were asked about relationships within their school (e.g. 'discuss professional issues regularly'), the percentages who 'agree' or 'agree strongly' were 80–90 per cent (ibid.: table 5.7, 46–7). In contrast, and unsurprisingly, relationships with the network (e.g. 'share work associated with network projects') received much lower percentages (45–60 per cent). Figures for collaboration were more mixed: higher when it dealt with attitudes to network colleagues, but lower when involving working with them (53–66 per cent). Inquiry-based joint work with those in the network (i.e. outside of own school) produced ratings of 30–40 per cent (e.g. share lesson plans, teaching activities with network colleagues: 38 per cent; Earl *et al.* 2006: table 5.8, 48). Earl *et al.* (2006) also list features that would enable networks to create and share knowledge, and two are of relevance: relationships and collaboration. Although their discussion of relationships talks of 'connective tissue' and social capital that both enable communication and disseminating information (ibid.: 26), the main focus of the discussion is on trust, which comes from strong relationships.[32] The discussion of collaboration cites the work of Little (1990) on sharing and the need to make teachers' work accessible to others, but there is no elaboration of this.

All this reinforces for us the legacy of these approaches focused on community elements that emphasise strong relationships through collaboration, but which have failed to give the insights from a wider conception of networks, particularly where they contrast with PLCs. It is ironic that the Networked Learning Group did not take more heed of the uniqueness of networks, as it was warned to do in a paper addressed to the group (Little 2005a).

> Despite evidence of the potential importance of network participation, the field knows little as yet about the interaction between a network-based professional community and the localized professional communities rooted in the daily lives of schools. We are only beginning to learn what exactly transpires in such inter-actions that constitutes resources for professional learning and school improvement. With few exceptions, research on professional learning communities takes the school or the within-school group (department, team, grade) as a meaningful unit of analysis. Similarly, research on networks concerns itself with the network as an entity, with participants from a particular school standing as a kind of proxy for the school itself. Yet these case boundaries, so convenient for research, do not correspond to the places and pathways traversed by the individuals and groups we study. Nor do they allow us to capture precisely the kind of boundary-spanning work that individuals and groups do when they move from one institutional space to another.
>
> (Little 2005b: 278)[33]

In a sense, this acts as an agenda for our concerns in this book! One contribution to the debate does try to tackle some of the issues identified by Little, and to which we have also pointed. This study, by an NCSL research associate, focused on weak ties (Lawrence 2007) and was published by the NCSL. It comes from his EdD work (Lawrence 2009) but does not investigate NLCs; rather, another initiative that links schools that want to learn from other schools. We will draw on this study in Chapter 7.

The NLC programme ended in 2006, and although the publications are sustained on the NCSL website, there is no apparent evidence of these networks.[34] Out of this focus on NLCs in England came the government-supported Primary Strategy Learning Networks. The Primary Strategy was a prescriptive directive that followed up a centrally determined and tightly specified curriculum and testing regime with directions on pedagogy.[35] The Primary Strategy Learning Networks came from the Innovation Unit (IU) within the Department for Education and Skills (DfES), working in conjunction with the NCSL, and provided £17,000 through the local authority (£12,000 to the whole network and £5,000 to the school that acts as the network fund holder) to enable primary schools in an area to form a network. The intention was that by 2008 the majority of primary schools would have the opportunity to be part of a network, with an estimated total of 1,500 networks (DfES 2004). One report said that there were 2,000 such networks with 7,000 schools involved (Jackson and Temperley 2006).[36] The head of the IU, Valerie Hannon, writing about these networks, uses the terms 'clusters', 'collegiates' and 'partnerships' (2005: 2) as a substitute for 'networks', and indeed partnerships is the strongest theme in the article, particularly as this is the term used in the *Five Year Strategy*: Education Improvement Partnerships (DfEE 2004). The article goes on to discuss three purposes, one of which (accelerating improvement and stimulating innovation) relates to the ideas discussed above: distribution of good practice, creating, validating and spreading knowledge about what works and creating PLCs. Combined with this 'PLC theme' is the idea of the network as a form of organisation; another purpose is 'creating new units of service delivery', in which 'schools work in close partnership to take responsibility for their children' (Hannon 2005: 4). The planning documents available to these primary school networks contain many helpful ideas and tools for planning a network, though there is much more focus on reviewing the schools to decide priorities for work within the network, than on the network processes themselves (DfES 2005b). One booklet within the documents, 'Effective networks', does stress '[o]rganising school-to-school visits so that learning transfers easily and rapidly between schools' (ibid.: 'Effective networks': 2) and some specific suggestions on new opportunities for adult learning:

> shared investigation of your schools' practice and strategies . . . school-to-school activities . . . dynamic and structured interactions between staff from different schools . . . these 'networked learning' opportunities are the places where teachers come together to engage in real tasks on behalf of the wider network. . . . Evidence suggests that they ['networked learning' opportunities] include
> - collective planning (e.g. steering groups);
> - joint work groups (e.g. project teams);
> - joint problem-solving teams (e.g. focus groups);
> - collaborative enquiry groups (e.g. enquiry teams);
> - shared professional development activities (e.g. learning forums or joint staff days);
> - structured school-to-school visits (e.g. 'learning walks').
>
> (ibid.: 'Effective networks': 4)

Most of these are directed at knowledge creation, with only the penultimate one being associated with sharing across the staff not directly involved in the various groups or teams.[37] Because the documents that formed the background for schools on networks are by Lieberman, Jackson and Hannon, they have the limitations to which we have drawn attention.

Once again, however, this apparent enthusiasm for networks shifted into the work of communities, and indeed the term 'networks' has disappeared from the IU lexicon, being replaced by PLCs.[38] Perhaps now networks are an innovation no longer in fashion?[39]

The starting point for our research

We started this research with some developing ideas on networks from David Hargreaves, some culs-de-sac in PLCs and some missed opportunities from NLCs. Our initial work reflected some of this, in particular that of Hargreaves, at least as laid out in the LHTL project proposal, to which he was party.[40] At the network level the research aim for the LHTL project was split into a number of sub-questions:

> Investigate how educational networks can support the creation, management and transfer of knowledge and skills of learning how to learn.
> (a) What variations are there in network structures, technologies and operation in ICT-rich learning environments?
> (b) What policies and practices help or hinder the development of networks as mechanisms for enhancing teaching and learning?
> (c) What are teachers' existing levels of competence and confidence in using network technologies?
> (d) How do the competence and confidence of teachers about networking through ICT affect the quality of their networking practices in specific relation to learning how to learn?
> (e) Do the demands for knowledge transfer drive new forms of networking within and between learning organizations?
> (f) Do such forms of networking reflect existing patterns of collaboration and interaction or are new forms developed?
> (g) What combination of organizational and technological factors maximizes the potential for generating and transferring teachers' knowledge and skills both about 'learning about learning' and about other aspects of teaching and learning?

Many of the sub-questions reflected a concern with technologies, and we had the experience and interest to pursue such questions. However, when we came to work on them we realised that they made some assumptions, such as seeing networks as entities and networks where ICT was a significant feature. Did we understand the nature of educational networks sufficiently to be sure that these were the right questions?

The issues

In the light of the overall aim for the research ('Investigate how educational networks can support the creation, management and transfer of knowledge and skills of learning how to learn'), and the discussion in this chapter, where does this leave us with regard to how to think about networks, both what they are and how they operate?

First, it is evident that PLCs and NLCs address knowledge creation through collaboration of a small group of those who participate directly in the communities associated with them. How others not directly involved benefit is unclear. At least there is some understanding of how knowledge creation can take place, although, as we shall show in Chapter 7, even here there are some problems. How knowledge is shared is almost completely missing – that is, what happens in such things as conferences, workshops and reporting? Is it possible to think of network structure in ways that do not necessarily see it as an organisation, but rather as deriving from the relationships among those in a network? Is it right to presuppose the existence of *a* network, or is it necessary to look at the networks within which teachers exist – in a sense, to look at just the aspects that the likes of Jackson and Temperley (2006) dismiss (as 'networking')? These kinds of issues and questions we take up in the next chapter, where we consider how to theorise about networks.

In addition, if we are to extend network learning (to use the NLC term) to others who are not involved in the collaborative activities, what do we mean by this learning and how does it relate to creation and sharing of knowledge? We shall take this up in Chapter 3, where we consider teacher learning and how that might relate to knowledge creation and sharing.

Chapter 2

Theorising networks

Introduction

The discussion of Hargreaves (2003a) in Chapter 1 indicated a number of ideas that are relevant to network theories and knowledge creation and sharing, including the importance of mobilising various kinds of capital, the transfer of knowledge through networks, and the role for information and communications technology (ICT) in these networks. Although some specific networks are indicated by Hargreaves (e.g. local authorities [LAs]), electronic networks seemed to dominate his thinking in relation to sharing (his fourth transformation, 'using ICT laterally'). For example, he refers to the working practices of hackers or open-source software developers who collaborate online. In arguing for the role of ICT, he talks of:

- schools as 'nodes', and 'hubs' and 'satellites' (to show relationships among schools);
- LAs as brokers for networks;
- computer-supported collaborative work, where teachers could work online;
- Napster peer-to-peer file sharing as a form of collaboration and sharing;
- fostering 'contagion' to enable the spread of innovation;
- the networks as being 'self-organizing', with a 'web' as the analogy to indicate how networks are managed.

As was noted in Chapter 1, these ideas draw on a number of network ideas, not all from the same theoretical base. Hargreaves is doing this quite legitimately, as the final idea of a 'web' indicates, namely as a metaphor from network theories. The network seen as a metaphor is a common theme in discussions on network theories, as we will shortly show, but Hargreaves (2003a) is somewhat 'mixing his metaphors', not all of which are likely to be compatible when their underlying theoretical roots are examined. We will examine Hargreaves' ideas directly or indirectly in this light by considering a variety of network theories. We will explore whether they provide specific analytic concepts or whether they are used metaphorically. Finally, we will review the literature on networks in education, which we feel takes us beyond that examined in Chapter 1.

The research questions we started with (Chapter 1) essentially assumed that the LHTL project team already knew something about the nature of educational networks. Indeed, the first question asks about 'variations in network structures', implying some knowledge of existing structures. None of them poses questions about what these networks are like, and many of the questions relate to network technologies and the use of ICT. This bias towards electronic networks in the LHTL project team's initial thinking was there because they were seen as possible ways in which schools would be able to share and possibly create knowledge. These ideas were influenced directly by David Hargreaves and Geoff Southworth, both of whom were involved in the original research proposal but who were not involved in much of the subsequent research work.[1] We came to the research with a variety of influences and research expertise in relation to networks, but the clearest was that based on the electronic networks. This gave us a predisposition to treat networks as entities – that is, representing all those individuals electronically connected wherever they were located. Such connected schools would be able to share classroom practice, as Hargreaves (2003a) envisaged. (We will explore what such notions mean in later chapters.) Indeed, our LHTL project website (www.learntolearn.ac.uk) was seen as an element of this, with the facility to store accounts of assessment for learning (AfL) classroom practice and to go beyond this sharing of practice to the possible creation of new practice through discussion forums. However, our initial contacts with schools, including those that were deliberately electronically connected (Virtual Education Action Zones [VEAZ][2]), indicated that although teachers were using the technology in their schools with their students, there seemed little activity related to the development of their own classroom practice. (In Chapter 10 we shall review our systematic research about the use of electronic networks.) Nevertheless, such networks were an obvious starting point, drawing on the ideas of Castells (1999), which see information technologies as central.[3] Subsequent research drew us to the work of Hakkarainen *et al.* (2004), who used the ideas of social network analysis to investigate innovative IT companies and the workings of knowledge communities. For them, knowledge building was of prime concern, albeit that the context was not education. From this we went on to investigate the various theoretical positions that underlay this and related work. Here we outline some of these influences, and in subsequent chapters we will examine how we used them to investigate the school networks we set out to understand, including how we developed our ideas.

Network theories

We indicated in Chapter 1 that the literature surrounding the networked learning communities (NLCs) did not focus on social relations as defining a network, but saw a network as a form of organisation, and hence a particular kind of structure.[4] The first of the theories we will consider, social network analysis (SNA), seeks to derive social structure from the relationships among people. The second picks up the anthropological tradition, in which the nature of the interactions that take place as a result of the relations is also a focus. We shall then consider social capital approaches to networks, picking up one of Hargreaves' ideas and examining how this is used to understand networks. Finally, we shall deal with his idea that we are all connected, using the 'small world' view of networks. Our intention is to understand the elements of these theories and to examine their bases. Here we only outline these theories, as they will be developed in later chapters.

Social network analysis

In the introduction to a classic text on social network analysis (Wellman and Berkowitz 1988a), the editors delineate the characteristics of network analysis as a form of structural analysis:

- Structure is defined by relationships.
- Structural analysis recognises that social structure can be represented by networks.
- A network is a set of nodes and ties depicting their interconnectedness.
- Social relations are not just between people but can be between groups, corporations, households, nation-states and other collectives (these are all seen as 'nodes').
- Ties represent flows of resources, symmetrical friendship, transfers or structural relations.

These form the basic ideas of SNA. Wellman and Berkowitz (1988a: 4) suggest that 'network analysis is neither a method nor a metaphor, but a fundamental intellectual tool for the study of social structures'. In arguing that such structural analysis has moved on from method and metaphor to theory and substance, Wellman (1988), in the same text, describes the two traditions of SNA. First, there is the British one from anthropology, where a network was seen as a set of social ties linking the social system's members across social categories and bounded groups. From this the SNA idea of 'density' emerged (a measure of the actual links as a ratio of the possible links in a network), which brought about the second tradition, from the United States, involving increased quantitative analysis.[5] This quantitative SNA enabled patterns of relationships in networks to be shown using graph theory (and its subsequent associated mathematical methods).[6] Within this tradition were two kinds of studies. One was *whole-network* studies, directed at the comprehensive structure of relationships. These were not always methodologically feasible, could deal only with a few hundred individuals and were unable to deal with naturally occurring settings where the population could not be defined. These problems led to the need for the second kind of study, of *ego-centric* (or personal) networks. In these, networks are shown as they are perceived by the individual (i.e. who is at the centre), investigated through surveys and interviews, although anthropologists who mostly use this approach favour ethnography. In such studies, individuals are asked to record the relationships they have (observation may also be used). As we will show in Chapter 4, the division of these two approaches within the quantitative tradition is more profound than just methodological limitations of the whole-network approach, as it implies that a network as an *entity* exists.

In presenting the case for structural analysis being 'more than a set of topics or a bag of methodological tricks' (ibid.: 30), Wellman examines five principles, two of which are of significance here. First, the structural social relationships are a more powerful source of sociological explanation than the personal attributes of system members. People belong to networks as well as categories (e.g. social class), and indeed this view sees categorical membership as reflecting underlying structural relationships, which give patterned differences in access to resources. This is important in analysing educational networks and, say, the impact of headteachers compared with a co-ordinator of a specific innovation in classroom practices (e.g. AfL). The relationships the co-ordinator sets up can give her or him better access to expertise and innovative practice than the headteacher has, even though the co-ordinator is not in the same managerial position. (In Chapter 9 the Juniper Primary School case study shows this.)

The second principle is that the world is composed of networks, not groups, which points to the importance of the internal and external links of the individuals within an organisation and the patterns the links form. In seeking structural analyses, sociologists are concerned to uncover the latent structure, and hence have been able to show that the traditional view of community, based on locality and place, has been replaced by one in which networks are communities (Wellman *et al.* 1988).[7] As we saw in Chapter 1, schools are taken as communities without there being any investigation of the actual links among those in them; this view also ignores communities outside a particular school that may not have a formal status.

Wellman presents analytic principles that are a 'mixture of definitions, assumptions, partially tested hypotheses, and empirical generalisations' (1988: 40), including the following:

- Ties are usually asymmetrically reciprocal, different in content and intensity (for example, the link may be involuntary but important, as is often the case of a school with a local authority or national ministry of education department).
- Ties link network members indirectly and directly, hence it is necessary to define the context of larger network structures (for example, where a teacher may have a direct link to his or her headteacher, who provides an indirect link, through regular LA meetings, to knowledge of the practice in other schools).
- Structurally, social ties create non-random networks, hence clusters, boundaries and cross-linkages are found (for example, members of a school department may be closely linked, but isolated from teachers in the rest of the school).
- Asymmetric ties and complex networks differentially distribute scarce resources (for example, someone who is well connected can often collect more information on an issue than someone who is isolated).

This long tradition of quantitative analysis provides ways of thinking that are useful in qualitative studies such as ours.[8] Examples include concepts of network structure and the location of a node in a network: centrality, degree and path distances (e.g. measures of individuals who are at the centre of things); and betweenness (of a node, indicating the amount of control it has over, say, resources going to others in the network). Others deal with descriptive data about ties: weak and strong ties (weak or strong relationships); size of a personal network (the number of people an individual is connected to); whom links are made with; and duration and diversity of links. These will be examined in later chapters.

Anthropologists' study of networks

Knox *et al.* (2006) give a contemporary view of anthropologists' work, but a much earlier work (Mitchell 1974) is instructive to those of us with a concern for educational networks, as it reviews the field after 'only' 20 years of empirical work. This review was of work that used social network theory in a *post hoc* way, after the data were collected.

LIVERPOOL JOHN MOORES UNIVERSITY
LEARNING SERVICES

Mitchell's view of the field concerns the role of network theory and how it relates to other theories that are used to make sense of the data. This is part of a larger argument about whether networks are used as metaphor or as a substantive (network) theory, something we will come to later in the chapter. Another part of Mitchell's view is the helpful division into what he calls structural and transactional perspectives. A *structural* perspective interprets behaviour of an actor in terms of patterns of links in a social network; behaviour is explained by the social network. The *transactional* alternative is to see the behaviour of an actor in terms of how he or she manipulates links to achieve an end. Some who use a network approach see transactions as a consequence of network structure, while others see network structure as flowing from transactions. Early work on social networks used the framework of structural functionalism, and more recent work (in the 1970s) took a transactional approach (e.g. political candidates mobilising support from voters). These two approaches (structural and transactional) lead to the use of network concepts of morphological features of a network (shape or pattern of links; e.g. density as a measure of connectedness, reachability in terms of number of links between two actors of concern), or interactional features (e.g. intensity of relationship). In terms of our concern for knowledge creation and sharing, the interactional ones are of most importance, and Mitchell particularly spells out the 'content' of social interactions as being the least well researched. He gives three categories of content:

- communication content – the passage of information, classically found in studies of diffusion of innovations;
- transaction or exchange – categorising types and multiplexity of links and how relationships can constrain actors' behaviour;
- normative content – an actor's construction of meaning of the relationship in terms of understanding other people's expectations of his or her behaviour.

The first of these will be examined in Chapter 7, and the third has some relevance both to a discussion of 'metaphor' versus 'concepts' of networks later in this chapter and to our discussion of teacher learning in the next chapter.

Social capital

We have already noted that Hargreaves (2003a) used concepts of capital in relation to how he saw the innovative work of schools in the creation and sharing of knowledge and the role of social capital in growing intellectual capital. Social capital is also a basis for network theory, with Lin (2001) arguing that a fundamental understanding is that social capital is captured from embedded resources in social networks, and thus social capital is seen as assets. Lin considers the access to resources individuals have, and the processes of mobilisation of these resources, as increasing social capital in a network. The particularity of the approach is that it views social capital as a development of ideas from the classical theory of capital (from Marx, among others) to human capital theory concerned with the returns that are made by individuals' investments, and cultural capital (Bourdieu 1990), where dominant classes are signified by the investments they make in symbols and meanings. Social capital is the investment in social relations with expected returns; individuals engage in interactions and networking to produce profits.

(This resembles Mitchell's transactional perspective, though without the idea of the 'economic human actor'.) Social capital facilitates the flow of information because social ties in strategic locations can provide the individual with useful information about opportunities, etc. otherwise unavailable. Alternatively, these ties can alert the organisation to other individuals, etc., which reduces the transaction cost for others to use the investment. Social ties also exert influence on agents who play critical roles in decisions involving actors, some with social ties in strategic places (e.g. uniquely connected to part of the network) and positions carrying more valued resources and exercising greater power on organisational agents' decision making (i.e. putting in the word). Social tie resources (e.g. who agents know who would be of use to an organisation) are social credentials, some of which represent the individual's accessibility to resources through social networks and relations. Thus, socially mixing with bankers or celebrities may be of use to a company seeking finance or publicity. Finally, social relations are expected to reinforce identity and recognition, and the assurance of worthiness acts as a reinforcement for the entitlement to resources.

We have elaborated these origins and ideas to show some of the contributory concepts that are brought with the social capital concept, not all of which may be obvious to those who use it. We wonder, for example, if Hargreaves (2003a) had in mind 'expected returns' of social capital and the competition orientation that some of social capital theory assumes. The development of these ideas led to theories about either resources or relations. For example, Burt (2001) shows how location in a network is key to social capital, such that individuals are seen in relation to how near or far they are from a strategic location (e.g. a bridge).

Burt's work is particularly influential and worth elaborating further. In his classical work on a structural theory of action he indicates that actors do not act alone – that is, independently of each other. Figure 2.1 depicts this (Burt 1982: 9) by indicating that an actor's actions depend on his or her position in the social structure (lines 2 and 3); and further, that the action taken in turn also affects the social structure (line 4). In his whole text, Burt (1982) tries to separately establish the empirical links in

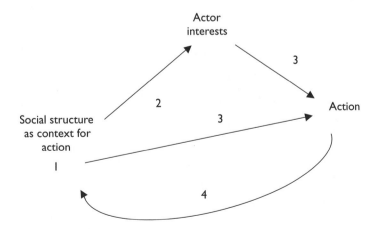

Figure 2.1 Components of a structural theory of action.

Source: Burt (1982: 9).

each of the lines (1–4, Figure 2.1), to enable the theory to be demonstrated in a more tractable way. His empirical work is based on two systems: large corporations involved in American manufacturing, and elite academics concerned with sociological methodology. The first step in the process is to establish the social structure, through examining network models to give the relational patterns among actors, which he argues captures the social context for action. The networks of relations are shown algebraically in adjacency matrices derived from a sociogram (Figure 2.2a). Each '1' in the matrix (Figure 2.2b) indicates a link in the sociogram. Thus, node '5' is linked to '9', indicated with a '1' at the intersection of 'row 5' and 'column 9' of the matrix; '4' is linked to '5' (shown in the same way). The intersection of 'row 5, column 4' does not show a '1', as the relationship is not reciprocal. Where a relationship is reciprocal, a '1' is found both ways. For example, the relationship between nodes '7' and '9' is reciprocal, hence 'row 7, column 9' and 'row 9, column 7' intersections both contain a '1'. These diagrams and matrices are the standard basis of SNA. Burt is able to develop mathematical methods to analyse various features of a network such as density (the extent to which actors in system are connected on average to one another). In fact, he proposes six modes of network analysis, each with its own concept of network structure. The importance of explaining this social action model and the use of network structures is to illustrate the underlying theory he draws on, and the fact that he aims to derive a mathematical basis for network analysis, in similar ways to Wellman and Berkowitz (1988a).

Burt (2001) examines two network structures that create social capital with two hypotheses:

1 what he calls the 'closure argument', where social capital is created by a network of strongly interconnected elements;
2 the 'structural hole argument', where social capital is created by a network in which people broker connections between otherwise disconnected segments.

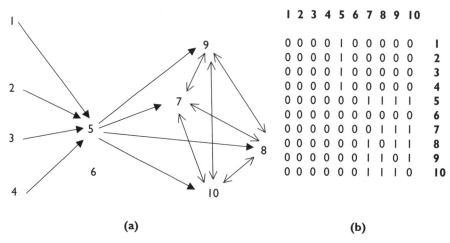

Figure 2.2 Sociogram (a) and adjacency matrix (b) for an advice network of ten actors.
Source: Burt (1982: 25).

In Figure 2.3, Jill is part of network A, which depicts closure – that is, a network where almost everyone is directly connected with everyone else. Jill makes the only link to networks B and C (each of them indicating closed networks apart from the link to Jill). If she did not make the link, there would be what Burt terms a 'structural hole'. Jill acts as a bridge, and hence a broker, for network A, enabling the knowledge from the other two networks to be shared with those in network A. Thus, the 'closure argument' is effectively saying that, with a cohesive group (see Figure 2.4, group B), one where all the people are directly linked together, and are linked to the same people external to the group, then the social capital from this 'closure' (strong, non-redundant social ties) is the maximum that can be created. Burt argues in the 'structural hole argument' that brokerage across structural holes is a source of added value by making the resources in the outlying parts of the network available to an organisation such as a school.

The social capital associated with structural holes depends upon the strength of weak ties, an argument made most convincingly by Granovetter (1973).[9] Weak ties are usually between those who are less likely to be socially involved with each other than is the case for strong ties (e.g. those between friends). Weak ties between actors are found in a low-density network (i.e. one where the connections are indirect), strong ties in a high-density one (where many of the nodes are directly connected). Without weak ties a network will be starved of information from distant parts of a social system. This relates to Burt's idea that weak ties that bridge are more likely than other weak ties to connect to significantly different kinds of people. Weaker connections can be seen as holes in the social structure (structural holes), and those who span the hole have an advantage (Jill in Figure 2.3). Brokering the flow of information between people and central projects can be done by bringing people together either side of a hole. Figure 2.3 illustrates this, where those in group A are brought together with those in B and C, with Jill acting as the bridge. These issues will be explored more in Chapters 5 and 6, when we consider nodes and links.

Burt examines the empirical evidence for the efficacy of these two arguments (between closure and structural holes), concluding that the bridging of structural holes is shown to create more social capital than relying only on within-network closure. However, he is able to reconcile them by showing that closure is needed to realise the value buried in structural holes. Diagrammatically, he indicates this by three configurations (Figure 2.4), where A is the one that produces the best performance

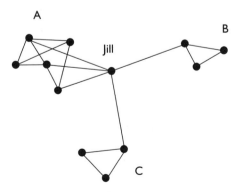

Figure 2.3 Network showing how Jill bridges structural holes.

because each node in the network has unique external ties, bringing in potentially more diverse and non-redundant information. This has important implications for the discussion in Chapter 1, where we indicated that focusing only on the strong links within cohesive communities (B in Figure 2.4) ignores the other weak links external to those in the cohesive communities. Group B in Figure 2.4 has external links but they are shared by everyone in the group, and this might reflect a school acting as a PLC or a group of teachers in an NLC. Burt argues that these communities will not function as well without these bridging external links. If a whole school, or even several schools in a network, involves a relatively small group of teachers with only cohesive (direct, close) links, they will not be as effective as they would be if they had links to others both *within* and *across* schools. Such links could be to schools and others not in the NLC or PLC. These are the very links that are largely ignored or unexplored by those who study and promote PLCs. They do not deny the value of external links, but they pay insufficient attention to them and have limited conceptual ways of dealing with them. Thus, they consider the group as a *community* and draw upon brokerage from Wenger (1998); Chapter 5 will show other forms of brokerage. Taking a social *network* analysis perspective offers another way of conceptualising external links, and this has ramifications for how knowledge is shared and indeed created. As we will show in Chapter 7, the advocates of PLCs and NLCs focus more on the creation and less on the sharing of knowledge, and are in danger of being less innovative.

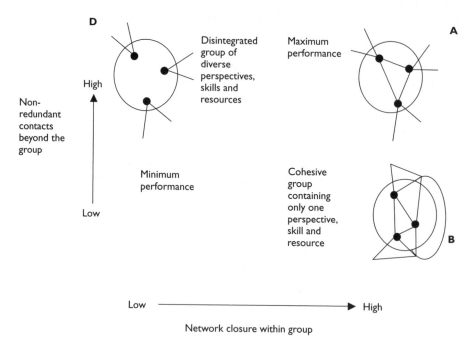

Figure 2.4 Comparison of network closure and bridging structural holes.

Source: Burt (2001: 48).

The 'small world' hypothesis

The idea that we live in a small world comes from the common experience of speaking to a stranger at a party only to discover that you have a friend or acquaintance in common. Erdös and Rényi worked on a related idea of our living in a small world in the 1950s and, as part of graph theory, were able to show the importance of clusters in the process of information passing from one person to another and then to all those in a room in a party (Barabási 2003). Milgram (1967) conducted a famous experiment to find the 'distance' between any two people in the United States by asking 160 people in two distant areas of the country to send a postcard to a target person in Boston (not someone well known) or, if they did not know that person, to send it to an acquaintance who might. Only forty-two of the cards reached the target person, but for those that did, the average number of postings (i.e. people through whom the contact was made) turned out to be 5.5. Hence, we have the commonly known idea of 'six degrees of separation': that any two individuals are only separated by six acquaintances (Barabási 2003). In considering the views of community, Clark (2007) recognises that this idea of a short chain of acquaintances (six degrees of separation) is compelling but not well grounded in empirical research.[10]

A more recent large-scale electronic version of the Milgram study, using email, confirmed the number of steps needed to reach a target to be between five and seven.[11] In seeking explanations of this small world problem, it turns out that clusters (groups of closely linked nodes) are often connected by one person, and it is this combination of close local links and distant ones that provides the answer. The significance in the studies of this 'small world' idea is the kinds of network theory that have developed from graph theory, and the fact that authors such as Watts and Barabási are interested in developing such graph theory.[12] The significant element of this theory is that there are ordered and random networks. The links people choose are usually ordered. If A has friends B and C, it is likely that B and C will know each other. On occasions there is a random element. A random graph is where connections are made entirely at random, and there will be no clustering. (The mathematics of the two networks, random and ordered, is different.) The ordered element exhibits clusters, which if combined with a random element will be connected by (random) links to other clusters. It is this combination that leads to the small world phenomenon. Watts (2003: 89) calls 'random' links to other clusters 'shortcuts', which form bridges, thus taking us back to the analysis of Burt (2005). To this is added the idea of some people being well connected, and that those we choose to link with is 'governed' by this. (Barabási [2003: 85] refers to such links as 'preferential attachments', governed by popularity.) The resulting networks are 'scale-free networks'. We will discuss such well-connected people (hubs) in Chapter 5.

There is one further aspect of networks that this approach reveals. The ordered networks reflect the social *structure* – that is, what we do is determined by the position we occupy in our surrounding social structure (Watts 2003: 72). However, we all exhibit *agency* that is not constrained by our social position; our decision making may reflect our individual intrinsic preferences and characteristics. (To go back to Burt's model in Figure 2.1, those decisions we take reflecting structure and those reflecting agency are represented by the two lines labelled as '3'.)[13] This neglect of human agency has been a criticism of network theories in the past, with either a structural determinism that ignores actors' beliefs and values, or structural instrumentalism that sees such beliefs in narrow terms, as is evident in the economic rationality of social capital ideas of Burt; a third approach, structural constructivism, relates actions in a network to identity as a constructed phenomenon (Emirbayer and Goodwin 1994). Watts (2003: 99) identifies structure with ordered networks and agency with random ones, arguing that the newer network analyses can include identity (Watts *et al.* 2002). Both Watts and Barabási are concerned with network theories that can be used to understand a wide range of networks, both social and natural (e.g. neural networks). These mathematical attempts to understand social and other kinds of networks drive a conception of the world of social interactions and lead to assumptions that enable models to be used in analysis and, as we will show in later chapters, these do not always match the realities we seek to understand.[14]

The final 'network theory' we will consider is that of 'actor-network theory', which is almost the antithesis of the SNA we have been considering up to now, particularly its mathematical basis.

Actor-network theory

The actor-network theory was derived from studies of science, where the work of scientists in action is followed. This is done by making a close study of all the various associations between the elements involved; these elements are actors and can be human or non-human (Latour 2005). Thus, a scientist and the artefacts she or he uses in the laboratory, etc. have associations that transform meaning. This identification of both human and material objects means that social ties alone are not the only concern, an immediate contrast with SNA. In some ways, however, actor-network theory (ANT) takes the idea of the revelation of social structure by SNA further, by rejecting overarching ideas that are used to explain these associations.[15] The network is the string of actions where each participant is treated as a mediator, who transforms meaning or the elements that are supposed to be carried in the interaction. (Mediators are contrasted with 'intermediaries' who simply transport meaning without transformation.) The aim of ANT is to produce accounts of these associations that trace the network; these accounts are the explanations and hence make visible the social. As such, it gives us a different conception of a network; it is not a thing out there like a telephone network. Latour acknowledges that the term 'network' in the ANT context is confusing, given the existence of technical networks and its use by those who study social ties (e.g. Granovetter 1983), and the work of Castells, where new technologies merge these two views of networks. In fact, he would prefer 'worknet', which indicates an active mediator, or 'action net', which indicates the work of laying down a network (here he has in mind a technical network) as a stabilised set of intermediaries. Latour (2005: 131) sees a network as 'a concept, not a thing out there. It is a tool to describe something, not what is being described'.

Although this is a general approach to social theory, it is also primarily a theory about how to study actors without imposing a social order on them – a method, not a theory (Latour 1999). Such an approach posed a real problem for our research in the LHTL project, because to employ ANT would have entailed using this approach exclusively from the start, and employing research methods (detailed case studies of particular knowledge production and sharing) that the general LHTL research design precluded.[16]

It certainly could not easily be used to enable *post hoc* analysis of our data. However, it does have some interesting ideas within its formulations that enabled us to reflect on our thinking and hence on how to research networks, ideas we will come back to in other chapters. This is particularly so as we, like those who studied science, were concerned with knowledge production.

Networks as metaphor or concept?

The question in the title of this section arises from a constant theme in the extensive literature over the past twenty years or so, and over the different academic traditions that have used networks as a way of thinking about their problems and theories. Mitchell (1974) contrasted 'network' as a metaphor, where social links of an individual are seen to ramify through society, against 'network' as an analytic concept that would enable sets of propositions about how 'knots' (nodes) in the network influence each other.[17] Mitchell is sceptical about achieving the latter, and he argues that in fact any theorising about these propositions is likely to come not from 'network theory' but from some other underlying theory of the area being studied (e.g. about the nature of social movements or of exchange). Mitchell's argument is that network theory supplements structural theories rather than replacing them. In part this relates to his point about its being too demanding to create a set of propositions that can be substantiated empirically through network theory. To do this, he argues, needs an underlying theory to relate behaviours and social links; from this the inference is that theory will come from the context of study, in our case the development of teachers' knowledge and practice.

Wellman and Berkowitz (1988a) have no such reservations, as we have already indicated. Wellman (1988), in his chapter on the issue of metaphor and concept, is unequivocal, stating that network analysis is not described by the mechanics of analysis; it is not just method. However, his case is based on the way in which network analysis is part of structural analysis, a particular concern for sociologists. Taking Mitchell's point, there is no implication that we need to see Wellman's certainty as equally valid in our concern with networks in education, where social structure is not the focus *per se*. Theorists such as Watts (1999, 2003) and Barabási (2003) see no such limitations, in that they go even further than explaining social structure using network theory, and seek to 'explain' a large range of phenomena, including the spread of disease, neural networks in the brain and marketing effects. We qualify 'explain', because what they are able to do is to show that the graph theory models are seen to predict, for example, the way a disease may propagate in a population. Although, for example, Barabási (2003) is able to show the importance of particular individuals who are 'well connected' and hence act as hubs in the spread of AIDS (i.e. those who have many sexual partners), he does not offer anything about the precise biological mechanisms for the passing on of the infection. This requires, as Mitchell says, a substantive theory, in this case from biology and related sciences.

Let us take an example from SNA that deals with something of concern to this book, namely the diffusion of innovation, in our case new classroom practices. Valente (2005) reviewed diffusion studies, which try to understand the factors that lead people (of a defined population, such as farmers or doctors) to adopt a new idea whereas others do not. Considering early work, Valente notes the realisation that social factors rather than economic ones were important influences on the process of adoption. The network diffusion models use the idea of contagion, or exposure; for example, in the adoption of a contraceptive device by women, the network model assumes that if an individual is linked to more people who have adopted the use of such a device, then she is more likely to adopt it herself. As was the case in anthropology, early studies were retrospective, and Valente concludes that work should have focused on 'collecting better data or reanalysing diffusion network data in which contagion are more likely' (2005: 99). Nevertheless, he concludes that our understanding of how diffusion occurs is limited, and that in a study of, for example, medical innovation, contagion via social influence was unlikely.[18] His concern is with capturing that influence in quantitative terms (as are his other colleagues in SNA), and hence being able to show the kinds of relationships that Mitchell was saying are so difficult to achieve. In Chapter 7 we will consider this issue further, relating it to the specific issues of educational practice creation and sharing, and what 'adoption' of a new practice means, and indeed whether 'adoption' is the correct conceptualisation of the process.

Despite the confidence of the SNA authors we have considered, Knox *et al.* (2006), in addressing the issue of metaphor and method, see the problem for SNA as methodological expertise being bought at the cost of oscillating between individualistic and structural perspectives. We have already noted the structural view. Knox *et al.* (2006) see the individualistic perspective as being represented in the work of Granovetter (1983), with his concern for embedded links and the study of individuals in their context (through ego-centric studies). This matches Watts (2003: 49), who discussed weak links in relation to linking individual to group-level analysis. Social capital theories similarly focus on individuals in this way. (We will return to the critique of SNA in relation to whole-network approaches in Chapter 4.) As with Knox *et al.* (2006) and Mitchell (1974), Diani (2003), in his review of social movements and networks, points to the strands of network thinking including the individual and structural perspectives (paralleled by ideas on agency and structure). In his view a distinction of the field of SNA is in its linking of social networks and culture – a network of meanings through which actors make sense of, and categorise, the social environment (drawing on White 1992). Passy (2003), in the same text, takes up the dichotomy of social structure and the individual, arguing that agency is ignored by structuralist approaches (echoing Emirbayer and Goodwin 1994). She thinks that the network can be seen to account for the construction of meanings from social interaction, and argues that networks are phenomenological realities: 'islands of meanings which define and redefine individual identities through interactions with other actors or groups' (Passy 2003: 26).[19] The network of meanings brings culture and agency back into individual participation, linking interestingly with Mitchell's third kind of 'content' ('normative content'; see 'Anthropologists' study of networks', p. 26), and with concepts of identity considered earlier in relation to small world theories. These are important ideas in relation to views of knowledge and learning, similar to those from the different research traditions in education considered in the next chapter, when we argue for learning as identity formation. Interestingly, the issue of identity is also the concern of Otis, who discusses the merging of the technological and the human in networks: 'the metaphor [of the network] invited all who encountered it to rethink their identities' (2001: 20).[20]

Knox *et al.* (2006) consider a sophisticated idea of the network metaphor by tracing some of the anthropological research, in particular that which stems from work on socio-technical objects. A concern for these objects is brought about in part by the growth of networks aided by ICT, and is one strand of how the network frames our thinking about such things as the working of communications systems. This is most strikingly seen in the study of such systems in the nineteenth century by Otis (2001), who shows how views of the brain and nervous system were interpreted through metaphors of a web, and that similar ideas prevailed in communication systems such as telegraphy. The metaphors were used to justify both centralised views, where communication could be controlled centrally, and the more familiar one of the network as a self-organising system (as Hargreaves [2003a] envisaged). This puts the focus on the character of network processes. Knox and her colleagues draw on the work of Riles (2000), who studied the networking activities of the Fijian women's movement. These women focused on the processes of collecting information, compiling documents and disseminating them, leading up to, during and following international conferences. The network was in itself the object of study, and not a way of analysing a culture or society; there was nothing to explain through the use of the network as a metaphor, as it was already understood by its members. Riles contrasts this with the usual anthropologists' use of network to provide analytic distance that enables models and accounts of complexity to be created.[21] Knox *et al.* (2006) conclude that if the network becomes a blueprint for the social relations of social life, it will lose its productive capacity to provide an analysis of them. The network as a 'blueprint for social relations' in a sense is the position of advocates of teacher networks and NLCs, which we considered in Chapter 1 (e.g. Lieberman and Grolnick 1996). They put emphasis on the network as a form of organisation, using it metaphorically to conjure up a set of conditions that constitute this form (e.g. voluntary participation and equal treatment). They do not use any of the concepts of network theories, and where they do invoke concepts, these are derived from those associated with 'community' and groups where only strong ties prevail.

These views of the network as an entity or object in itself go further than the view of 'whole-network' studies (which similarly envisage a definable network, from which they effectively sample). Such views have, as indicated earlier, been given added import by the development of ICT, and we now turn to this idea of 'the network' by considering the work of Castells.

Networks as entities

In his classic text on the network society, Castells (2000a) seeks to examine social structure and the way knowledge and information processing can be seen as the basis for a new socio-technical paradigm. His hypothesis is that the control of knowledge and information decides who holds power in society. The dominant interests in this view are those of scientific–technological rationality rather than of economics. In line with sociologists who use SNA, he seeks to show how social structure can be looked at in terms of relationships; his concerns are with '[t]he organizational arrangements of humans in relationships of production/consumption, experience, and power, as expressed in meaningful interaction framed by culture' (Castells 2000b: 5). As with some of the other theorists we have just examined, 'meaning' is an important concept in relation to networks; he sees the network society as 'constantly produced and reproduced through symbolic interaction between actors framed by . . . social structure and at the same time acting to change or reproduce it' (ibid.: 7).

His enterprise of detailing the network society is beyond the scope of this book, but within his theorising there are important ideas that at the very least are influential in the common discourse on networks (e.g. Hargreaves 2003a). He also provides some specific ideas that we found important. One of the features of his analysis is the role he saw for the socio-technical paradigm (also called the new technological paradigm) 'constituted around microelectronics-based information/communication technologies, and genetic engineering' (Castells 2000b: 5–6). Castells argues that these technologies accelerate the production of knowledge and information in a self-expanding and virtuous circle. He sees a network as a set of interconnected nodes, with ICT transforming them into information networks. Further, the network as a form of structure has no centre, and the importance of any node lies in its ability to process information more efficiently than others. The relevance and relative weight of nodes are related to their ability to be trusted by the network with an extra share of information. The main nodes are not *centres* but *switches*, part of what Castells (ibid.: 16) calls a network logic rather than a command logic – that is, they do not have a hierarchical relationship to other nodes, but attain their status because they process information for the network more efficiently than do other nodes. Ironically, even though Hargreaves (2004) supported a network logic, by publishing in a volume with this in the title, his view of hubs, namely that they have an almost hierarchical relationship to surrounding nodes (schools), is not like Castells'. Such hubs, 'innovative schools', are certainly not identified by other schools because of the information on practice that they can supply more effectively, but are identified separately as 'leading edge' schools (Hargreaves 2003a: 38).[22]

In examining three features of the 'new economy', Castells (2000b: 10) argues that it is networked, and this represents, in his terms, connectivity in a new form of economic organisation, what he calls the 'networked enterprise'. These networks focus on projects that make a network enterprise programmed to attain specific goals. The firms that are part of this network are the nodes (units of capital accumulation) in global networks of financial flows. These networks are flexible and based on corporations sharing information. He also argues that there is a pattern of networking in the cultural realm, with ephemeral symbolic communication based on electronic media, including the internet. Hypertext structures the symbolic environment, and this 'virtuality . . . [becomes] a fundamental dimension of reality . . . from which we think and thus exist' (ibid.: 13).

The 'flows' in a network are not just financial. Indeed, Castells argues that societies are fundamentally made of such flows exchanged through networks of organisations and institutions. These flows are 'purposeful, repetitive, programmable sequences of exchange and interaction between physically disjointed positions held by social actors in economic, political, and symbolic structures of society' (2000a: 442).

The structure between networks and positions is related to these network flows, enabling power holders to control 'less important' nodes. He contrasts the 'meaning and function of the space of flows', which depend upon the flows processed within networks, with the 'space of places', where meaning, function and locality are closely interrelated. This is similar to the contrast of traditional views of community based on place with, say, modern urban society, where networks that transcend place operate (Wellman 2001). We will return to the space of flows in Chapter 8 when we consider spatial and temporal dimensions of networks.

Castells sees the 'space of flows' as the material form of support for dominant social practices that are described by a combination of three layers, which specify its content. The first layer describes the electronic network itself, what we would call the *electronic map* – that is, the electronic connections and how various servers, server systems and exchanges might interrelate and switch electronic traffic around. The second is concerned with mapping networked resources such as web pages, what we call the *information map*, which offers the potential to make resource discovery more efficient and effective. This is the kind of analysis that Google uses as a search engine. A third layer is concerned with the use of the network by actors and groups, what we would call the *actor map* ('the spatial organization of the dominant, managerial elites' [Castells 2000a: 445]). An example would be an analysis of the nature of email exchanges for network activity (or those on an electronic discussion forum). Indeed, as we move from the first to the third layer it is necessary to use measures, and hence 'data', to analyse the network that are increasingly conceptual or abstract representations of links and activity. Social network analysts would argue that their work provides concepts with which to analyse such social relations. What is striking is the way in which these layers are used metaphorically in discussions of networks in the educational literature. For example, when Hargreaves (2003a) discusses the use of ICT laterally (his fourth transformation), he appears to talk of it as a single kind of connectivity, starting with Milgram's six degrees of separation (layer 3), moving on to hubs (layer 1), then sites such as Amazon.com (layer 2), and then computer-supported collaborative environments (layer 3), as if they are all artefacts of a single kind of network facility, 'ICT'. It is likely that the nature of the practice (classroom teaching and learning), and the kinds of relationships that exist, will mean that a more careful use of the idea of the 'networked society' will need to be considered in relation to educational networks.

To return to Castells' ideas, it is interesting to note that his focus on relationships, which determine social structure, relates to a discussion of Wenger (1998), which we will come to in the next chapter:

> This social structure is formed by the interplay between relationships of production/consumption; relationships of experience; and relationships of power. Meaning is constantly produced and reproduced through symbolic interaction between actors framed by this social structure, and, at the same time, acting to change it or to reproduce it. By meaning, I understand the symbolic identification by an actor of the purpose of her/his/their action. The consolidation of shared meaning through crystallization of practices in spatio-temporal configurations creates cultures, that is systems of values and beliefs informing codes of behaviour. . . . Meaning results from symbolic interaction between brains which are socially and ecologically constrained, and, at the same time, biologically and culturally able of innovation. Meaning is produced, reproduced, and fought over in all layers of social structure, in production as in consumption, in experience as in power.

(Castells 2000b: 7)

This draws together some of the earlier quotations from his work to show a complex interrelationship of views on social structure, networks and meaning. Whatever questions may surround any network view drawing on technology, it is clear that in the world of 'Web 2.0' it would be unreasonable to ignore its impact on educational networks. In Chapter 10 we will return to these kinds of networks, to examine their role in the creation and sharing of practice.

Educational networks

In Chapter 1 we examined some educational networks but concluded that they are seldom informed by any clear network thinking. Most of this work focused on collaboration but did little to examine the relationships within or between schools in any detail, or to explore the sharing of the results of the collaborative work with those not involved in it (we quoted from Little [2005b: 278] to this effect). We pointed to the limitations of reviews such as those by Kerr *et al.* (2003), Stoll *et al.* (2006) and NLG/CUREE (2005) in focusing on 'community' views of networks. Work of this kind does acknowledge some of the network ideas that we have considered in this chapter.

Adams (2000) investigates the effectiveness of a teacher network for mathematics education, conceived very much in the Ann Lieberman tradition (Lieberman wrote the foreword to Adams' book) and citing the professional learning community research. Although he reviews a modest amount of the network theory literature, his model of analysis of how curriculum change is implemented (Adams 2000: 26–9) includes character of relationships (e.g. reciprocity), frequency of interaction and strength of network (i.e. whether members have multiple types of relations with other actors in the network). Yet in the actual analysis of the implementation, the evidence presented on these features of the networks is weak. For example, in discussing the relationships among network members he cites some data on rapport, supportiveness and acting like peers, and showing that social and professional relationships were reinforcing, but acknowledges that there was very little information on the 'strength of relationships among network members' (ibid.: 143). The idea of a 'linker' is used (ibid.: 138–9): someone who serves as a link among network teachers and schools, and connects them to the larger world of professional experience and expertise. Despite citing Burt (1982) in reviewing the literature on networks, Adams makes no connection to his ideas on brokers, and this linker is in fact the network co-ordinator. Nevertheless, as we will show in later chapters, this role does resemble some of the functions of the LHTL school co-ordinators (e.g. as shown in Chapter 9 case studies). In a study of practitioner research in various NLCs in England, McLaughlin *et al.* (2008) explore the network literature, again largely from that of PLCs, but with references to Granovetter (1973), Nardi *et al.* (2000), Castells (2000a) and to some of our own work from the project. The bulk of the discussion, not surprisingly, given that it involves teachers researching their own classrooms, reflects the views of networks we discussed in Chapter 1. McLaughlin *et al.* do, however, note a number of times the importance of sharing, and the difficulty this presents, concluding in their final chapter that in their studies of NLCs 'there was very limited evidence of extensive resources being invested by the networks in this demanding task of sharing validated good practice' (2008: 198). They were able to cite examples of this sharing, but did not use any of the network thinking we have discussed to understand the processes involved.

In this chapter we have explored a range of network theories and now turn to an examination of the research that has used it in an educational context. Our concern is not with educational networks for students, but educational networks for teachers and schools as organisations (both within and across schools). There is in fact a wide range of network research, much of it taking an SNA approach, though the bulk of it is concerned with leadership in a variety of forms. Work has also been done on change and diffusion, collaboration and support for newly qualified teachers.[23] We will examine these areas as they relate to schools.[24]

There are a number of leadership studies that consider distributed leadership (Cole 2008; Warfield 2009), informal leadership (Fraser 2008; Hancock 2008), the influence of leaders (Palmer 2008) and how school leaders use networks for resource acquisition (Hite *et al.* 2006).[25] A concern for leadership also relates to some of the work on change and the diffusion of innovations. Thus, Bidwell (2001) sets out a case for the study of networks of teachers' informal relationships that affect both the local cultures of practice within a school that may be resistant to change, and the role of teachers' links to those in other schools. Aston (1997) studied the strong and weak ties of teachers and how these relate to teacher beliefs on educational change, finding that social networks had more impact on teacher beliefs than school experiences. O'Rourke (1999) used SNA to identify opinion leadership, which is related to the diffusion of innovations. Most opinion leaders were not part of the formal leadership structure, and hence made up an informal structure. Pitts and Spillane (2009) are concerned to identify who in a school are instructional leaders – that is, whom teachers go to for advice on teaching and learning – though their study is largely a methodological one to validate an SNA instrument. Studies of diffusion also related to ICT and the role of technical assistance networks (Tate 1998) and instructional technology resource teachers negotiating roles with opinion leaders in schools (Pixley 2008).

Studies of change look at the community aspects and, in particular, ideas on collaboration and trust. In a conceptual paper, Lima (2001) is concerned to expose more directly what happens within schools, responding to a critique by Little (1987), who was sceptical about much of what passes for collaboration. Lima argues the case for considering the role of friendship in relation to change and also the role of both strong and weak ties. In a later article, Lima (2007) investigates two departments and how their social networks relate to their potential for knowledge sharing and development. By revealing the way teachers relate to each other, he shows how some departments can be isolated, with poor connections within them and with the rest of the school, thus revealing that teachers have different views regarding the idea of 'the whole school'. He shows that an isolated department engaged in almost no talk about teaching and very little joint work with colleagues. These insights open up the idea of 'community' in the kinds of way Little (2005b: 278) called for in a passage quoted in Chapter 1. Lima extends this work on departmental cultures by looking at distributed leadership (Lima 2008) and support for student teachers' views on and practices of collaboration (Lima 2003). Both of these latter studies uncover the actual relationships that exist within the schools he studied. They reveal differences in the collaborative environments that leaders of departments are able to create, and the support they give to teachers' professional development, and hence the difference in their leadership.[26] Newly qualified teachers are also studied by Baker-Doyle (2008a, b), who shows the importance of informal support people for these teachers, coining the terms 'intensional professional network' (*sic*) for this support through strong ties, and 'diverse professional allies' (e.g. parents, volunteers and students) who bring diversity to teachers' networks. (Chapter 6 will deal with intensional networks.)

All of these studies are important for opening up the internal workings of schools, in the way Hakkarainen *et al.* (2004) have done for innovative companies. They also explore the extent to which 'cohesion' exists both to generate knowledge within the school and to utilise any knowledge gained from elsewhere (as Burt [2005] argued). In particular, they reveal the kind of evidence that would have been helpful to NLCs in understanding both their internal collaborative processes and how they could share the results of them.[27] However, these studies focus on particular schools, rather than across schools, which was our concern in the LHTL project. Recent work by Daly and his colleagues, from a leadership perspective (Daly and Finnigan forthcoming a, b; Daly *et al.* 2009), investigates networks at the district level (in the United States). In the study of teachers they acknowledge that there is little empirical work at this level, and they use both SNA surveys and qualitative interviews to explore the social networks and their role in school reform (Daly *et al.* 2009). Their concern is with the relationship of work-related and social networks of teachers, investigated through SNA surveys of teachers within schools (recording their frequency of relationships on three areas, such as lesson planning), and with one other teacher in another school in the district. They also interviewed twelve teachers who reflected demographically the teachers in the district and the various positions teachers occupied in the social networks (from SNA surveys). They found that there were quite different patterns of engagement, communication and collaboration based on social interactions, with grade-level teams[28] having different social structures, which are ignored in the reform movement in the district. Similarly, there were various patterns of interaction between schools in terms of reciprocity and engagement with collaboration; where there was more interaction, there was more co-construction of lesson development. Interestingly, school principals were important in the way the reform was interpreted within the school (with either a technical or a learning-oriented focus), irrespective of the particular social interactions within the school. Daly *et al.* argue that such SNA data will give an understanding of social structure to enable those who are more central in a network to be best placed to 'move knowledge and practice throughout the system' (ibid.: 21). They also argue that knowledge of the social interactions at school level would enable school leaders to support and design reform, although, as we shall see later, this raises ethical problems.

In a second study, Daly and Finnigan (forthcoming a) investigate the next level up – that is, how district and school-level administrators relate to each other – showing that many school principals (headteachers) may be isolated and have insufficient interaction with the district office or each other. In view of the finding of the importance of principals in influencing their schools, this is significant. Obviously the details of the impact of these social structures will reflect the particular education system in the United States, but Daly and his colleagues illustrate the utility of this kind of work.[29]

The evidence of all these studies of educational networks from an SNA perspective, although instructive and revealing, does not provide a panacea for understanding networks. They all make assumptions about the nature of the network, and the entities within it. They use quantitative measures to represent relationships that may have validity challenges (some, such as Daly *et al.* [2009], Lima [2007] and Baker-Doyle

[2008a], also employ qualitative methods), and of course they assume the extent of the network (a school or district). As we have indicated, in discussing the pioneering work of Daly *et al.* (2009), they also make assumptions about the nature of knowledge and assume that it indeed can be 'moved'. In the chapters that follow on mapping networks (Chapter 4), the nature of nodes (Chapter 5) and links (Chapter 6), and the nature of what 'flows' in these links (Chapter 7), we will discuss some of these assumptions and examine the ways the different views of networks might help us to understand and research them.

Chapter 3

Teacher learning

Introduction

Chapter 1 ended with a question about the nature of teacher learning, particularly in relation to 'network learning', and so in this chapter we will examine how to conceptualise 'learning'. An obvious question might be: 'Why consider teacher learning when the focus of the book has been on knowledge creation and sharing?' It was evident in Chapter 1 that many of those concerned with educational networks and professional learning communities (PLCs) discussed these ideas in relation to teacher learning. Examples include Lieberman and Wood (2004) on the role of teacher learning in relation to networks and professional communities, Stoll *et al.* (2006) on PLCs, discussions of 'network learning' (e.g. Jackson and Temperley 2006) and Veugelers and O'Hair (2005a) and the enhancement of teacher learning through collaboration in professional communities. Similarly, discussions of continuous professional development (CPD) are concerned with teacher learning, for example policy documents (DfEE 2000) and reviews of literature on CPD (e.g. McCormick *et al.* 2008; Wilson and Berne 1999).

Many of these authors were concerned with the creation and sharing of educational knowledge, though few of them articulated the nature of the learning process; rather, they identified many characteristics of how these communities and networks operated that were in a sense equated with the 'learning process'. One early account of teacher learning in the context of professional development opportunities reflected on the fact that the research and development of views of *student* learning was not evident in the literature on *teacher* learning (Putnam and Borko 2000). They referred to the student learning literature, where a situated view of learning had become common, and discussed the way in which cognition was *situated* in the physical and social context, and *social* in that knowledge and learning were the products of interactions of groups of people. They also acknowledged that cognition was *distributed* across people, places and symbols. In making these points they referred to some key discussions in the learning literature. Some of these ideas have clearly entered into the thinking of the literature we discussed in Chapter 1, even if those who discuss PLCs and networks do not contain articulations of the underlying theories. For example, notions of 'collaboration' and 'joint working' are seen as key elements, without their relationship to a particular theory of learning being discussed.

We now explore conceptualisations of these processes of learning to answer the questions posed in Chapter 1. However, we cannot assume that the knowledge creation and sharing that, for example, Hargreaves (2003a) described is the same as 'learning'; indeed, in the earlier account of the 'knowledge-creating school' (Hargreaves 1999), he discusses a different kind of theory drawn from work in innovative companies. We will therefore examine this strand of thinking (through the work of Paavola *et al.* [2004]), which distinguishes itself from the usual ways in which learning is depicted.

Views of learning

The account of Putnam and Borko (2000) referred to some of the discussions that were taking place in the literature between two views of learning: one based on individual cognition ('in the head', as it were) and the other on social aspects.[1] Putnam and Borko seemed to focus on the latter view, often referred to as the situative (or situated) perspective. The two views, developed with regard to student learning, were conveniently captured by Sfard (1998) in two metaphors for learning: the *acquisition metaphor* (AM) and the *participation metaphor* (PM).

Metaphors of learning

The *acquisition metaphor* takes a symbol processing view of mind, as a manipulator of symbols. These symbols are learned and stored in memory; when confronted with a problem, a person searches the memory for symbols to represent the problem and then manipulates them to solve the problem. There are of course different views of how these symbols are learned – that is, of what constitutes the learning process. At one end of the spectrum is the information processing view, where the learner is a passive processor of information. But the most widely held view sees learning as a knowledge construction process – that is, individual learners make meaning from experiences. This places learners in an active role, with problem solving as a central process in knowledge construction, a process carried out by an *individual* learner, with the focus on individual cognition.

Through the latter part of the twentieth century there were those theorists who focused increasingly on the social aspects of knowledge construction and the social nature of knowledge. This led to a group of theories labelled as social constructivist. Central to this view of learning is the role of others in creating and sharing meaning. All constructivist approaches have some social element in the construction process. Thus, Piaget, although focused upon individual internalisation of knowledge, saw a role for peer interaction to produce cognitive conflict that would result in a change in the thinking of the individual, leading to the internalisation of a concept or idea.[2] By challenging the role of others in the construction of knowledge, social constructivists, to varying degrees, challenged views of the nature of knowledge and of culture.

Those who view learning as a process of *participation* in cultural activity see a different role for the interactions with others, with 'participation' as a central process. This approach stems in part from Vygotsky and action theory (Lave 1996; Bredo 1997). Meaning is created through participating in social activity. In this sense there is no individual notion of an idea or concept, but a distributed one. Rather than seeing learning as a process of transfer of knowledge from the knowledgeable to the less knowledgeable, we have engagement in culturally authentic activity. Such activity is part of a 'community of practice'. From this view of situated learning comes a central focus on collaboration (between peers and others) and problem solving. Unlike the AM view, problem solving in a situated view is a shared activity even when it involves an expert; expert and novices jointly solve problems. In Sfard's account of AM and PM there was an emphasis on how the two perspectives give different views of knowledge: the former as an 'object' (e.g. a concept) that we can possess, the latter as practice or activity in which an individual can participate.

The AM sees knowledge as a commodity (an object) that can be developed (for example, we talk of 'concept development', with the concept as a basic unit of knowledge) or constructed. Whether knowledge acquisition is seen as a transmission process or as a construction process, the individual accumulates it, like some kind of material. Typical words used that display this metaphor are knowledge, concept, conception, idea, notion, misconception, meaning, sense, schema, fact, representation, material and contents. There are a number of processes (the mechanisms of learning) that we use to describe how learners make knowledge their own: reception, acquisition, construction, internalisation, appropriation, transmission, attainment, development, accumulation and grasp. These processes may of course be different, but in the end the knowledge becomes individual property that, once acquired, can be applied, transferred and shared. The PM avoids referring to knowledge as an entity and replaces 'knowledge' with 'knowing', and 'having knowledge' with 'doing'. Through the use of ideas of participation and discourse, 'participation in activities' is important, not 'possession of knowledge'; 'becoming a member' replaces 'learning a subject'.

At the time she wrote this paper, Sfard (1998) was arguing that both metaphors were needed to reflect the complexity and incompleteness of our understanding of learning. Although Putnam and Borko (2000) took the PM stance, one of the authors in a more recent publication apparently building on this earlier work seemed to support both kinds as dual perspectives on learning (Borko 2004). She argued that, as with bifocal lenses, both perspectives were necessary to 'see' the world of learning. In later work, Sfard (2006) has seen the PM as the most complete account of learning and uses it to explain her empirical work in mathematics education. We also take a PM approach, casting this more broadly in the socio-cultural approach to learning, and draw on Wenger (1998) for the most complete account of this. As we will show, this view does not ignore the individual (reconciled through the concept of learning as identity development). We recognise, however, that the AM is ingrained in our vocabulary, and, further, that the complexity of the learning process is such that it is unlikely to be captured by any one theory.

Communities of practice

Wenger developed the idea of communities of practice, used in discussions in Chapter 1, although many authors refer to the original work (Lave and Wenger 1991). The significance of the Lave and Wenger (1991) account is that it was built around case studies of apprenticeship as a way of conceiving learning. Novices (or newcomers) are enculturated into the practices of the community of practice and move from being able to participate peripherally in the practices to being able to participate centrally when they are competent in the practices. We shall outline some of Wenger's ideas used in this chapter and later in the book – in particular, practice, meaning, community, learning, identity and learning community (Wenger 1998). We shall also briefly examine the nature of knowledge and issues of the boundaries around communities.

Wenger (1998) argues that communities of practice create and sustain practices that reflect a particular enterprise and the related social relations. For teachers, this would include classroom and school practices in which they participate as part of everyday activity. This concept of *practice* is not just the 'official' activity that is laid down, say in any procedures, regulations, schemes of work, lesson plans, etc., but what teachers might do to make the task of teaching manageable. In Wenger's view, such practices are always social and have a history and context that give them meaning to teachers. There are explicit and implicit elements to practices, yet both elements are socially negotiated. Thus, a particular approach to grading in the school might reflect a particular headteacher's ideas, or those of a working group that created a policy. However, the science and mathematics departments might 'unofficially' have adopted a variation of this (e.g. using a 100 per cent scale when the school uses letter grades), or the English department might reward effort even though doing so is not part of the policy.

In Wenger's view, practices are not just routines, and hence even when apparently manual tasks are carried out, the doing and the knowing are not separate; practices are not therefore inherently unreflective. Members of a community of practice negotiate meaning through engagement in these practices. Meaning is in the dynamics of interaction, and hence doing and thinking are not separated. Participation in practices is central to making meaning from activity, but need not be equated with collaboration; isolated individual activity can be seen to have a social element. Teachers' practices largely take place when teachers are working on their own in a classroom, but they are part of the community of practice of teachers.[3] Objects can capture elements of practice, as is the case with a scheme of work, which will co-ordinate the practices of a group of teachers. Wenger calls such objects 'reifications', which give a focus for negotiating meaning. Symbols and tools of the community of practice are all forms of reifications. Thus, a science teacher might use a scheme of work that delineates the sequence of science concepts and associated student tasks that will be introduced for a particular age group. The scheme of work can shape the teacher's experience of the lessons that result,[4] but meaning will only be contextualised through participation in the teaching of these concepts. Wenger sees 'participation' and 'reification' as complementary in that if there is only a reification of practice, then it will not have meaning without participation. In his words:

> With insufficient participation, our relations to broader enterprises tend to remain literal and procedural: our co-ordination tends to be based on compliance rather than participation in meaning. . . . With insufficient reification, co-ordination across time and space may depend too much on the partiality of specific participants, or it may simply be too vague, illusory, or contentious to create alignment.
>
> (1998: 187)

Again, a scheme of work or an assessment strategy may not have a universal meaning and will depend upon the local practices of a school or a department in a school (as already illustrated), requiring an individual to participate in these practices to see their full meaning. If a new teacher comes into the school, then the reification helps the teacher to see what is required; without it, negotiating the meaning of the practice for a particular lesson topic could be difficult. Without this scheme of work, a new teacher would have to work alongside a teacher who had been operating in the school for some time, and this could be an inefficient way of learning the local practice. Lesson plans can operate in the same way; they are not the lesson but an abstraction of it. It is evident that making a classroom practice explicit in a lesson plan requires a transformation of participation but does not do away with the implicit element of the practice. Just as reification and participation are not a dichotomy (they are a duality), so it is with implicit and explicit knowledge. These two concepts of participation and reification are central to understanding knowledge sharing, in that reifications 'travel' whereas participation does not – something we will examine in Chapter 7.

Strangely, although *community* is the best known of Wenger's concepts, it is often not used by others in the way Wenger describes it. By associating it with 'practice' in the term 'community of practice', Wenger defines a community by its shared practices. Three dimensions of practice give the community its coherence: mutual engagement, joint enterprise and a shared repertoire. In the discussion on PLCs, for example, these three dimensions are rarely dealt with.[5] (In view of the evidence from social network analysis [SNA] we reviewed in Chapter 2, assuming that any grouping of teachers working in a PLC or a 'network' form a community warrants an investigation of the nature of the relationships that actually exist.) Here we give a brief outline of the three dimensions.

Mutual engagement implies engagement in some activity – that is, a community of practice is not a social category, a network of interpersonal relationships[6] or those in geographical proximity. This gives an interesting view of teachers as a community. They mutually engage in a whole range of activities, not all of which would be regarded as teaching, which contribute to the practices of the community. Attention has to be given to these as much as to the teaching activity itself. This mutual engagement does not imply that there are no specialisations and diverse roles in the community. The difficulty comes in defining at what level of grouping the community of practice exists: teaching group (age group, subject department), school, district or nation – an issue we consider in what follows.

Joint enterprise is the collective process of negotiation that creates the community of practice. The practice is shaped by participants, it being their response to the conditions. This joint enterprise may not correspond with any organisational (or employer) definition of it. The community's practice would include the reconciliation of the competing demands on participants from the job, the organisation and their own needs; what 'makes the job habitable' (Wenger 1998: 46). This also involves negotiating judgements on quality that are shared but not easily reified, leading to a regime of mutual accountability.

A *shared repertoire* is built up over time through the joint pursuit of the enterprise, creating resources for negotiating meaning. These will be routines, terms, tools and ways of doing things, which will be both reified and participative. Though this repertoire creates meaning through shared points of reference, it does not impose meaning on community members, and hence ambiguity will still exist. This takes us back to the earlier discussion of reification and participation. We can see in schools the differences in repertoire between a science teacher who has to enable practical work and that of an English teacher who has to enable dramatisation of scripts. Whatever else they may share, there are some tools, etc. that may distinguish their practice.

In this example of English and science teachers, there are hints of some of the complexities of defining a community of practice. It is not 'all teachers', as it is evident that the repertoires are only partially shared across different school phases and, even within a phase, between teachers of different ages (e.g. reception class teachers and those who teach 11-year-olds) or subjects. But do science teachers in all secondary schools belong to *a* community of practice or do we have to consider the level of *a* science department in *a* particular school? Wenger discusses this issue through the idea of locality, indicating that there is an issue of level of analysis; a specific interaction cannot be seen as a (transient) community of practice, nor can a whole nation or culture be seen as one. There would need to be too much reification in the latter two and only participation in the specific interaction (and not 'practices'). Thus, we reify classroom practice by considering that all teachers 'teach', but the specifics of this for any locality may be so varied that this word does not really give an indication of the mutual engagement, joint enterprise and shared repertoire. A subject association can be seen as a community of practice of, say, science teachers. We will return again to what counts as a community of practice shortly, when we consider some of the critiques of Wenger's idea of it.

All communities have *boundaries* between them, and these provide a focus for understanding practice (the notion of legitimate peripheral participation is premised on moving from a boundary of a community to full participation at its centre). Boundaries define both continuities (connections) and discontinuities, but two forms of connections are of particular importance: boundary objects and brokering. *Boundary objects* co-ordinate perspectives of various constituencies for some purpose. For example, a statement for a child with special educational needs is a boundary object for teachers and educational psychologists (or other local authority [LA] staff); the national test results will be a boundary object for headteachers and LA staff, or school inspectors; the National Curriculum for a subject or phase is a boundary object for many of the communities of practice within (and outside) education. Such objects (reifications) provide connections between communities of practice that otherwise have no specific shared practice, and hence act as 'bridges', but they do not necessarily bridge the different perspectives and meanings of the various constituent communities.[7] (It is evident that there are different interpretations put on the meaning of such objects as those listed above by the different groups.) *Brokering* occurs when a participant from one community of practice (A) enters another (B) and persuades this latter community to adopt an interpretation of a procedure from the former community (A). This is exactly what we are trying to do when we ask secondary teachers to work with primary teachers to encourage them to use a particular procedure of, say, assessment for learning (AfL). More probably, we ask secondary English teachers to work with secondary science teachers on an assessment procedure the latter already use to encourage the former to develop their practice. It is also possible to use reifications of practice as a form of brokering, which is what our LHTL project staff (all former teachers) did when they presented a primary school exemplar of practice to a group of secondary school teachers. So, it is possible to see brokering in terms of participation and reification; the latter 'travel' better, but uprooted from the practices in which they function they have reduced impact. There are ways of having participative connections through multi-membership of communities or working with someone from another community in a third community (e.g. members of A and B working in C).

Wenger's view of *learning* extends beyond the movement from peripheral to central participation in a community's practices, as indicated earlier. He sees practice as a shared history of learning, with practices being reinvented even in an apparently routine job. Wenger encapsulates the idea of an emergent structure in the phrase 'Learning is the engine of practice, and practice is the history of that learning' (1998: 96). Tracing this emergent structure may be a way of understanding how learning takes place in the introduction of a new pedagogic approach or a feature of student learning in a school, LA or even the profession. For teachers this will occur because different classes and individual students within a class will require different variations of a classroom practice, and perhaps even a new practice not tried before. In his study of claims processors he said that they talked of 'change' rather than 'learning'; their ability to engage in practice changes.

An example of the situation described above occurred when the teachers in the King's Medway and Oxfordshire Formative Assessment Project (KMOFAP) were trying to make meaning out of the research that indicated that four areas of classroom practices would benefit from an AfL approach. Indeed, to move from something like the ten principles of AfL (ARG 2002), which are extremely reified practice, to actual classroom practices (participation) requires considerable negotiation of meaning. The meaning of AfL did not pre-exist for the KMOFAP teachers to take on board; rather, they had to negotiate its meaning. The researchers they worked with were clear about the principles of AfL and were able to give accounts of research experiments and studies that showed the basis of these principles and even particular associated practices, but they had no more idea how to turn the general ideas (reifications) into specific practices than the teachers initially had. Meaning for these teachers was to be found in the interaction of these ideas (the thinking) and the doing. The ideas of AfL are reifications that find meaning in participation in practices. Even when these teachers produced accounts of classroom practices that could be used by others (Black *et al.* 2002), these accounts were themselves reifications that could then enable others to negotiate meaning through trying them out and developing them in classrooms. Indeed, the LHTL project built on such accounts and ideas for classroom practices to create workshop activities that would enable this participation to take place (James *et al.* 2006a). Nevertheless, even these workshop activities were themselves reifications. These ideas are central to a consideration of what is 'flowing' through a network, and we will look at them in detail in Chapter 7.

In most of the discussion so far, it seems that the individual is lost, and that learning is entirely social. Wenger uses the concept of *identity* to move the focus to the person, by seeing individuality within the context of practices of a specific community. Participation is a source of identity, and learning to participate is to develop an identity. For Wenger, identity stems from the unique experience of engaging in practices. Individuals are likely to be members of a number of communities of practice, and this multi-membership is reconciled at what Wenger calls the nexus of an individual's identity. The nexus is not just a mix of elements of the different identities but will require work of reconciliation to establish meaning in activity. Recognising the autonomy of your own child (as father or mother) has to be reconciled with how you treat the autonomy of children in your classroom (as a teacher). For a particular community of practice there are various kinds of participation and indeed non-participation: full participation; full non-participation; peripherality; marginality.

Wenger sees identity formation through different 'modes of belonging', where he identifies three 'modes': *engagement, imagination* and *alignment* (1998: 173). The sense of belonging in *engagement* can be identified when a teacher taking part in a CPD activity on AfL shares an understanding of the purpose of the workshop activities. The teacher may want to share this understanding with others and so be active in making learning explicit (an important strategy in AfL). This is a way for the teacher to enact being a teacher skilled in the use of AfL strategies. *Imagination* is not just about how we see ourselves now, but what our vision of self is for the future. The teacher needs to see her- or himself as a competent AfL teacher, a view beyond the current state of practice, perhaps in reference to some account of practice by a skilled teacher in these AfL practices. *Alignment* is the co-ordination of our actions to 'fit' within a 'broader enterprise'. The teacher may see that a current classroom technique of putting up lesson objectives, while not being all that is involved in AfL, nevertheless can contribute to mastery of AfL techniques. The negotiation of identity is how teachers 'make sense of' the practice within which they find themselves.

But the development of identity is also learning, and, as noted, it is identity that, Wenger (1998) argues, links the social and the individual. Learning is a trajectory of becoming, and this trajectory is an individual one, even where that identity is one shared with a community. The identity associated with the new practices in a community is little elaborated, and this remains an area for research.[8]

Wenger's idea of a *learning community* deals with the community of practice as a living context both for newcomers to gain access to competence, and to explore new insights and hence knowledge that can be created (by 'old-timers'). This idea is based on the relationship between 'experience' and 'competence', which are both constituents of learning and thus knowing. Competence drives experience for newcomers, who transform experience until it fits with competence as defined by the community of practice. Experience may drive competence by forming new experience to be reified and then getting others in the community of practice to participate in this experience. Thus, a new classroom technique of, say, 'questioning' (in the sense understood in AfL) will be a competence that an early-years teacher may be introduced to, from a description of it by a colleague who has developed it (a reification), and learning takes place as her 'knowing' is transformed by a change in alignment of the experience and competence. As this technique is shared in the community it becomes a shared practice and part of the experience of the community of practice. This is at the heart of the idea of knowledge creation, and we will return to this when we consider it more completely later in the chapter.

Critiques of communities of practice

We have already noted that there is an issue with defining the community in terms of local and global ideas about it. Our concern here is how these communities are seen in relation to knowledge creation and sharing. One criticism, implied at the outset, is that learning only concerns those who are newcomers to a community of practice – who learn through a process of apprenticeship.[9] Engeström (2007) mounts a critique of communities of practice, arguing that the traditional apprenticeship cases presented in Lave and Wenger (1991) are not good models for modern collaborative communities. He considers three forms of production, comparing craft (which is what he sees Lave and Wenger [1991] dealing with), mass production and finally what he calls social production. In particular, he thinks that these modern communities, which are part of social production, have less fixed boundaries. This gives challenges: from a high level of technical division of labour and diversity of knowledge and skills; from authority that relates to knowledge and expertise, not to status; and from the need for the values to be examined in open discussion to orient all members of the community. Like Hargreaves (2003a), he looks to the software development communities who produce the Linux computer operating system as illustrative of social production. Such communities, he thinks, are more like mycorrhizae, which are invisible organic structures under fungi, symbiotic with the roots of a plant ('filamentous growth' [Engeström 2007: 48]). However, at this stage in the development of the idea, this has a similar status to Hargreaves' (2003a) ideas, with metaphorical rather than conceptual leverage.

Nevertheless, this criticism, and others (e.g. Fuller *et al.* 2005; Hughes *et al.* 2007), are based on the idea that communities of practice in contemporary workplaces may not be so parallel to those in the original formulation of Lave and Wenger (1991), which drew on traditional craft production. Wenger's later work (1998) was based on a relatively contemporary workplace of insurance clerks (compared to the traditional crafts of the Lave and Wenger text). It is reasonable to acknowledge the differences in workplaces, particularly those that involve more complex knowledge and skills. In an overview of the critiques by Hughes *et al.* (2007), Fuller (2007) gives six themes deriving from research in workplace learning, four of which are relevant to our discussion. First is the focus on learning as participation: that it fails to account for construction and transformation, because of the idea of enculturation. Fuller draws on Edwards' (2005) analysis of the PM, where she discusses activity theory in relation to the view of learning from Lave and Wenger (1991). Unfortunately, Edwards (2005: 57) does not actually develop the argument, but simply states that for the production of new knowledge we need to turn to the concept of expansive learning, which we will return to shortly.

A second of Fuller's themes is that there are both narrow and broad definitions of a community of practice: one which sees it as a tight-knit group and another that is concerned with more general 'participation, belonging and social relations' (2007: 23). Although the latter is not in itself clearly broader than the former, it nevertheless resembles a contrast of communities and networks that we will return to in our final section of reflection on networks.

Fuller's fourth theme concerns the simple division of novice and expert in the learning situation. She argues that research on workplace learning indicates that novices can be more expert in certain areas than 'old-timers'. In her view it is more important to see many different types of trajectories and hence identities, something she acknowledges that Wenger (1998) developed after his earlier work with Lave. She cites work in music education to show that there are many identities being developed by musicians, not just one corresponding to a single community of practice (Nielson 1997). We would agree with this, hence our interpretation of learning in terms of identity development, and we cite other work that illustrates the development of a variety of identities in apparently singular communities (Tonso 2007; Hughes 2008).

Finally, in her sixth theme, Fuller (2007) describes learning across different social spaces that lead to participation in multiple settings and networks that enable boundary crossing and hence more expansive learning. Although Fuller does not develop the network idea, this is compatible with the ideas of networks we have put forward in this book.[10]

Critically, from our point of view, Wenger is concerned with learning as it relates to a community, and his ideas are relevant to the situation with which we are concerned: where there is no curriculum as such (even if there are ideas that have to be implemented), and where there are no experts who can provide the 'teaching'.[11] Teachers concerned to develop new AfL practices, either new to them or where no examples exist for the age group and the context they are in, have to 'learn' new practices. This situation is what Engeström (2001: 138) referred to as 'new forms of activity which are . . . literally learned as they are being created'. Despite criticisms of 'communities of practice', our use of Wenger does not in any case depend upon the apprenticeship idea of learning, but upon his more general idea of learning as meaning-making and the development of identity, expressed as a trajectory of becoming. However, there are those who say that in the case of knowledge creation, what we need is not a metaphor (or theory) for learning but a knowledge-building metaphor.

Knowledge creation

A third metaphor?

Chapter 1 noted that Hargreaves (1999) uses a theory by Nonaka and Takeuchi (1995) as a parallel for teacher knowledge production in a school. This theory has a major focus on turning tacit knowledge into explicit knowledge that can be shared, which then becomes implicit in everybody's practice. This Japanese research concerned companies that were knowledge producers, as is often the case for hi-tech companies of the kind Paavola *et al.* (2004) were concerned with (in the commercial information technology sector). The latter's argument is that Sfard's AM deals with 'ready-made' knowledge, not something new that has expanded the knowledge available (however it is manifest, including within products). As we have indicated already, Paavola and his colleagues argue that because the PM approaches to learning are concerned with stable communities and the movement of novices from peripheral to central participation, these approaches are insufficient to account for the requirements of 'innovative knowledge communities', and hence they argue for a third 'knowledge-creation' metaphor.[12] They examined three models of how knowledge is created in such innovative communities, including Nonaka and Takeuchi (1995), Engeström (1999)[13] and Bereiter (2002). This is not the place to detail these approaches, and hence we will be highly selective in our account of them. We have already indicated that Nonaka and Takeuchi describe processes of going from implicit to explicit and back to implicit knowledge in a 'knowledge spiral' (Paavola *et al.* 2004: 559). This assumes that the source of the innovation is in the implicit knowledge of individuals that needs to be explicated for use by others in the community. Engeström uses activity theory[14] as a framework of explanation for an expansive learning cycle with seven stages, starting with individual participants questioning and criticising existing practices and including creating a new model to deal with problems (1999: 383–4). Finally, Bereiter (2002) proposes a knowledge-building theory that is concerned with conceptual entities such as theories and ideas. Bereiter argues that modern enterprises systematically produce and develop conceptual artefacts, rather than 'learn'. Such artefacts are shared knowledge and result from problems or new thoughts, with the focus being on creating new knowledge. This approach has been used with school students as well as in other organisations, and has also spawned software to enable knowledge building (Knowledge Forum[15]).

Knowledge creation in schools

Each of these approaches, and the knowledge-creation metaphor itself, are useful in both focusing on knowledge creation and examining the ways in which knowledge is created within organisations. However, there is an apparent assumption that these processes are the same in different contexts, despite some of the critiques being that the original formulation of learning by Lave and Wenger (1991) assumed a workplace that did not reflect contemporary ones. One of the critiques by Engeström (1999) of the cycles of implicit to explicit knowledge in the knowledge-creation process advocated by Nonaka and Takeuchi (1995) was that they were concerned with only large-scale processes. This does not throw any light on what happens in teams working in a manufacturing plant such as Engeström researched, which required an analysis at a lower level of detail. Such detail should be sought within the school setting to see whether the work of the teams of teachers (e.g. in a department) can be analysed in the same way. Engeström and his various colleagues have conducted research in a number of commercial and public service providers, including health practices (e.g. Engeström *et al.* 2007) and a middle school (Engeström *et al.* 2002), indicating that their activity theory approach can be used to capture the creative processes of teachers. In the case of the middle school, as is the case for a number of these activity theory studies, the approach is to intervene in the situation and for the researchers to carry out an analysis that is fed back to the groups being studied. This intervention is part of revealing contradictions, and is a driving force of change and development in activity theory (Engeström 2001). Equally, the initial questioning and analysis of a problem can start a cycle, which he calls 'expansive learning'.[16] The issue is whether the various contexts of innovation and knowledge creation over a range of activities are all the same – for example, designing products that satisfy market demands or indeed creates new demands;[17] uncovering contradictions between health providers and patients in a health practice; or the kind of knowledge building that a science researcher might develop for a new theory. And are any of these situations the same as that of teachers trying to develop new practice of AfL on the basis of some general principles from research and other teachers' descriptions of classroom practices that may not work in their case? Detailed empirical work is needed to establish whether that is the case, and we will return to the point shortly. First we look again at Hargreaves' account of knowledge creation in schools that we considered in Chapter 1, as this draws on some of the knowledge-creation metaphor ideas.

In his accounts of knowledge creation, Hargreaves (2003a) deals with general processes, for example in his use of Nonaka and Takeuchi (1995), and, in referring to the software development of Linux and hacker culture, he notes the importance of collaboration. In other accounts he notes the importance of reflection, dialogue and inquiry (Hargreaves 1999, 2001). Most of these are well-founded elements of effective professional development, as we have already indicated in Chapter 1 (e.g. as reported by McCormick *et al.* 2008), and Cordingley *et al.* (2005a, b) have shown how CPD based on collaborative inquiry has a positive effect on student outcomes. But few accounts of research investigate the details of the processes by which new classroom practices are created. As part of the LHTL project, a staff questionnaire was employed to gauge teacher AfL practices in the classroom and their experience of processes that supported teacher learning (Pedder 2006). Three factors relating to teacher learning were derived from the questionnaire:

- *inquiry*, i.e. using and responding to different sources of evidence; carrying out joint research and evaluation with colleagues;
- *building social capital*, i.e. learning, working, supporting and talking with each other;
- *critical and responsive learning*, i.e. through reflection, self-evaluation, experimentation and by responding to feedback.

These factors correspond well to the literature on CPD. Pedder related them through regression analysis to the reported practice of the teachers as captured in two factors of positive AfL practice:

1   *making learning explicit*, i.e. eliciting, clarifying and responding to evidence of learning; working with pupils to develop a positive learning orientation;
2   *promoting pupil autonomy*, i.e. a widening of scope for pupils to take on greater independence over their learning objectives and the assessment of their own and each other's work.

What Pedder shows is that all three of the teacher learning factors show associations with the classroom practice factor 'making learning explicit', but only in the case of 'inquiry' is the association strong; 'building social capital' and 'critical and responsive learning' had only weak and non-significant relationships. For the most important classroom practice factor (as we will show in Chapter 7), 'promoting pupil autonomy', there was only an association with 'inquiry'. In other words, 'inquiry' is the most significant predictor of successful classroom AfL practice. Again this link corresponds with the literature reviews on collaborative inquiry cited above (Cordingley *et al.* 2005a, b).

More empirical work would be needed into the details of such factors to see what takes place in relation to how new practices arise.[18] Despite our knowing quite a bit about the general *conditions* of effective teacher developmental work, including collaboration (Borko 2004), it is evident that the fine-grain work on the *processes* is still to be done. Little carried out such detailed work with a group of teachers and used communities of practice ideas to create a framework for analysis of this research, and concluded:

> Prior research in education has yielded typologies that differentiate between strong and weak professional cultures in schools, and that distinguish strong teacher traditional communities from those organized for improvements in teaching and student learning. However, such typologies do not go far enough to explain the

nature of teacher learning resources made available (and not) through daily participation in professional communities.

(2002: 937)

As part of their investigation of activity systems, Engeström and colleagues included detailed video recording of teachers (or medical workers) going through the expansive cycle, along with associated documents and interviews of participants, and this goes some way to giving an account of these processes. Engeström (1999, 2001) also makes some interesting links to actor-network theory (ANT), and we will return to this issue in Chapter 7, when the processes of creation and sharing are dealt with in more detail.

Even with this work, we still have to deal with the problem of scaling up what Borko (2004) raises. Borko's examination of the various phases in research on professional development indicates that particular kinds of professional development in a particular site have been shown to be effective. However, there has been insufficient work on the effectiveness of particular kinds of professional development work in multiple sites with multiple facilitators (let alone research on multiple kinds of professional development in multiple sites). The problem she sees in this 'scaling up' is of fidelity versus adaptability – that is, when multiple sites and facilitators are involved, how much does the particular professional development programme change to meet local conditions (adaptability) and how true does it remain to the original conception or implementation? This is, in our view, to completely misunderstand what happens when a CPD programme is scaled up. This is exactly what we were doing in moving from the intensive KMOFAP work to LHTL, where the LHTL project deliberately did not replicate how the original work was executed (e.g. we did not replicate the extent of the support to teachers, as this would not reflect the situation where all schools adopt AfL, the essence of scalability). Indeed, if teachers are *learning*, then we cannot easily carry out the kind of research that Borko (2004) sought in her depictions of the map for research on teacher development; for fidelity to exist would require slavish implementation of a particular professional development approach.[19] Wenger (1998) warns of practice being 'literal and procedural', as we saw earlier. As we will show in Chapter 7, such a 'literal adoption' version of fidelity does not result in effective AfL practice being implemented.

Learning or knowledge creation?

The knowledge-creation metaphor requires us to consider a range of issues that relate to how organisations innovate. Given the critiques of communities of practice considered above, should we still insist on using 'learning' as the central process in this innovation – that is, in the creation of new classroom and school practices? We have already indicated that our focus in the account of learning by Wenger (1998) is on learning as meaning-making and the development of identity, expressed as a trajectory of becoming. It is nevertheless instructive to look at what Wenger says about knowledge creation. One line of his argument comes from identity – in particular, imagination – which, when translated into student education, involves exploration. He describes it thus:

Educational imagination is . . . about not accepting things the way they are, about experimenting and exploring possibilities, reinventing the self, and in the process reinventing the world. It is daring to try on something really different, to open new trajectories, to seek different experiences, and to conceive of different futures. In this sense, it is about identity as a creation.

(ibid.: 273)

Although here Wenger is discussing student education, it is no less important an element of teacher education. (He makes the point that education is not just an initial socialisation but something individuals and communities should continually do to renew themselves.) Wenger reinforces this in his discussion of learning communities: 'The transformative practice of a learning community offers an ideal context for developing new understandings because the community sustains change as part of an identity of participation' (ibid.: 215).

The other strand of his indication of creation as part of learning is in the relationship between competence and experience. We noted earlier that Wenger argues that experience may drive competence by forming new experience, and in the discussion of learning communities he uses this relationship:

A history of mutual engagement around a joint enterprise is an ideal context for . . . leading-edge learning, which requires a strong bond of communal competence along with a deep respect for the particularity of experience. When these conditions are in place, communities of practice are a privileged locus for the *creation* of knowledge.

(1998: 214; emphasis in the original)

These ideas lead us to believe that 'learning' and situations where a 'learning community' exists (as indicated by Wenger) are adequate general theoretical principles to construct explanations of the processes teachers go through to create new practice. Whether such explanations exist we will consider further in Chapter 7.

Even after this consideration of learning and knowledge creation, we are still left with the 'sharing' element. How do teachers who are not part of the knowledge creation learn from its results? This is just where we left the situation at the end of Chapter 2 except that, given the ideas on learning we have outlined, it looks very much as if these teachers will indeed be *learning* even in the process of sharing others' practice. This implies negotiating meaning from the reifications that teachers will come into contact with as part of the 'creation' of new practice or when they come to share such practice. Wenger's views of boundaries as the locus for the production of radically new knowledge (1998: 254), and hence the role of boundary objects and brokers, are one way of looking at this. Our contention is that networks give us a further sophisticated insight, particular in the case of sharing practice, and we will return to this in Chapters 5 and 7.

Reflections on networks

We argued in Chapter 1 that the accounts from the literature on educational networks almost all discussed communities, not networks as we have tried to depict them in Chapter 2. This chapter has in a sense gone along with arguments about communities of practice and their role in learning, and so we would do well first to examine Wenger's views of networks on the one hand, and on the other consider again whether communities can indeed be viewed as networks.

We part company with Wenger when he says networks are undeveloped communities (i.e. '*merely* personal networks' [1998: 126]). He does acknowledge the work of SNA (citing Wellman and Berkowitz 1988b), and in particular the role of 'strong ties', but seems to confuse some of the concepts by effectively saying that a community of practice could be viewed as *nodes* of strong ties in interpersonal networks (Wenger 1998: 283). Elsewhere he talks of a community of practice as a node for disseminating, interpretation and use of information (ibid.: 252). We have some sympathy for those who wonder about communities of practice, and about Wenger's view of networks. Does it mean that network learning, or learning networks, can be considered as just learning communities?

The idea of 'network learning' was proposed by members of the National College for School Leadership Networked Learning Group (e.g. Hadfield 2005), who see the network as a form of organisation (Chapter 1). In this sense the network forms a site for learning. Tynjälä reviews perspectives on workplace learning and organises it around learning by individuals, communities, organisations and, in her words, '[e]ven networks and regions' (2008: 136). One of her sources is Knight (2002), who herself reviews the literature on network learning, and she too takes a view of a network as an organisational form. Her focus is on networks that are 'strategic' (legally autonomous organisations with a high level of interdependence and co-operative working) or 'wide networks' (loosely bonded collectives of organisations linked by geographical proximity, similar interests or activities or participation in, for example, production of a product). Knight draws up a matrix to explore levels of learning and context of learning, each described by individual, group, organisation, dyad (of organisations) and network of organisations. Thus, an individual learns in the context of a group, organisation or network. She acknowledges that this gives some difficulties with the idea of group learning in the context of an individual, and this only serves to indicate to us a simplification of context. The thrust of her discussion is to arrive at a definition of 'network learning' in which the network itself learns, as indicated by changes in attributes of the network, such as interaction processes and structures, and shared narratives. This definition distinguishes network learning from 'learning network', where members of the network are learning and not the network itself. While the idea of network structures developing as a result of learning is a useful focus, it is unlikely that, for example, the networked learning communities (NLCs) would see any use in being preoccupied with network learning of this sort. The whole point for such an NLC is for practice to improve in the schools that are part of it. In addition, Knight treats groups and organisations as unitary entities – that is, connections between organisations are from one to the other, and not, apparently, among particular individuals within the organisations.[20] This is the problem that Little (2005b) drew attention to in the quotation from her we gave in Chapter 1. What is needed is a more detailed and inside view of relationships within networks, in the way we have tried to suggest.

There is another strand of network learning that emanates from those who study electronic networks in education and usually refers to any learning taking place in an electronic web-based environment (e.g. Jones [2004] talks of it as an alternative to 'e-learning'), although some of this work does relate to the ideas we explored in

Chapter 2 (e.g. Jones *et al.* 2006; Ryberg and Larson 2006). We will consider this work in Chapter 10.

We have already noted the argument deriving from SNA that 'community' has changed and that using networks as an analytic concept is a more productive way of thinking about community. Wellman (2001) argued that communities have moved on from that which is 'door-to-door' (where people could walk to visit each other as in a village), through 'place-to-place' (where community is geographically scattered), to a 'person-to-person' community facilitated by electronic networks. This current state Wellman refers to as the rise of 'networked individualism', where interpersonal networks are important. Wellman (ibid.: 241) ends his discussion of this by asking the question 'Can true community be found online . . . ?' Given our initial pessimism about the future of electronic networks when we started our research, it still remains open to question this development in relation to teacher communities of practice. It seems, however, that networks are worthy of as much attention as communities. In a sense, this was Engeström's argument in presenting the alternative 'mycorrhizae'. Wenger (1998) himself had the idea of 'constellations of practice' to deal with broad, diverse and diffused configurations that cannot be treated as a single community of practice. If the network becomes the entity that the likes of Riles studied (Chapter 2), then it may be that we are likely to replace the idea of a 'community of practice' with a 'network of practice'. The discussions in Chapter 2 on the role of meaning-making in networks, and also of identity, indicate that there is some convergence taking place. Brown and Duguid (2000: 141–3) compare 'networks of practice' with communities of practice, seeing the latter as consisting of a closer-knit part sub-group within the former. Members of a community of practice have direct links with each other and would thus exist within a network of practice, where links can be indirect. (Burt's ideas on structural holes and closure come to mind again.) For Brown and Duguid (2000), the role of information technology is important where communication is enabled among people who may not know each other – an interesting contrast with the way Wellman (2001) sees its impact on 'community', where direct contact is maintained by technology. The situation looks confusing, with on the one hand a community focus leading to teacher learning (seen usually as local), yet we have shown evidence from the SNA work in schools that in social relations terms, schools do not necessarily function as communities. On the other hand, we have ideas of networks that can exhibit the same meaning-making and learning that we have hitherto attributed to communities. We will return to this in Chapter 11 when we have examined more of the details of the networks we have researched, including the electronic ones in Chapter 10. Despite these puzzles, we remained convinced that the concept of learning that comes from Wenger's work is important in understanding the creation and sharing of knowledge.

Chapter 4

Mapping networks

At this stage in the book we are in a position to investigate the LHTL data from teachers and others in schools and local authorities, using the problems in the current literature on educational networks and the general theoretical ideas on networks and on learning (Chapters 1–3). Our concern so far has been on what the literature says, but now we need to turn to investigate how it might further our analysis of the educational networks that we uncovered and also to a further understanding of such networks more generally. This will be done over this and the next three chapters, and here we want to look particularly at the mapping process and what it revealed.

The central research investigation in which we engaged was through a 'mapping' activity intended to explore respondents' conceptions and perceptions of their communication networks and of the elements within them. This exploration was particularly important as it was evident that we had little understanding of educational networks involving schools, as discussed in Chapter 1. These respondents included headteachers, local authority (LA) staff and teachers (based in schools) whose role extended beyond their remit to support the development of assessment for learning (AfL) practices in their schools and authorities (described for convenience here as 'co-ordinators'). The extension included the development of networking, liaison with other schools, or representation of the school at networked learning community (NLC) events. A total of forty-eight co-ordinators took part in the activity, including seventeen headteachers, sixteen teachers and twelve local authority staff (across five LAs). Three additional respondents were members of an experimental 'virtual education action zone' which linked schools in two geographically separated regions of the United Kingdom in a programme of professional development and school improvement activities. In total, eighteen schools drawn from across seven LAs were represented. Some of the schools were part of NLCs (two of which we will deal with in Chapter 9).

The mapping task we developed (Fox *et al.* 2007) was open-ended, and respondents were not asked to draw representations of specific networks or entities; nor were they constrained in how they represented the elements of the network. In this respect our approach differed from more structured approaches used to generate status-order networks where the relative status of individuals is ranked (Whyte 1943), sociograms (Moreno 1932; Katz 1953) or advice networks in which respondents specifically report individuals who are sources or recipients of advice and information (Krackhardt 1996; Hakkarainen *et al.* 2004). The key request that framed the task was:

Show how you visualise the networks in which your school/LA/VEAZ [virtual education action zone] are involved. Please show who and how communications are made.

Teachers were encouraged to use pictures and to explain what was foremost in their mind as they drew the maps, and why they used different particular modes of representation: was the direction of arrows, the thickness of lines or the use of images rather than words significant, for example? This commentary was recorded and transcribed and, together with the map itself and other sources of data collected, formed an initial dataset. Interviewers maintained a non-directive approach throughout the activity, encouraging respondents to expand upon and clarify what they were drawing. Thus, typical interviewer questions asked, 'Is it significant that these arrows are one-way?', 'Are these examples of links, or does each of these represent a particular link?' and 'Is the relative size of these [labels, illustrations] important?'

The tool itself was inspired by Mavers *et al.* (2002), who used a similarly structured mapping task with pupils to encapsulate their conceptualisations of the virtual world of computers and computer systems. They in turn drew upon the rich literature on concept mapping originating from Novak and Gowin (1984), where the focus was on the concept map as a representation of a person's knowledge about relationships between concepts related to a specific topic. The concept map would then typically be a series of words or phrases to represent the concept (as a node), and some line joining it (a link) to another concept expressing a relationship of the two. This can be used either as an instructional strategy to help the learners explore and review their own understanding or as an assessment tool. Our view of mapping aligned more with that of Mavers and colleagues than with conceptual mapping as a means of externalising concepts or mental models: it was primarily concerned with *perceptions* of interpersonal relationships. What we discovered, however, was that in many cases our respondents' *conceptualisations* did indeed shape their framing of the task, their selection of what was 'mapped' and the modes of representation they employed.

This approach is comparatively rare in network analysis, where, for the most part, other data are used to generate models and representations of networks: cast lists inform the network analysis of the Internet Movie Database (Watts 1999); historical documents are used to construct social networks of powerful elites (Wasserman and Faust 1994: 61–2); interviews and observations inform models of kinship and allegiance (Whyte 1943); and email contact is used to explore networks within organisations (Ahuja and Carley 1999; Gloor *et al.* 2004). As we were to discover, however, the different representations produced by respondents, together with the open nature of the task we set, was to make this difference a less significant issue than we originally thought.

Respondents interpreted the task in ways based not only on the experiences and relationships they wanted to express, but also on their ideas about the nature, role and scope of networks. There were rich (but also highly variable and somewhat eclectic) representations and accounts. Some of the respondents wanted to *set up* networks, others' role was to *support* networks and yet others described themselves as *respondents* in networks (such as an NLC). At the same time, when we initiated discussions, respondents referred to network concepts (like 'hub', for example) and the concept of 'the network' as a whole with some confidence. So, our respondents' conceptualisations

of 'the network' clearly also had *metaphorical* value that would lead to different interpretations of the task and promote diverse representations by different respondents.

Outcomes of the mapping task

Initial analysis of the maps allowed a number of dimensions of variation to be identified.
This range was the first sign that, while it was tempting to look for underlying network
forms in the maps (the majority of which were centrally arranged networks with
elements linked by lines), our opportunities either to aggregate or to compare maps
might be limited. Maps varied in the respects outlined in what follows.[1]

Centrality

The respondents drew a range of representations, of which the majority placed
themselves or their institution (school or LA) at the centre. For the school-based
respondents, twenty-six of their maps had a clear centre with radiating links; of these,
nineteen showed the school at the centre, four showed the respondent at the centre
and three had other central elements, including one with a learner at the centre (Figure
4.1). A further five maps were drawn around two recognisable but distinct centres, as
in Figure 4.2, suggesting complex relationships between headteacher and school,

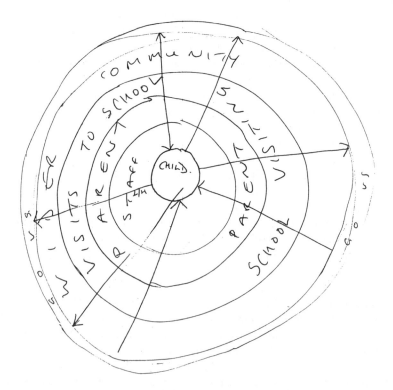

Figure 4.1 A school-based respondent's map with the learner at the centre of the
network.

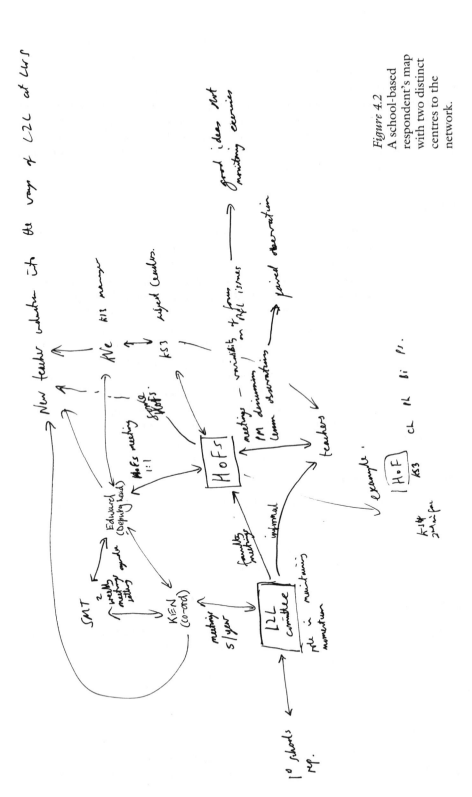

Figure 4.2
A school-based respondent's map with two distinct centres to the network.

school and respondent, or groups and teams within the school. The remaining four maps used different representations with some notion of hierarchy or tiers. Of the LA respondents, seven of the sixteen placed the organisation at the centre of a map (Figure 4.3); three others, whose roles involved maintaining online environments and resources for the network, placed themselves, or the website for which they were responsible, at the centre. Alternatives included multi-centred maps representing the LA's directorate structure (which in one case brought education and children's services together with this relationship drawn as a central element), and organisational maps, one of which (Figure 4.4) took the form of a 'jigsaw'.

Metaphors

Here the focus is on the overall 'metaphor' that was used. While many of the maps took the form and used the visual conventions of 'concept maps' (see Figure 4.5), many combined this with representations of geographical space and distance. So, for example, geographical features such as school grounds, the local teachers' centre, the LA offices and the River Thames appeared alongside conceptual and organisational elements (see Figure 4.6). This was not simply an issue of heterogeneity: one map contained a globe oriented to show Australia, not merely as a geographical marker but also as a reference to the research orientation of some network respondents who had attended an international conference. References to geographical locations were often loaded with meaning – references in maps to 'Woughton House' meaning not only the physical location of the LA offices, but the powerful individuals based there. Other metaphors (the child at the centre, the jigsaw, the tiered nature of the organisation) also represented important perspectives and ideological positions on the part of respondents.

Actors and artefacts

What was represented in the maps varied widely, including individual people (named); roles (such as 'SENCO', 'Headteacher'); groups ('Senior Management Team'); places (named and generalised); organisations; projects; concepts and commitments ('Formative Assessment', 'Inclusion'); and processes, together with the documents and other material artefacts that accompanied them.

Symbolism

Some respondents' maps included attempts to represent numbers of links (secondary schools with radiating links to 'feeder' primary schools, for example), while others simply showed single labels marked 'schools'. Other respondents indicated relative importance, or the volume of communications, by showing links in darker grey, or as wider lines between network elements.

Boundaries

Notions and representation of 'boundedness' varied; some respondents explicitly marked a boundary around a section of their map, often representing the school or

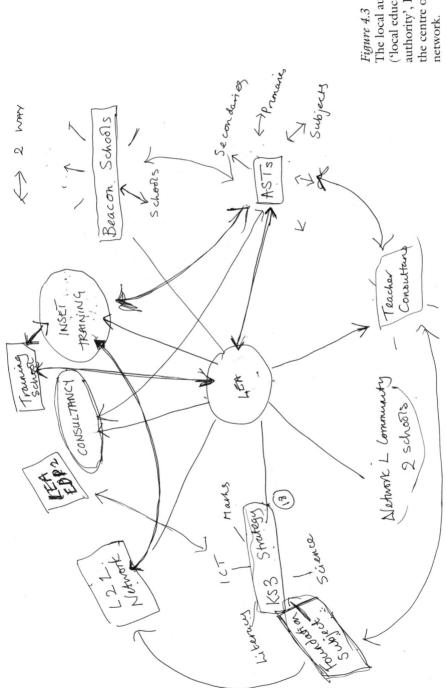

Figure 4.3
The local authority
('local education
authority', LEA) at
the centre of the
network.

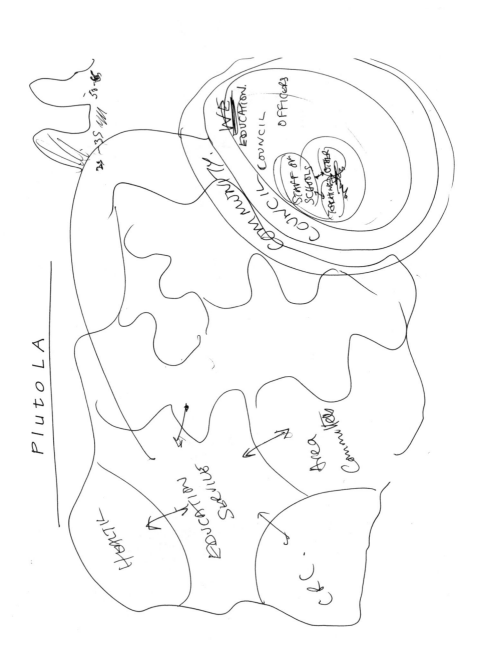

Figure 4.4
The local authority as a 'jigsaw'.

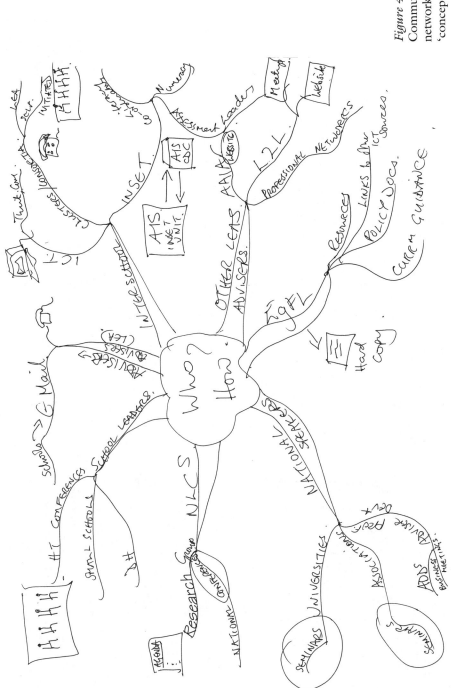

Figure 4.5
Communications
network as
'concept map'.

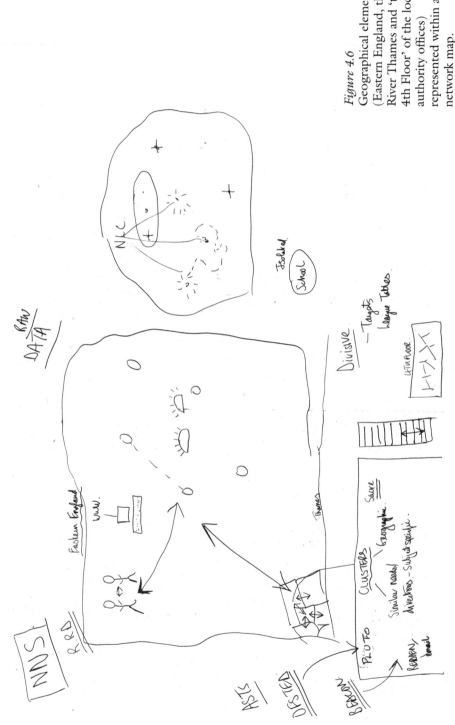

Figure 4.6
Geographical elements
(Eastern England, the
River Thames and 'the
4th Floor' of the local
authority offices)
represented within a
network map.

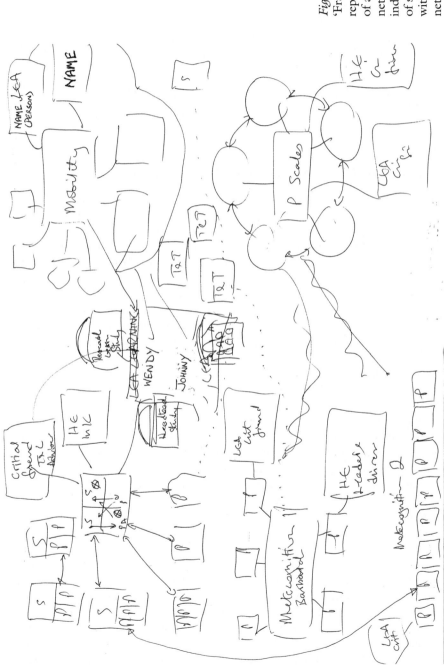

Figure 4.7 'Fractal' representation of a network of networks with indicative clusters of schools, each with their own networks.

LA, with a clear 'outer' ring of information providers, support agencies and regulatory bodies. Others deliberately illustrated networks which continued either 'over the horizon' or through a representation reminiscent of Morgan's (1997) 'fractal' model of organisations, suggesting that each element (school, for example) would have its own sets of networks analogous to those being drawn in detail in the main section of the respondent's map (Figure 4.7).

Faced as we were with this variation not only in conceptualisations but also in representation, it was apparent that the different analytical approaches discussed in Chapter 2 would themselves also reflect particular perspectives on networks and networking.

The variation in scope and representation of networks was, on the one hand, revealing of the varied conceptions and experiences on the part of respondents. On the other, it meant that we had to be very careful, almost guarded, in our application of concepts and measures derived from social network analysis.

Social network analysis: an analytical framework?

In effect, while our respondents had, in many cases, drawn representations of networks, we had to 'translate' these in order to effect any kind of social network analysis (SNA), just as we would have done had we only had access to interview or survey data. Two approaches were used. One was a re-analysis of a subset of the maps collected in a particular LA, converting each map by reducing the range of labels used on what were represented as 'nodes', or other entities, so that they all used the same terminology. So, for example, all representations of the LA were consistently described, as were school structures ('Senior Management', 'SMT [senior management team]' and similar) and individuals who appeared on several maps, sometimes referred to by name, sometimes by role. This allowed some comparisons between maps to be made, and also the construction of aggregated maps in an attempt to develop a single representation of 'the network' within which all the respondents operated. This was largely unsuccessful. Variations in representation went further than simply nomenclature, extending to: the level of detail shown; the representation as 'nodes' of specific people; representative 'personas' ('the child', 'adviser'); groups and organisations; conceptual entities ('assessment for learning', 'inclusion'); documents; and other elements. Furthermore, on many of the maps, what were drawn as 'nodes' and 'links' were interchangeable, or were inconsistently applied even within a single map. People could appear as nodes ('someone I am connected with') or as links ('someone who connects me to . . .').

A second, less ambitious approach was to attempt to map and describe using SNA only small sections of an even smaller number of maps, specifically those where a group of respondents shared some experience or referred to each other, and where maps were comparatively rich in detail. This reduced the problem of widely diverging descriptive frameworks, and revealed differences not only in the perceptions of the network structure and the nature of communications, but also in the individuals' views of their own positions and roles in a small region of a network. An example of this approach, and the interpretations that arose from it in the case of a single school, is described by Carmichael *et al.* (2006) and elaborated further in Chapter 9. Even then, these data were difficult to compare, let alone aggregate, and revealed more about the different experience of individuals than about the nature or structure of a shared network to which they all belonged. (We will show in Chapter 6 how this led us to be able only to raise questions about the differences across groups of respondents, rather than draw conclusions.)

This strategy aligned our work more with a perspective on SNA that is 'ego-centred' rather than 'whole network' in character (Wasserman and Faust 1994). As we have discussed in Chapter 2, 'whole-network' studies and analysis techniques are founded on a 'closed-world' premise that the whole of a network can be known, and that links are bimodal (they either exist or they do not) or are quantifiable. This was clearly not the case with our map data, even when they initially appeared to be representations of well-understood and bounded networks. Ego-centred approaches are characteristically exploratory, the boundaries of the network and potentially the nature of the network elements being studied only emerging as data were collected (Marsden 2005). In SNA there is an assumption that such ego-centred analyses represent samples or perspectives on a network that can be progressively elaborated; the variations in many of our respondents' maps seemed to preclude even this, however.

With social network analysis now seeming to offer us fewer opportunities to interpret the maps in a quantitative sense, we reviewed which of the concepts from SNA were potentially useful as qualitative categories. These include:

- the distinction between *position* in a network and the *role* and *prestige* this brings;
- the idea of *directedness* of links (one-way, two-way or unspecified);
- special network functions such as *cutpoints* (nodes which, if removed, would 'break' the network), *bridges* (links between components of the whole network) and *broker* (bridges and bridge builders).

Other apparently intuitively useful concepts such as *density* (how many of a node's possible links existed in reality) were difficult to apply with any confidence, and others such as *path length* (how many 'degrees of separation' there are between network nodes) could be applied with caution – if only to show that some forms of communication were mediated by 'third parties' (as when contact between a respondent and the LA, for example, takes place through a school manager or specialist such as a special educational needs co-ordinator [SENCO][2]).

We also drew extensively on the work of Hakkarainen *et al.* (2004), whose work used selected SNA concepts (density, centrality), although their use of highly structured research instruments within the closed networks of a company allowed them to apply these with more confidence than we could. Other important concepts they employed are *affiliation networks*, in which individuals share a commitment to concepts, principles or communities; these, like personal *embedded links*, are imported into workplace settings and may be as important to individuals as formal networks of organisations within which they work (or indeed more important). (We will deal with these concepts in later chapters.)

At this point the focus of our analysis broadened to include not only the maps themselves but also the transcripts of the accompanying discussions. An initial coding scheme was drawn up that included:

- not only those concepts from SNA that were thought still to be relevant, together with other categories relating to particular kinds of network elements (e.g. people and places);

- practices and processes of networking;
- barriers, drivers and outcomes related to networking activities;
- more general beliefs about networks and networking.

Cross-coder reliability was established through an iterative process of individual analysis and discussion across the research team. Each team member carried out a close reading and coding (using Atlas.ti qualitative software) of the transcript of the same single mapping activity. During this process the map was consulted and, where possible, links established between what was being drawn and what was being described in the transcript. This involved identification of areas where it proved difficult to apply the coding scheme or where the scheme was found to be inadequate as a means of representing the networking concepts expressed by the respondent.

In such cases, additional categories grounded in SNA and other literatures were identified, and their inclusion in the coding scheme was discussed across the team. As well as self-identified areas of difficulty, an automatic analysis of all coded transcripts was carried out using the Atlas.ti software. The intention here was not to achieve some specific level of inter-coder reliability, but rather to highlight areas of agreement and difference; the latter being taken as an indication of a concept or groups of concepts worthy of further discussion leading to a consensus or at least an agreement to add analytical 'memos' to terms where the meaning was contested or open to multiple interpretations. With many terms used by respondents having multiple meanings according to different theoretical positions (such as 'broker' or 'hub'), or everyday meanings at odds with those in SNA (such as 'strong' and 'weak' in relation to ties), or meanings that were relative and ego-centred (such as notions of centrality or proximity), there was inevitably a need to categorise respondent comments in a distinctly non-'*in vivo*' way. Rather the opposite, in fact, as transcript fragments were annotated with comments of the type 'I think they mean . . .' or 'perhaps [another category] instead?'.

Once a stable set of categories was identified, the remainder of the transcripts were analysed using Atlas.ti and reports generated across codes and code families. Again, disparities in how codes were being used provided a basis for discussion, not only of respondents' conceptions of networks and networking, but also of our own more nuanced reading of what networks and networking involved, and how different theoretical perspectives could contribute to our understanding.

Methodological challenges

With our selective and qualitative reading of SNA concepts, our concerns were now not those of network analysts frustrated by partial and unreliable data, but rather those of qualitative researchers more generally. At the same time, we were faced with the prevalence of networking terminology in the maps and accompanying commentaries, and of everyday terms with specific meaning in SNA. This meant that we had to be cautious so as not to enthusiastically interpret respondents' representations and accompanying comments from transcripts as exemplification or confirmation of the concepts from SNA. Finally, there were specific issues and challenges arising from the educational context in which our explorations were taking place. Networking terminology was not simply a reflection of participation in a 'network society'; it also reflected a powerful rhetoric in a changing educational landscape in which networking formed part of a governmental response to issues of school improvement, teacher professional development and raising of standards, as Chapter 1 indicated.

Our decision not to pursue any form of quantitative methods, or to employ SNA in its usual sense, located our work as a particular kind of qualitative inquiry. Hence, we were aware that it opened our interpretations to critiques levelled at qualitative methods more generally: namely, lack of operationalisation of concepts, an inability to use 'control' methods to rule out alternative explanations of observed phenomena, and a lack of a basis on which to generalise findings (see Hammersley 2008: 32–3). While we did draw upon the maps, transcripts and, in some cases, other data collected from schools in the course of our work, there was, indeed, no formal triangulation of these data with quantitative measures (though some subsequent work did attempt to use the mapping task as an element in a more explicitly multi-method approach). Similarly, our approach did not provide us with generalisable models of networks or recommendations as to which forms of networks, or networking practices, were effective in terms of knowledge creation and sharing or of organisational success. Rather, the widely divergent interpretations of what networks comprised, what functions they fulfilled and the relationships they supported pointed to a need for qualitative inquiry into the nature of respondents' conceptualisations of networks and of the socio-cultural practices employed in establishing and maintaining communications channels, brokerage functions and other characteristics of the networks our respondents described.

We were also aware of a more specific issue in relation to the mapping task itself: whether it was sufficiently robust and reliable. This was particularly important as the influence of contextual factors (those introduced not only by the project researchers but also by contemporary discussions about the importance of networks in student and teacher learning and professional development) was clearly evident in the maps drawn by respondents and in accompanying discussions. However, rather than seeing this as an 'irremediable obstacle' to the approach's providing any useful insights, the data generated from the mapping task do help us understand how concepts associated with networks and networking are differently understood and operationalised in the light of continuing disagreements about the nature, role and scope of networks. Within such a contested and complex field it is doubtful whether *any* research approach (interviews, maps, grids or direct observation by the research team), no matter how robust and rigorous, could have adequately described either the experience of individual respondents or the networks within which they located themselves.

While it was possible to apply some concepts from SNA, and many of the respondent accounts did align well with high-level network metaphors and concepts ('hubs', 'brokers', 'centrality' and so forth), we did find examples of conceptualisations which suggest that other perspectives might be useful in our analysis. Some respondent accounts suggested that the networks in which they were involved were more malleable and transitory than the more structural, material interpretations of Castells (2000a) or Wellman (2001). As a result, the maps that they drew would inevitably be 'snapshots' representing their current understanding of situations that were themselves changing. One respondent felt completely unable to draw a map because he thought it would change from day to day.

At the level of what was actually represented, significant challenges to even our qualitative reading of social network concepts emerged:

- 'nodes' that were widely heterogeneous and included people, organisations, locations and concepts, and in many cases were vastly different in scale;
- adjacent nodes representing a single person and an entire organisation of many hundreds of individuals (effectively a locality or even a network in its own right) were 'collapsed' into a single network entity.

A further issue emerged concerning the heterogeneity not only of nodes but of links, which varied in terms of strength, frequency and the value that was ascribed to them by respondents, as we will show in Chapter 6.

The respondents themselves identified difficulties in *representing* their networks that were indicative of related challenges to the *analysis* of those network representations. Even though we left the nature of the representation open to respondents, some struggled to apply their chosen visual metaphor and to apply their approach consistently as they began to elaborate on their map. They identified problems or limitations with the broad representational strategy they used:

> I would have to say they are more tenuous, I think, and more sporadic in that there might be links on specific projects but no links in other fields. . . . I would find it difficult [to represent that] so perhaps I'll just put a few kind of rather haphazard links.
>
> (Keith Tiler, LA co-ordinator)

> [P]robably the easiest way to start it is with your standard triangle, equilateral triangle. Because I think there's a perception that there certainly is a hierarchy within the LA . . . [some time later] so we've got, we're just going to have like a spider's web really.
>
> (Julie Humber, LA co-ordinator)

> [I]t's a massive mind map, in fact it would be better off done as a mind map, but I mean that's, that's my personality thing, I think.
>
> (Ben, co-ordinator, Mulberry School)

Others raised issues of adequately representing structure:

> I think most of them I could put arrows all over the place really.
>
> (Nell, headteacher, Oak Infant School)

> [Asked if she was happy that the links are shown in the way that she wanted them to be] No, because I really need a 3D chart.
>
> (Maureen Edge, LA co-ordinator)

> Of course, none of this stands alone . . . but they all link across. . . . It can't, and so diagrammatically, it's virtually impossible.
>
> (Henry, headteacher, Yew Community School)

The last of these respondents, having struggled to represent the complexities of his school's communications networks, reflected that the task highlighted the difficulty of any one person having oversight of all the initiatives and activities within the school:

It is a problem of representing it. It is a problem of knowing it.

> (Henry, headteacher, Yew Community School)

Changes over time, or the expectation of changes, caused problems for some:

> Well, this is as you can see, this lot about the website, I mean it's virtually there but it's not there quite yet. This [another activity] *is* happening.
>
> (Elise Downey, LA co-ordinator)

For some respondents the task was difficult because it highlighted issues related to their own role, position and commitments, and they were careful to make clear that this represented a personal view, or one that reflected a particular perspective:

> I'm going to put myself in there because I think that at the moment this is quite personally generated really.
>
> (Elise Downey, LA co-ordinator)

In a few cases, respondents explicitly questioned whether communications systems such as websites or email lists or events that brought individuals together constituted networks – a clear indication of difficulty of dealing with a term that had both metaphorical and practical meaning:

> Well, this isn't strictly speaking a network, but one of the big things we do is INSET [in-service] training, and that's got to be part of the links, hasn't it?
>
> (Kay Fisher, LA co-ordinator)

Alternatives to social network analysis

In attempts to address not only these voiced concerns but a broader question of how adequate SNA might be as a basis for the interpretation of our data, we turned to a number of other perspectives on networks and networking. Most important among these in framing our analysis was Burt's work (1992, 2000) on the relationship between social capital theories and networks; actor-network theory (ANT) (associated with Latour [2005], Law [2004], Law and Mol [2002] among others); and Hardt and Negri's (2000) perspective on networks as a means of responding to organisational constraints and asymmetrical power relations. From Burt we gained insights into specific networking practices, notably brokerage; from ANT an approach to the heterogeneity of the networks that were described by our respondents; and from Hardt and Negri the idea that networks were strongly 'intensional' and represented a key means by which individuals could exercise agency and contribute to innovative practice in organisational settings where other structures hindered or actively prevented this.

An influential extension to SNA is the synthesis of ideas from that approach with ideas about 'social capital', which we started to explore in Chapter 2, notably those of Burt (1992, 2000). Burt asserts that

> perspectives on social capital are diverse in origin and style of accompanying evidence, but they agree on a social capital metaphor in which social structure is

a kind of capital that can create for certain individual or groups a competitive advantage in pursuing their ends. Better connected people enjoy higher returns.

(2000: 348)

Burt describes different types of network structures associated with levels of social capital, notably the 'entrepreneurial', 'clique' and 'hierarchical' types, and associates them with characteristic network metrics, models of management and, implicitly, with views of, and opportunities for, practitioner learning. Cliques (the term does not necessarily have its usual pejorative meaning in the context of networks) are discussed further in Chapter 5. Burt discusses how small-scale studies and 'lab experiments' can be carried out in order to explore network roles and the emergence of structures, patterns and networking practices, and can be combined with census studies and archival and survey data in order to illuminate how social capital is accessed and utilised in the course of individuals' career development. These multi-method approaches inform the role of networks and specific networking practices (such as job seeking and information sharing) within a broader social framework, and enable the exploration of the particular in order to make statements about networks more generally.

Burt also argues for the central importance of 'brokerage' in networks and, as discussed in Chapter 2, identifies social capital 'as a function of brokerage across structural holes . . . resources accumulate in brokers, people with exclusive exchange relations to otherwise unconnected partners' (ibid.: 357). Burt's model of brokerage goes further than simply seeing brokers as well-placed individuals with many con- nections and a high degree of what SNA terms 'betweenness'. His models of brokerage, as with his account of social capital in networks more generally, blend quantitative methods drawn directly from SNA with qualitative accounts of the social practices and accompanying discourses of brokerage activities, which range from fostering knowledge exchange to facilitation of intensive cross-disciplinary and cross-domain collaboration.

Both school-based respondents and those based in LAs identified brokerage functions as important and in many cases explicitly talked of them being not only about links but also about *making* links, particularly in relation to knowledge sharing and potential collaborations. This aligns well with Burt's model of brokerage in particular, a theme we shall return to in Chapter 5.

Perhaps the most obvious feature of ANT is its recognition of the importance of human and non-human actants which are subject to 'symmetrical analysis'. As articulated by Law (1992), this challenges the notion that networks of 'unmediated human bodies' exist, and is exemplified in Suchman *et al.* (1999) and famously in the study by Callon (1986) of the various actants in the networks of the fishing communities of Saint-Brieuc. Callon's tracing of the associations between human activities and a range of biotic and abiotic factors in the locality shows how both human and non-human actants are capable of action, and it is through their relations with other actants that each takes on its particular form and role. When we look at the maps drawn by respondents, it is indeed evident that they represent widely heterogeneous sets of human and non-human elements, the latter including organisations (e.g. systems), buildings, artefacts and concepts. These in turn define and circumscribe the role of human actants, including the respondents themselves, in relation to other network elements.

In some maps and their accompanying discussions it was evident that elements or localities in many individual networks were effectively 'black-boxed' in ANT terms – their role, nature, function and importance submerged and unchallenged until circumstances made them evident and brought them into sharper focus. Good examples of this were: the representation, particularly among less senior staff, of national government or the LA as a single node; in others, the local teachers' centre[3] was represented in the same way. The teachers' centre is a particularly good example: in some maps it was represented as a single dot, circle or label, in others as a recognisable building, hinting at the complexities within. For those respondents who were involved in activities at the centre, it had greater significance, serving as a focus for continuing professional development (CPD) activities, acting as a site where one could access the internet and other resources, and, in social network terms, acting as an area of high density within a sparser network. (As we will show in Chapter 8, such sites are important in their physical and social sense.) But any discourses and controversies about its role, governance and relationships to schools and the local authority were, for many, invisible – 'black-boxed' until some event or controversy revealed their complexities.

The 'black-boxing' metaphor has unfortunate associations with a notion of materiality, as though the 'box' can be used to monitor the complex flows within a system or network. In fact, the most significant feature of the methods of ANT (which borrows from other approaches, including visual sociology, discourse analysis and ethnomethodology [Latour 2005]) is its focus on the relationships, 'controversies' and interplay that is part of the creation of the network, rather than just its material expression. According to Lanzara (1999: 332), 'This formulation of the problem, rather than "opening the black-box" to study the process that made it stable, "tracks the process before the box actually gets closed".' So, rather than seeing the teachers' centre as a stable locality or microcosm of local authority-wide activity, any exploration using the characteristic approaches of ANT would also (ideally) study the discourses and controversies that shaped its role.

ANT has been criticised (e.g. Amsterdamska 1990; Collins and Yearley 1992; Whittle and Spicer 2008), not least for its ascribing of agency and intentionality to non-human actants. One response is that it is not the specific actants that have agency but rather the *associations* of those heterogeneous actants. According to this perspective, the most effective 'networkers' in our study were those respondents who were able to engage and mobilise other networked actors and actants in support of an activity, using what ANT describes as 'mediators': actors capable of magnifying the impact of some activity on the part of respondents.

One final contemporary account of the nature and role of networks is set out in Hardt and Negri's work *Empire* (2000) and subsequent discussions and responses to it (Negri 2007, 2008). This represents a significant attempt to broaden the focus of study from specific networked settings to carrying out a more general analysis of networks as they have become important in globalised society. Comparable in breadth and scope to the work of Castells (2000a), Hardt and Negri's account is a 'creative revision' of the dialectical approaches of Marxism, in which they draw on Foucault and Deleuze: both their use of deconstructionist methods and their characterisation of networks as 'smooth spaces'. This does not see networks as new forms of material organisation, but rather as the boundless sites of continuing tensions between a global 'empire' and a 'multitude' for whom networks represent a vital form of expression and action. Conceived as a means of theorising and informing anti-globalisation movements, this account still sees networking as giving access to social and intellectual capital but within a radical and transformative framework. Dyer-Witheford (1999) uses Negri's ideas to explore the role of electronic networks in particular and argues that diverse and 'heterarchic' (non-hierarchical and potentially subversive) networks need to be developed to support local activity, innovation and knowledge creation. We see some indications of this kind of networking in the maps and other contributions of respondents who described how developing networks represented a response to organisational constraints, geographical or intellectual isolation, or limited opportunities to engage with innovative practice. This implies a strongly 'intensional' approach to the development and maintenance of network ties and proactive development of networks (as suggested by Granovetter [1973] and Nardi *et al.* [2000]), although in this case it goes further and is oriented towards the circumventing or even subversion of existing organisational structures.

The educational context: of what landscapes are these maps?

As we have described, the various approaches to analysis revealed such a wide range as to make a reductionist approach to maps impossible. The maps that were drawn varied not only in the metaphors they employed and the respondents' own position, role and representation in the maps, but also in the micro- and macro-political issues they reflected. A specific map might represent a particular person's 'ego-centred' view of a network, but might also express a school, LA or other organisational perspective. In some cases this perspective itself employed network concepts and specific representations, which themselves were imported into the individual respondent's map.

Perhaps the best example of this was in one LA in which a particular representation of the authority-wide networks (which could be seen adorning the walls of the authority offices) also reappeared, slightly edited but clearly distinguishable, in several individual maps. One interpretation of this pattern is that this network did indeed exist as an organisation and was conceptualised and experienced by respondents; hence it appeared in their maps. Another interpretation is that this was a specific, almost iconic, representation that represented personal affiliation with the LA's 'self-image' of itself as a networked organisation (see Figure 4.8). In other cases, organisational structures such as clusters of schools (often with a secondary school surrounded by a number of primary schools) or representations similar to organisational charts, showing hierarchies, patterns of line management, funding streams or multi-agency collaboration, appeared as clearly structured network localities within maps, or even as the framing for the entire map. Once again, whether these represent ideal models, planned structures, organisational perspectives or individual experience was often difficult to discern.

That our inquiry was taking place against a policy background in which the role of the LA, and associated advisory services for education, was shifting was evident in maps from LA staff. We shall discuss the substantive nature of their contributions subsequently, but it was clear that their responses to the tasks were frequently not neutral accounts. Rather, they pointed up either the many roles they played (which were not always recognised), in the case of LA advisers, while headteachers were, in some cases, keen to assert the extent to which their role had expanded far beyond the school context into areas previously considered the responsibility of the LA.

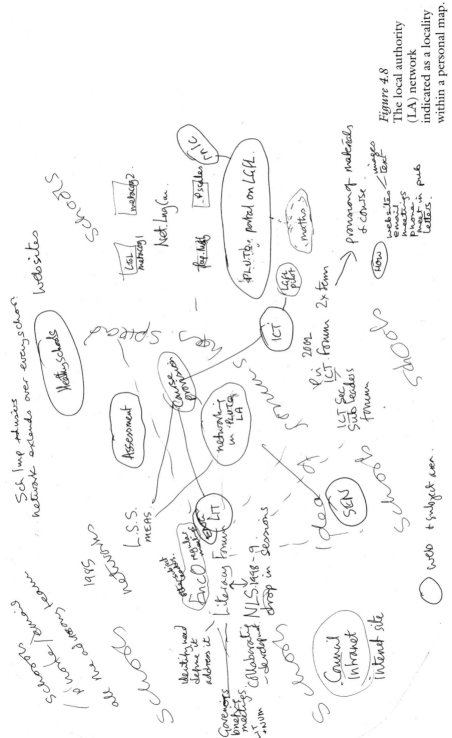

Figure 4.8
The local authority
(LA) network
indicated as a locality
within a personal map.

Summary

The activity in which we engaged our respondents was initially framed so as to reflect a dominant view: of networks as material constructions, as organisations with distinct structures and individuals as members of multiple groups. However, our emerging understanding and engagement with a wider range of interpretational framings means that, in terms of the various perspectives described above, it is closer to an *ego-centred* perspective than a *whole-network* one. This acknowledges the *heterogeneity of networks* and explores the *particular* rather than seeking universal measures of network activity or position; it is not an exercise in SNA but is better seen as part of a more general qualitative inquiry. While this meant that we did not have to engage with some of the problems associated with the reductionism of SNA, it raised a new set of problems more typical of visual methods, interviews or other qualitative approaches.

Hybrid and multi-method approaches may represent a way forward. The work of Flap *et al.* (2003) and Van der Gaag and Snijders (2003) in the Netherlands in particular has shown how qualitative accounts can be used to complement and extend quantitative survey and census data. In a subsequent application of the mapping task described here (Morales and Carmichael 2007), an initial mapping task provided the source data for further analysis of part of a 'closed' network of the kind described by Palonen *et al.* (2004) and Hakkarainen *et al.* (2004). Lists of individuals and organisations mentioned in the mapping activity within a networked organisation (in the case of Morales and Carmichael, a Higher Education Funding Council 'Centre for Excellence in Teaching and Learning' spanning three higher education institutions) were collated into grids that were used for a second activity in which respondents were asked to record the frequency and nature of interactions (Morales and Carmichael 2007). This allowed SNA measures such as centrality and advice size to be calculated for this small, high-density network. A key finding to emerge was the fact that 'advice size' was non-reciprocal: some respondents whose advice was highly valued and widely sought by others did not identify themselves as *providers* of valued information – and possibly did not recognise their importance in the working practices of others or in the functioning of the network as a whole. (We will take this up in Chapter 6.)

The following chapters describe the outcomes of our analysis using this hybrid model of network analysis that draws in part on SNA and in part on other conceptions of networks and networking.

Chapter 5

Network nodes

Entities or relationships?

This chapter moves from the structure of the network, i.e. network morphology, discussed in the previous chapter, to consider the nodes that form the basis of relationships that give it the structure. We do not take this division of nodes and links (the relationships between nodes) as unproblematic, but it is a convenient way to examine the details of networks. This examination starts with a consideration of a 'descriptive' analysis of the LHTL project data, whose basis we established and questioned in the previous chapter. This analysis is not purely descriptive, as we were implicitly influenced by the literature on networks, and so in the second section of this chapter we examine how various theories represent 'nodes'. The uniformity that social network analysis (SNA) attributes to nodes enables the creation of measures associated with nodes indicating their position and centrality. Nodes are not always individual (e.g. people); they can be made up of groups, and we will focus on cliques as a case of strongly connected people, typical of professional learning communities (PLCs), at least in their ideal form. At this point it will be evident that there are assumptions made about nodes that may not reflect the needs of those concerned with educational networks, and we therefore examine these assumptions. Whatever our reservations, particularly about SNA, brokers and experts are well recognised in education and other studies of how knowledge is created and shared (e.g. Hakkarainen *et al.* 2004), and so we examine both their conceptualisation in networks and other theories. At times we will take on the assumptions of SNA approaches, even if ultimately we may not accept or use their quantitative definitions of concepts. As we have said a number of times, some of these concepts used qualitatively have resonance in our LHTL data and are worth exploring. These concepts are used, in the case of brokers and experts, to make sense of the LHTL mapping and interview data. Finally we return to the issue noted above, the division between nodes and links, in preparation for the next chapter.

Nodes in the LHTL maps

The LHTL mapping exercise that was described in Chapter 4 asked teachers and advisers to '[s]how who and how communications are made', hence making an assumption that links were made with *people*. In fact, there was quite a range of 'entities' involved in the maps produced, as Chapter 4 illustrated. In order to try to obtain a general picture of teachers' and advisers' maps, and hence to achieve what we thought might be a better understanding of the nature of educational networks, we categorised these entities using the following exclusive categories: *role*, such as headteacher or local adviser; *named people*; *group*, formal or informal; *organisation*; *community*, meaning any collective that was more general than a group but not an organisation; and *construct*, for conceptual entities (e.g. 'children', 'parents' and 'staff', which did not refer to specific individuals, groups or roles in these kinds of groups). We followed the general convention in SNA of referring to these entities as 'nodes', and our categories mainly reflected this approach. However, as we will show, different network theories view nodes in different ways and designate different kinds of entities as nodes. The types of node from the LHTL project data are approximately ranked in Table 5.1.[1] 'Roles' and 'organisations' nodes were the most common, probably influenced by asking respondents to think of their school's or local authority's communication, rather than their own personal communication. Examples of roles include local authority (LA) advisers, headteachers and consultants employed to support the school with a particular student group or element of the curriculum (e.g. Key Stage 3 consultant;[2] literacy adviser). Examples of organisations were LA, the DfES (the government department responsible for schools), the National College for School Leadership (NCSL) and universities. The least common node, 'communities', was not represented by examples of communities of practice as discussed in earlier chapters (e.g. a subject association). Instead, respondents referred largely to cultural communities within which the school was embedded, e.g. local Somali or Croatian communities.

> [Talking of wider community] [I]n fact, it's bigger than religious leaders because we also have the multicultural link with various community groups as well.
>
> (Alexandra, co-ordinator, Gingko Primary School)

Table 5.1 Average percentage of nodes according to their type (48 respondents, both LA/VEAZ and school based)

Node type	Rank	LA-based respondents	School-based respondents				
		All (n = 15) Mean % of nodes	All (n = 33) Mean % of nodes	Heads (n = 17) Mean % of nodes	Co-ords (n = 16) Mean % of nodes	Primary (n = 25) Mean % of nodes	Secondary (n = 8) Mean % of nodes
Roles	1	23	<u>36</u>	<u>39</u>	<u>28</u>	<u>41</u>	13
Organisations	2	<u>32</u>	22	22	23	18	<u>32</u>
Constructs	3	20	10	8	13	10	10
Groups	4/5	9	18	20	16	17	21
Named people	4/5	14	12	8	19	12	13
Communities	6	2	2	3	1	2	2
Total %		100	100	100	100	100	100
Total mean no. nodes		38	37	46	28	36	39

Note: Underlined values indicate modal group of node type for each category of respondent.

This apparently contrasts with the discussion of professional learning communities (PLCs) in Chapter 3, where communities are seen as central, although it could be simply viewed as a labelling problem, with practitioners using 'communities' in an everyday sense rather than one laden with 'theoretical' significance. Even where other schools were indicated (as organisations), these were not in terms of a group of teachers in the other school working with those in the school of the respondent.

Comparing maps generated by staff from an LA with those from school-based staff shows similar average numbers of total nodes per map. There were different average proportions of types of nodes, with LA staff indicating more 'organisations', and school staff more 'roles'. LA staff could thus have access to a wider range of knowledge resources through access to the organisations represented on their maps than could those in schools, which could reflect the formality of role of the LA. Why school staff appear to rely more heavily on roles (as indicated by the number on their maps) may reflect their way of representing formal activity. Some drew a map that resembled an organisational chart.

The most striking difference between primary and secondary school staff maps is the relatively high proportion of nodes by 'role' for primary schools. The reasons for this are not clear but it may be that primary schools, being more local in their orientation (indicated by the proximity of nodes; see Fox *et al.* 2007), tend to refer to internal roles (multiple roles, formed by the same person taking on more than one role) and LA roles, rather than named individuals.

Secondary school respondents, however, included more 'organisations' than those in primary school. It may be that these were an expression of the formal links they need to make in respect of the 14–19 curriculum and links with the further education of their students, or that they are indeed connected to a wider range of resources (similar to LAs) – for example, national links to the Learning and Skills Council (a government agency), local ones to a further education college or Education Business Partnership covering a local area.

Primary and secondary headteachers' maps included a higher proportion of 'roles' than LHTL school co-ordinator maps, perhaps reflecting the range of people they relate to in the course of their job. Co-ordinators represent similar proportions of organisations, despite their reduced possibility for networking, as classroom teachers with relatively little non-contact time (compared to headteachers). It may be that in this case they are combining their personal professional networks with those of the school in general.

In addition to identifying nodes, respondents also generated their own symbols for them (e.g. Figure 5.1). Researchers of social network diagrams argue that symbols convey meaning about nodes and should not be overlooked (Moreno 1932; Freeman 2000). Sack argues that any analysis of open-ended social network diagrams must focus on the symbols used to determine to what extent they 'present' rather than 'represent', for example, any feelings and emotions they convey (1980: 29). Some respondents did include value-laden images such as that shown in Figure 5.2. The use of different symbols could be considered to be the respondent trying to construct a hierarchical legend whereby each type of symbol represents a layer of parallel status nodes. Others explained, without using different symbols, that they were trying to show a layer of nodes as an overlay on others (a 'palimpsest', as one respondent described it). As noted in Chapter 4, in addition to using more symbol types on a map, almost three-quarters

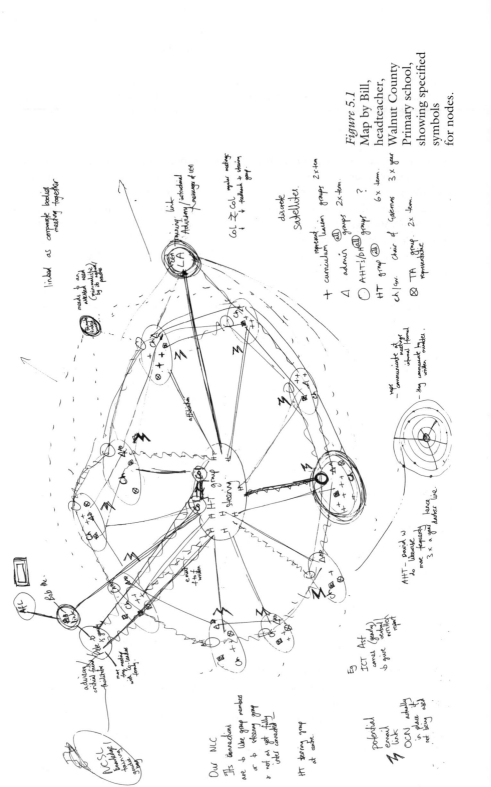

Figure 5.1
Map by Bill,
headteacher,
Walnut County
Primary school,
showing specified
symbols
for nodes.

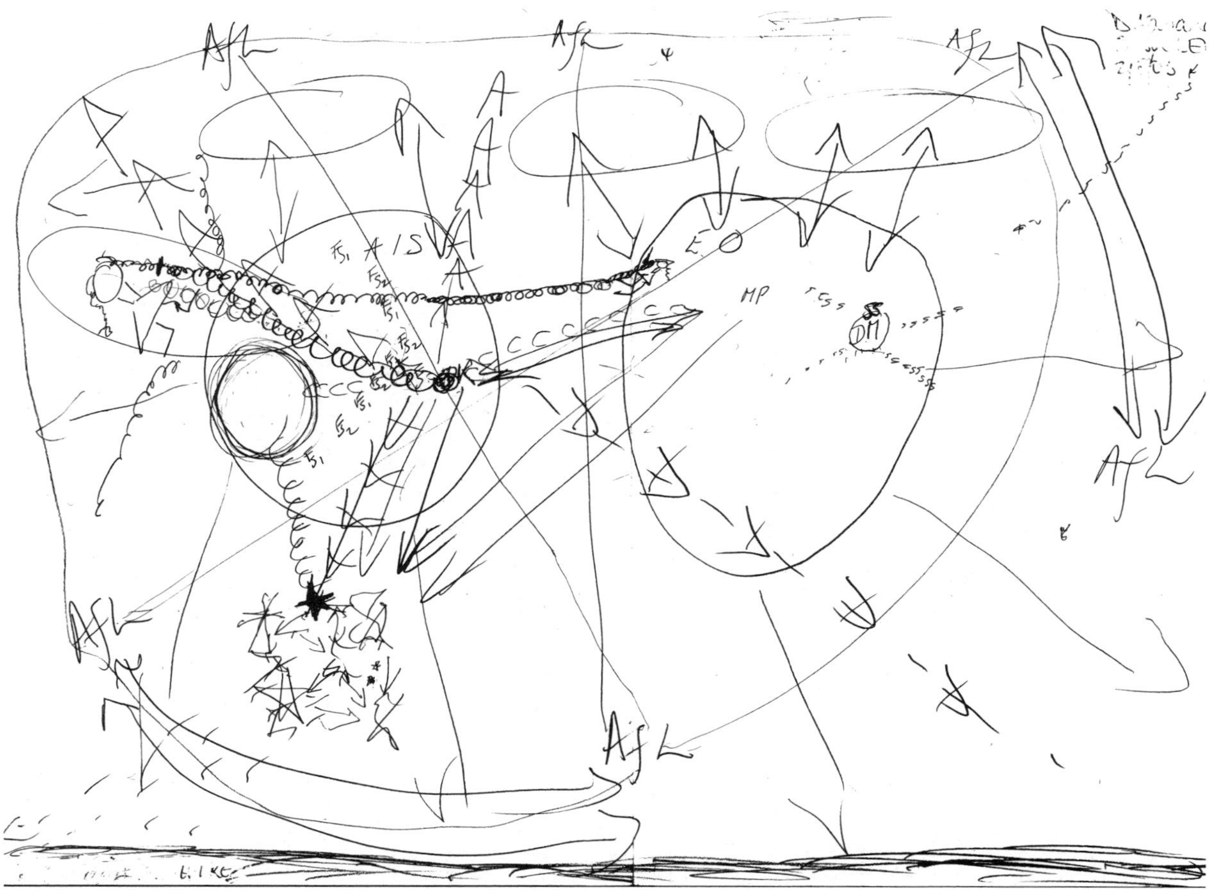

Figure 5.2
Map by Eileen Laws, LA co-ordinator, showing the use of graphics.

of local authority or virtual education action zone (VEAZ) respondents included a wide range of other graphics including classrooms, buildings, the River Thames, stairs, an office plan, a globe, a web page, people, a bag, a diary, stars and pigtails (e.g. Figure 5.2). There are at least three different explanations for this use of symbols and graphics:

1   Less direct contacts require more symbols.
2   These symbols are significant in terms of identifying key places, people and events and provide some information on attitudes to, and the value of, nodes.
3   They represent respondents' predilection for visualisation.

There are of course limitations with this 'counting' of nodes on the map, apart from limitations of non-representative sampling, which qualify any associated quantification. Not least, it ignores the descriptions that the respondents gave while they were drawing, which puts the entity into context, along with any symbolic significance given to the graphic. In addition, counting is somewhat arbitrary and not grounded in either the respondents' ideas or any particular theoretical orientation. This quantitative approach suffers in the same way as the conversion of the maps to a standard set of labels to enable aggregation (described in Chapter 4) – an approach we abandoned because of the variations that existed and the interchangeability of nodes and links for some respondents. This quantitative approach therefore has severe limitations and, as Chapter 4 indicated, we moved away from this direct SNA analysis. The comparisons and ideas discussed above do, however, raise interesting questions that can be further researched. These difficulties arise because there are many ways of considering what counts as a node or indeed identifying it in these abstract ways, as the next section indicates.

Theoretical views of nodes

The language of 'nodes' and 'links', as Chapter 4 indicated, is very much in the tradition of SNA, as is the visual representation in graphs as a 'ball and stick'. Wellman and Berkowitz say that 'social structures can be represented as *networks*, as sets of *nodes* (or social system members) and sets of *ties*' (1988a: 4; emphasis in the original). The nodes in these representations can be individuals, groups, corporations, nations and other kinds of collectives (the LHTL project data largely reflected this). As their concern is with social structure, all the nodes involve people, and all nodes are identical (except in the particular case of two-mode analysis, where nodes can be individuals and events, for example; Faust 2005). A variety of terms is used to capture these 'social entities' (Wasserman and Faust 1994: 3), but commonly they are referred to as 'actors', though in SNA they interestingly do not necessarily have to act: 'Actors are discrete individual, corporate, or collective social units. . . . Our use of the term "actor" does not imply that these entities necessarily have volition or the ability to "act"' (ibid.: 17). This definition would be rejected by those who use actor-network theory (ANT), where 'action' is required: '*any thing* that does modify a state of affairs by making a difference is an actor' (Latour 2005: 71; emphasis in the original). Although this focus on action is similar to Burt's (1992) model (Figure 2.1), 'actor' does not imply the causality Burt had in mind (with the defined direction of causal relations of the lines in the model): 'To use the word "actor" means that it's never clear who and what is acting when we act since an actor on stage is never alone in acting' (Latour 2005: 46).[3] ANT adds a more radical element to the notion of actors: they can be human or non-human objects (Chapter 4). This idea was developed from work on science studies, where the interaction of humans and machines, etc. is studied. The details of this argument are less important here than the idea that a network can be made up of a variety of entities, not just 'social' ones (the latter is an idea that Latour [2005] would reject). Although our categorisation did not include 'non-human' objects (as much because we use the formulation 'with *whom* all communications' in our mapping task, which implied humans), it will be evident in Chapters 6 and 10 that teachers do use websites and other electronic communication technology (and those in VEAZs specifically mentioned using them to distribute material).[4] Just as important, ANT alerts us to the variation in types of nodes that may be present in the network, evident also in the maps by teachers and LA advisers. SNA researchers would argue that they are clear in their focus on particular types of actors arising from their previous research and the hypotheses they are investigating, and hence such a 'human' focus is justified. Critiques of ANT argue that its approach focuses on the loud voices because the potential nodes are unlimited, driven by its concern with power (Miettinen 1998, cited in Nardi *et al.* 2000: 24). In a situation where little is known about educational networks, taking a singular approach to conceptualising a node as a 'social entity' is premature, even in the case where the focus of the study is teachers.

Position in the network

In whatever way we see the 'action' of the actor, a central idea of a network perspective is to see the *position* of the actor in a network (accepting that the existence of *a particular* network may be problematic). SNA distinguishes between social 'position' and 'role' in a network:

> In social network analysis *position* refers to a collection of individuals who are similarly embedded in networks of relations, while *role* refers to the patterns of relations which obtain between actors or between positions. The notion of position thus refers to a collection of actors who are similar in social activity, ties or interactions with respect to actors in other positions.
>
> (Wasserman and Faust 1994: 348; emphasis in the original)

Although social position and role are related, we will focus in this chapter on position. This concept of position creates different classes of actors through attributing structural similarity to each class. In SNA this 'similarity' is translated into 'equivalence' – that is, any two nodes that have *identical* ties are equivalent (ibid.: 392). This is termed 'structural equivalence', where the nodes are equivalent within the structure of the network. The mathematical methods for defining this structural equivalence are the basis of this rigid requirement, but our interest is the qualitative idea to understand the networks we collected, and hence we are relaxed about this requirement, given the variety of maps in our data. It would give us an interesting way of comparing, for example, two of the LHTL school co-ordinators in a particular networked learning community (NLC). In theory they might have access to the same range of members in the network, though of course their connections internal to their school will be unique. Do they link with members of the network that indicate a different position

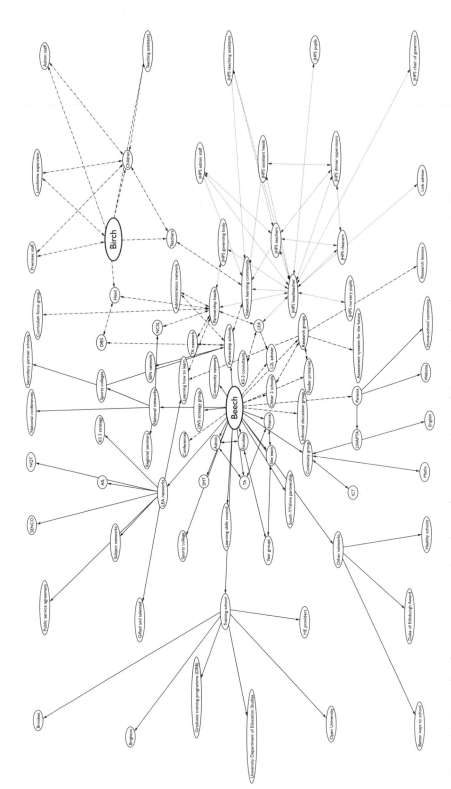

Figure 5.3 Example of a computer-combined map from respondents of three schools in the same networked learning community.

Note: JHPS refers to Walnut Primary School.

in the NLC? This kind of question can be answered only if we have some mapping of the NLC, and the best we were able to do was to combine maps of people in the same NLC through a computer program. Our attempts at this, as indicated in Chapter 4, were of limited use, in part because there were too few respondents to enable meaningful interpretation in this way and also because of the invalidity of trying to standardise nodes and links (see Figure 5.3).[5] Using a more conventional SNA approach we could have employed a name generator instrument (where respondents can select names to indicate strength or relationship, etc.) or used a list of all the members of an NLC, or some manageable subset (such as those involved with the central organising team of the NLC, along with, say, the headteachers, etc.), and then asked everyone to indicate with whom they had links.[6]

Centrality

An SNA approach derives specific quantitative measures based on algebraic formulations of definitions, which enable other characteristics to be attributed to a node. One of the most easily understood is that of *centrality*. The idea of someone 'being at the centre of things' is a familiar one, and measures of centrality assign a value to this. The important concept behind centrality is that those in a central location in the network can control the flow of information and resources to other nodes. One such measure of centrality is *degree*, based on how many links the node has as a proportion of all the possible links it could have. Thus, in Figure 5.4a, node A has the highest degree of centrality; there are six possible links and A has six links, so its degree is 1.[7] The other nodes (B–G) each have one link and therefore have a centrality of 1/6 (0.167). If 'A' was a teacher in a school and these were the links she had to other teachers in the school, then she would potentially be in the best position to influence the staff in the school. Figure 5.4b, on the other hand, shows a situation where all the nodes (e.g. teachers) have equal direct links to other nodes, so all have the same degree, i.e. two out of the six possible (0.33). In the third diagram (Figure 5.4c) the centrality of five of the nodes is 2/6 (0.333), but for the end two nodes (A and G) it is 1/6 (0.167).

Another measure is *betweenness*, which measures the amount of control any one node has over the others – that is, how many pairs of nodes a particular node comes between. Thus, again in Figure 5.4a the betweenness of A is higher than that of all those linked to it; indeed, the information (or resources) from any two nodes has to go through A. The betweenness of all the other nodes (B–G) is zero, as none of them is between any other pair of nodes. In Figure 5.4b, again all the nodes have the same value of betweenness.[8] In Figure 5.4c the betweenness of the nodes in the middle is higher than that of those at the end, with D having the highest and A and G having zero betweenness. Thus, the more actors a particular actor is between, the higher its betweenness is said to be.

'Degree' is rather a crude measure of how easily information can be communicated to others in the network (as it only relies on direct links), and so *closeness* gives an indication of how 'quickly' a node can interact, directly or indirectly, with others. It measures the minimum number of steps or 'distance' between two nodes, and the closeness is greater with less distance. In Figure 5.4a the central node, A, again has a closeness of 1 (only one step to any other node in the network), and all the rest have

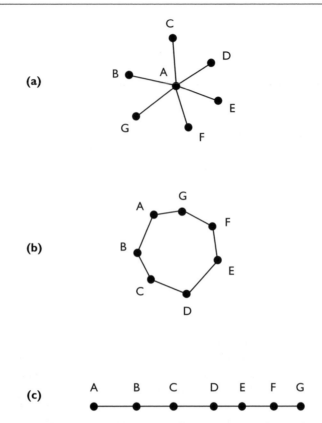

Figure 5.4 Networks showing nodes with different degrees of centrality.

a lower and equal closeness. (Unlike in the case of the betweenness measure, a node can have zero closeness only when it is not connected to another node.) In Figure 5.4b, again all nodes have the same closeness, and in Figure 5.4c the two outer nodes have the lowest closeness and the others (B–F) have the same closeness.

These measures, 'actor indices', are attributed to a node. There are refinements of these that make different assumptions about paths that are taken between nodes and also about directionality (of the link). Indeed, when only links *to* a node (incoming links) are considered, the measure is not of centrality but of *prestige*. These indices for nodes do not imply a value judgement about whether centrality is good or bad, as this will depend upon the situation being studied. Nevertheless, assumptions about 'ease of information flow' generally imply that it is positive, though if the network is concerned with keeping good ideas within the school, easy information flow (to other schools) might be bad. It is likely that in any case the relationships will be complex even with knowledge sharing, as we will indicate in Chapters 7 and 8.

Watts (2003) criticises measures of centrality as reflecting a view that authority or control must lie with key people. There may be no such key people, at least none who are always key. This relates to his second criticism: such measures present a static view of a network. A dynamic view does not assume a simple cause and effect, because something random may trigger an event and a 'centre' may emerge. Watts illustrates this through examining revolutions: leaders may cause revolutions, but equally, revolutions may cause leaders to arise. Watts (ibid.: 54–5) indicates two kinds of network dynamics:

1   dynamics *of* the network, where its structure may evolve with new ties being made and 'old' ones broken;
2   dynamics *on* the network, where people do something (e.g. adopt a new practice) and they are influenced in this decision by their neighbours.

An illustration of the second kind of dynamic is the creation of synchronised clapping at a concert. People start applauding and a core of people (leaders) influence those around them, and synchronised clapping spreads. On another occasion the core may be made up of different people. In a dynamic network there is a reciprocal relationship, which Watts (ibid.: 55) illustrates by the analogy: 'Your happiness affects your network, and your network affects your happiness.' There are different ways of dealing with this, and Watts adopts mathematical solutions in ideas of 'random' and 'scale-free networks', whereas qualitative sociologists are concerned with understanding human agency and personal and network histories. We will return to this shortly.

In practice, networks are more complex than the ones considered in Figure 5.4 and, with so little network research specifically related to schools (including the links both within and between them), it is difficult to discuss the nature of such measures in practical terms. The two studies by Daly and his colleagues, discussed in Chapter 2 (Daly and Finnigan forthcoming a; Daly *et al.* 2009), would be interesting to consider in terms of network dynamics. It might be that particular kinds of reform and the way they are implemented change the nature of the networks. For example, a reform instituted under conditions of accountability pressures (e.g. as a result of a 'failed' inspection) might result in different configurations of social relationships than if it were part of an internally and collaboratively agreed initiative to develop practice.

Although SNA measures of centrality are all based on quantitative definitions that produce indices, they can be given a qualitative interpretation. Identifying the most central nodes can be determined from qualitative data. To do so with any certainty requires quantitative data and computation, with all the attendant issues of validity associated with reducing links to numbers, assuming all links are of the same value, and working with identical nodes. Nevertheless, it is evident from the brief reviews in Chapter 2 that research using such ideas on nodes could aid understanding of how innovations develop in schools. When Ken, the co-ordinator in one of the LHTL schools (Beech School), was drawing his network map, he discussed a problem with the effectiveness of the learning to learn committee, which he chaired (responsible for the assessment for learning [AfL] initiatives in the school):

Ken: There's a [learning to learn] committee which meets . . . five times a year . . . and [it] discuss[es] new things that we're going to do and how things are going. . . . I don't think it's yet a particularly successful group. Even though it's got an obvious focus, it doesn't have an obvious role and its job is [inaudible] taking to achieve. But the key players, I think, in making things happen are the heads of faculty and they drive forward [the] group's development in the school, led by [Edward, deputy head]. . . . I think this committee at the moment doesn't have a definite remit.

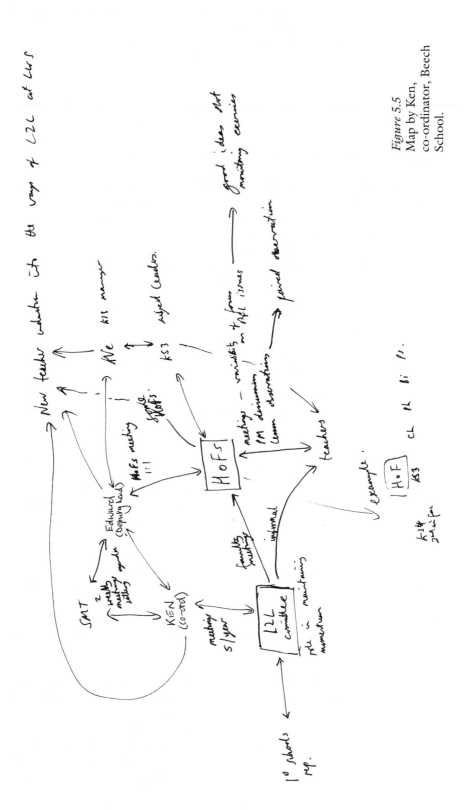

Figure 5.5
Map by Ken,
co-ordinator, Beech
School.

. . . There's very variable practice [in the school], depending on the leadership of heads of faculty, and some is fantastic and again, there's variable practice amongst teachers. . . . And it's quite difficult, I think, to have a group, a special group of people that need to do something if that doing something is keeping it going and making sure that it continues to do that . . .

Researcher: And its line of communication is the faculty meetings?

Ken: [T]here'll be some informal discussion with individual teachers. . . . But that's probably a big weakness, that there's no clear way for this committee to make an impact.

(Ken, co-ordinator, Beech School)

In fact, drawing the map made him realise that the learning to learn committee did not have any formal connection to the heads of faculty committee (see Figure 5.5). Instead, it relied on contacts with heads of faculty, primarily by members of the learning to learn committee raising issues in their own faculty meetings, or informal connections with individual teachers. Ken felt that the group's position in the school network was inadequate for the task of changing practice throughout the school. It was evident from this ego-centric mapping that there was a need for some other direct link to heads of faculty meetings. If an SNA exercise had been carried out, even with members of this committee, it would have enabled them to see the 'closeness' they had – what Ken labelled as 'informal' in the link between his committee and individual teachers. If a whole-school exercise were carried out, then a more robust view of how these members might influence the school could be determined.

A recent study of how heads of faculty managed the development of AfL in their school focused on how each faculty operated and how their management related to school policies and developments of AfL practice (Moore 2009). A considerable amount was found out about faculty differences and how, for example, the staff composition of a faculty with regard to individual member's reactions to AfL affected the progress of the initiative in the faculty. This work could be extended to a network analysis to explore both the intra- and inter-faculty relationships and how individuals affected those not in their own faculty of the kind undertaken by Lima (2007, 2008).

Hargreaves (2003a) used the idea of a 'hub' (Chapter 1) in his consideration of networks, and in SNA terms this is a node with a high degree – that is, a 'well-connected person' (Hargreaves was referring to schools as hubs). Barabási (2003) sees these hubs as very important, arguing that they arise from what he calls 'scale-free networks', because of preferential attachment of one node to another. Such hubs exist in all kinds of networks, not just social networks. Indeed, Barabási's mathematical analysis indicates that there is a power law that can model the existence of such hubs in any particular network (see Figure 5.6). This law indicates that most nodes have a few links, but a small number have many links. He assumes that *a* network exists, but he has examined parts of some very large networks, most notably the World Wide Web and the internet.[9] Barabási explores the significance of hubs in diffusion studies (discussed briefly in Chapter 2) – for example, the diffusion of the use of a particular drug, and how hubs are important in this process of diffusion (something we explore more in Chapter 7). There are some obvious implications of hubs or central nodes for educational networks. For example, a school about to launch a new development initiative, such as AfL, could sensibly consider starting with 'hubs'. Schools in the

LHTL project employed various strategies to start with: introducing it to all staff at the same time; picking a particular group of teachers predisposed to innovation (or this innovation); picking a particular department or year group of teachers who were willing. The reasons for choosing one approach rather than another are likely to be very local to the particular school, but it may be that basing the choice on 'keen innovators' or a 'willing group' pays more attention to the developing of new practices than to how any developments will be shared with the rest of the staff. Following on from the earlier discussion on hubs or other nodes with high centrality, it might be interesting to try to use staff who were 'well connected' to spread the word about the new practices. This entails carrying out an SNA by asking each member of staff what kinds of links they have with whom. But it also makes assumptions about how new practices spread (examined in Chapter 7).

Burt (2005: 28–38) gives an example of a new head of the supply chain of a large electronics company who wanted to get up to speed with thinking about and communicating a strategy for integrating the supply chain. Burt collected data on the links of the supply-chain managers (in various divisions and geographical areas) through an elaborate web-based questionnaire that enabled managers to say what was their best idea for increasing the value of the supply chain, whom they discussed it with and who were the people with whom they most often discussed such ideas. For each of these latter two sets of names, they were also able to rate how often such discussions took place. His focus was on determining something about the value of brokers, but it illustrates an interesting way of finding out who might be the right people to involve initially in developing new practices as well as how these practices will be spread throughout the school. Palonen *et al.* (2004) give an account of how this was done for team interaction within a telecommunication company. They asked each member

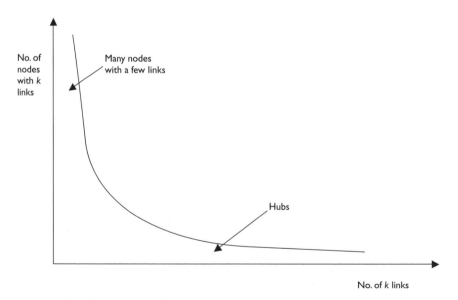

Figure 5.6 The 'power law' for nodes and links.

Source: Barabási (2003).

of the company to answer the following questions for all the other members of the company, effectively indicating the strength of the links with each member (from weakest [1] to strongest [4]) (ibid.: 279):

1 To whom do you go to ask for advice?
2 To whom do you go to ask for new information?
3 With whom do you have informal discussions?
4 With whom do you carry out your most important collaboration?

The SNA studies in education, reviewed at the end of Chapter 2, indicated variability in relationships. Any attempt to introduce new practices into a district or school might well be improved if those who were more 'central' in an area or school were trained first (assuming, of course, that they could be identified). Within a school, finding out and using hubs could be important in spreading ideas around the staff.

What the earlier account by Barabási misses, however, is the fact that the nature of the hub is affected not just by the number of links but also by what kinds of links they are, including to whom (or what). This extends the idea of network position, to take in how a node might link to specific nodes in parts of the network that themselves have a particular structure or grouping (e.g. a tight-knit group). Such groupings might be of those who are well connected to each other, but less so to other parts of the network. This is particularly important when we think about Burt's ideas of brokers, briefly examined in Chapter 2 and earlier in this chapter. We will consider brokers as nodes of special concern in network analysis, but first let us look at some of these sub-groups, which are themselves structural units. One such structural unit is the 'clique', a term that conveys the idea of a closely connected group (although in SNA it has no pejorative connotations).

Cliques

The variety of nodes has already been noted, and the fact that some may themselves be networks, understood or represented as a single node. For example, see the representation by Bill of 'LA' as a node (Figure 5.1, right-hand side). He actually indicates a 'link adviser' who in effect represents the whole local authority, because this person is well linked within the authority and also to the school. If the school is linked to this adviser, it is also linked to the rest of the authority (at least, that is what is assumed). It may also be that Bill's representations of the schools (the 'satellites' around the central headteacher group) he thought of as well-connected entities. SNA uses the concept of the 'clique' (meaning a small set of interconnected nodes as part of a network of localised high density) to explore this structural unit, which Bill represents as a node. The Chapter 2 discussion of closure (Burt 2001) was in effect discussing a clique. Three nodes all interconnected would form a clique, with a density of 1. In practice, networks would have many cliques all overlapping if the requirement for a clique was that it was a part of the network with a density of 1, and so this requirement has to be relaxed (Erickson 1988). This is done by specifying some minimum level of density or a group linked to all but a specified number of nodes. Erickson (ibid.: 107) argues that the choice of definition of a clique should stem from the theoretical goals of the network study, though in practice people use intuitive criteria that may be based on pragmatic decisions (much as happens with definitions of 'whole networks'), with ambiguous theoretical implications. In addition, the clique is refined if the strength of links is taken into account, and then the cut-off can be used in relation to a pre-defined level of strength, related of course to the purpose of the study. It is likely that the PLCs we discussed in Chapter 1 would be made up of cliques, at least within a school, where the strength might be indicated by the fourth question that Palonen *et al.* (2004) posed to members of the telecommunication company discussed earlier ('With whom do you carry out your most important collaboration?').

Identifying cliques can be a basis for both setting up such communities and researching them, using SNA. The research could reveal how they are functioning, and details of how people actually collaborate, and with whom. Investigating Bill's various 'curriculum liaison groups' (Figure 5.1) using an SNA approach might reveal whether they were cliques where effective collaboration took place, or simply meetings that people attended in some routine way. Of course, there could be other dimensions of cliquishness that are not indicated by the measures of strength of links Palonen and her colleagues used – for example, friendship cliques or smoking cliques (formed by those who meet regularly outside the school building to avoid the 'no smoking' rule inside!). These might relate to ideas on contagion, which we will examine in Chapters 6 and 7.

Assumptions about actors

It is important to have a clear view of the way actors in a network act, in terms of the assumptions built into the theoretical models. Burt (1992), concerned with a market, sees the actor with social capital giving a company advantages within the market, for which the actor is rewarded. His action theory, examined in Chapter 2, indicated a view where bridging structural holes released their social capital. This theory also recognises that the actor is subject to the social context as well as affecting it (encapsulated in the 'circular' nature of Figure 2.1). General SNA approaches assume an awareness of the network and, indeed, stochastic approaches (e.g. Snijders 1996) are

> based on the idea that actors evaluate their position in the network and strive for the 'best' possible configuration of relations. All actors are assumed to have full knowledge of the present state of the network, and given this state, all actors are assumed to behave independently.
>
> (Huisman and Snijders 2003: 255)

It is not clear that a teacher looking to improve her practice would view her actions in the way Burt assumed or takes such a strategic view of the network as a whole as is envisaged in the above quotation.

Castells (2000a) also sees a market operating, based on the networking of information, arguing that the importance of a node relates to its ability to process information more efficiently than other nodes, hence it becomes more central. However, as was indicated in Chapter 2, Castells uses the idea that these main nodes are not 'centres' but 'switches', in contrast to the more common idea of a hub. Nodes can be excluded from the information network if they are not used by other nodes, emphasising the competitive environment within which he considers that actors act.

As noted in Chapter 2, it is not clear that the functioning of a market or competition within a network applies to educational enterprises. Nevertheless, a criticism of Hargreaves' idea of 'leading-edge schools' (that take a lead for a group of schools in knowledge creation [Hargreaves 2003a]) is that it assumes, perhaps, a benign climate among schools. There is a tension in the model he proposes: on the one hand it is a collaborative regime, yet there are lead schools that work to level up those they are linked with. It is evident that the current situation in England, where schools are in competition for students at a local level and where they are compared in public examination league tables, creates a climate where they are less likely to collaborate with local schools that are in effect their competitors. Thus, the pessimistic reading of the situation is that the market orientation underlying some of the SNA and social capital approaches does exist in education. Whether there are any rewards for individual teachers, as Burt (2000) is able to show for managers who have social capital, is something that requires more empirical work.

Another issue is the view of actor agency in a network. Chapter 2 outlined different views on structure and agency, which we will consider in this chapter in relation to brokers. Emirbayer and Goodwin (1994) indicate how different network approaches view the actor differently in these respects. They review three models of network analysis with different views of the relationship between networks, culture and agency:

- *structural determinism*, where the actor's beliefs, values and normative commitments are ignored (e.g. Wellman 1988);
- *structural instrumentalism*, where actors do have agency, but this is seen through limited instrumental dimensions (e.g. money, power or status [Burt 1992]);
- *structural constructivism*, where agency is conceptualised as a process of identity change.

The structured instrumental view of agency sees actors as 'homo economicus' (Emirbayer and Goodwin 1994: 1428). Despite the comments above on competition in schools in reference to Hargreaves' view of hubs (Hargreaves 2003a), it is unlikely that a teacher involved in changing practice is such an actor. Structural constructivism has a more complex view of agency and acknowledges that the actor's goals and aspirations are complex and historically determined. Emirbayer and Goodwin argue that this approach enables the evolution of networks to be understood and to see why they come about in particular ways; to see networks as dynamic. They refer to White (1992), and agency through 'identity', as a way of seeing the dynamic nature of networks. Action is thus an expression of identity as well as having a source in the network structure, with the actor seeking to create meaning. (This is an alternative to the ideas of Watts [2003] on random and ordered networks; see Chapter 2.) Passy's (2003) view of individuals constructing meaning from their interactions within the network, rather than just responding to what they see others doing, provides a counter to the SNA approaches of structural determinism or instrumentalism. Inevitably, this view requires a qualitative, ego-centric perspective on the network rather than the quantitative whole-network approach of SNA.

Fox *et al.* (2010), investigating support of early-career teachers, were able to show how individual teachers, through their use of their personal networks, varied in how proactively they used the available support. Fox and her colleagues argue that this was the teachers' exercise of agency. They also link this to 'identity' as discussed in the professional development literature, and to tensions between structure and agency. Reflecting on the LHTL project network data, it is difficult to take a view of teachers' personal networks in the light of this discussion on meaning-making. Some respondents had evidently thought about networks, and used the word unprompted in reference to their maps of communication relationships; others had not thought about communications or interactions in this way. It remains an empirical question whether their agency is expressed in the network. They could, when prompted, assign value to links, the beginnings of attaching meaning to them. This, however, takes us to the issues of the nature of links, the subject of the next chapter. We will later discuss evidence that potential brokers find it difficult to spot the structural holes that will realise social capital from within the network (Burt 2005), an indication of a lack of actor awareness.

The characteristics of nodes attributed to structural location are rather general and, although they have qualitative interpretations (e.g. of a well-connected person) that are relevant to educational networks, it was difficult to obtain this kind of evidence from the mapping exercise we carried out. (We have already indicated how more quantitative methods could be used to derive, for example, measures of centrality.) Our work did, however, enable us to examine two particular kinds of nodes that were important in the maps, namely experts and brokers. External experts are particularly important in knowledge creation in the commercial sector (Hakkarainen *et al.* 2004), and we have evidence from the LHTL project data that enables us to examine who these experts are and what they do in education. We have already discussed the basic idea of a broker as explored by Burt (2000), and it evidently is also a commonly recognised role in the educational literature.

Brokers

For Burt, a broker is someone who bridges structural holes in a network. Brokers can connect otherwise disconnected segments of a network across the structural holes, including bridging between cliques (where closure exists), which are possible areas of collaborative activity. How does this view of broker match that of Wenger (1998)? There are some similarities in the sense that Wenger sees brokers working across two communities of practice, but he assumes a broker participating in each community, and hence strong links between them. We have already discussed the fact that Burt (2005), drawing on the ideas of Granovetter (1973), argued that weak ties were particularly important to obtain information from distant parts of a social system, and that such weak links connect to significantly different people. The metaphor for Burt is a 'bridge' and for Wenger a 'translator', a person able to align the communities' perspectives. We have coined this latter view 'the "two worlds" perspective' (the broker 'lives' in the two worlds of the communities [McCormick and Carmichael 2005]). Wenger's account sees socially generated boundary objects (reifications) as the bridges. We have already noted that Wenger's ideas on a community of practice present a high hurdle for researchers to identify such communities (and so usually they do not apply Wenger's criteria). Likewise, it is a tough definition to satisfy the conditions of a broker. However, as we will show, Wenger's idea is more common in the education literature, where there is some attempt to conceptualise 'broker'.

From the point of view of networks it is worth focusing on Burt's ideas of a broker (Burt 2005), whom he sees as an opinion leader, or rather an opinion broker, and also that of the network entrepreneur; this gives individuals competitive advantage, as part of his market view of networks. Being opinion leaders, with access to non-redundant sources of information (which contrasts with that inside a clique), enables brokers to have what Burt calls a 'vision advantage' (ibid.: 60). They are more likely to have creative ideas, as these ideas emerge from engaging in selecting and synthesising across structural holes, with unintentional learning being a feature of the process. Brokers are thus agents of internal change by bridging from new practice elsewhere in the network to current practice in a tightly knit group or clique.

Burt (ibid.: 61) identifies different levels of brokerage that go from the lowest to the highest level of creating value,[10] some of which touch on the 'two worlds' view:

- making people both sides of a structural hole aware of interests and difficulties in the other 'group';
- transferring best practice (by being able to see practice in one group that will be useful to the other);
- drawing an analogy between groups that seem irrelevant to one another;
- synthesis arising from familiarity with both groups and identifying new beliefs and behaviours that combine elements from both groups.

For a school looking to keep its practice at the forefront, brokers are clearly a must, but can we identify or create them? Brokers do not set out to build bridges; rather, brokers become such as a by-product of other ends (their normal work within the network); so they are not consciously brokers. Opportunities for brokerage are not obvious, and people vary in their capability to detect holes, though experience does improve it. Burt (2000, 2005) has examined contingencies that might affect the strength of association between social capital and performance for individuals such as managers. These contingencies were personality factors,[11] culture (are some cultures more successful than others?) and kinds of relationships. If these contingencies explain the association, they have a bearing on the extent to which such individuals can be 'produced' or exist in some situations rather than others. None of them did explain the association between social capital and performance. As noted, however, experience at spotting structural holes does help, even if 'training' to become a broker is unlikely to be successful. But Kossinets and Watts (2006: 90) conclude that caution is needed in relating differences in outcomes measures, such as status or performance, to differences in individual network position: 'Bridges, for example, may indeed facilitate diffusion of information across entire communities. . . . However, their unstable nature suggests that they are not "owned" by particular individuals indefinitely; thus, whatever advantages they confer are also temporary.' They also cast doubt on whether an individual can strategically manipulate their position in large network. However, Kossinets and Watts do concede that the subjects in their research (higher education academics and students) may not need to manipulate their position and hence it was not evident in their results.

Nevertheless, Burt's picture of brokers is a rich one and potentially productive to schools. However, as was indicated earlier, it is not one found in much of the literature on education. In a search of almost fifty articles on brokers, eleven dealt with brokers from Wenger's perspective, whereas only two indicated Burt's view (of these two, one mentioned the idea of a 'bridge' but did not theorise it; the other included ourselves: Carmichael *et al.* [2007]).[12] A review of leadership literature by Miller (2007) is somewhat of an exception. His concern was with the specific role of 'boundary-spanning leadership' in university, school and community partnerships. In the literature, this had names relevant to our discussion, such as 'network co-ordinators', 'internal networkers' and 'bridge people'. His typology of this role focuses very much on specific individuals' characteristics that echo ideas in the network literature:

- well-connected bridge builders (between disparate communities), with numerous points of contact (hubs) and hence high social capital;
- establishing collaborative environments with clear and regular commitment;
- serving as information brokers that can make sense of different types of information, scan environments through various modes and filter information to decide who gets what.

He also attributes other individual qualities to them: having credibility; being knowledgeable, with significant social and personal skills; and being able to move freely and flexibly. (We have thus another instance of agency verses structure, as Miller sees these 'bridge people' as agentive, whereas Burt [2005] and Kossinets and Watts [2006] seem to take a structural view.) None of Miller's literature sources includes that from PLCs, NLCs or general SNA literature, yet they reflect some of the ideas Burt puts forward, and those we found in our LHTL data.

On the other hand, an example of the Wenger perspective is a paper by Hartnell (2006), who discusses teachers brokering across classroom and school boundaries viewed in terms of communities of practice. A large number of the 'broker' sources searched also included the idea of an outside organisation acting as a broker, for example Hadfield (2005: 186), who identifies the NLC programme core team as a broker for schools and NLCs by making connections for them. In describing this role, Hadfield quotes Wenger (1998) and discusses the latter's ideas of boundary objects in relation to frameworks that the core team produced. Other examples of brokers occur in a major study by Fielding *et al.*, who give examples that show a network perspective:

> Many [headteachers] regard it as part of their role 'To find out what is going on, know who to ring up', though one head reflecting ruefully on the observed practices of his fellow heads remarked: 'I am surprised at how few heads do [take opportunities to pick up on practical work of value presented at conferences]. They expect gurus! You should take the opportunities that are there and broker for other teachers, give an atmosphere of encouragement and celebrate minor practices.'
>
> (2005: 46)

> A deputy head in another school was, in effect, carving out a 'new' role for himself as a talent scout-cum-broker of good practice both within and outside his school. He appeared to be constantly looking out for good teachers and instances of good practice to fill his mental rolodex, from word of mouth among staff and students, or from conferences, seminars and meetings he attended, with a view to developing particular teachers' work or putting people in touch with each other as necessary.
>
> (ibid.: 47)

Other examples these authors give are of heads of departments and senior leadership teams providing *internal* brokerage by putting teachers in touch with each other within a school. But the main focus of Fielding and his colleagues is on brokerage by *external* agencies such as LAs, and they consider five elements and roles of this (ibid.: 49):

1   brokering practices (knowing about and making information available);
2   brokering relationships (putting people in touch);
3   enabling fruitful dialogue (providing context for practice sharing through creating a sense of audience and community);
4   resourcing joint work (providing resources for sharing);
5   being a catalyst.

Their focus is in fostering collaborative work (an element of Miller's view), and hence there is an understandable focus on the 'two worlds' perspective. For example, for Fielding and his colleagues, '2' above involves spotting where people think along similar lines and could work together; '3' includes creating a wider sense of community; '4' is about providing resources (including funding) to enable teachers to have the time, etc. to engage in collaborative activity; '5' is to foster new forms of collaboration. However, '1' is more clearly an example of Burt's idea of bridge building, and Fielding and his colleagues give examples of the use of websites to show services and names of useful people, along with a discussion area where schools could share the networks with which they were involved. Similarly, '3' includes bringing headteachers together to discuss shared interests, and events hosted by outside agencies where networking can take place through the making of fruitful contacts. There seems to be some tension in these elements: in '3', people are brought together because they are 'like-minded', whereas the catalyst role in '5' encourages doing something new, although the mechanisms for the introduction of the 'new' are not clarified. Fielding *et al.* (ibid.: 73) recognise the need for more clarity and make recommendations on brokerage:

> [B]rokering practices . . . emerged as a key element in the development of collaborative professional learning. However, despite its promise, existing provision appears patchy and the notion of brokerage seems conceptually under-developed and empirically of uneven quality. . . . Further study is required to develop a robust intellectual account of brokerage, that summarises the current state of our empirical knowledge in this domain, and recommends a number of fruitful ways forward.

Our analysis, based on the network literature and on the LHTL project data, enabled us to identify examples of brokerage roles of both kinds (Burt and Wenger). There is, however, a tendency for school-based respondents to describe mainly 'two worlds' roles and LA/VEAZ respondents to describe both 'two worlds' and bridge-building roles, as we will show in the next section.

Characterisations of brokerage in LHTL schools

Only one of the respondents in our study explicitly described themselves and their organisation (a VEAZ) as a 'broker', in the context of information exchange and access to expertise:

[T]hey will e-mail in here saying, 'Look, we want to get some modern language work going using software and curriculum. Is there anywhere you know where we can go and look?' So, if you like, they use us here as the broker.

(Nancy Iver, VEAZ co-ordinator)

[The VEAZ] probably is the broker because the schools would say to you, and quite rightly, that *they* are the [Virtual Education Action] Zone.

(Nancy Iver, VEAZ co-ordinator)

This resembles the Fielding *et al.* (2005) 'brokering of practice'. However, there were many instances in which the respondent used other descriptive terms that related brokerage to network position, centrality or boundary locations (such as 'exchange', 'hub', 'interface' or 'point of contact'); or where the nature and outcomes of brokerage functions were described. These illustrated some implicit understanding of the network ideas on brokerage role that we have discussed.

Although respondents provided examples of both the 'two worlds' and the bridging perspectives, within these accounts there was a variation in the degree of agency and autonomy in the roles. At one extreme were accounts of acting as *conduits* for information simply by virtue of network structures or their own position within them:

[I'm] in the centre, not because I regard myself as the most important, but because most things actually come through me one way or another.

(Sam, headteacher, Alder Primary School)

But there are also conduits for information about links with others:

We have a community development officer . . . who has, as it were, established actual links – so that means he knows . . . he has names and telephone numbers of key people, specific things that are set up.

(Nick, headteacher, Beech School)

Respondents also identified other examples in which they were primarily *representatives* of a school or other group on committees or in negotiation with other agencies:

I am the headteacher representative for the secondary schools of the ten . . . boroughs [LAs]. . .you get quite a few college reps [representatives]; there is this guy who runs the airport, a number of industrialists, all sorts of people . . . discussing what the role of the [Learning and Skills Council] should be.

(Ed, headteacher, Redwood High School)

Representation of this kind may be considered to be a brokerage function but, as with other aspects of networking, a general commitment to discussion and collegiality does not necessarily lead to the brokering of anything of value. A formal organisational role does not imply any informal activity, and how an individual interprets the role can vary. So, these events might be considered to be 'sites for brokering' within which associated brokerage functions might not be enacted, as one of our respondents ruefully explained in the context of teachers attending a one-day in-service session:

People come in, they listen, they go back to school. Whether it actually happens in the classroom as a result is another matter.

(Kay Fisher, LA co-ordinator)

In other cases, respondents described a more active *rapporteur* role in which they were involved in communication of information from one individual or group to another. Some were very clear that they were simply acting as messengers rather then fulfilling any more complex or continuing mediation role, while others reported back on individual or group activity:

One of my TAs [teaching assistants], who's a representative and goes to meetings, wants to see me now on a regular basis to feed back to me what they've been . . . you know, the elements of their activity.

(Bill, headteacher, Walnut County Primary School)

In some cases this involved a deliberate 'filtering' process on the part of the broker, who was encouraged to identify valuable resources, information or outcomes:

We just say can you bring back five points that you think are worthy of sharing with the staff, for whatever reason. They could be things that could affect your practice or they could be things that you think that we need to be thinking about for ourselves in the future.

(Jane, headteacher, Gingko Primary School)

Other respondents, predominantly those from LAs and the VEAZ, described a *mediation* role in which they regularly convened meetings, passed selected information from one source to appropriate recipients, or gathered information from disparate sources to address a specific need. In some cases this involved drawing on the expertise of others, or on personal prior experience, or on the collective resources available to an organisation:

I will take into that meeting . . . resources they might want to access, like useful websites . . . publications and those sorts of things. I will take along things that I think would be really useful to them.

(Una Hills, LA co-ordinator)

This mediation role went beyond simply presenting materials, but involved a moderation and interpretation role as well, resembling the Wenger perspective on brokers:

[I]t generated an awful lot of requests from schools to come in and actually mediate those materials with staff . . . we had set them out to be materials so schools could mediate their own staff meetings but somehow they still wanted the message to come from someone else outside.

(Una Hills, LA co-ordinator)

While it could be argued that the request, presumably from a school leader, for the LA representative to provide the 'message' to staff might be seen as an attempt to *bridge* a 'structural hole', clear examples of this alternative perspective on brokerage were less common. Some respondents described how they saw this bridging as a specific function of their school leadership role (as Miller [2007] argued), made achievable by their being active in networks, as this headteacher indicates:

> But what I am able to do is identify – through discussion, through reading, through contact – areas where good practice is happening and actually bring the best of them into the school and put the staff into contact with other people.
>
> (Sam, headteacher, Alder Primary School)

This is similar to the example from Fielding *et al.* (2005) quoted earlier. Among LA advisory staff the practice of systematically collecting instances of practice, or bringing together teachers who are interested in such things as 'inquiry', suggests the emergence of brokerage roles, though these were conflated with other functions such as mediation and critical friendship (see 'Pete D' at the top left-hand side of Figure 5.1), and were often couched in terms of 'facilitation' or 'keeping channels open'. These LA respondents were frequently keen to stress that it was school-based participants who had to be the active participants in a process that they simply enabled or catalysed:

> I facilitated it, but the fact that it grew was [because] people were convinced because of what was happening in their classrooms.
>
> (Eileen Laws, LA co-ordinator)

> I'd see it as part of the general role which is to listen to the networks and to try and make sure that things happen to be enabling for them.
>
> (Wendy Dix, LA co-ordinator)

When *bridge-building* activity was described in detail, the identification and 'closing' of structural holes was often dependent on a specific individual being charged with the co-ordination of a specific innovation. This is the case for the LHTL school co-ordinators, and in Chapter 9 we will show a case (Juniper Primary School) where the co-ordinator represented the main link to all those involved in AfL, both within the LA (which had an NLC) and beyond. When this co-ordinator left, all the personal relationships she had with those in the other clusters were broken. Some of the links would still exist, but the personal relationships associated with them (and hence the social capital) were lost.

Another example involved a teacher who had been seconded to work on a project that involved bringing designers and animators into schools, and who was on the lookout for potential recruits:

> We have had people who have come in . . . who have supported some IT work, working with animation and making very short animated clips for Year 4 children [aged 8–9]. This was excellent, the children were so pleased with it. . . . That was brought about because that teacher was seconded by the borough [LA] . . . to do that sort of thing. And because [our ICT co-ordinator[13]] had been at a meeting and that had come up and [the seconded teacher] said it would absolutely be right for our school.
>
> (Barbara, headteacher, Juniper Primary School)

At an LA level an example of bridge building was an ICT manager talking of sharing video resources between schools:

> Well, I've got [a teacher] who is working on this at Redwood High School. I've got [a primary school] working on this and I've got a teacher here who is working on that . . . making the connections. Perhaps we are connection makers. Connections were made at a personal level, but then the practicalities were dealt with by the teachers concerned.
>
> (James Noon, LA co-ordinator)

This last issue is of particular interest, in that it reflects an awareness that brokers as 'connection makers' have only partial knowledge about the contexts in which teachers are working; their role is to establish links on the basis of 'promisingness' or common aspects of the brokered relationship, but beyond that, the 'practicalities' of the situation are best dealt with by teachers themselves. This is a contrast with the 'two worlds' perspective, where the level of mediation is likely to be higher (as the broker has to interpret for each of the communities), though this is also the case with Burt's fourth level, 'synthesising', discussed earlier (Burt 2005).

An important impact of effective brokerage is the establishment not only of relationships between two individuals but also of links between those individual's networks. The identification of individuals with many links of value (and access to, or influence over, other network elements) leads to *gatekeeping* and *multiplier effects* in which the critical dyadic relationship (which may, of course be brokered by a third party) 'opens up' many new network paths. Setting gatekeeping within a network perspective extends the idea of the 'filter' role that Miller (2007) identified. An example of a school-based gatekeeper acting with an external agency gatekeeper, with multiplier effects at 'both ends' of the bridge that is established, was cited by Brian, the headteacher of Hawthorn High School, when describing the development of innovative induction procedures within the school, with the help of the NCSL:

> Last summer, [the deputy headteacher] and a few people . . . got together to say they were interested in a National College [NCSL] pilot. . . . Anyway, it was piloted down here with funding from the National College and it fitted in, you see, very much into what we want to do anyway. That really was me, me talking to Johnny Stanton [at the National College], saying that we were keen on doing this work and gossiping . . . I had pretty much a social conversation with Johnny that this was an area of interest. Johnny obviously latched on and was very enthusiastic, and that provided us with some contacts which we . . . hadn't known about and out of it all we have opened the links with the National College.

An initial relationship between Brian and Johnny had led to the brokering by Johnny of a longer-term collaboration between a programme team at the NCSL and a team at the school, led by the deputy headteacher, in which school staff had access to NCSL resources and networks. The place of the school within LA networks led, after a year's pilot activity in collaboration with the NCSL, to the adoption of similar induction activities more widely across the authority:

We used it to run our own programme in induction week, which we are currently reviewing for next year, so we've now got our own school-based induction policy . . . and this has been now taken on across the borough [LA].

(Brian, headteacher, Hawthorn High School)

The observation by Hakkarainen *et al.* (2004) that effective brokerage is mutually beneficial to all participants appears to be borne out in this example. In addition to the ultimate beneficiaries of the enhanced induction procedures, school staff networks have been extended, the status of the school in the LA has been reinforced, and the NCSL has increased the reach and impact of its initiative and potentially enhanced its reputation as enabler and supporter of change.

We became interested in brokers and brokerage not only because of their role in the dissemination of specific AfL practices or in promoting particular kinds of links, but also because they had a role in supporting and sustaining networks more generally. Some respondents explained this broader commitment to networking and network building. LHTL LA co-ordinators, who work with a number of NLCs in their LA, including one for AfL that included LHTL project schools, explained:

I don't see it as separate because my role as co-ordinator is for all the networks, which isn't just for the assessment for learning network and within that very small group of schools. So I wouldn't see it as separate. I'd see it as part of the general role, which is to listen to the networks and to try and make sure that things happen, to be enabling for them.

(Wendy Dix, LA co-ordinator)

[T]eachers are in there working with a very specific group of people. . . . It's a function of people [who are] not working in that way, to make sure that they maintain networks to inform each other.

(James Noon, LA co-ordinator)

The headteacher who described the role of the NCSL in the establishment of the school (and later, authority-wide) induction development reflected:

[T]hat is an example of good networking, it has given us a link to the National College and we are keen to continue this.

(Brian, headteacher, Hawthorn High School)

Overview of brokerage in LHTL schools

The range of brokerage functions described here mirrors Burt's levels, discussed earlier (Burt 2005: 61–2), as indicated in Table 5.2. There is a variety of expression of brokers' work (conduit, rapporteur, mediator) extending network capability, but there is little explicit awareness of this broker role in schools. Perhaps, as Fielding *et al.* (2005) noted, it is only part of LA thinking. In situations where the LA is less important, or where it only provides specific services, rather than adopting a more paternalistic role towards schools, then schools themselves need to be more aware of the potential of the broker role. Earlier, we indicated ideas that schools could adopt to determine who

Table 5.2 Examples of different levels of brokerage

Burt's level	Example from LHTL project
Making people aware of each other's existence	Community development officer with telephone numbers of key people (Nick, Beech School)
Identifying and helping transmit 'best practice'	What our respondents described as acting as 'conduits' (Sam, Alder Primary School)
Relating one person or group's needs to another by analogy	The kind of 'matching' role exemplified by the case of the seconded ICT teacher recognising what might be 'right' for a school (Barbara, Juniper Primary School)
A creative synthesis in which both sets of participants benefit but in which new insights or approaches are generated and contribute to the available repertoire and social capital of the extended network	Working with NCSL on an induction programme (Brian, Hawthorn High School)

might be well-connected people (with high centrality), and the use of network mapping more generally might reveal networks external to the school to which staff are connected. Burt (2005: 22–3) indicates that it takes skill to see structural holes, but there is evidence that, with experience, people can learn to see them (though again note the caution by Kossinets and Watts [2006]). Our research on teachers becoming middle managers gave case-study evidence that some had not yet seen the importance of making links to other teachers and schools, and they found that such invitations detracted from what they saw as their leadership role (McCormick *et al.* 2006). Fox (2008) suggests mapping of external links to reveal useful resources using the weak links in staff personal networks, and we will return to the importance of such brokerage to 'distant' sources in Chapter 7. There is evidently scope for researchers to work with schools in growing broker roles and in researching their effects.

With respect to experience with brokerage, Burt's view of expertise is similar to Bereiter and Scardamalia's (1993) association of it with the capacity to recognise the 'promisingness' of particular courses of action. If indeed the capability for brokerage is related to perception, then it may also be related to structural position within a given network. This blurs the distinction between the two perspectives (those of Wenger and Burt) to some extent; a broker who is at the boundary of two network components (e.g. cliques) or communities of practice and who can 'translate' between their domain-specific discourses may be better placed to recognise 'promising' opportunities for brokering across the structural holes that exist between the two. This in turn means that it is necessary to see the transformation of weak links into strong 'bonding' links. However, this might offset the value of weak links in reaching alternative perspectives as noted above. Hakkarainen *et al.* (2004) distinguish between weak links used to search for information and strong links to exchange it, and this may be the key to when a broker needs these different kinds of links – an issue we will return to in Chapter 7.

Experts

Expertise is central to all ideas about the creation and sharing of knowledge, and most conceptualisations of it in the literature concern the role of experts *within* an organisation, the nature of their expertise, how it is developed and how it is distributed within the company (see Hakkarainen *et al.* 2004: chapters 2–4). Hence, for example, it is possible through SNA to find out those people who are seen as experts by members of an organisation (by asking whom they seek advice from, etc., as shown earlier). Such people have high 'advice size'. Distributed expertise is a particular issue for organisations, but in the context of schools this may be somewhat problematic. It is not clear how schools see themselves as having to share knowledge to conduct their normal business of teaching and learning, as opposed to in specific professional development activities.[14] Whatever the situation within schools, the focus of our part of the LHTL project was the link *between* schools, and here the literature on networked expertise is weaker.[15] In the LHTL project we sought to understand who respondents saw as experts, the types of experts, and who and what were seen as experts. In the coding of experts in a network map and associated interviews, it was not always possible to use a respondent's view of expertise in identifying experts, although this is the ideal perspective; we used a combination of views, including specific labelling by respondents.

In what follows, the types of experts, what they offer, how they are known or found and their impact are first discussed in general terms. Then profiles of various kinds of experts are given, using simple categories of national and local location, and recognition.

Types of experts

Experts were seen in terms of a number of characteristics that at times overlap:

- where they are *located* or are seen to operate;
- how their expertise is *recognised*, or its basis;
- *what expertise* they offer in terms of the form and subject;
- how the organisation *knows* about them;
- the *impact* they have.

Location

Experts can be seen in terms of whether they are international or national figures, the latter being identified in terms of their role (David Bell as Her Majesty's Chief Inspector[16]) and reputation (e.g. Shirley Clarke[17]), and international figures in terms of reputation (e.g. Bill Rogers[18]). This implies that their sphere of influence or work is at these two levels, national and international. Similarly, there are experts who work or are known at the local level, either within a LA or among other schools – that is, they work across schools. Of these local experts, some are simply identified and work internally to a school, and indeed may be the headteacher. Some of these local, and internal, experts work nationally in that they may be used by national organisations.

Role/basis of expertise

The international or national experts are usually recognised by reputation, which may stem from their personal activities as a speaker and writer (e.g. Shirley Clarke) or researcher (e.g. Dylan Wiliam[19]). Some, as is indicated above, are recognised by their national role (e.g. David Bell). These characteristics are seen as the basis of their expertise (in the eyes of our respondents). Others have their expertise recognised in their job title, for example advanced skills teachers (ASTs),[20] LA advisers or support services. Some are seen as 'lead teachers', or are recognised as teachers with expertise (by their school or other schools). Recognition can also come from a specialist organisation (e.g. the Association of Christian Teachers), where an individual is used by them as, say, a consultant. In some cases the expertise is not with individuals but with the school itself, leading to visitors being brought to the school. All the references (direct or indirect) by respondents to external expertise were to individuals (named or by role title) rather than to institutions, although, as we shall show, there are examples of schools seeing themselves in this role. Fielding *et al.* (2005: 13) discuss external expertise in relation to Beacon schools, which take a lead in a local area in spreading 'best' practice; they refer to such schools as 'all-purpose' advisers.[21]

What experts offer

Experts can be used for consultation, demonstrations, advice, to observe classrooms (or be observed), present at conferences or to give workshops or in-service training. In some cases they can be available electronically and pose and answer questions. In many cases the subject of the expertise (i.e. what it is about) is not specified; in other cases it is a 'school subject' (literacy, mathematics, English, ICT). At times it is more generally related to 'practice', or to some special aspect of education (e.g. AfL, emotional capacity, Christian teaching).

How are they known or found?

For those with a national or international reputation, then this reputation is how they are known, reflecting the SNA idea of 'prestige' discussed earlier (such people have many incoming links). In few of these instances can we tell how contact was made (though there is an example of someone searching on the web and finding telephone numbers). More often, experts are known through personal contact (e.g. by ringing up headteachers they know), or the known role they have (e.g. AST).

What kind of impact do they have?

The question of the kind of impact they have is seldom explicitly answered. When it is, it is usually in terms of the immediate effect rather than through the impact on teaching and learning. Thus, respondents gave evidence of teachers talking about what the expert said or that they were impressed.

Profiles of experts

Profiles are not clear-cut, but can be organised around the basis of the expert's expertise: national or international reputation/role; local role, reputation or recognition; school as expert.

National or international reputation

Not surprisingly, there are few people with a national or international reputation and, given the context of the LHTL project, they are mostly related to AfL, as the examples given earlier illustrate. Because of this, few were international experts. On one occasion a respondent referred not to an individual in person, but to their publications:

> Apart from reading Shirley Clarke's book and the Dylan [Wiliam] and [Paul] Black research . . .
>
> (Wendy Dix, LA co-ordinator)

In almost all of the cases, experts were invited to a conference in the school or LA/VEAZ to give a presentation. In few cases did they work with the school, although in the case of Dylan Wiliam, he initiated the work of the LHTL project with a school or authority.[22] In one case his relationship continued, not just because he was part of the project, but beyond this.

As was noted earlier, these experts were generally known because of their reputation, though in only one case did we have direct evidence of a respondent's view of this reputation:

Interviewer: Can you explain how she came to become a speaker?
Wendy: I think because she's such a national well-known figure and we wanted a high-profile person.

> (Wendy Dix, LA co-ordinator)

This person (Shirley Clarke) was described as 'hugely appealing to teachers' as a practitioner and researcher. Our other pilot work on events, such as conferences, indicates that teachers might attend a conference on the basis of the reputation of a speaker. (This 'events' research will be discussed more fully in Chapter 8.)

The impact of such experts was seldom specified, and usually only in general terms. Thus, respondents referred to its being a 'stimulating day' (involving Bill Rogers) or the fact that staff were arguing about what the person had said for weeks after the event (involving David Bell). In one case a personal reaction was given:

> And you sat there and you would think to yourself, and I was, you know quite heavily challenged, as sort of . . . a somewhat mature headteacher, with some of the things Dylan [Wiliam] was saying.
>
> (Brian, headteacher, Hawthorn High School)

Because few of these experts get involved in the school, beyond giving a talk either within the school or at a conference at which staff attend, these constitute a 'weak link' in a school's or LA's network. Nevertheless, they are seen as important by those who make these links. Given the preponderance of focus on 'strong links' in schools this is not unimportant. (We have already argued for the value of weak links through brokerage, and the value and strength of links will be discussed more fully in Chapter 6.)

Local role

The most obvious of these roles is that of LA adviser. In the following example an adviser describes how she uses her expertise:

> But, increasingly, I also see my role in it [the LHTL project] as maintaining the impetus for the schools that are involved in terms of their need, in my perception, and in the way that they have represented it to me, a level of developmental input. So, it is not only about maintaining contact to keep the momentum going, but as critical friend overseeing perhaps and giving some guidance on the process of development.
>
> (Una Hills, LA co-ordinator)

In this case the adviser is referring to her role as an LHTL LA project co-ordinator, and hence the focus is AfL. She indicates that she takes the initiative and visits schools, but she gave no evidence of impact. In another case the LHTL LA co-ordinator talks more generally about the advisory role, also referring to going into schools:

> Within the adviser and support service we have different teams, for example, as well as specialists. To give you one example, we have a team which particularly leads on failing schools of concern. . . . If one of my link schools went into that category, a task group would [be] set up. It would involve me, it would involve this officer [referring to the map]. The overall responsibility for failing schools of concern would feed in as well.
>
> (Eileen Laws, LA co-ordinator)

This particular adviser had an AfL focus and ran in-service support for primary schools, including not just those in the project but those in an NLC, within which only some of the schools were in the project.

References to local services or adviser roles from school respondents covered the usual list of those provided to schools, namely ICT support, special needs support services, behaviour management and special programmes such as the Duke of Edinburgh's Award Scheme.[23] Although it might be argued that these services are not specifically 'expertise' in the way considered so far, it is clear that school respondents saw them as sources of knowledge and practice. In some cases the expertise of the adviser (or LA specialist role) is utilised outside of the authority:

> I am the regional co-ordinator for [ICT] training for the Technology Colleges Trust and we meet very regularly at Warwick University to share best practice, and [name] and I also both speak at the Technology Colleges Trust annual conference. We link in, of course, with Becta and the DfES[24] and a range of . . . people.
>
> (Bryn Yardley, a VEAZ webmaster[25])

In all cases the expertise was provided by visits to the school, but in one the telephone and the use of an electronic environment (though the exact form was not indicated) were mentioned:

> It [the electronic environment] will help me do better my task, which is to help teachers. And I leave it as broad as that because you can help teachers in a whole host of ways. One might be they'll ring up and say, 'Where do I get X, Y, Z computer program?' That's a fairly mechanical task. And another thing might be to say, 'Well we'd like to improve the amenities of the Teacher Centre', which one group of teachers has worked upon. And I'm working with them on that. . . . I'll say, 'Well, are all your visuals five years old? You might want to think about how you're going to improve that. The actual ceilings are too high so you'll get echoes which you'll hear.' So, lowering the ceilings will definitely help those people who've got hearing problems.
>
> (James Noon, LA webmaster)

This indicates a useful 'weak link' that is seen as effective, at least by the person offering the expertise.

Local teacher experts

Local teacher experts can range from teachers with a designated role to act as an expert (e.g. ASTs), to those with some informal recognition. Of the three references to ASTs, one indicated their subjects as ICT and mathematics. In another reference the idea that 'ordinary' teachers could fulfil this expert role was also mentioned:

> We buy in consultants, but I also, I've approached other schools and said to other heads, 'Do you have anyone who's got a bit of a background who can help us with this, or do you have an AST?'
>
> (Alexandra, headteacher, Gingko Primary school)

More commonly, the informal designation of 'leading teacher' was used, as this same headteacher indicated:

Alexandra: The leading teachers, the leading mathematics teachers and the leading English teachers are people who belong to a forum, belong to mathematics forums and English forums, and they've been identified because of their good practice.
Interviewer: By you?
Alexandra: By myself, but also by other people . . .

> (Alexandra, headteacher, Gingko Primary school)

The leading teachers in one local authority give demonstration lessons and speak at conferences:

> The other thing that we're getting is . . . our leading teachers in different schools. And leading teachers are there that people can visit to look at demonstration

lessons . . . and that's been quite helpful in letting people go and see good practice in other schools.

(Roger Newland, LA co-ordinator)

We had an inclusion conference recently and so we've . . . the SEN [special educational needs] team identified some good practice that was happening in one of our schools with regard to planning for SEN children. They contacted the school and that person got up and spoke for fifteen minutes about where they'd started and where they were at now.

(Roger Newland, LA co-ordinator)

The impact of these teachers was not usually indicated, though in one case they were seen to give confidence and were of importance and value to other teachers. However, we had one graphic example of a teacher who became an expert:

Alexandra: She also does demonstration lessons for a particular piece of research that we were doing last year on carpet drama. . . . There was this new research coming out of America about providing nursery children with opportunities to talk and write. We were shown this video about a year ago and our nursery teacher, who's absolutely stunning, was highly motivated.
Interviewer: So where did the video come from?
Alexandra: The adviser came with the video and had invited all of the local nursery schools to watch this video and talk about this innovative practice. My nursery teacher was so inspired by this we talked with the advisers about how we could extend that opportunity so more people could see it working in practice rather than the video. So she agreed to be the guinea pig, if you like, to work with the authority to develop the practice and then offer that out as a demonstration lesson for people who hadn't seen it. It involves herself [tran]scribing the stories but it also involves our bilingual assistant now, who was quite nervous to begin with, but she's grown in the role, and she translates the stories as they're being told. And we have nursery staff coming to watch that frequently. I mean that happens probably once every two weeks.

(Alexandra, headteacher, Gingko Primary school)

The same respondent went on to indicate how such experts were used by teachers and the importance of the culture of learning from them:

I think inevitably the wider staff would see those people who are demonstrating lessons, or those people who are successful at things, and would tap into that and use that as a resource, saying for example to Jo (Jo's the nursery teacher), 'How did you do that? Come and show us, or can we work together and plan a carpet drama? Perhaps you could do it first and then we'll plan it together and we'll share and then I'll take over and you tell me how I did?' So I think that culture exists where people just tap into the expertise of those particular individuals, and I think everybody has a sense that they've got something that's important and something that is providing a value that they can offer to the school.

(Alexandra, headteacher, Gingko Primary school)

LIVERPOOL JOHN MOORES UNIVERSITY
LEARNING SERVICES

As we noted earlier, in some cases the headteachers who responded were themselves used as experts, in most cases at a national level, for example as consultants to a professional association. This expertise included speaking at conferences, for example for the Specialist Schools Trust,[26] or teaching in university courses (on school improvement). It was also the case that LHTL school co-ordinators who were co-leaders of NLCs acted as 'experts' in presenting practice in their schools to others, and Chapter 9 will show an example of this (Pluto NLC).

Interestingly, on only three occasions were university staff mentioned as experts (apart from the one already indicated as someone with a national reputation); schools did this to widen the pool of expertise for courses:

> I think there were occasions . . . where I suppose we would feel within the authority the courses haven't always been differentiated in the way that you would do within a class. And so sometimes we have found it has been more valuable to go places like the Institute in London [an HEI].
>
> (Hilary, headteacher, Deodar Primary School)

In one case a school had made links with a Swedish university, and the headteacher had visited to learn more about bilingualism and multiculturalism.

Apart from the earlier reference to Dylan Wiliam, these references leave out the interventions that LHTL project staff (all from universities) made in their work with schools, either as researchers collecting data or as critical friends (a point noted earlier). The latter was a role in which each school had a member of the LHTL team allocated to help them work with the project, its ideas and materials. This was what we described as 'light touch' support, involving only a few days over the course of the project. Swaffield (2007) has written about this role (light-touch critical friendship), offered mainly to the LHTL project school co-ordinators (occasionally involving other staff). She identifies some of their activities relevant to expertise: presenting and training; supporting reflection; questioning; supporting development; spreading and critiquing practice. Of these, 'presenting and training' is an obvious 'input' kind of expertise using project materials (e.g. for initial presentations to staff, or subsequent workshop activities). Similarly, in 'supporting development' they fed in ideas and thinking that would encourage personal development, such as 'references to follow up, literature to read, web sites to explore or materials to consider' (ibid.: 209).[27]

The school as 'expert'

The idea that a school has leading teachers who can provide expertise to other schools can be more extensive, such that the school is itself the source of expertise. This reference was to the school as having 'expertise' by virtue of people wanting to visit:

> I had Dylan Wiliam on the phone saying he wanted to bring someone from the OECD[28] here to see the AfL work.
>
> (Brian, headteacher, Hawthorn High School)

Sometimes this expertise derives from its status as a specialist school (which may have derived from its reputation with regard to a specialism):

So that's the agenda and that's the government funding networks and hubs where we see sports colleges as providing the expertise and the hub and the momentum for all this development to happen.

(Nick, headteacher, Beech School)

Again we will show this in more detail in the Pluto NLC case in Chapter 9.

A reflection on the experts used by schools

The range of experts that schools have access to seems somewhat limited, with the bulk being teachers in other local schools and those who work in a local area. These are supplemented by special events such as conferences held locally or nationally. It is reasonable to assume that the expertise being sought is that which corresponds to the teacher's own identity. Hence, teachers of mathematics will look to skilled local mathematics teachers, and an infant teacher to experts in early-years education or numeracy and literacy consultants. Most of the references to experts in our LHTL data see experts in this way. Schools thus have access to a relatively small 'advice size': the amount of advice that an individual, group or organisation provides for others in a network. The relative lack of university staff does not by itself indicate a failure to use experts, as it is just as likely to reflect school staff views of the value of their expertise. Indeed, a reliance on other teachers is viewed positively. It is in stark contrast to the PLCs, which are based on partnerships with universities (Veugelers and O'Hair 2005a), although some are anxious to see practitioners acting as a source of expertise (e.g. Lieberman and Miller 2008a). This contrast is especially great given the fact that LHTL project staff deliberately acted as 'light-touch' critical friends, with much less input than is typical of the university staff support given to PLCs.

The lack of examples of electronic means to access experts reinforces the idea of the small advice size available to schools; the source of experts that could be reached can be increased by electronic means (the focus of use was, as we will show in Chapter 6, mainly related to obtaining classroom materials). The small advice size may also reflect the lack of weak links to experts more remote from the school (local links to teachers are likely to be stronger), and this may limit the sharing of a wider range of knowledge. This is all the more significant specifically because the teachers use electronic means less than we expected (Carmichael and Procter 2006), something we will return to in Chapter 10.

Nodes: entities or relationships?

The examination of brokers and experts in this chapter epitomises the two orientations towards 'nodes'. Expertise can be seen as something deriving from an individual or an organisation (in the way that Fielding *et al.* [2005] talk of 'originators' and 'partners' in the transfer of knowledge) or as something that derives from relationships established. The focus of the traditional work on professional development, and the PLCs considered earlier, reflects relationships that are largely strong, emphasising collaborative work among schools and those they work with, and hence the focus is on brokers, for example through relationships (recall the 'linker' from Chapter 2; Adams 2000). The evidence from the LHTL project reflects the idea of the 'expert' as an entity, being in part an artefact of our mapping exercise and in part how respondents thought about expertise. Our discussion of brokers is more ambiguous. Undoubtedly we have focused on individuals or organisations as those who take on a brokerage role (as did Miller [2007]), but even this statement indicates a process (brokerage), and we have defined the LHTL examples in terms of their *functions* (e.g. mediation and bridge building). It is clear from the way Burt (2005) discusses such individuals that they are defined by their position in the network, and hence by their relationships. Although it is convenient to discuss brokers as entities, their relationships are more important, and hence the processes they undertake. Similarly, when access to expertise is considered as 'advice size', it is more related to the whole network that an individual or school is connected with, rather than with particular expert individuals or organisations. Nevertheless, the focus is on the function of providing access to valuable information. In the end it is likely that, as we indicated in Chapter 4, nodes can be represented by links and links by nodes. It is with this idea in mind that we turn in the next chapter to consider network links and the relationships they represent.

Chapter 6

Network links

Interactions or transactions?

Introduction

At the end of the previous chapter we questioned the simple division of 'nodes' and 'links', as it was evident that some of the positions that 'nodes' have in a network are identified by their function – what they do in the network. If we take the map of any LHTL respondent and ask them to talk about the people or other elements with which they link, it is unlikely that they would want to respond only along the dimensions in the questions Palonen *et al.* (2004) posed ('To whom do you go to ask for advice?' etc.). If respondents were talking about brokers or experts, they would want to describe their relationship with each of them in different ways (as our evidence showed in Chapter 5). Even if a social network analysis (SNA) researcher is focused on a specific issue of collaboration, reducing relationships to a limited set of dimensions raises questions in our minds about the validity of the representation. We shall argue in this chapter that links cannot be seen as simple representations of the type used by SNA. We will go further and argue that links are better seen as encapsulating processes, especially in the context of knowledge creation and sharing by teachers. In this chapter our focus is on Mitchell's (1974) 'transactional perspective', which in some views of networks considers behaviour in terms of how an actor manipulates links. Actor-network theorists would go even further in the transactional perspective by defining actors in terms of the process of transformation, with a 'meaning' being the substance of that transformation (Latour's mediators as actors; Chapter 2). Meaning-making is at the heart of the process of *learning*, which, we argued in Chapter 3, is the most productive way to understand knowledge creation and sharing. Such a process is more than a relationship, indeed more than an interaction; rather, we argue that it should be seen as a transaction. This anticipates to some extent the discussion in the next chapter, but first we need to establish that links are indeed processes.

In interpreting our LHTL project data from the mapping exercise, we were faced with a similar dilemma to the analysis of 'nodes', in following the classic SNA representation of networks as nodes and links. Strength of ties is, as we have shown in previous chapters, an important way of thinking about links among nodes. For example, in Chapter 5 we discussed the work of Palonen *et al.* (2004), who measured 'strength' of relationships between members of a company by indicating to whom they go when asking for advice, new information, informal discussions or collaboration, indicated by individuals for every other member of a company. The educational SNA studies reviewed in Chapter 3 used 'frequency' to indicate strength of ties; for example:

- along a variety of dimensions – exchange of materials, joint development of materials, joint planning (Lima 2008); or
- by a '1–5' rating of the impact on another's professional development; or interpersonal relationships – 1 for an acquaintance, 5 for an intimate friend (Lima 2007).

Each individual does this for all those in the department (as was the case in Palonen *et al.* 2004), and hence direction can be indicated on a network visualisation.[1] If links are reciprocal, then they are taken as strong, whereas one-way links are weaker. Thus, although 'strength' is often the dimension being measured, an indication of this is through 'frequency' and 'direction' of communication. In all of these studies, however, the quantitative social network data were combined with interview data, which gives a more context-rich account from a smaller sample of respondents. In quantitative terms, directionality and frequency are the common SNA categories assigned to ties that represent the relationships in the network. Given this kind of familiar background, we were prompted during the project to investigate both directionality and frequency in the LHTL maps. However, we were initially concerned about the role of technology in supporting the creation and sharing of knowledge among schools, and so 'mode of communication' was analysed. We realised that such analyses of 'mode', 'frequency' and 'direction' from the whole-network studies typical of SNA were not easily applied to ego-centric data in a graphical form (as argued in Chapter 4). In particular, it is difficult to quantify aspects of links because of the incomparability of them (as was the case for nodes in the previous chapter), although we did so for selected smaller, consistent samples, for example based on a local authority (LA). In the next section we present our data analysed in these terms, pointing out the difficulties we encountered. But tie 'strength' can be seen in a variety of ways, and we consider the LHTL data in a different way to explain how it can be seen from an ego-centric perspective (drawing in particular on the interviews associated with the mapping exercise), and linked with what respondents considered as the 'value' of a link, seen to some extent as independent of strength. We continue this qualitative application of SNA ideas by investigating some other ways of viewing links that draw on the informal interactions that network analyses are so useful at uncovering. In particular, we consider affiliation networks, intensional networks and social contagion. Through these considerations of our data we will show that viewing links as processes is a more authentic interpretation, one that will enable us to consider how these relate to the creation and sharing of knowledge, which is, in Mitchell's (1974) terms, the 'content' of transactions.

Classifying links

We will consider first the three indicators of strength of ties to which we were led by the literature and our research questions: physical mode, frequency and directionality of communication. Then we will consider how these indicate strength as it relates to knowledge creation and sharing, drawing on the major work of Hakkarainen *et al.* (2004). We did also explore an analysis of power in terms of hierarchical relationships, although we were not initially alert to this. Blasé (1987, 1991), among others, has used micro-political perspectives to focus on formal and informal manifestations of power and politics within the workplace. Some of these aspects we looked for in our data, such as power being enacted through what we termed hierarchical relationships. Although the evidence offers possible lines of further inquiry, we do not think it warrants including here.[2]

Physical links

We began our analysis by establishing how the nodes were physically connected as an indication of the mode of communication. This related to our interests in the extent to which education professionals were electronically connected, and also what educational resources might be involved. Evidence of the modes of communication used came from an initial survey of teachers in eleven of the project schools, followed later by data from the network maps and related interviews of forty-eight respondents (in thirty-three schools). The survey asked respondents (teachers) to rank the order of importance in their school of various modes of communication (for details, see Carmichael and Procter 2006). The most highly ranked responses by 269 respondents are summarised as Table 6.1. Within-schools communications are dominated by face-to-face interactions, followed by paper-based means of communication and telephone conversations. Even though the prompts included person-to-person email, email lists and web-based discussions, these were not highly ranked. Differences between primary and secondary schools are probably attributable to size and physical dispersal, telephone and email being more reliable means of contacting staff than depending upon face-to-face contact in bigger, sometimes split-site schools. Primary schools characteristically have a single staffroom, and they reported using notice boards more than their secondary counterparts. It is worth noting that all of the primary schools were large, with rolls of 300 or more; even more face-to-face communication would be likely in the case of smaller schools.

To some extent this evidence matched data gathered through the network mapping task and interviews, which covered a wider range of school and local authority respondents than the survey (see Table 6.2). Again face-to-face methods were dominant, with secondary schools appearing to use more face-to-face communication than primaries. This may be in the form of internal meetings, reflecting the larger staff and implying more meetings, and also that secondary school teachers have greater opportunities to meet others out of the classroom.[3] In addition, the staff responding (co-ordinators and headteachers) tended to be more senior, with less student contact time. This data set

Table 6.1 Summary of within-school modes of communication ranked by 269 primary and secondary school teachers

Primary schools	Secondary schools
Meetings	Meetings
Informal face to face	Telephone
Notice boards	Memos
Memos	Individual email
Newsletters	Newsletters
Individual email	Informal face to face

Table 6.2 Summary of modes of communication within and beyond organisations, extracted from forty-eight network maps and related interviews

Link method	Rank	LA-based sources All (n = 15)[a] Mean % links per method	School-based sources All (n = 33)[b] Mean % links per method	Heads (n = 17) Mean % links per method	Co-ords (n = 16) Mean % links per method	Primary (n = 25) Mean % links per method	Secondary (n = 8) Mean % links per method
Face to face	1	58	50	63	40	50	60
Paper based	2/3	10	18	22	13	19	9
Email	2/3	12	13	9	21	13	16
Telephone	4/5	7	11	6	16	10	11
Website use	4/5	12	4	2	7	5	4
Notice boards	6	0	1	2	0	1	0
Fax	6	0	1	0	2	1	0
Total % links		**100**	**100**	**100**	**100**	**100**	**100**
Total number of links (mean)[c]		**44[d]**	**37[e]**	**40**	**31**	**34**	**28**

Notes
a Only 7 of the 15 LA maps provided enough information to produce quantitative data on link method.
b Twenty-seven of the 33 school-based maps provided data by method. The 6 maps that did not provide enough information on link method included 3 headteachers and 3 co-ordinators, of which 3 were primary and 3 secondary sources.
c The total number of links, however, refers to the entire sample.
d If maps alone were considered, the mean is reduced to 37 links per map; we included the associated transcript evidence as well.
e If maps alone are considered, the mean is reduced to 33 links per map.

indicated more paper-based communications in schools than in local authorities, although insufficient information was collected as to whether these were mostly being 'received' or 'sent out' by schools (as not all respondents gave directionality). In contrast to what Table 6.1 shows, primary schools appear to have more paper-based communication than secondary schools. This is likely to reflect the greater external links, through a raft of LA and national primary school strategies at the time of the study; these involve documentation being passed to and from schools. Email was more prominent than in the survey: equal access for both primary and secondary teachers. LA/virtual education action zone (VEAZ) sources in particular indicated website use (as shown at the centre in Figure 6.1 and on the lower right-hand side of Figure 6.2). In the VEAZ a central website was seen as an efficient method for communicating with the many linked organisations, particularly schools, to give access to material. This was our first indication of the 'non-human' nodes, discussed in Chapter 5.

In a more recent study with beginning teachers (Fox and Wilson 2009), websites and other socially created resources were regularly represented on maps of network support (e.g. Figure 6.3). In this study, eleven secondary school science teachers in their second and third years of teaching were asked to represent their communications with people, groups and resources; all of them included websites and/or other resources. There are at least two explanations for the differences between these more recent data and those from LHTL. First, LHTL respondents were asked to represent *organisational* communication, whereas in the Fox and Wilson (2009) study the focus was on *personal* communication, which may be more likely to involve the use of the web. Second, teachers are now more likely to use electronic communication than previously. Although the second explanation is no doubt true, their purposes are no different from those of LHTL respondents, namely that the use of the web is to obtain classroom materials for use with students, rather than for their own professional development (Carmichael and Procter 2006). Fielding *et al.* (2005: 12) discuss the importance of personal contact for 'transfer' of practice, and use the idea that teachers are 'people people'. This has a ring of truth, although Wellman's (2001) argument that the use of computer and mobile technology has created networked individualism (Chapter 3) would not preclude 'the "person connection" in practice transfer' that Fielding *et al.* (2005: 12) focus on. This may mean that 'mode of communication' as a single indicator of 'strength' of ties has limitations.

Returning to the LHTL data (Table 6.2), it appears counter-intuitive that head-teachers, with more desk time than classroom teaching staff, use telephone and email less than co-ordinators do. The greater extent of paper-based communication perhaps reflects headteachers' view of the administrative interactions of the school and that, internally and externally, they are able to use more face-to-face communication with others than their classroom-bound colleagues. School coordinators, who usually have a strong classroom role, displayed the greatest diversity of methods of communication. Their lesser reliance on face-to-face interactions perhaps reflects the time pressures on classroom teachers: they use email and telephone more than do headteachers, and paper-based methods of communication less. Email and telephone are easier to use during the working day than formal meetings or events, allowing them to control when they initiate or respond to communications. This is more of the person-to-person communication of Wellman's networked individualism, and it relies on their own personal networks. (Nardi *et al.* [2000] argued that in a modern, free-market view of

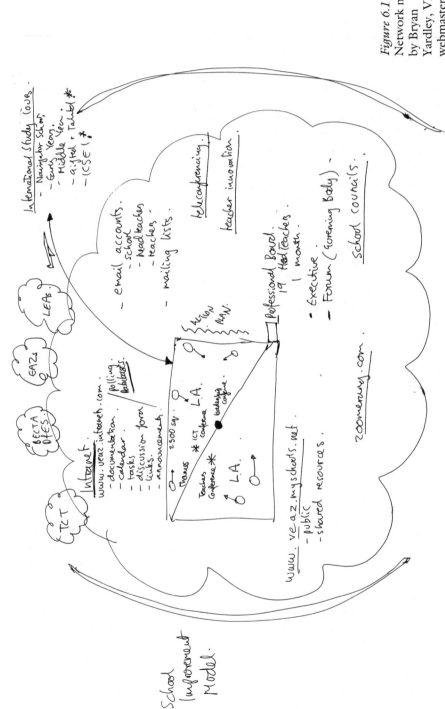

Figure 6.1
Network map
by Bryan
Yardley, VEAZ
webmaster.

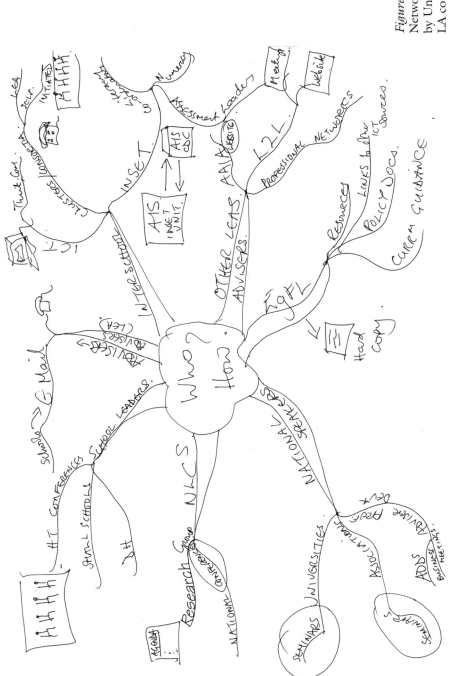

Figure 6.2
Network map
by Una Hills,
LA co-ordinator.

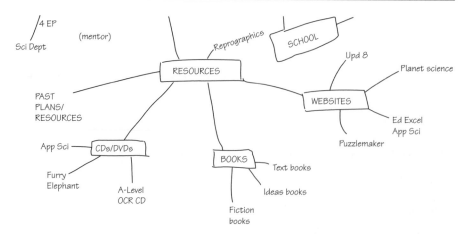

Figure 6.3 Extract of a beginning teacher's network map showing links with resources.

the world, people should be very consciously using their personal networks – a view developed later in this chapter.) The LHTL project mapping task, focusing on organisational rather than personal communications, underrates these personal networks, hence the approach in the later study of beginning teachers (Fox and Wilson 2009).

Frequency of links

Although respondents were asked to reflect on 'frequency' after drawing their maps, individuals did not consistently offer such information. Table 6.3 represents frequency data, using both map and interview evidence, for four individuals within one LA that offer some consistency of representation (to reduce the problems of 'counting' noted in Chapter 4). The most frequent links were between internal members of the school community, as might be expected. Governors' and parental links with the schools varied from respondent to respondent. The headteacher, referring to daily contact with governors, is likely to be meeting with individual governors, and those reporting 'fortnightly' to 'intermittent' interaction imply a different relationship, some seeing governors only at meetings.

LHTL respondents may not have been personally involved in all reported links and hence they estimated frequency. Even for their own communication, individuals offered only an estimate, and this limits the reliability of the data, also a feature of SNA studies not based on diary studies. A more recent study asked trainee teachers to keep diaries recording with whom they interacted, to gain a more detailed and reliable account of frequency.[4] Three secondary initial teacher trainees kept weekly diaries, recording every interaction along with a summary of its purpose. This is very intensive for the respondents, and even within a week they resorted to an estimation of frequency of interaction. Collecting this kind of information solely to indicate the strength of a link is difficult to justify, and methods based on retrospective estimates are almost inevitable.

Table 6.3 Frequency of links for four respondents from both network map and interview data

	Daily	Weekly	Fortnightly	Monthly	Half-termly	Intermittently	Termly	Annually
Head of Deodar Primary	Head with staff (×2 in staffroom) (open door at end of day) Head with pupils (assembly)	Line managers with those managed Evaluation from phases to phase leaders/SMT SMT meetings INSET for all (including TAs) Whole-staff meetings (rotating chair) Staff plan together	Those with responsibility points meet Newsletter to parents with input by staff and parents Head into classrooms to see pupils	Middle managers meet	Governor working parties meet (including HT, DHT, Ass. HT)	Governors into school	Parents' evening Other open evenings for all Parent–Teachers' Association events Governors meet (including HT, DHT, Ass. HT)	Transfer meetings for parents with staff Maths evening for parents
Head of Gingko Primary	Staff with parents	A governor plays piano and teaches music	Head on governor committees or subcommittees Staff using parents as a resource		Newsletter to parents	Link adviser into school (×4 yearly) meets with HT	HT report to governors Visits into school by governors	

continued overleaf

Table 6.3 Continued

	Daily	Weekly	Fortnightly	Monthly	Half-termly	Intermittently	Termly	Annually
Co-ord. at Juniper Primary	Internal – subject co-ords, year group, phase group, whole staff, SMT, head, pupils, governors			AfL project co-ordinators meet		With parents and Friends of school		
Head of Hebe C of E Primary[a]	HT and staff with pupils	Full staff meetings Newsletter to staff and parents Head and chair of governors informally twice-weekly	Management or key stage meetings (alternating) Head and school council meet Head and governing body working groups meet		Head with full governors meet Headteacher steering committee of LA with director		Head report to governors	

Note
a C of E is 'Church of England'. Such schools are mainly state funded, but with a church affiliation and partial funding.

Directionality of links

Part of the network mapping task required respondents to represent directionality, but this proved too difficult for them to do consistently across a map. We exemplify an analysis for headteachers and project co-ordinators from five schools in the same local authority for which the most complete data were given (Table 6.4).

In such a semi-structured interview situation it was not helpful to 'push' respondents to indicate directionality for each and every link. Even when indicated, it was not clear on what basis individuals attributed directionality, or whether individuals represented it consistently. At times, arrows on links related to information flow, but it was often unclear what links without such attribution meant. Ego-centric mapping methods require investigating respondents' meaning of directionality, along with a way of reviewing this for all links to give both less ambiguous and more reliable data. Whether *all* links by the Hebe co-ordinator (see Table 6.4), for example, were in fact strong (indicated as two-way) would be difficult to establish for these data, and it would be unsound to conclude, on the basis of the map representation, that they were. As was the case for frequency, it is easier to collect directional data in bounded networks, where nodes had been identified. An ego-centric study of this kind cannot give parallel systematic evidence of directionality as in SNA whole-network studies but can investigate the meaning of such evidence. The conceptual problem with 'directionality' is that for knowledge creation and sharing it implies 'knowledge' moving along the links. If we view links as part of learning, and hence as transactions, it is unlikely that directionality, in the sense that it indicates strength, has sufficient meaning. (Again this point will be developed in the next chapter.)

Table 6.4 Directionality on network maps from one LA

School: role	Direction			Number of links on map
	No direction (% of links on map)	One-way (% of links on map)	Two-way (% of links on map)	
Hebe primary: head	0	7	93	59
co-ordinator	0		100	21
Deodar primary: head	0	33	66	33
co-ordinator	0	53	47	19
Juniper primary: head	21	11	64	28
co-ordinator	27	27	46	61
Hawthorn High: head	40		60	27
Redwood High: head	56		44	24
co-ordinator		61	39	66
Mean	16	21	62	37.5

Indicators of strength

The importance of strong ties, particularly for collaborative work among teachers, has already been explored in our discussion of professional learning communities (PLCs). The SNA studies of non-educational settings focus on the importance of these strong ties, and Hakkarainen *et al.* (2004) note that they are multi-modal – that is, that they use a variety of means and that they are reciprocal, and frequent. In addition to individuals interacting repeatedly and intensively face to face, they explain that face-to-face meeting is likely to be supplemented by other modes of communication such as email, telephone and the sharing of resources, and indicate the 'effort' invested in such links. Educational SNA studies make similar assumptions about the importance of 'reciprocity' and 'frequency', in part related to developing trust within relationships, which enables collaborative knowledge creation. However, recent SNA research indicates that the picture is more complex for some SNA measures, particularly 'reciprocity'. Moolenaar *et al.* (2009) show that the relationship between trust and a measure such as reciprocity in a social network is not so straightforward for teachers and schools.[5] Using measures of density and reciprocity from SNA and a questionnaire on trust, they were able to show that although denser teacher relationships are related to higher levels of trust, and those with higher numbers of relationships are more likely to trust their colleagues, reciprocity does not correlate with trust, and indeed at a school level there is a negative relationship. The problem, as noted earlier, is with cliques formed through reciprocal relationships that excluded others. Moolenaar *et al.* (forthcoming) carried out a parallel analysis of the data to show that an orientation towards innovation is also not related to reciprocity.[6]

Hakkarainen *et al.* (2004) examine strong and weak ties through the exchange of knowledge, drawing on their earlier analysis of explicit and tacit knowledge. Tacit

Table 6.5 Nature of knowledge exchange and strength of ties

Characteristic of knowledge exchange	Strength of ties	
	Strong	*Weak*
Information flow	Redundant/reciprocal information	Non-redundant/ asymmetric
The nature of knowledge exchanged	Usually complex	Simple and accurate
Form of knowledge	Often non-codified or tacit	Often codified
Relation to knowledge environment	Context bound, i.e. a part of a larger knowledge structure	Often context free and independently understandable
Type of communication	Thick and encapsulated, including chunks, expert terms and scripts	Thin and easy to understand
Management of network connections	Demanding of resources	Little need for resources

Source: Hakkarainen *et al.* (2004: 75)

Table 6.6 Further attributes of strong and weak ties

Strong	Weak
Large element of knowledge sharing rather than flow of new information	Information gained useful for updating the knowledge base of strong links
Provide opportunities for sharing in-depth expertise	
Important in the process of innovation after extended, intensive communications between strong ties	More likely to guarantee an 'adequate' number of ties
Increasingly likely to be tacit/non-codified information if links are embedded	Information can also refer to distributed practices, although not necessarily of 'best' practices, which may act as a memory in absence of codified knowledge
Parties meet often and intensively (therefore linking to the density and cohesion of the related network) as the actors may need several opportunities to assimilate the complex knowledge	Relationships require less effort
If embedded, more likely to assimilate via negotiation and adjustment	
Possibly inertial, if over-embedded, i.e. if weak ties absent, those in strong ties are in danger of group think biased to internal, inertial practices and beliefs	Can speed up projects
May provide socio-emotional support, if embedded	More likely to be used in looking beyond existing contacts, allowing the possibility of exchange of knowledge between networks

Source: Adapted from Palonen *et al.* (2004)

knowledge they see as particularly important for innovation (the division of knowledge in this way was questioned in Chapter 3). Table 6.5 is their characterisation of strong and weak ties in terms of knowledge exchange, indicating that strong ties enable reciprocal, complex, tacit and context-bound knowledge and information to be exchanged. Table 6.6 shows the use of knowledge through these two types of ties. From both of these tables it is evident to Hakkarainen *et al.* (ibid.) that the really important ties are strong ones, and although they acknowledge the value of weak ties in brokering and in searching for innovations, it is their view that the strong ties enable innovations to be created. Indeed, they see weak ties as having to be developed into strong ones if they are to be of long-term use. This is very much the position of those who advocate the collaborative PLCs examined earlier. The interesting research issue is whether the arguments put forward by Hakkarainen *et al.* (ibid.) for commercial teams working within an organisation are the same as for teachers working within and across schools. In particular, we need to know whether the conditions they advocate for knowledge creation and sharing are the same as for teachers developing and adopting new classroom and school practices. This is particularly so if, as we argued in Chapter 3, this development and adoption involves teacher learning. Although Moolenaar *et al.* (2009: 25) assume that their measures (e.g. trust) relate to teacher learning, they do not examine this learning directly (as a process). Similarly, their measures of innovation may or may not relate to actual changes in practice.[7] Such studies are very important in investigating how aspects of trust and innovation relate to social networks, but the authors acknowledge that further research is required and, in our view, one strand of this must be to examine personal networks in relation to particular innovations and efforts to change practice. In Chapter 7 we examine this in more detail with evidence that somewhat complicates the role of trust in sharing practice.

Thus, strength of ties is not a straightforward idea either in terms of how it is measured or in its effect on knowledge creation and sharing. As Clark notes in his discussion of the mathematical complexity of social networks and how this may distract us from the social relations underlying the representation,

> some theorisation about social networks, such as the relative value of strong and weak ties, remains empirically weak. For example, perhaps weak ties are more important than strong ones for maintaining social cohesion, but it may not be the number or type of tie that is important, but rather what that tie is for.
>
> (Clark 2007: 21)

This reflection is particularly important in relation to a view of changing practices and the teacher learning involved, something we will come back to in the next chapter. Our research also revealed that teachers applied another dimension that operated independently of strength, namely value, which we examine in the next section.

Strength and value of links

An oft-quoted phrase from the title of Granovetter's (1973) article, 'the strength of weak ties', in a sense tries to capture some element of the value of the ties in a network. As we have shown in earlier chapters, value is attributed to ties on the basis of a network analysis (e.g. Burt's evidence, considered in Chapter 2). In the LHTL project our respondents attributed value to links as they spoke about them, 'value' being described in terms of 'quality', 'satisfaction' and the relevance and impact they had on practice. In this section we will explore how they articulated the relationship of strength and value, considering the two in their different combinations.

Weak and valued links

We have already argued for the importance of weak links in the way that Granovetter's article presented the case, and when LHTL respondents talked about such valued weak links, they included in some cases links with parents, governors and local residents.

Such groups, beyond the school's internal network, interacted with the school in a meaningful way; for example, the governor who came in to teach music lessons (see Table 6.3, head of Gingko Primary School), and parents who act as interpreters in certain situations. Although these are not as strong as some within-school links, they were valued. Other weak links are more pertinent to learning new practices, as these headteachers of primary schools recount:

> I went to a cluster meeting for the [name] LA schools a few weeks ago that Elise Downey [LA co-ordinator] arranged and there was a lady from the [name] School in Letchworth, who are not part of the LHTL project, but they have been doing similar things in their school and she gave us a presentation – it was really interesting to listen to that; there were a few things to think about and how she had managed getting everybody on board in a large school was very interesting.
>
> (Christine, headteacher, Quince JMI School)

> We get together [in a cluster of schools], we've been able to share practice. We've asked different people to come in. Last time we met together we had a secondary school teacher come in to speak to us about what they'd done in their establishment and as a result I've then come back to school and as a senior leadership team we've taken on board some of their ideas about presenting that learning to learn [LHTL] information as a separate policy other than just being part of the teaching and learning policy.
>
> (Teresa, headteacher, Chestnut Primary School)

Although websites are less frequently used for teacher learning, here a headteacher shows how such links can be important, as well as ones for use in the classroom:

> Some of the websites we will suggest to them will be for their own professional development. Some of them would be for them to use with children. . . . Someone will say, 'Oh, I've seen this great website and it teaches children to . . .', whatever it might be, so we might look at that at the beginning of the staff meeting. If it's websites for staffs' personal or professional development then we turn to . . . well, just this week I sent out a list of lots of really good ones, and you know, 'Have you thought about looking at this one, and the QCA [Qualifications and Curriculum Authority[8]] one about the activity, [it] is a fantastic website.' But nobody actually looked at it because they don't have time. Unless you can point them into the direction of a really good website and the teachers are actually going to get something out . . . if they can just access the bit that they need and it's just taking a little snapshot of the website. On the QCA site there's just a fabulous statement at the beginning about creativity, about how all children have this as a right in their education and it just makes you think and, 'oh wow, yes', and it makes you want to read on. So it's that sort of website that we look at.
>
> (Nell, headteacher, Oak Infant School)

Given the context of a lack of time and indeed inclination, it is evident that teachers could see this as a valuable link, but it will not be strong in the sense that they do any more than go to it once, and it may not be a link they have always made (i.e. in terms of frequency). Other respondents valued links operating intermittently, for example an LA adviser with her role on the Association of Achievement and Improvement through Assessment (AAIA) executive.[9] She explained that at times she worked closely with her colleagues around the country to help disseminate ideas about 'good practice' – gathering evidence and putting reports together, often working to tight deadlines. Then she would not hear from them for several months. If these colleagues did call, she would prioritise responding to them, as she valued and trusted their opinions and the relationship. This kind of relationship is typical of intensional networks, in that they can be activated as necessary (we deal with these later in the chapter). This was similar to occasional contacts with key figures from elsewhere in the educational world, such as academics as speakers at conferences or working on projects associated with the school or LA. Two advisers reflect on such highly valued, but infrequent, links:

> A colleague of mine is absolutely excellent at grabbing every national speaker there is and saying come . . . and talk to us. And that has had some, not just from the point of view of knowledge and understanding but one of the things I've put down here was inspiration and motivation . . . you know, getting excited about Michael Barber[10] coming down . . . that shot in the arm every now and then to get some inspiration.
>
> (Una Hill, LA co-ordinator)

> Can I put in another strong link, but again although it's not that frequent is certainly my links with higher education and King's College and Paul Black. I mean that is usually the kind of link that would in a conversation or an email would have spin-offs for setting up or for leading into other things or for what I do with other people.
>
> (Eileen Laws, LA co-ordinator)

Thus, the second quotation is disassociating strength and frequency for this respondent, and, interestingly, sees 'Paul Black' as a bridge to other things.

Granovetter (1973) theorised that weak ties could also benefit individuals through creating new opportunities and enable resource and information diffusion. Timperley argues that such external expertise is necessary for schools to enhance professional development and school improvement: 'External experts need to be able to challenge assumptions and present teachers with new possibilities; challenge the social norms by which collegial groups operate, wherever these norms constrain professional learning' (2008: 20). In Chapter 5 we considered such external experts, including LHTL project staff, as part of the development role of the project. Many of the respondents did indeed cite critical friends assigned to schools, and even researchers, as weak, in terms of being occasional, but highly valued, links. Here it is important to focus on the activities they engage in:

> I think [named researcher] to a degree, I would ask for certain types of advice. . . . He's part of the refocusing. You know, when he comes, it refocuses everybody. It gives us something to come back to.
>
> (Helen, co-ordinator, Deodar Primary School)

The activity is giving advice but it is part of a refocusing process for the staff, and it is this that gives value to the link.

Weak and unvalued links

Table 6.5 indicates that weak links are asymmetric and unidirectional, and examples in the LHTL data were, for example, as this headteacher describes:

Researcher: What about [links with] local education authority officers or advisers?
John: That disappeared ages ago. All you get is when they want something, he comes in.
Researcher: And what about to the rest of the county council [LA]?
John: Very few communications with them. It's one-way traffic basically.
Researcher: Which way?
John: In [to the school].

(John, headteacher, Ironwood Community Primary School)

A school co-ordinator was more specific about such links with the LA that were not valued, when talking about its role in a networked learning community:

Angela: The LA play a role as well and . . . the only time you really get any contact with the LA is when they want you to do something for them.
Researcher: And has that been your experience with the LAs?
Angela: Or to remind them, you know, there's a conference and can you do something, or you haven't booked your place yet, or, I'm sorry, but they should be playing, you know, a significant role, and I just feel, they kind of, it's all a bit kind of glossy.

(Angela, co-ordinator, Redwood High School)

Trust is often associated with strong links (Hakkarainen *et al.* 2004), but in these cases it is less a lack of trust that make the links less valued than a lack of respect for what the LA does for the school. If previous experiences had been positive and useful, then the links and transactions associated with them were more highly valued. If doubt and scepticism crept in, then the links were considered less valuable. Child (2001) notes that establishing trust is set against any challenges to that trust. Many of the other school co-ordinators and headteachers had positive experiences of their LA co-ordinators, so such unvalued links with the LA were not typical of these relationships.

A weak link might remain so if whatever it offers is not of a high enough priority in a busy timetable of school activity, as the same LHTL school co-ordinator indicates with respect to a networked learning community (NLC), in part caused by how it is run:

Well, two people were appointed to run it from two schools by the LA and it kind of just happened. . . . I'm not saying that I would want to run it; I wouldn't, I haven't got the time . . . and I've got other things that I really want to be doing. But . . . apart from getting sent information about . . . 'this is the next meeting', that's it. So if there weren't meetings I might as well not be in this Pluto network learning community because I have no contact at all, other than via emails telling me 'oh the next meeting's on . . . , or the conference is on . . . , or you haven't booked your place at the conference, why haven't you . . . ?' Well, actually I'm a bit busy.

(Angela, co-ordinator, Redwood High School)

Strong and unvalued links

We started by challenging the hypothesis that all strong links are likely to be highly valued and noted that several respondents spoke of the low-value but high-volume links of statutory information coming either from the DfES (the government department for education) and the Qualifications and Curriculum Authority (QCA) or to schools from the LA classed as 'routine businessy things'. This information reached school via email, meetings, mail or associated telephone calls. Such links might, in terms of being frequent and using multi-media, be classified as strong. However, such information was codified, context free and easily transferable, perceived as more to do with 'system maintenance' than with the knowledge creation discussed by Hakkarainen *et al.* (2004), and in this sense could be classified as associated with weak links. These kinds of links lie somewhere between weak and strong, but are of low value. One primary school headteacher reflects how she had decided to deal with such information and directives coming from the DfES:

> [W]e have had a whole heap of government initiatives which . . . you could kick and rail against for all sorts of reasons. But in fact, if you have got to get on with it . . . therefore you have got to deal with it fairly positively, so we have looked for the positive all the time within whatever we have had to implement.
>
> (Barbara, headteacher, Juniper Primary School)

She saw such initiatives as being of low value, and explained how she tried to maximise the value of them for her school in every case.[11] In a way normally attributed to weak links by network theorists, she appears to see the value of such links as being limited to updating an individual's or group's knowledge base, or ensuring an awareness of changes in the wider professional community.

Hakkarainen *et al.* (2004) argued that the repeated use of weak links would be unproductive, and that they should be developed into strong ones; here a primary school co-ordinator wonders about this:

Researcher: Have you had any links with the . . . infant school?
Sophie: Next door?
Researcher: Oh yes, of course.
Sophie: We don't have very strong links with them, to be honest; things are strengthening up lately, they've had the change of head[teacher] recently and that's helped to exchange information between the schools, but we haven't shared any of this, no. Not at the moment.

(Sophie, co-ordinator, Eucalyptus Junior School)

In this case there was a problem with the previous headteacher of the neighbouring infant school (ages 5–7); with a new headteacher there was a possibility of developing a stronger link.

Strong and valued links

There was also much evidence of strong ties as characterised in Table 6.6. A good example was the research being carried out by teachers *within* a secondary school where the assistant headteacher describes its cross-school impact:

> [T]he links that are being established between a very small research group who kicked off the assessment for learning thing, then the link between them and the teaching and learning styles group has just really grown in strength and then that's just kind of gone over to heads of department meetings because we've actually got a lot of heads of department representing their department at the teaching and learning styles group now more than ever. At one of the last meetings I counted up how many people who attended the meetings were heads of department and it was high. Whereas it's not intended to be . . . it can be anybody [who attends], it doesn't matter what their experience is. It could be an NQT [newly qualified teacher], it could be absolutely anybody, but the fact that when you compared the make-up of the group from say a year ago to now, heads of department kind of wanting to come to that group, they want to you know so that's a really strong. . . . So, from this small core thing to then the teaching and learning styles group and then that's having an influence over other areas of the school, that's really important.
>
> (Angela, co-ordinator, Redwood High School)

This school's experience with their 'teaching and learning styles' group is in contrast to the lack of links of the 'learning how to learn' committee and the heads of faculties group that Ken at Beech School recounted (Chapter 5, p. 91). Research lessons, an approach used in PLCs, are a vehicle for developing strong links within a school:

Sally: So we were using research lessons in the school and very interesting work across departments. We had a science teacher with a . . . science class whose kids couldn't get the answer in SATs questions[12] because they couldn't understand the questions but they knew the science for the answers. So an AfL teacher worked with that teacher on questioning techniques, decoding language, all that kind of approach and they did all sorts of little things . . .

Researcher: They decided what the focus was going [to be]?

Sally: Yes. And they did a series of three research lessons and they shared that work in their department and this is ten kids . . . out of a whole year group. This is the bottom year and four of them got a level five,[13] which isn't bad, is it?

Researcher: . . . that's very good. Is this ongoing? Do I understand the use of research lessons as again one of these embedded features of teacher learning here?

Sally: No it's not, but it hopefully will be. This was a one-off project and, although the learning has been shared in science, it's not come out into the school yet. I was going to do it on the training day when you came but there was too much in it so we didn't.

(Sally, co-ordinator, Hawthorn High School)

In both of the above extracts it is evident that the research team work closely together to create new ideas, then share their expertise with others in the department. The research team are dealing with complex information and ideas rather than in codified or 'reified' forms (e.g. questioning techniques).

Another example of complex, sustained interactions is a headteacher talking about the link between his school (operating as a Beacon school) and partner schools[14] becoming a strong one:

> *Ed:* [N]ow we're more clear that the purpose of these links is to bring about improvement here and in other places. That's the purpose, and then sustained links, where there's a focus on changing classroom practice, are the way to go. Therefore, deeper links, over a longer period of time, are more important . . .
> *Researcher:* And deeper in what meaning?
> *Ed:* Deeper in the sense we maintain the contact over a longer period and the focus is on the classroom.
>
> (Ed, headteacher, Redwood High School)

This example offers an interesting variation on 'frequency' as a measure of strength, as here 'time over which the link is sustained' is what this headteacher values. Opportunities for such rich discussions are another feature of some of the strong links identified. An example of these was a school co-ordinators' meeting with colleagues in other NLC schools as they started on similar work together. At these meetings, advice on how best to proceed was sought from those who had already started AfL work and led to sharing of initial changes to practice after they had been trialled. It cannot be claimed that all links between co-ordinators at these meetings were strong, as noted earlier when Angela commented on such meetings in the Pluto NLC. However, the strength of links made as part of being in a NLC was not solely dependent on these co-ordinator meetings. Another headteacher spoke of the value of visits by teachers at her school to other schools and how this enabled them to reflect on and adapt their own practice. We found one example where the students were also part of these strong links:

> That's one of the exciting things that we'll be taking forward, is [name], who is the L to L [learning how to learn] co-ordinator, with myself, has been invited, with two of her children, two of her Year 4 children [aged 8–9]. . . . One of the other schools in the project is taking two. . . . In fact, the school that we went to visit yesterday is taking two of their Year 6 children [aged 10–11], one of their teachers. And another school is taking one of their Year 2 [aged 6–7] children and one of the teachers. And they're going to get together to talk about, with the children, what they feel is a 'good learning classroom', and come up with the criteria involving teachers and children. Which I think's fantastic.
>
> (Jacqueline, headteacher, Service Tree Primary School)

It appeared that these opportunities for strong links do not always have to be face to face. An LA adviser's links with some schools involved high-value transactions:

> I would have some quite lengthy phone calls. It depends, a lot of it is face to face, but we don't have a huge amount of time in school, you know. So it would be time in school and sometimes quite lengthy phone calls and those are unlikely to

be during the day; they are more likely to be at the end of the day, say five or six o'clock and, if I am not here, they would certainly be in the evening at home.

(Eileen Laws, LA co-ordinator)

Value is implicit in how much time is invested in the call, and the acceptance that this might need to extend beyond the end of a normal working day. The schools this adviser was talking about as strongly linked to her fell into two categories: those that had taken the initiative to reactivate the link with her with a concern or a query, and those with which she needed to work more closely because of concern identified by herself and the LA team. In both cases, actions resulting in change are to be expected and required from such a link.

In looking back over the combinations of strength and value of the various links in the LHTL data, it is evident that they can indeed be seen independently. Because strength is not synonymous with value, the assumptions that are often made about 'strength', especially in discussions about collaborative work, need to be questioned. To emphasise this, we think it would be useful to use a graphical illustration (Figure 6.4) to focus researchers on the process within a link that makes it valuable.

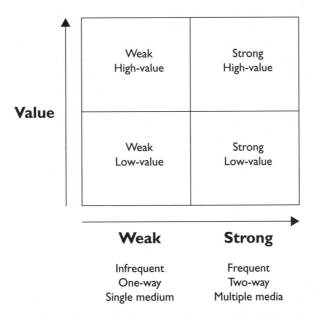

Figure 6.4 Model of the relationship between the strength and the value of links.

Strength, value and processes

It is instructive to reflect on the kinds of processes that teachers and LA staff are referring to when they are describing what they value in both strong and weak links. Some processes are explicit in the link (e.g. sharing practice; challenging assumptions) or are associated with the link in some subsequent activity (thinking after a presentation). The idea of a link either as an instant or as on ongoing activity is too

Table 6.7 Comparison of the processes associated with the examples of strong and weak valued links in terms of 'intensity' of activity

	Intense	*Less intense*
Strong links	Worked with teacher on questioning technique Visit classrooms with pupils and discuss 'good learning' criteria Share practice (at meeting) and put into policy document	Influence (teachers)
Weak links	Challenge assumptions Refocus Thinking	Inspire Motivate Create excitement

simple, as it is evident that there are many different time sequences and events taking place. For example, the visits to another school by teachers and students are not in themselves the link (Service Tree Primary School), so much as the discussion with the students afterwards and the production of criteria for a 'good learning classroom' (*strong, valued link*). Nor is it the case that strong, valued links produce intense activity and weak, valued links less intense activity. Thus, a strong link involved teachers working on questioning techniques and a weak link 'challenged thinking' or 'refocused activity'. Similarly, a strong link resulted in 'influencing teachers', just as a weak one might give 'inspiration'. Table 6.7 indicates this variation by representing the references to processes in the sections on weak and strong valued links, in terms of the intensity of the activity. Inevitably, judgements about intensity are highly inferential, but they beg questions that can usefully be investigated. General questions might be: 'What happens when a link is made? What are the processes involved?' Specific questions would require more details of particular processes: 'What is involved in "working on questioning techniques" with another teacher?' It is evident that large-scale quantitative or even large qualitative studies cannot yet be used to answer such questions without first engaging in some detailed case studies of particular links. It is evident that these processes involve transactions. In part, this is the argument in Chapter 7, which will indicate that more research is needed. These questions also invite a return to actor-network theory (ANT) approaches, where, for example, research could be carried out on what happens when a teacher makes a link to a 'QCA website' that Nell (Oak Infant School) was trying to encourage her staff to access. What happens when teachers see a 'fabulous statement . . . about creativity'?

Formal and informal links

Whatever the limitations of the SNA approach to strength, especially with qualitative ego-centric data, there are many ideas about links that derive from quantitative studies and give insight into the nature of such links. Its stress on personal networks is particularly useful, and stands in contrast to those who consider networks as an organisational form. The danger in viewing NLCs as organisations is that this underrates personal relationships and assumes (formal) relationships where none may exist (or at least only unvalued ones, as Angela at Redwood High School experienced). Thus, when school co-ordinators attend an NLC meeting, the value may be as much in the informal links they make as in the formal business of the meeting. They may make contacts with others at the start of the meeting or in the coffee break that give new ideas, practices and resources. In Chapter 1 we quoted Little (2005b), who indicated the need to look at the interactions that transcend the boundaries of school or network as entities, and it is these that are almost relegated to 'informal' processes. However, little clarity as to the distinctions between formal and informal has been reached in the literature. Buchberger *et al.*, when evaluating the success of a range of European educational networks, concluded that there was likely to be some blurring between formal and informal processes: 'While many conceptualizations stress the informal character of social networking, [this] does not always hold true in the field of educational innovations, where networking can be sometimes arranged formally and be the main way of organising work' (2003: 3). UK studies have also noted the significance of informal relationships in social networks without explicitly defining them (e.g. Goodyear 2001; Thorpe and Kubiak 2005). Hargreaves sees informal links as significant to individuals in contributing to overall social capital within organisations:

> Culturally, social capital is the level of trust between head and staff and among the staff, between staff and students and among the student body as a whole. Structurally, it is the extent and quality of the internal networks, such as networks of teaching teams as well as informal networks of friends. A school that is rich in social capital has a strong sense of itself as a community, but also has many external networks with ties to other communities.
>
> (2003b: 7)

Hargreaves' view identifies a number of network links: formal teaching team links, 'informal' friendship networks and external (professional) networks. LHTL respondents often used the term 'informal' themselves to describe their relationships and activities. Other language clues included 'casual', 'who you bump into', 'fleeting', 'chatting over lunch', 'ran into somebody', 'unofficial', 'just bump into somebody', 'outside meetings', 'pop in and see', most interestingly referring to interactional processes. One approach is to turn to the literature on formal and informal learning, where ideas of 'conscious' or 'unconscious learning' are discussed, as a better representation of the distinction (Hoekstra *et al.* 2007: 191). However, the scope of such a debate takes us beyond network relationships.[15] The idea of 'consciousness' has an echo in the work of Baker-Doyle (2008a), considered in Chapter 2, with her idea of the 'intensional professional network'. We will shortly come to such intensional networks, but it is worth noting here that there can be unnecessary distinctions between personal and professional links and networks. A vocabulary and conceptualisation are needed to think about these 'informal' links, some of which derive from 'formal' links. SNA has developed several that are of relevance: affiliation networks, intensional networks and social contagion. These are helpful to this discussion and we will consider them in the light of our LHTL data.

Affiliation networks

The idea of affiliation is a familiar one, and it lies behind 'old boy' networks of people who do each other favours or when people who are on several boards of directors informally operate in their own interests. Film stars who have acted in the same movies or academics who have co-authored articles both represent versions of these affiliations (noted in Chapter 4). Affiliation networks are formally defined in SNA in terms of actors (film stars or academics) being related by events (movies or articles), or events being related by actors. Wasserman and Faust (1994) explain that where people find themselves in a group (termed a 'collectivity'), they affiliate as actors (mode 1 networks), but when they do so through events it is a mode 2 network. Watts (2003: 121) contrasts these latter networks with those that are usually analysed by simply seeing how actors relate, taking them as pairs (a mode 1 analysis to give adjacency matrices, encountered in Figure 2.2). From this the social structure is determined, but without its being known why relationships are formed. Introducing affiliations anticipates the structure. He also argues that the more affiliations, and the stronger they are, the more likely it is that individuals in them will interact. If teachers are members of various committees, they are affiliated through their joint membership. Figure 6.5 illustrates this for ten teachers in a subject department in a secondary school, some of whom are members of a teaching and learning committee, some a pastoral committee, some the senior management team (SMT) and one the head of faculty committee. Two of the groups (teaching and learning committee and SMT) have some common membership; one group (pastoral) connects three teachers, but has no overlap with other groups; and one teacher is the only person in the group. These groups (which are effectively cliques) provide affiliations that may affect discussions in the department or the way ideas move around it.

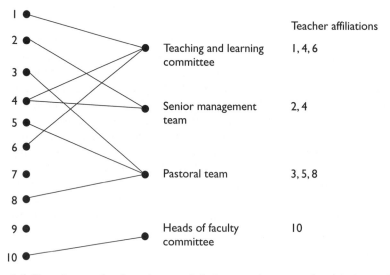

Figure 6.5 Bipartite graph of teachers and their committee membership in a school department.

Hakkarainen *et al.* (2004: 76) identify affiliation networks where actors meet repeatedly as members of several groups or committees and knowledge transfer is achieved through these repeated meetings, as they get to know one another well and develop trust in each other. In educational networks this applies where people meet regularly according to their role or a task, for example headteachers, LA advisers, secondary school subject co-ordinators and transition (students moving from primary to secondary school) staff. Hakkarainen *et al.* (ibid.) argued that in these situations, profit accumulates in these actors as a result of their membership of such networks, offering an informal and unplanned dimension to actors meeting formally. Head-teachers usually get the most chance to attend professional meetings that enable affiliation networks to be set up and used, as this one indicates:

> I would then ring people and ask, 'What do you do with so and so?' or you know, 'Have you ever had to deal with whatever?' . . . Yes, it is partly because I have been around for a while so that I probably know most of the longer-standing heads reasonably well.
>
> (Barbara, headteacher, Juniper Primary School)

Heads may actually use the occasion of the meeting to use their affiliation network:

Researcher: So are the gaps [spaces] between things as important . . . as the agenda and the formal aspects of the meeting?
Alan: Yeah, I think so because . . . it's often those set meetings that are the points of contact that generate relationships that can spin into other areas of interest and so on, and so . . . we might find it could even come up in the formal business of the meeting that, say, a school has had a certain approach to something and you just flag it up and catch [them] a bit later and say, 'I was interested in that, could I come and have a look?', you know, 'can we have a talk about it?'.

> (Alan, headteacher, Hebe Church of England Primary School)

In this example the contact at the meeting arises out of the business, but the head is aware of the other types of contact that can occur. In other cases, opportunities were created for those in similar roles to come together in groups that meet occasionally:

> Actually there's a couple of other informal things which have started recently which I'm finding very useful which are just informal discussion groups . . . where there are four either deputy heads or assistant heads who are in a similar position to me and we meet once a half-term just to discuss various issues. . . . I find those really useful, listening to people who are trying to tackle the same sort of problems that we are trying to tackle here.
>
> (Ken, co-ordinator and assistant head, Beech School)

> We also have [a] consortium of heads, which is a collaborative group, and we meet informally on a half-termly basis, for a morning, or an afternoon . . . we just meet to talk about common shared interests in the . . . consortium.
>
> (Dave, headteacher, Goldenrain Junior School)

This second example illustrates how an affiliation might be extended into another form, or it might be the start of an affiliation network as it draws headteachers together in a new affiliation. One headteacher spoke of how a group of heads formed a new affiliation through a peer support group for headteachers of the larger primary schools in the locality:

> On a personal level I think that we set up ourselves . . . we call ourselves the Big Heads Group and we're all headteachers of large schools. That's been very, very valuable. . . . There were two new heads who'd got appointed as headteachers of large schools, who'd never really taught [or] worked in large schools and were floundering. And so we said if we set up a support group . . .
>
> (Hilary, headteacher, Deodar Primary School)

Despite having informal origins, this group can now be considered formal, with meeting agendas. As a result of a successful research bid, its members had recently all travelled to the United States to make a comparative study of similar schools there. However, they are accountable only to themselves, and meetings and activities do seem highly flexible and involving increasingly 'embedded links' with a social dimension. This, then, forms part of an affiliation network. Socially embedded links, based on extended relationships, allow people to become more committed to one another and therefore to the task in hand, such that they are prepared to do more than is set out in any actual contract (Hakkarainen *et al.* 2004).

Affiliation networks are also ones that a person can transfer from one work context to another, as they are personal to the actor. One LA adviser talked of how he continued to use links with his former LA colleagues rather than more proximal colleagues in his current job; a new headteacher continued to meet socially with those in the LA with whom she had worked as a network co-leader in support of her new role as headteacher despite no longer having direct formal relationships with these advisers and colleagues (see the Pluto case study, Chapter 9, p. 200). Hakkarainen *et al.* (ibid.) observe such links as often being related to 'thick' information flows, associated with actors engaging in intensive negotiation and adjustment. These are the characteristics of strong links.

In affiliation networks, use of formal contexts overlaps with the use of (informal) embedded links, which can encourage knowledge flow. These are embedded links because they are personal and involve friendship, as this example illustrates:

> I have actually established a whole link and group of friends through playing football basically. Obviously the more formal meetings too, but the informal discussion that goes on has been far more productive . . . because you basically tend to be like-minded individuals sharing my views.
>
> (Sam, headteacher, Alder Primary School)

The examples of the affiliation networks in education illustrate the point made, namely that it is unproductive to assume that professional and personal networks are unconnected.

The consideration of affiliation has focused on external networks, but Little (1990: 528) considered external and internal school affiliations to what she described as 'naturally occurring reference groups'. Little's analysis gives another view of the idea we quoted from her in Chapter 1, which criticised taking the school as an undifferentiated unit of analysis and pointed out the salience of sub-groups within the school. The naturally occurring groups may not reflect the formal organisation of the school, and represent multiple affiliations. These groups can exhibit differences in professional beliefs and practice and hence express different identities for teachers, which might be at stake in any collaborative endeavour. Moreover, when collaborative activity is introduced into a school in pursuit of a new programme of work (such as AfL), it may cut across these reference groups. Similarly, external affiliations may aid or hinder a teacher's motivation towards the school and its innovations. Although Little is able to indicate research on internal groups, she says the effect of externally referenced groups on the school's work is largely unexamined. This more negative view of affiliation (Little does not use the term 'affiliation network', but her account reflects this concept) is in contrast to our considerations drawing on both network theories and the LHTL data. Little's work also has implications for collaborative activity within schools, and we will return to her ideas in Chapter 7, when considering knowledge creation.

How, then, do these affiliation networks relate to the idea of links as interactional processes? These networks provide the context (the social structure in Watts' terms indicated earlier) for the interactions that take place among those who are affiliated, and hence form the context for the resulting processes.

Intensional networks

Nardi *et al.* (2000: 3) define intensional networks as '"egocentric" networks that arise from individuals and their communication and workplace activity'. These networks arise, they argue, from rapid structural change that means that they are used rather than the existing formal organisational methods of working being relied on. They chose the term 'intensional'

> to reflect the effort and deliberateness with which people construct and manage personal networks. The spelling of the term is intended to suggest a kind of tension and stress in the network. We found that workers experience stresses such as remembering who is in the network, knowing what people in the network are currently doing and where they are located, making careful choices from among many media to communicate effectively with people, and being mindful to 'keep in touch' with contacts who may prove useful in the near or distant future.
>
> (ibid.)

These authors assert that a personal network is likely to overlap with the networks of others and may be extended using these networks, resulting in unpredictable assemblages of people and roles. This view therefore contrasts fundamentally with bounded and structural views of networks, and places individuals centrally in control of their networks. Such networks, Nardi and colleagues argue, empower workers to solve problems for both the workers and their organisations, and act as a resource for the individuals and their career development. Adding new nodes to the network to increase the pool of available resources means that it is necessary to keep in touch with current nodes and activate sub-networks when tasks are to be completed. Because of this effort and the personal connections made, Nardi *et al.* (ibid.) argue that these have some persistence; the shared experience of joint work serves to establish relationships that may form the basis for future joint work. This is a very conscious view of networking, seeing it as being personally generated, with a key role for informal activity in communicating with others, while not ignoring the potential to benefit from planned, formal opportunities to get to know and work with others.

It is not easy to show data from the LHTL project that illustrate the creation of intensional networks, as our focus in mapping was for a 'snapshot' of the network, whereas these networks operate over time. The example given earlier of valued weak links, where an LA adviser worked with colleagues in the national organisation, the AAIA, is indicative of the way an intensional network can be activated to complete a task.[16] It was evident that school co-ordinators, who did not have an established management role (which might have given them affiliation networks), had to set up new contacts for AfL. Sometimes this came through the NLC or an LA consortium, as we saw in the data on the strength of links. There is nevertheless some evidence of other elements of intensional networks, namely remembering and activating these networks. For example, an LA adviser explains the potential utility of being aware of already established relationships with people now working in other geographical areas:

> I have links with other authorities that are party to the assessment and learning how to learn [initiatives]. For example, I come from LA [E] so I know of Adviser [X]. I know of Adviser [Y] at LA [R]. So I know what's going on in those authorities but I haven't met up to see how those things are developing but I know that there are those links that I could develop.
>
> (Kevin Vine, LA co-ordinator)

From an organisational perspective, one headteacher acknowledged the existence of his staff's individual personal networks and his awareness of the value of them to the school in general, when activated:

> Now our staff connect with a huge number of other schools informally. Their partners work there or their kids go there or their best mate used to work there, but now he's moved on and he teaches somewhere else. . . . I guess we've received a significant amount of informal information in schools as a result.
>
> (Nick, headteacher, Beech School)

This again indicates how personal and professional networks intertwine. A school co-ordinator (Ben, a deputy headteacher) is able to tap sources of expertise for use as external consultants:

Researcher: How do you decide who to call in?
Ben: We have our own contacts. So regular . . . professional contacts . . . plus personal [ones]. So, for example, my father is an English consultant that we use in that way.
(Ben, co-ordinator, Mulberry School)

This view ascribes an agency not normally attributed to nodes, which Watts (2003) saw as part of the random element in networks (Chapter 5). It is interesting to see how the affiliation networks of headteachers (who have opportunities to set up affiliations) are added to by the intensional networks of the likes of the LHTL project school co-ordinators. The combination can greatly expand a school's access to useful networks to developing practice, and it is likely that the loss of such co-ordinators results in a structural hole in the school's network (as we noted in Chapter 5). In terms of our argument for links as interactional processes, the creating, maintaining and activating of affiliation networks are in themselves such processes, and when they are activated, the links will themselves become interactional processes.

Social contagion

In Chapter 2 we considered the work of Valente (1995) on contagion in relation to diffusion of innovations. This discussion pointed out that 'influence' to adopt an innovation was related to 'exposure' to those who had already adopted it. This influence operates through close ties, for example friends. Hakkarainen *et al.* (2004: 76), on the other hand, say influence operates through weak ties, and cite Marsden (1998) and Levy and Nail (1993), who review the state of the field on contagion. These two sets of researchers consider the work mainly of social psychologists, and both agree that the state of the field at the time they were writing was confused, with Marsden (1998: section 1) noting that there was 'an absence of agreement among researchers as to the particular mechanism that underlies social contagion'. We will consider this mechanism in more detail in Chapter 7, but for the moment we want to consider the kinds of ties that contagion implies. If it describes a process whereby individuals adopt the attitude or behaviours of others who influence them, then the 'knowledge flow' can be thought to be in one direction. As we have already argued, if weak ties are at work, then social contagion has a great potential to permeate a wide range of settings.

Overall, we found patchy evidence of such contagion in the LHTL data. Sometimes key speakers may do enough in presentations to inspire changes in the practice of those who have attended. For example, Shirley Clarke, speaking nationally to schools about AfL practices, was noted to have had a significant impact in a number of the LHTL project schools. Teachers referred to practices she advocated that were considered for adoption in schools:

> We had a group of people went to hear Shirley Clarke. . . . The co-ordinator and two others we managed to send as well. That slotted things into place for us. So those three came back and fed back to the rest of the staff and just clarified especially some of the things like WILF – What I am Looking For – and that being put into children's language so getting that bit clarified.
>
> (Barbara, headteacher, Juniper Primary School)

Clearly, however, the ground had already been prepared for 'adoption'. Examples of respondents speaking specifically of inspiration from presentations included the following:

> At the national conference for Key Stage 3 strategy last December, there was a headteacher talking about practice in his school, and mentioned that what had really sparked him off, and what had been instrumental was hearing about, and

he described it as an inspiring input from a head of science from an [LA name] school.

(Kevin Vine, LA co-ordinator)

I think the whole thing about informal/formal sometimes depends on the quality of the person you've got . . . if you've got people like Dylan Wiliam, well he's so engaging . . .

(Kate, co-ordinator, Juniper Primary School)

As noted in Chapter 5 ('Experts', p. 108), the impact of experts is seldom specified; for example, a respondent referred to interactions at a 'stimulating day' with reference to an in-service event led by Bill Rogers, and another commented that 'staff were arguing about what the person had said for weeks after the event' in the case of a talk by David Bell. From such examples we conclude that any such inspiration to make changes in practice does not appear to rely on long-term exposure to the practice of others, or intense interaction. Whether or not such contagion exists from one teacher to another in relation to the adoption of new teaching practices we will consider in Chapter 7. For the moment, all we can conclude is that the processes involved in social contagion are 'influence' and 'inspiration', which is not a very satisfactory level of understanding.

Relationships, interactions and 'flow'

Representing a link as a single dimension such as 'strength' appears to be inadequate. The problem of representation is exacerbated if this dimension is further limited to a simple rating of strength, or to a list of activities from 'asking for advice' to 'collaborating with'. These measures are useful, whatever their limitations, when patterns of interaction are needed, of the kind that SNA produces. Nor is 'strength' easily captured by 'reciprocity', a proxy for a mutual relationship. The example of one teacher working on questioning technique with another (where the first had developed this in her practice) does not imply a mutual *relationship*, as the one with developed practice may not change her practice (even though there is mutual *interaction*). Although we have argued for refining the consideration of 'strength', to be complemented by 'value', the nature of the different processes involved in valued strong or weak links is not defined by this dual categorisation (value and strength). Characterising links as 'informal' is also in itself insufficient, but the use of SNA ideas of affiliation and intensional networks, and social contagion, expand our conceptual tools to understand what informal links might mean. The interactional processes involved in each of these are problematic, as little work has taken place using this 'interactional' idea within education. We noted that affiliation networks act more as a context for interactions, following Watts (2003), whereas for intensional networks the processes seem to be more in the creation, maintaining and activating of the networks, rather than what is done with them when they are 'used'. Here the focus is on 'networking' itself, rather than on the substance of its operation.

Drawing a line on a network map or sociogram can represent many different interactional processes in any particular ego-centric network, and some may indeed not even be 'relationships' – for example, a link to a website. If this link is taken as

Castells' layer 2 (see Chapter 2), it cannot be assumed that there is any information 'flowing', even if a file is downloaded. Reading the 'information' online is no different from downloading (at layer 2), but the important process is the thinking or response to the 'information'. How, then, are we to capture such processes?

Links are better viewed as processes instead of channels – as interactions in which *transactions* are central. Some talk in terms of flow (e.g. in diffusion of innovations; Chapter 2) others in terms of intangibles: 'With an intangible . . . you can trade it and you still retain possession, meaning you can extend the same intangible to someone else' (Allee 2003: 178). In the context of business, Allee states that human competence – knowledge of internal systems and knowledge relating to networking itself – can be shared, and she goes on to talk of the potential for this to have a multiplier effect: '[W]hen you engage in an economic knowledge exchange both parties gain the other's knowledge and can actually create more knowledge of value to both of them' (ibid.: 178). The teacher who shares a resource may have taken note of the different context in which the second teacher thought it could be used, and this second teacher may produce something completely different (e.g. her own policy document). The teacher working with another on the second's practice does not 'give' her practice to the second teacher. The teacher giving advice on a problem may have been forced to re-evaluate the advice or information she gave, or even reflect on whether the problem raised is also relevant to herself. With this view of links as transactions, it is not possible to locate the object and conclude where it went after the connection. Instead, it allows a focus on the transaction as an opportunity for meaning-making. Actor-network theorists would want to investigate the associations involved in the process. People can interact with objects and ideas in isolation from others and change the meaning attached to the object, and so further their understanding – Latour's (2005) 'transformation'. How does this sit with a view of networking as interactions one with another? This chapter has raised as yet unanswered questions, ones that need some view of how the processes relate to teacher learning, which we argued in Chapter 3 lies at the heart of our concern with knowledge creation and sharing. These questions and their associated issues are developed in the next chapter.

Chapter 7

Network traffic

Creation and sharing

Introduction

If we are to consider the links between nodes in a network as transactions (the argument of the previous chapter), then it is clear that we will have to re-examine some of the ideas from network theories about the 'flow' down tubes or 'pipes'. This chapter will therefore try to reconcile some of the potentially conflicting ideas encountered so far in the book – for example, that learning is central to creation and sharing of knowledge, that relationships are the basis of networks, and that at times it is thought that an object or substance is 'flowing along pipes' within these networks. To do this we will consider, first, the nature of the 'substance' that is being created and shared within a network, namely 'practice'. We will examine the assessment for learning (AfL) practice that was the subject of the LHTL project, including how it was formulated as part of the project. Second, we will consider the issues arising from the need for this practice to 'move', and in particular how this relates to views of knowledge that stem from our view of learning put forward in Chapter 3. At this stage we will then be in a position to examine the nature of 'creation *and* sharing of knowledge', including their relationship, and how we can think about and study them.

What is the 'substance' that is being created and shared?

There is a danger of seeing 'practice' as somehow unproblematic, or at least as all of a oneness. Fielding *et al.* (2005), in a major study of the 'transfer of good practice', address the idea of the substance of what is transferred, but they say relatively little about the composition of this substance. The closest they come to this is to ask the question 'What do we mean by practice?' (ibid.: 56), which is answered in the context of the transfer between two teachers:

- a new addition to a teacher's repertoire;
- a principle (e.g. quality) or a general concept (e.g. constructivism), which is capable of being interpreted in a wide variety of ways;
- a set of skills developed over time, such as learning to learn, critical thinking or learning in groups; or
- a cluster of activities and/or learning materials, which constitutes the main body of the curriculum for a particular subject.

There is nothing inherently wrong with this, but it is somewhat limited in scope, largely because they confine their consideration to transfer between two teachers. Their review of the literature starts with an acknowledgement of what they call 'three units of scale in which practice is enacted . . . : individual classrooms . . . a small group of classes . . . and a whole school' (ibid.: 85).[1] Indeed, they go on to consider schools as entities in their empirical work, although, as we will show in the next section, the focus on two teachers reflects their concern with a particular type of relationship in the transfer process (close collaborative relationships). The LHTL project developed and studied practice at all levels, as the title of the project indicates (Learning How to Learn in classrooms, schools and networks). To be clearer about the nature of practice, we will consider the AfL practices and how they were represented in the LHTL project.

The LHTL project focused on teachers' development of AfL and learning how to learn (LHTL) practices and principles. These teachers would then be able to help their students to become autonomous and independent learners.[2] Of central importance (James *et al.* 2006a: 1) were practices that:

- help learners to understand learning objectives and to know what counts as high-quality learning;
- help learners to build on strengths and overcome barriers in their previous learning;
- help learners to know how to act on constructive feedback about how to improve, and develop the motivation to do so;
- help learners to use the help of others, including through peer assessment, to enhance their understanding and take responsibility for their own learning.

An initial presentation was given to schools by a member of the project team, usually associated with a discussion or workshop. This initial session included the overall idea of AfL, some of its underlying principles, the research upon which it was based and some examples of actual classroom practice. From the above list of practices a series of workshops were developed by the project team that could be run in schools (see the list below).[3] The workshops could be led by members of the project team or by teachers within the school. The workshops presented teachers with practical examples of how AfL practices could be used within their own classrooms, along with the associated research evidence. These new practices could be challenging for teachers, and thus schools sometimes ran workshops over a number of weeks. The advice to school co-ordinators was to tailor the input to suit their schools and their strategies of implementation. Teachers who were engaged in the project were expected to develop AfL practices and resources in their classrooms, reflect on their practice and share their experiences and resources in the times between workshops with other project teachers within their own school. In some cases, initial development was limited to a core team of individuals or departments, and in others the whole school was involved. The project team encouraged the building of relationships between small schools in the same geographical area, and between primary and secondary schools in the same area. The project also organised opportunities for school co-ordinators to meet and share practice.

Four workshops were initially developed with the following headings:

- developing classroom talk through questioning;
- feedback;
- sharing criteria with learners;
- self-assessment and peer assessment.

A fifth workshop was developed that dealt with how people learn, at the request of teachers in schools who wanted to update their knowledge of learning theory. Schools could choose the extent to which they were willing to engage in the project and whether they would try to take on practices from each of the workshops or whether they would choose to focus on one area of AfL practice within their classroom, for example questioning. Although the first four workshops primarily dealt with classroom practices, they did relate to school policy issues. For example, the workshop on feedback (which deals with marking student work) led one primary school to draw up a school marking policy, and in another the idea of 'comment-only marking' was included in an explanation of the school assessment policy for parents.[4] In addition, secondary schools often worked in their department groupings and so could decide common strategies for the department. Similarly, primary schools could derive common strategies for an age group (e.g. early-years). The fifth workshop focused on more theoretical ideas about learning and encouraged teachers to discuss these, but also required teachers to plan a topic of work based on one or more of the theories presented.

One of the important developmental issues concerned the fact that the research and the examples of classroom practices made available were often very specific to the context from which they were derived. The examples of questions (in the workshop on questioning strategies) might come from primary science teaching, the commenting on student work from secondary students' work or the sharing of criteria from secondary English language teaching. Thus, teachers of early-years children, for example, would have to try to work out appropriate classroom strategies for involving them in peer assessment, something that might be thought suitable only for older children; teachers of religious education would have to devise a questioning strategy drawing on the ideas from examples given in science. In other words, few of the examples of practice could be used without some development work, and the workshops were intended to begin that work. One example of how a strategy was changed by teachers involved the 'traffic-lights' strategy (ibid.: 47); this strategy invites students to reflect on the current state of their learning in relation to a particular task or activity. If they feel confident that they understand a given piece of work, they use a 'green' indicator; if they are not quite sure of their understanding, they use 'amber'; if they are very uncertain, they use a 'red' indicator, thus reflecting the sequence of traffic lights. The idea here is that 'traffic lights' are used as an expression of a learner's confidence in their learning; they are not intended to be used as just another scoring system to assess their performance. Rather, the system should be the basis for working with students – for example, the 'amber' and 'green' students can work together on the problems identified by those who see their understanding as 'amber', and the teacher can work with those who are 'red'. An indicator for traffic lights could be a marker, a coloured pencil or crayon, a card or a sticker.

Teachers were imaginative and adapted the strategy to the context of their own class-rooms (drawing on ibid.: 99–100)[5]:

1   Traffic lights were replaced by 'smiley faces' ☺ ☺ ☹, to indicate varying degrees of confidence.
2   Students wrote, on the bottom of their written work, R if they found it really difficult, O (orange) if they were unsure and G if they were happy with it.
3   Teachers found that young children were sometimes unsure when to use amber. They found that a twofold version with red and green had the desired effect.
4   Teachers developed a version of traffic lights to monitor work in progress, often providing children with coloured cards which children would place beside them as they worked.
5   Other teachers adapted this approach for whole-class discussions or the end-of-lesson plenary.
6   One primary teacher reported how the process was so well established that 'props' were no longer needed and the class was asked to display a big smile, a straight face or a frown at a lesson review point. This had the advantage that students would be unaware of what faces other students would be showing and thus reducing the chance of peer pressure affecting student self-assessment.

To enable other teachers to be able to develop strategies, they might only have available a brief teacher description of a strategy – for example, for the approach in (6) above:

> During my plenary session, I then ask them to think about how well they think they have achieved the objective. They can either be really confident and ready to move on, fairly confident and happy that they have more or less achieved the objective, or not ready to move on and need more help/practice. I turn my head, count to three and ask my class to be ready with a big smile, a straight face, or a frown, depending on how they feel. The kids love it, and because they are all facing me, they don't feel worried about their peers seeing their expressions. The grins are getting cheesier and the brows more furrowed in the frowns!
>
> (ibid.: 100)

This approach of providing examples of practice had its roots in the early work of Black and Wiliam (1998b: 146), who advocated 'living examples of implementation, as practiced by teachers with whom they can identify and from whom they can derive the confidence that they can do better'.[6] This was because they assumed teachers were too busy to translate the general principles of formative assessment into everyday practice; only a few would be able to undertake such work. Subsequently, Black and Wiliam undertook a development project with mathematics, science and English language teachers to build up a research base for what worked, and produced the 'living examples'. These were told through the testimony of teachers in a popular form for use by schools (Black et al. 2002) and more extensively in book form (Black et al. 2003). However, this still left the development of the work by teachers using the examples, as noted above, and also the sharing of them with others throughout the school system. Black and Wiliam (1998b: 147) had also advocated the dissemination of formative assessment practice to all schools, though they recognised ultimately that 'each teacher must find his or her own patterns of classroom work'.

All the authors cited above have used the words 'development', 'translate' and 'dissemination' to indicate the nature of the processes of creation and sharing of knowledge involved in this 'movement' of practice; first from general principles in research studies (which were themselves examples of classroom practice), to a parallel range of examples of practice in different areas of the curriculum, and finally to any school or classroom. But what are these processes?

Some theoretical issues on 'movement'

Views of knowledge

Following the argument of Chapter 3, the basis of the processes is that of *teacher* learning and, when this learning extends beyond the single classroom, *school* learning. The socio-cultural view of learning advocated in Chapter 3 leads to a quite particular view of knowledge and, on the face of it, a problem for a network made up of nodes connected by pipes through which 'knowledge' can flow. Table 7.1 contrasts the views of knowledge of the two metaphors of 'acquisition' (AM) and 'participation' (PM) we considered earlier.

The AM is easily accommodated to a 'flowing' idea of knowledge in a network, but not so, apparently, the PM. Indeed, many who discuss the sharing of educational practice point to the problem of tacit knowledge bound up in practice, which makes it difficult to share except through direct contact between the 'originator' and the 'recipient' (e.g. Hargreaves 2003a; Stoll *et al.* 2006). This gives rise to the idea of embedded knowledge, used in both industrial (e.g. Hakkarainen *et al.* 2004) and educational systems, where the context and the knowledge are bound together (one of the assumptions in a situated view of knowledge). This means that when knowledge is removed from its context it can become inert and fragmented, making it difficult to

Table 7.1 Metaphorical mappings for 'acquisition' and 'participation'

Acquisition metaphor		Participation metaphor
Individual enrichment	Goal of learning	Community building
Acquisition of something	Learning	Becoming a participant
Recipient (consumer), (re-)constructor	Student	Peripheral participant, apprentice
Provider, facilitator, mediator	Teacher	Expert participant, preserver of practice/discourse
Property, possession, commodity (individual, public)	Knowledge, concept	Aspect of practice/discourse/activity
Having, possessing	Knowing	Belonging, participating, communicating

Source: Sfard (1998: 7).

'transfer'; it requires shared practices, or frames of reference to be disseminated. The solution proposed by Nonaka and Takeuchi (1995), which we discussed in Chapter 3, is to go through a series of steps making implicit knowledge explicit to facilitate its sharing and then for that to be subsequently made implicit again when put into action.[7] Making knowledge explicit leads to innovation (Hakkarainen *et al.* 2004), which we examine in the next section through a comparison of industry and education, and the possible differences in the role of innovation and knowledge. Hargreaves' third transformation considers this issue of transfer and advocates a person-to-person approach, with an emphasis on exchange and reciprocity (Hargreaves 2003a). Stoll *et al.* (2006: 217) make a similar point to Nonaka and Takeuchi (1995) when they argue that tacit knowledge is constantly converted into shared knowledge through interaction. This can work *within* a school or other organisation, but becomes more problematic *between* schools. It may well be a problem even within schools, because each subject tradition will have its own shared understandings that are not held by teachers of other subjects; similarly, in primary schools, early-years teachers may have underpinnings of practice not shared by those who teach 11-year-olds.

Whatever the complexities of these issues, we wonder whether there is a continual tendency to conflate the *creation* and the *sharing* of knowledge. In raising this question of transfer versus creation, in the context of the work of professional learning communities (PLCs), Stoll *et al.* (2006: 234), quoting Fielding and his colleagues, say:

> The question is whether 'transfer of good/best practice' is ever appropriate or even feasible or whether, in effective PLCs the intention is and *modus operandi* should always be exchange (a commitment to reciprocity between two staff members where one is an 'originator' and the other a 'receiver') and practice creation (two individuals that 'create new practices that are inspired by and energised by their dialogic encounters') (Fielding *et al.* 2005: 104).

That there is a similar kind of work going on in both 'sharing' and 'creation' may be the case (Stoll *et al.* talk of active construction and deconstruction of knowledge), but it would be helpful not to always assume the conditions of creation in *all* cases of sharing. We will explore this in the next section, particularly in relation to different strengths of relationship, but before that we want to go back to the discussions in Chapter 3 on reification and participation, which will help us to think about these issues more fruitfully.

Reification and participation

The earlier discussion indicated the way Wenger views reification and participation as two complementary concepts, and although reification does not 'capture' practice (e.g. in a lesson plan), it can act as a focus for negotiating meaning. Taking the description earlier of the use of the traffic lights strategy at the end of a lesson, another teacher could use this as a basis for contextualising it into her or his own classroom through trying it out (participation). The description can therefore be seen to 'travel'. When practice is reified (in a description), it can travel across a network, but this is not the same as the practice being able to move across the network. Any 'reification must be re-appropriated into a local process in order to become meaningful' (Wenger 1998: 60). Thus, teachers receiving the reification must develop their own meaning from it as they develop their own practices. Rudduck *et al.* (2000: 265) refer to this as 'borrowing' and 'contexting', where practices 'need to be re-thought – or tried out and then re-thought – to see how to make them fit and flourish in a different context'. Thus, a policy (or ideas and practices) can be made to 'fit and flourish in a different context' (ibid.). Any practice in the form of a reification will thus need to be recreated by a 'receiving' teacher in a network. Even though this could be seen as re-creation, for the receiving teacher at that time it is a 'creation' and a negotiation of meaning from that reification. This is what Stoll *et al.* (2006), Hargreaves (2003a) and other authors who discuss 'transfer' as a creation process also say, but they do not seem to give any significance to the idea of a reification. They appear to want to reproduce a creation process by having two teachers develop a 'shared' practice through close contact and exchange.[8] This is not the same as one sharing practice with another, as we will shortly argue.

First, though, let us look at examples of sharing of practice in responses to the LHTL mapping exercise. In many cases it was ideas or reported practices that 'flowed', and these were mainly through orally communicated 'objects'. We found relatively few examples of physical resources shared. Local authority (LA) co-ordinators told us of electronic mechanisms they were setting up for the creation and exchange of physical resources, but we found no evidence of this in schools. Nor was there much evidence of schools sharing their own resources directly. We had only one example of sharing practice that involved *joint teaching*, where one school was working with another in a support role:

> And there is another school, a secondary school to which we have given most support, with some of their teachers coming up here and with our teachers going up there. Last Tuesday we had both our cohorts of year 7s doing literacy-based activities together.
>
> (Brian, headteacher, Hawthorn High School)

This is one of the few examples of high participation, where teachers are involved in practice. The teachers involved in the joint teaching no doubt employed lesson plans associated with some discussion prior to their carrying out the joint lessons, and could have shared practice in the classroom and then discussed this practice after the activities. This illustrates the complementary nature of reification and participation. They are also faced with a need to share their experience with colleagues not involved.

More frequent in responses to the mapping exercise were visits to schools to *observe* some practice, and we had two such examples, one being prompted by a desire to see ideas (from books) in action:

Dave: I went to [name of a school] in Tonbridge, because they're an EAZ [Education Action Zone] school, and they were, I said to you this morning about our guided reading and that was where we got the books from. Well, I wasn't just going to go and buy books, I wanted to see it in action so I went to [name of a school] in Tonbridge to have a look at their work . . .

Researcher: So you invited yourself . . . ?

Dave: I just phoned them, and said, 'I've heard that you do wondrous things in terms of literacy. Show me what you do.' I went to have a look at literacy at [name of another school], I've been to look at one of the Headlamp colleagues,[9] to have a look at her school literacy.

(Dave, headteacher, Goldenrain Junior School)

We quoted in Chapter 6 (p. 134) Jacqueline, a headteacher whose teachers and students visited another school (to derive criteria for a 'good learning lesson'). Visits are not uncommon, but to carry them out on a large scale for a school or group of schools is not easy, as we observed in a networked learning community (NLC) where considerable financial costs were involved (for teacher cover when they visit), including the need for a system of administration. More commonly, teachers are involved in various kinds of professional development where a *teacher talks* about what he or she does in the classroom (though we do not know the details in the following case):

One of the things that works really well on INSET [in-service training] is having teachers coming in to talk about what they've been doing. When you do evaluations at the end of the course, the things that always make me smile are little comments like 'It's really nice to have a real teacher come and talk about what they are doing.'

(Kay Fisher, LA co-ordinator)

One example of professional development focusing on AfL (feedback strategies), led by a higher education institution involved in the project, included such things as planning classroom activities and discussing how they should be conducted. The workshop involved resulted in school action:

We've looked at feedback which has given a bit of impetus again for the workshop, the Cambridge workshop, and that is in turn turning into the marking policy.

(Kate, co-ordinator, Juniper Primary School)

Although getting teachers to talk to other teachers is useful, it is usually not feasible to extend this to a large group of schools, and so local authorities will often create case-study material that can be used in such workshops:

You have got colleagues from other advisory services and other authorities and teachers and from schools with very practical case-study workshops . . . the things I go on that have the most impact is where you get those practical examples.

(Una Hills, LA co-ordinator)

Such materials enable practice to be shared more widely and perhaps be co-ordinated over a wider area (indeed, their use at a national level can have this intention, as is the case with the government's national strategy materials in England). Interestingly, the LHTL project material (discussed earlier) is the most frequently mentioned material. In most cases the material has been downloaded and printed, in one case for use in a school but in two others for use with a school not involved in the project (i.e. sharing broader than the project):

. . . so now I surf the Learning to Learn [LHTL] website and also that's where I downloaded . . . the workshops.

(Kate, co-ordinator, Juniper Primary School)

Resources can include those that form a 'script' for a classroom activity or that try to capture some of the action:

Well, as I say, we do make reference to these particular groups or particular contacts or particular agencies, and if somebody has been using a source and it has resulted in particular materials, maybe worksheets or photographs, those will then be stored as part of that particular project box.

(Alexandra, headteacher, Gingko Primary School)

The classroom worksheets reify the students' activities, though they clearly do not give any indication of the supporting activities and associated talk of the teacher. Similarly, photographs can convey activity, but these need more description or perhaps an audio tape of the interactions for a 'stranger' to negotiate meaning.

Ideas are probably the most reified way in which practice might be shared:

So, for example, Tracy and I have traded ideas . . . I've then developed, she's then developed . . .

(Ben, co-ordinator, Mulberry School)

None of these examples is very surprising, but they indicate that there is almost always some reification taking place, something that appears to be discounted by those who advocate the close collaboration by teachers to overcome any of the problems with the use of decontextualised practice. The interesting question is the extent to which such advocates show evidence of what actually occurs, even where the focus is on the creation of knowledge.

Many of those who advocate collaboration and joint development do so to ensure that there is none of the disadvantages of reification, but it is instructive to examine their accounts to see whether this is indeed the case. As we have shown in Chapters 1 and 3, those who research PLCs are part of this group, and Stoll *et al.* (2006: 226–7), in reviewing the literature on such communities, examine the characteristics that make them effective:

- reflective professional inquiry, which includes the examining of teachers' practice, through mutual observation and case analysis, joint planning and curriculum development;
- 'Collaboration. This concerns staff involvement in developmental activities with consequences for several people, going beyond superficial exchanges of help, support, or assistance . . . for example, joint review and feedback.'

Each of these characteristics includes some form of reification: observation records (or characterisations of the interaction through talk); the depiction of a 'case'; planning documents; record of feedback. One reaction to this might be talk of 'knowledge of practice' being what is involved. However, we would prefer to use 'reification of practice', as it is when participation becomes involved that it becomes knowing. Others, as we see next, use 'representations of practice'.[10]

Accounts of practice 'creation'

In reading the work of advocates of teacher networks (which Stoll *et al.* 2006 say has similar assumptions to those on professional learning communities [PLCs]), there is limited evidence of the work on the 'fine grain processes', as we noted in relation to the quotation from Little (2002) in Chapter 3 (p. 53). In writing about such communities, Stoll and Louis (2007b: 6) quote Little (2002) in their discussion about the need for a better understanding of the collaborative processes in PLCs, asking, for example, '[W]hat does ["thinking together"] mean when colleagues actually get together?' As we noted in Chapter 1, the National Writing Project (NWP), described as 'one of the oldest and arguably most successful [of the teacher] networks' (Lieberman and Wood 2003b: 478), has yet to show these 'fine grain processes'. Gray (2000), who directed one of the net-works in the NWP, chronicles the development of the project, and his account gives details of one of the major activities in the five-week summer institutes for teachers, namely the teacher demonstrations. Examples of some of these are given, and they consist roughly of:

* a presentation of a particular classroom approach by a teacher (e.g. short-piece writing);
* a demonstration of student activities where the teachers act as students and, as it were, simulate the activity (e.g. they write a short piece as students would);
* a look at the demonstration teacher's students' work (e.g. examples of students' short pieces);
* a discussion about the approach.[11]

Those who organised the institutes provided teachers with coaching in how to run these sessions, which were then the basis of what they did when the teachers themselves ran professional development sessions (subsequent to the institute) in their own areas. Gray also discusses some of the teachers acting as researchers, which included observing their students, etc., but this appears to be more about their own learning than that of their colleagues. No details are given of whether or not the observations and associated data were shared with other teachers. Lieberman and Wood (2003a) give a research account of the NWP, but give no more details of these demonstration sessions. They describe six case studies of individual teachers who had been to the summer institutes, but the focus is on their personal learning, including tracing the results of their experiences at these institutes back to their classrooms (which Lieberman and Wood observed). One teacher attended local sessions in her early days and she talked of trying out ideas that various presenters had given when they presented at these sessions. Lieberman and Wood also discuss NWP teachers taking a leadership role in their own schools and districts, but again no details of this are included. They acknowledge that more research is needed, particularly on a larger scale. We therefore must await this research to understand the details of both the creation of new practices and how it is shared with other teachers who are not 'NWP teachers', at the level of detail that is needed to understand the processes involved.

Little was particularly concerned about the content of collaboration, which she thought resulted in detailed accounts (e.g. by ethnographers) that emphasised form over content. In her view, these were not

> substitutes . . . for a more close-grained account of the moral and intellectual dispositions that teachers bring to or develop in the course of their relations with one another; . . . [they had not] been well-informed by careful scrutiny of the actual talk among teachers, the choices teachers make in concert, or the ways in which individual actions follow from the deliberations of the group.
>
> (1990: 524)

Little followed this in her later work of a detailed study of teachers collaboratively trying to improve their teaching, by advocating a framework which includes '*representation* of practice, *orientation* to practice, and *norms of interaction*' (2002: 934; emphasis in the original). The first of these concerns what is made visible or 'rendered public in exchanges among teachers' ('going public') and how complete and specific it is in relation to the practice in the classroom. Her worry was that the way teaching is organised is such as to limit observation of practice, and hence its transparency is low. Further, 'relatively little research examines the specific interactions and dynamics by which professional community constitutes a resource for teacher learning and innovations in teaching practice' (ibid.: 918). Little followed this, first, in a study of these representations of practice, where she notes the way in which teachers decontextualise classroom practice and recontextualise it in the course of their interactions in a professional community; in their co-construction of representations of practice, they reify the language of practice (Little 2003). Further, she found that there was what appears to be an inevitable insularity of such communities of practice, which we see as having implications for any subsequent sharing of practice developed in this community. In a later article she has shown how student work can be part of the support for teacher learning (referred to in the quotation above) that she finds lacking (Little 2004). She also acknowledges other work, in particular 'lesson study', which is pertinent to the first example given above from the LHTL project, where teachers undertake joint teaching (Fernandez 2002). Lesson study combines the *inquiry* element of knowledge creation (Chapter 3), with teachers jointly planning a lesson in detail. One teacher teaches the lesson and the others observe. They then revise the lesson plan on the basis of a discussion of the observations, and another within the group teaches it, with the rest again observing. Different pedagogical issues or problems will involve different numbers of cycles of this planning, observing, revising and re-teaching.[12] Here the lesson plan and the observations (which can be recorded on the lesson plan) are reifications, illustrating that even where participation is high, there is still an element of reification needed to co-ordinate practice among a group of teachers, whatever the degree of mutual understanding.

Little's (1990) worries about collaboration (noted in Chapter 6 on affiliation networks [p. 141]) were part of a more general critique of the lack of understanding or recognition of the processes involved. She frames her discussion by seeing the various forms of collegial relations on a continuum from complete professional independence to interdependence, with 'story telling and scanning' at the 'independence' end and 'joint work' at the 'interdependence' end, with 'sharing' in between (ibid.: 512).

Storytelling and scanning take place in opportunistic encounters with quick exchange of stories or specific ideas. Joint work involves 'shared responsibility for the work of teaching' (ibid.: 519), but that '[q]uite apart from their personal friendships or dispositions, teachers are motivated to participate with one another to the degree that they require each other's contribution in order to succeed in their own work' (ibid.: 520). She argues that professional autonomy makes collaboration difficult and that when teachers do engage in collaboration, the micro-politics become visible and conflict can occur. This autonomy means that there are few real interdependencies, and that it is only these that will motivate teachers to engage in joint work, concluding:

> To the extent that teachers find themselves truly dependent on one another to manage the tasks and reap the rewards of teaching, joint participation will be worth the investment of time and other resources. To the extent that teachers' success and satisfaction can be achieved independently the motivations to participate are weakened.
>
> (ibid.: 523)

This puts in context her support for lesson study in her later work that we discussed above.

The general outcome of our consideration of the 'creation' of practice is that there is insufficient work on the way practice is rendered to enable the creation process to take place. Hence, if this 'sharing' of practice *within* a collaborative relationship is not understood, then sharing with those not involved in it becomes even more problematic. Little (2004) advocates ethnography to shed light on these processes, anticipating the call of Latour (2005) in his case for actor-network theory (ANT) for studying the associations in a network. In Chapter 11 we will return to this and consider how the tracing of associations might help, along with alternatives such as activity theory, as suggested by Miettinen (1999).

In contrast to these ethnographic and ethnomethodological studies, Lima (2004) argues for a broader approach using social network analysis (SNA). As we discussed in Chapter 2, he advocates studies of social relations at a more general level than Little is calling for, with measures of density, centrality and fragmentation. These measures indicate the extent to which teachers in a school tend to work in cliques based on departments or whether such cliques are made up of teachers from two or more departments. Lima argues that cliques tend to form around departments, and his other work indicates how departments can be differently related to others in the school (Lima 2007). The argument from Little (1990) on affiliations, which we looked at in Chapter 6, indicates a more complex picture and explains her concern for the use of ethnographic studies. Our view is that both approaches are necessary.

Sharing

This lack of understanding of the collaborative processes essentially takes us back to where we left things towards the end of Chapter 1, namely that while we may know something about the processes involved in creation (and, as we have just argued, even this has problems), we know insufficient about sharing, at least in the educational networks discussed. Little's view of collaboration extends into her rather pessimistic view of 'sharing', which requires less professional interdependence than joint work (1990: 518–19). The quotation from Little (2005b) in Chapter 1 as an agenda for the book, and her insights discussed above, leave us with a need to see whether the 'mainstream' network theories discussed in earlier chapters can help us to understand knowledge sharing. First it is worth looking at the 'knowledge networks' that are discussed in commercial and industrial sectors, rather than education. The general arguments that are given for the knowledge economy and its importance in industrial innovation seem on the face of it to be important, but not all are indeed so relevant. Where these arguments centre on the role of ICT and information flow, we do not think they are of prime concern, as there is little evidence that ICT changes the way practice is created and shared. (However, we will return to the role of ICT in sharing practice later in the chapter and consider electronic networks more fully in Chapter 10.) More pertinent are knowledge networks, as found in industrial and commercial sectors. One such example is Küppers and Pyka (2002) on innovation networks, which they see as the third phase of production (the first being craft and the second mass manufacturing). Networks are a way of working in a situation where products are complex and require the dynamic interaction of parts (i.e. where changes in one will affect changes in the others). Küppers (2002), as part of this discussion of complexity, self-organisation and innovation networks, indicates that the context is one of responding flexibly to turbulent markets. This kind of literature, and some of the associated literature on knowledge management, we feel is not so relevant to education. This is because it is not easy to see how innovation is needed in quite the same way as it apparently is in industry, where responding to a market with unique products is the major incentive. Hargreaves (2003a), of course, argued for innovation as part of his transformations, but his framing of this did not have a market orientation. Quite the opposite: he saw schools collaborating and sharing. However, as we will shortly show, some of the research on innovating industrial companies does have relevance because it uncovers processes that are relevant, but different from those discussed by Pyka and Küppers (2002).

As Chapter 6 indicated, Allee (2003) is concerned with knowledge, and, on the face of it, of relevance to education, as she deals with the practical issues involved with ensuring people have the everyday knowledge they need to do everyday tasks. Her prime concern is with networked enterprises, where ICT is central, that employ a form of decentralised patterns of organisation (in what she calls a living network). She considers how knowledge follows social interactions (hence the importance of SNA) and the forms of knowledge creation (e.g. through communities of practice). Her identification of intangibles in a value network does not seem to be linked to these processes of creation, or indeed in the sharing of knowledge. The intangibles can be knowledge assets, but we are given insufficient insight into how they are shared or used to create new practices. Her contribution is in encouraging the idea that knowledge of practice can be discussed and, in the process, it is not lost or handed over; it can be adapted and offered again in further discussion.

Using a socio-cultural view of learning, Brown and Duguid (2002) warn of problems of 'moving' knowledge around because it is embedded in practice ('sticky knowledge' [ibid.: 28]). They argue that it is easier to move this knowledge between companies, assuming that it is moving *within* a community of practice, what they elsewhere refer to as 'networks of practice' (Brown and Duguid 2000: 141). They assume, however, that the processes of the community of practice are the source of creation and hence do not add any more to our understanding than does Wenger (1998).

We have already detailed another strand of work, that of the Finnish researchers (Hakkarainen *et al.* 2004; Palonen *et al.* 2004), who have studied the work of innovative IT companies. Their use of communities of practice and SNA, including affiliation networks and social contagion (which we considered in Chapter 6), emphasised embedded links and strong ties. We also noted that they argued that weak ties should be converted into strong ones. Their focus was largely on knowledge *creation within* an organisation, though they were also concerned with external links and with the ideas of Burt (1992) and others on brokerage. The importance of complex knowledge, and hence of strong ties, leads them to consider that weak ties allow searching for *information*, but not for *knowledge* exchange. However, they place less emphasis on the point that Burt (2005) makes about the need for weak links across structural holes, whose resources can then be capitalised upon through the strong ties of closure in a close-knit team or department (see Chapter 5). Nevertheless, they do conclude that 'the optimal structure for an organisation may be a combination of arm's length and embedded ties' (Hakkarainen *et al.* 2004: 78).

Part of the problem here is with a lack of details about the nature of the knowledge at stake (which we considered at the beginning of the chapter) and hence theories of exchange that stem from the substantive area under consideration, namely education and its associated practices (the point Mitchell [1974] was making; see Chapter 2). We will return to this shortly when we consider the application of SNA diffusion studies to education, but first it is worth considering a specific study of weak ties in education (Lawrence 2007).

Lawrence investigated schools that were part of the Specialist Schools and Academies Trust (SSAT) 'Raising Achievement and Transforming Learning' project, which put mentor schools in touch with partner schools that might be interested in the practice of the mentor schools. The SSAT enabled schools to link up through a website, conferences and the use of consulting headteachers. Once contact was made, the schools negotiated their own relationships and working arrangements. The main finding was that in all the cases Lawrence studied, the relationship between the mentor and partner schools could be characterised as a 'weak tie'. In all cases the link was with a headteacher or member of the senior management team (SMT), and the practice focused not on classroom practice *per se*, but on the organisational processes that underpinned such practice. Lawrence speculates that had there been a wider range of teachers involved in a relationship (including those from the classroom), then it could be that a strong link was necessary. Another major finding was that trust did not have to be developed or be pre-existing for 'transfer' to take place. There were several reasons for this, including the fact that teachers tended to trust other schools (as a mark of their professionalism) or that the project itself lent trust to the whole enterprise. In the end the partner schools (or, more properly, the senior teachers in these schools) relied on their own judgement to learn from a particular practice in the mentor school, rather than to have to rely on the mentor to identify what is needed, etc. through a trusting relationship.[13] In Chapter 6 we acknowledge the importance of trust in strong collaborative links typical in knowledge creation, and Hakkarainen *et al.* (2004: 70) also indicate its role in knowledge sharing within an organisation. In this case this sharing seems to be closer to being part of the knowledge creation process, rather than sharing from one organisation to another. Finally, Lawrence (2007) coins the term 'catalytic practice' in contrast to the 'joint practice development' studied by Fielding *et al.* (2005). Thus, the practice illustrated by the mentor school acted as a catalyst for developments in the partner school, rather than both schools having developed new practice collaboratively.[14]

SNA does address the issue of sharing knowledge, though characterised in terms of the study of the diffusion of innovations. Diffusion deals with the adoption of a specific practice, product, ideas, etc. by exposure through social contagion. Studies of this consider how innovations diffuse through interpersonal contacts and seek to understand the factors that lead some members of a population to adopt a new idea and others not to. Adoption is related to the number of network contacts through exposure. Valente (1995) gives a classic account of a network approach to diffusion, in which he investigated the empirical evidence of adoption rates and network features, comparing three studies of, respectively, doctors using a new drug, farmers adopting a new seed and women adopting birth-control methods. These studies asked the doctors, farmers and women to identify those with whom they were friendly and with whom they discussed such issues (drug treatment, farming and birth control), and these were related to adoption rates. Valente examines two basic approaches to considering diffusion: relational and structural. The relational approach views exposure through direct contacts with those whom a person is in close contact with, and hence communication. Innovativeness is related to the number of direct ties sent or received;[15] it turns out that early adopters have many ties and are perceived as opinion leaders. It is evident, however, that indirect contacts are also important; for example, those with contacts outside their immediate relationships are more likely to hear about an innovation early, something that follows from the ideas of the strength of weak ties, and brokers who span structural holes, noted previously. This leads to the structural approach that considers the pattern of communications and the position of an individual in the social structure; among people who are structurally equivalent, contagion is more likely. Interestingly, Valente (1995) saw this as a 'network theory' rather than a 'diffusion theory'. Nevertheless, people who are central in a network are important in both relational and structural approaches. In comparing the empirical evidence from the three studies it is evident that each had different characteristics reflecting the differences both in the innovations and in the behaviours of the groups involved (ibid.). In our view, it is important, as we noted previously, to remember Mitchell's (1974) point about the need for substantive theories to explain the mechanisms at work (in his case exchange theory), rather than to see them in terms of network theories. Although this appears at odds with Valente's view, his more recent review of SNA methods (in which he acknowledges both that these methods have grown in sophistication since the 1950s, and the undoubted importance of diffusion studies) is more circumspect: 'Social networks are fundamental influences on human behaviour and conduits for the diffusion of ideas and practices, yet their roles are varied and complex and defy easy categorisation' (Valente 2005: 113).

One obvious issue is that the idea of 'adoption' of a practice is treated in the quantitative studies as an 'all or nothing' event: a doctor uses a drug in treatment or does not; a farmer plants a particular seed or does not. We have already noted the idea of transformation of ideas that Posch and Mair (1997) argued takes place when teachers visit colleagues' classrooms (Chapter 1, note 7). Our view of knowledge creation and sharing as part of teacher learning indicates that this process of 'adoption' is not straightforward in education, as we will shortly show in relation to assessment for learning. Inevitably, Valente (2005) feels that more research is needed (a point noted in Chapter 2), and we would agree with him in relation specifically to educational networks. We have already indicated the importance of mapping such networks to understand how they might operate, and it is evident that there could be some useful studies to look at how teachers learn about and adopt new practices, rather than assuming that some change strategy introduced from the school management is what matters. Little (1990) indicated a need to understand 'teacher influence', and this takes us on to a consideration of learning at both the individual and organisational level, which we have argued is at the heart of this process.

Individual learning

Our consideration of individual teacher learning will examine what the LHTL project revealed about how AfL was implemented in the classroom by teachers who had been 'exposed' to some kind of school programme, in part stimulated by the project. Not all teachers were able to use the strategies in the way that was intended by the research team. Marshall and Drummond (2006) observed twenty-seven video recordings of lessons, but only about 20 per cent of the teachers observed were able to grasp and implement the 'spirit' of AfL in their lessons.[16] Marshall and Drummond (ibid.: 137) characterised this spirit 'as "high organisation based on ideas", where the underpinning principle is promoting pupil autonomy'.[17] This contrasts with 'those lessons where only the procedures, or "letter" of AfL', were evident (ibid.). They go on to state, 'Evident from the data, was the very real difficulty of transforming AfL procedures or strategies into classroom cultures that promote pupil autonomy' (ibid.). Teachers who adopted this 'letter' approach to AfL practice limited the scope of tasks and had fewer opportunities for current and future pupil independence compared to those who had captured the spirit of AfL. For example, a teacher of English who intends to develop the sharing of criteria and self-assessment might simply give out the criteria that focused on technical right and wrong answers (the 'letter') and explain them, then ask students to carry out a self-assessment, whereas a teacher who followed the 'spirit' of AfL would involve the students in developing criteria and help students see what quality means. Teachers can attend a workshop on AfL ideas, be shown practical strategies, and develop, share and discuss their own resources and experiences of AfL, but it can still be challenging to apply these practices in ways that promote pupil autonomy in their own classrooms. It could be argued that there should be an initial focus on principles, and then the development of practices (LHTL introduced general AfL ideas, but focused on practical strategies in workshops), but there is likely to be no single 'correct' approach. Teachers' classroom practice of AfL did appear to depend upon their beliefs about pupil autonomy and on the extent to which the teachers felt they had the agency to improve the situation (rather than being the victim of students' 'lack of ability' or of influences outside the classroom). That does not imply that these beliefs are what has to be changed first.

Further, there appeared to be subject differences in how (secondary) teachers responded in the classroom, according to self-reports of their AfL practice (James *et al.* 2007). Teachers were statistically clustered in ways that showed their implementation of AfL practices (e.g. the extent to which they promoted learning autonomy and made learning explicit), and the subject differences indicated that there were more who were successful in English language, creative arts and physical education; teachers in science and mathematics were least successful (ibid.: 182–4). In an earlier comparison of two subjects, mathematics and English, Hogden and Marshall (2005) examined the extent to which there was indeed a subject specificity of formative assessment (their label for AfL) practices. They indicate that although formative assessment has generic ideas (in the four areas: questioning, feedback, sharing criteria, and self and peer assessment), they are manifest differently in different subjects. These differences reflect the 'guild' (community of practice) differences that students are being introduced to in each subject. For example, as Marshall (2004) argued, criteria for assessing work in English reflect 'English' as a subject. Indeed, she concludes that '[m]uch of the practice which appears to be formative on the surface arises more out of the subject discipline than it does out of a specific desire to be formative' (ibid.: 112). Hogden and Marshall discuss some of the problems for mathematics in implementing formative assessment:

> In our view the formative assessment within the mathematics lesson described here is good and considerably better than the current practice in the majority of mathematics classrooms. However, we feel that this practice is itself limited in the particularities of school mathematics in England. School mathematics tends to be taught as formal and abstract concepts.
>
> (2005: 172–3)

Such subject differences are not confined just to an innovation such as AfL. It appears that in trying to foster communities of learners in the classroom, teachers also exhibit such differences. Fostering such communities was a pedagogy devised by Ann Brown and developed by her and Campione (Brown 1997; Brown and Campione 1996), and involves students trying to reach a deep understanding of disciplinary content.[18] A 'big idea' of a subject is chosen and split into topics, and each topic is assigned to a student group to research and become 'expert' in that topic. New groups are formed containing one student from each of the expert groups, and the students share their understanding of the topics to develop their understanding of the big idea (jigsawing). This then enables them to complete a task that is dependent on the students all understanding the ideas they have been learning. In essence this is a generic pedagogy that Brown and others were able to show improved student performance in some selected areas of the curriculum, premised upon the organisation of knowledge as disciplinary knowledge.

Recently a group of researchers explored the way in which this generic pedagogy is developed across a range of subjects: social studies, biology, English and mathematics (respectively: Mintrop 2004; Rico and Shulman 2004; Whitcomb 2004; Sherin *et al.* 2004). What emerges from these studies is that the details of how to foster communities of learners depends upon the particular subject domain, and that there are sometimes conflicts between, on the one hand, what the discipline would encourage and the principles of fostering communities of learners (FCL) and, on the other, the 'default' pedagogy of teachers of a particular subject (much as the quotation from Hogden and Marshall [2005] indicated). Thus, one of the English teachers resorted to her more familiar school subject teacher-directed approach, rather than involving the students. Science teachers could create the big ideas, but in the research phase, despite the traditions of science, they resorted to the usual science education approach of focusing on grasping a body of facts, undermining the FCL approach. The social studies teachers investigated could not create the big ideas easily because they did not have sufficient discipline knowledge across the range of social sciences, and although they could set up the jigsaw groups, they could not maintain students' clear focus on these big ideas. Another English teacher, anxious to create discourse in the jigsaw process, had to go back to first principles for this to create dialogue, and was unable to rely on generic procedural approaches. As one team of investigators put it, 'Our experiences suggest that it is possible to teach mathematics through FCL pedagogy, but that doing so requires a reconceptualization of mathematics instruction as well as some rethinking of essential FCL features' (Sherin *et al.* 2004: 229). It is not just that there have to be 'subject-specific' interpretations of the pedagogy, but that there is mutual change in the subject pedagogy and that of the 'generic' pedagogy. These findings, and that from the LHTL project, were concerned with secondary school teachers who have subject identities, but it turns out that there is some evidence that primary school teachers, who are unlikely to have this subject identity, also exhibit subject differences in their teaching. A study of elementary teachers teaching mathematics and social studies in the United States indicated that the teachers adopted different pedagogy depending upon the subject, and the researcher concluded that such subject differences need to be taken into account when advocating reform of pedagogy in an education system (Stodolsky 1988).[19] Similarly, Jones and Moreland (2005), working with primary teachers involved in AfL practice, concluded that it was important that teachers knew the characteristics of the subject and the specific teaching and assessment practices of the subject to work successfully.

Our desire in this 'diversion' to examine subject differences is to underline the importance of seeing the issue of teacher learning of a new pedagogical practice as likely to be complex, and seeing that SNA assumptions about adoption, and hence diffusion, may indeed be difficult to apply. Nonetheless, there is merit in thinking about how such diffusion takes place and the role of social and other contacts that teachers have, within and outside the school.

School learning

The school also introduces another layer of complexity for the adoption of new practice, as changes are more usually part of a strategy undertaken by the staff as a whole, with steerage from the SMT and those who work in management roles beneath them (middle managers). One way of looking at this is through the ideas of organisational learning, which, according to some researchers, would entail 'creating routines and standard procedures' and also involve organisational renewal (Palonen *et al.* 2004: 272).[20] This view corresponds to an educational literature that uses terms such as 'embedding' and 'change'.[21] Swaffield and MacBeath (2006) represent this view, and their work resulting from the LHTL project enables us to examine the issues of the organisational level in relation to creation and sharing.[22] They see embedding as 'a vision, a set of procedures which become integral to the structure and culture of the organization. Over time, sooner or perhaps later, new ways of seeing and acting become habitual, reflexive and ingrained in practice' (ibid.: 202). They recognise that the concept is not straightforward and that often there is a model of change which is implicit in a view of embedding (e.g. that there is a gradual shift in practices, or that change is a steady state). Swaffield and MacBeath examine two approaches to embedding: structural and cultural.

A structural approach focuses on defining organisational structures, roles and communication patterns and uses accountability procedures to exert control over the practices. Thus, a school introducing 'comment-only marking' (i.e. not giving grades to students' work, only comments to help them improve) might ask middle managers (e.g. heads of subject departments in secondary schools) to check a sample of students' work for the teachers for whom they are responsible, to make sure that the school policy is being implemented. Similarly, classroom observations, as part of performance management, might be used to check that teachers are implementing a questioning strategy. It is evident that if teachers are not conforming, then it is likely that structural sanctions will not be the best way to improve the implementation, and a head of department is likely to want to work with her or his colleagues by suggesting activities or approaches to take. This engagement reflects the cultural approach to embedding, illustrating that the two approaches are unlikely to be independent of each other. A school co-ordinator illustrates this through what she sees as a management approach:

> I don't think it [is] desirable to say, 'go away and do whatever you like', because in the past when people have done that . . . there is no unification of ethos in a school. You have to have the basic ethos and tenets of the school clear, and that is the job of the head. The head is the person who takes on the ultimate role of saying, 'This is my school, this is what I believe, this is my philosophy', but how they disseminate that philosophy and how they take staff with them is about their skill to select people in the next two layers down who will work with them, who in turn can take it down to the people in the next levels of management. And that comes through the skill of senior management to disseminate that ethos and bring people along with them through developing this kind of corporate approach to management; where people . . . are cleverly guided down the route you want them to go to; but do feel they have joint ownership, because in the discussion that goes along the way they are allowed to . . . make their contributions and to be able to make them honestly and that they are taken notice of, even though they may not always sway the argument their way. Because at the end of the day the head is the head and the head has a vision, but then if they are rigid and say, 'No, this is how I am going to do it . . . ', you get people leaving all the time.
>
> (Helen, co-ordinator, Deodar Primary School)

The cultural approach deals with the underlying norms, values, beliefs and traditions that are part of the operation of teachers and the organisations they work in. Thus, when the LHTL project introduced AfL to a school staff, the research team engaged them in discussions and activities that asked them to examine what they did and to question the underlying assumptions of both their practice and that which underpins AfL. Our earlier discussion of the importance of teacher beliefs for implementation in the classroom indicates the importance of this approach. Interestingly, Swaffield and MacBeath note that embedding through a cultural approach places 'a greater emphasis on the informal flow of activity and conversation' (2006: 204), and hence we think this makes network ideas more salient. Such an approach would endeavour to encourage teacher ownership of any initiative to change, so that engagement could be encouraged and resistance overcome. Inevitably, cultural norms will become embedded in accepted procedures (such as 'comment-only marking') and will be subject to accountability mechanisms to check that staff are conforming to the norms. In a study of the role of middle managers in the implementation of AfL, Moore (2009) shows how those who started with a cultural approach changed over time when it appeared that some individuals, or indeed their whole department, were not implementing AfL practices that had been discussed and agreed at department level. They resorted to invoking school-level structures and policies to try to change resistant staff, despite this not being their preferred approach.

Swaffield and MacBeath (2006) also reported the embedding strategies used by schools in the LHTL project, including:

- professional collaborative activity (e.g. professional development days, peer observation);
- external influences (e.g. inspirational speakers, workshops run by outsiders and networks such as NLCs);
- integration with management mechanisms (e.g. short feedback on practices at the beginning of a staff meeting, integration into policy documents and documentation for new staff);
- cultural leadership (e.g. leading by example, building it into expectations).

This consideration of the school level adds to the complexity we examined in relation to individual learning and the change of practice, to further reinforce the view that any network analysis of diffusion has quite an agenda of issues to contend with. Although the LHTL project looked at individual teachers and their changes of practice in the classroom (e.g. Marshall and Drummond 2006), and also considered the role of networking at a school level, we were not able to relate these to the network maps (which sampled a different set of respondents).[23] Further research could usefully trace how individual teachers have changed their practice and the extent of their links with others in encouraging them in this. As we noted at the end of the section on theoretical issues, the need to cope with the complexity of both the process of learning at the individual level and embedding at the school level might indicate that an approach using the methodology of actor-network theory (ANT) could be suitable, if demanding. In the time since the LHTL project approach, the study of trainee teachers discussed in Chapter 6 ('Frequency of links', p. 122) charted three trainees' interactions with others and the value of these interactions on a weekly basis in both network diaries and blogs (Fox *et al.* 2010). The trainees also drew termly network maps to capture snapshots of their personal networks, and they and their mentors were interviewed about their use of support. In addition, they were observed teaching each term. The details of what support was given and accepted, along with evidence of changes in practice, are still being analysed, but this could address some of the issues discussed.

Thinking again about 'traffic'

Here we reflect on the chapter so far to come to some view about how to conceive of what constitutes 'traffic' or 'flow', given what we have argued about its role in teacher learning. We will do this by borrowing from ideas in the electronic world and by examining how these ideas can help us to understand some of the data in the LHTL project relating to teacher networks. At the outset of the project electronic networks seemed to be important, so we set up a website in part to enable the sharing of practice (see Carmichael and Procter 2005), and therefore wanted to think about how objects, as reified practice, should be conceptualised and indeed described in electronic terms.[24] Despite his faith in the role of ICT, Hargreaves (2003a), like many authors, feels that websites are a weak means to use to share practice because they can only contain disembodied practice. We have argued that if artefacts are considered as reifications of practice that need associated participation, then they have a role in sharing practice because they become the basis for a negotiation of meaning. At the beginning of the chapter we discussed the importance of 'examples of implementation' for promoting AfL in schools, and indicated how a simple strategy like 'traffic lights' had many manifestations developed by teachers from an initial example of practice (contained in the LHTL project materials available to all project schools). We will therefore return to this AfL strategy to explore what happens when it is documented in some way and becomes an 'object'.

One department (English) decided to adopt 'traffic lights' as a common classroom strategy, and, following some success, it was incorporated into the school's 'assessment handbook', which was rewritten to take account of the developing awareness of AfL issues and approaches. By the time the project team researchers visited the school, in the following term, the handbook had been distributed and staff had received further school-based professional development. As a result of this development, staff in departments which had not initially been 'research departments' taking part in the LHTL project had also adopted the 'traffic lights' strategy and were producing materials to support it, including posters and flashcards with smiling, indifferent and confused faces for use as part of classroom displays and for children to use.

The handbook and the flashcards themselves act as reifications of practice and are objects from which practice can be constructed. But how can the events that brought about their development, and the reports we collected through logs and research visits, be characterised? They were the LHTL project's tangible evidence of developing practice and teacher learning, and it is these transactions that we wished, first, to capture, and second, to encourage their production by teachers as part of the sharing process. Some of these transactions were concerned with classroom practice, as in the various 'versions' of the 'traffic lights' strategy. Others were concerned with broader organisational change as part of 'embedding' – for example, the idea of identifying 'research departments' in a school which take the lead in examining practice before disseminating their findings, and in this case producing a 'handbook'. In the context of an electronic environment, where we wanted to make practice available, the transaction with most impact and relevance for other schools would be not an uploaded version of the handbook but a posting describing how and why it came to be developed, together with a pointer to an online version of it. The handbook is interesting; the *idea* of producing a handbook even more so.

In the course of a project such as LHTL, a resource may be developed that is the 'artefact of certain practices [which] embodies a long and diverse process of . . . reification' (Wenger 1998: 55). Our concept of 'transaction objects' captures the idea that they are the means by which this 'long and diverse process' takes place. Our task within the project was to provide appropriate mechanisms to facilitate negotiation, collaboration and 'tinkering' (to use the term from Hargreaves [1999: 130]; he is quoting Huberman [1992]) not with resources but with the thinking of teachers as they developed their practice in response to project initiatives and their own professional priorities. The development of resources such as the 'assessment handbook' or the 'flashcards' described above was certainly to be encouraged, but more significant was the extent to which they were indicative of changes in practice, classroom and school culture. Whatever the prospects of electronic environments in providing the medium for sharing of practice, we feel it will be fruitful to think of the objects involved in sharing in terms of these transaction objects. The particular medium or type of resource is less relevant than the idea that it is an object to stimulate a transaction.

The argument in this chapter leads us to the conclusion that a *network* analysis of the creation of knowledge may not in fact be a distinctive analysis. How the innovation 'comes' to the school (e.g. through brokerage), who is involved in any process of working with that innovation (e.g. collaboration) and how it is subsequently shared within and outside the institution can be thought of as network processes. However, it may be false to see this overall process as a series of stages (as just delineated), as it is evident that they are interconnected; for example, attending a talk by a national speaker and then returning to the school with ideas to develop in school are not separate parts of the process. Similarly, working on some new practice as a group in a school is not independent of school climate and other organisational elements. Often, any development is part of a school strategy to embed the development in the institution. Subsequent sharing outside of the school might in many cases be disconnected from these earlier elements, unless of course the original impetus for the innovation came from an NLC. These processes are in need of research, which, as we indicated earlier, we will return to in Chapter 11.

Chapter 8

Networks in context

Spatial and temporal issues

Why space and time?

There have been several strands in the book that have indicated the importance of spatial and temporal dimensions in networks. Network theorists like Castells (2000a) contrast the 'space of flows' with the 'space of places' – the latter being replaced by the former through the role of new communications technologies (Chapter 2). Wellman (2001) made a similar argument for the change of the relevance of place in relation to views of community; moving from a 'door-to-door' community to a 'person-to-person' one, although his is not an argument for ignoring place, rather for its no longer being the dominant feature in social networks. Larsen *et al.*, who are concerned with mobilities (produced by transport and communications technology), argue that Wellman and 'small-world' theorists do not pay enough attention to where meetings take place and the travel to them:

> As societies are more spread out with connections at-a-distance and people are less likely to bump into their contacts, so scheduled visits and meetings are more significant . . . when people meet face-to-face this involves longer distance travel, especially as there is less likelihood of quick, casual meetings which occurred when work, family or friendship networks overlapped.
>
> (2006: 5)

They specifically examine meetings and their importance, concluding:

> [W]e showed that . . . meetings are significantly about establishing and maintaining networks, and indeed that places are increasingly about providing opportunities for meeting and networking. We also examined the possibilities of substituting various kinds of communications and virtual encounters for physical meetings. Overall we concluded that there are some possibilities here but many things get done within co-present meetings that mean they are here to stay for a good time yet.
>
> (ibid.: 56–7)

This seems to be so for teachers, as it was for the range of professionals that Larsen and his colleagues studied, as we indicated in Chapter 6 in referring to them as 'people people'. Indeed, when we considered links, we noted that physicality was a part of teachers' representations on maps, and that visits to other schools, conferences and other kinds of meetings were an important part of network relationships. All these face-to-face encounters were part of both weak and strong valued links.[1] In terms of relationships and networks, we were particularly concerned in Chapter 6 with the 'informal', considering this through affiliation and intensional networks and social contagion. We did not explore the physicality of where these kinds of relationships took place, though much of the evidence we presented from the LHTL data did mention locality, or at least employ it. Recall the affiliation network of Sam, the headteacher of Alder Primary School, who met with friends for football – clearly in different surroundings as compared with the formal meetings he also had with them, but, as he noted, with more productive discussions (see p. 140). An important part of attending meetings and conferences is not just the formal elements, as we noted in Chapter 6, and this adviser's view is a common one:

> I have to go to events and conferences in London where people are in a similar role to me and, although there's an agenda for the day, it's often the coffee break or the lunchtime which are informal [times] . . . sometimes I formalise it by saying to a particular individual, 'could we have ten minutes at lunchtime?' but even that's quite informal because it's organised at coffee time.
>
> (Roger Newland, LA co-ordinator, LHTL final interview)[2]

Note that the physicality is not only about location but also about time and, although we were aware of such issues, we did not initially develop ways of theorising or even talking about them as part of a network analysis. Our subsequent work has thrown some light on where informal transactions take place and on how they are seen in temporal terms, and in this chapter we will explore this work and some of the LHTL data of relevance.

Larsen *et al.* (2006) drew to some extent on the work of geographers such as Massey (1994), and it is in this tradition that much of the theorising has been developed. Such theorists add another dimension to the analysis of social relationships as the connections of social processes that we have discussed so far: 'It is not spatial form in itself (nor distance, nor movement) that has effects, but the spatial form of particular and specified social processes and social relationships' (Massey 1984: 5).

To better understand the significance of networking, some social scientists assert that the social and the spatial should be analysed together. A room commonly used for formal meetings might be only that – a set of walls, ceiling, floor and fixtures and fittings – until it is occupied. If the room is to be used informally, it might be arranged differently. Making the room meaningful will be related to people's activities in the space, which develop over time. In Wenger's terms, a group meeting in a room will have a history of participation that will relate to how they have experienced the room in a particular form of participation, which will affect what they do on any particular occasion.[3] They might associate meeting particular people in that room, adapt the seating in the room to facilitate interacting with others or use displays or materials to facilitate discussions or to allow for further interactions beyond the meeting time. The way the space is used needs to be understood, then, in terms of professional learning. McGregor (2004) draws on Massey's geographical perspective in considering teacher collaboration and has collected empirical evidence on spatial issues indicating that where people meet affects their social relationships as part of this collaboration.

An alternative theoretical approach that comes from socio-cultural views of learning expands the link between learning, space and social relations, including that between space and identity (Solomon *et al.* 2006). Solomon and her colleagues drew on the work of Nespor (1994), extending it not just to workplace learning spaces but also to the 'in-between' spaces associated with the workplace. These spaces included places where coffee and lunches were taken, the sharing of transport to and from work, and time spent around reprographics departments, which they investigated in the workplace of further education teachers. Solomon *et al.* (2006) were drawing on actor-network theory (ANT) and its concern with space-time relationships, networks and human and non-human relationships. This is a different link to network theories from that of Larsen *et al.* (2006). As we will show, these different theoretical perspectives give us a way of thinking about space and time in relation to network interactions. Before using these kinds of theories to bring greater clarity to a discussion of space and time, we want to examine the typical events described by the LA adviser Roger Newland, quoted above, who reflects many of our LHTL respondents when they talked about conferences and other places they went to for formal and informal events. We will do this through an examination of events such as conferences and one-day workshops.

Events

Despite academic work on teacher continuing professional development (Wilson and Berne 1999; Lawless and Pellegrino 2007; Bolam and Weindling 2006), events such as conferences rarely feature. One specific study of conferences (with a focus on ICT), acknowledges that '[p]rofessional conferences, both academic and non-academic, are an under-researched domain. Given their importance and frequency in the life of those who attend, it is remarkable that they have been the focus of so little study' (Jacobs and McFarlane 2005: 317). There is some research in areas other than education:

- Within healthcare, Festner (2006) argues that individuals need to be consciously aware of any knowledge created at such events or activities and make conscious decisions to transfer this practically into their workplace.
- Investigating farm managers, Kilpatrick (1998) recognises the importance of events in small business managers' learning 'networks', although her survey approach to examining farmers' networks did not investigate any details of the processes involved.

There are also evaluations of specific events, usually conducted by organisers (for a general account of the evaluation of continuing professional development (CPD), see Goodall *et al.* 2005). Because of this lack of research, we conducted some pilot research on events and conferences for both university academics and school leaders. We draw on this pilot work in this chapter, focusing mainly on the school leaders (Fox and McCormick 2009).[4]

Let us start by looking at the thinking of a London headteacher prior to an event, in this case a National College for School Leadership (NCSL) workshop on leadership development in London:

> I have heard of the speaker, John West-Burnham, and he is quite good. He presented at an NCSL faith schools event I was at. The topic is one I want to look

at and should be useful to me. For this type of event it will need a powerful speaker. I am very selective about the events I go to but like to go to NCSL events as I know they are coming in at the right level of expectation for me as a headteacher. I also know it will be an opportunity to meet other heads. As a head of an independent school[5] I can find myself quite isolated if I am not careful. . . . I hope to come out with something to do that will help me do something better or, at least, different in the future. I expect there will be opportunities to network and share on very practical aspects of how to do things. . . . I have no clue if there is going to be anyone there I know as, unlike some events I go to, it will just be attended by those to whom it appeals. You never know if you will know someone at these events but it is possible, as it is likely to have a range of London-based headteachers. . . . Other factors that affected my choice of attending were: the days I could go out of school [and] the travel issue, i.e. this is a local event and . . . it was not expensive, especially to hear such a well-known speaker. As a head, you need inspiration from somewhere and I thought that this would be a good chance to step back and ask, 'What am I like?'

(Headteacher, Leadership Development Workshop, interview pre-event)

The requirements of this head are for good formal sessions (which will inspire: important, as Chapter 5 indicated), a chance to reflect, an opportunity to network and that the event should meet practical requirements in terms of time, expense and travel. But how does the event location relate to her requirements? To examine this, we turn to the two venues we studied for school leaders, the NCSL purpose-built conference venue and a hotel the NCSL uses for its one-day events.

The NCSL Learning and Conference Centre

The centre is advertised as follows:

The NCSL Learning and Conference Centre was designed by award-winning architects Michael Hopkins and Partners. The centre offers conference and meeting facilities for up to 250 delegates, including 90 comfortable and modern bedrooms, 16 conference rooms, 15 syndicate rooms and conference room and hospitality services of a very high hotel standard. The centre also strives to act in the interest of conservation, with environmentally friendly equipment and procedures throughout. With its lakeside setting and landscaped surroundings, it truly provides a relaxing and inspirational environment.[6]

The building is constructed around two atria (Figure 8.1), each surrounded by seminar rooms with glass walls towards the inner open area, above which are accommodation rooms. The West atrium (shown in Figure 8.2) is used mainly for day events laid out with comfortable chairs around coffee tables, and planting and resource cases to divide up the space. This links directly into the surrounding rooms, which at the event shown were used for multiple presentations in parallel sessions. A lunch buffet is also served in this area. The other atrium (the Central atrium), where participants are greeted, has a bar. This is where evening sessions of events, and participants staying overnight, can meet. There is also a main lecture theatre and a high-quality restaurant. Figure 8.2

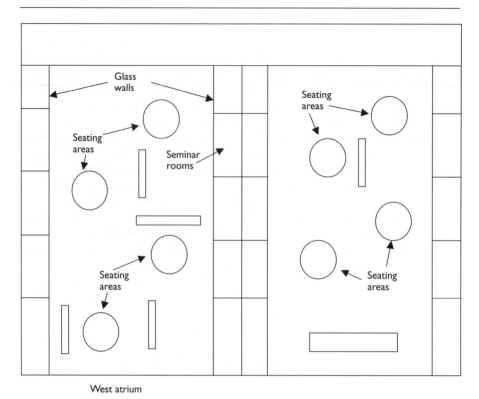

West atrium

Figure 8.1 Plan of the National College for School Leadership's 'Learning and Conference Centre'.

shows school leaders meeting up in the West atrium at the start of the event. Two of these leaders reflected on how this particular venue met their needs for this event and their previous use of the centre:

Headteacher 1:
We've always found the fact that you have central communal areas outside the workrooms, so you have a very open workroom environment with the glass walls, and then, whether it's being in a meeting or a training session, or today there could be the presentation sessions, actually coming out [from] all [of] those meetings to the Central atrium is really useful, because you walk out and walk straight into other people and you start the next set of conversations. So, I think the structure physically of the building allows that kind of process of short-term meetings and a focused piece of work.

Headteacher 2:
I also feel that the actual feeling of light and space, and the openness, it does generate a feeling of openness between people.
(Research Associate conference, March 2007)

These leaders were local to the event, from neighbouring schools, and explained how they met up as often as possible at events targeted at their leadership role. They had

Figure 8.2 School leaders meeting up at the start of a Research Associates event in the West atrium.

travelled independently, as they had not been specifically expecting to meet, but were grateful for the chance to catch up over a coffee and plan their participation at the conference together. (Providing lists of participants in advance, as is often done, would have allowed these leaders to arrange to share lifts to the event and hence prolong opportunities to interact.) They reported how the layout of the event allowed them to continue conversations with one another from formal to informal parts of the day. They referred to how the quality of the venue affected their attitude towards interacting with one another:

Headteacher 1:
We find that having a good-quality dinner together the night before, and there's a chap who works in the bar who actually looks after us very, very well, and he's always welcoming and has a huge impact on our general feeling of well-being and feeling valued, and to have a nice restaurant to go to, to have a nice place to come and stay, puts you in the right frame of mind for your own learning and the work we want to do.

Headteacher 2:
It is that being treated, being valued as a professional. I think the environment here, and the staff and people, like the bar manager, that make you feel valued as professionals, and that you're taking professional time to do a professional activity.
(Research Associate conference, March 2007)

It is evident that the place matters. In particular, it facilitates networking through participants knowing who is there, and by providing the ambience for informal communication and a sense of openness. The place also indicates that the participants are valued. One of these headteachers had even returned to his school and tried to model the atmosphere created for an internal staff development day. He gathered all the soft furnished chairs and coffee tables he could find in the school and arranged them informally in a space to encourage an environment of professional dialogue. He reported that he found this change in layout to be well received by his staff. Such a purpose-built facility as the NCSL uses is rare and it is more common to use hotels to reproduce a similar environment.

Hotels

Hotels (along with shopping malls) were decried by Castells (2000a) as non-places devoid of uniqueness and a sense of locality, implying that they do not offer opportunities to feel truly located somewhere. They do, however, provide locations for professional development. First, they offer participants an atmosphere of being valued by being offered comfort and a sense of luxury, which may improve the productiveness of the event:

> We didn't want [these conferences] to be at the [local] teachers' centre. We wanted them to be in a higher-level venue, somewhere that was nice, that people felt they were leaving their own environment.
>
> (Kate, school co-ordinator, Juniper Primary School, LHTL final interview)

This effect becomes a theme in conference venue advertising:

> **Ground-breaking** – boring business environments are so, well boring really. Good job we've put so much thought, design, love and flair into ours then. The result is simple – contemporary, vibrant and surprising eating, networking, partying and relaxation environments.[7]

The company concerned (etc.venues) explicitly offers conference organisers a purpose-built space in which to locate social and professional interactions (Figure 8.3):

> We only cater for business events and have set the venues up accordingly – from the way delegates arrive, to the way they are served their food, to the chairs they sit on, to the AV equipment that surrounds them, to the amount of natural daylight that illuminates their training room.

A second reason hotels support professional development is that they offer organisers a chance to badge the location to their ends, a response to the blandness Castells (2000a) so bemoans. Banners, marketing materials and poster boards can be brought in to market the event as belonging to a particular organiser, as shown in Figure 8.4. Here an organisational logo banner (at the back, by the table lamp) and related 'research briefings' for the Teaching and Learning Research Programme (in the foreground) are stationed around the entrance to the main lecture theatre (between the two wall mirrors).

Figure 8.3 The marketing slogan of etc.venues.

Figure 8.4 Badging of an educational conference in a hotel lobby area.

Finally, there are practical issues relating to travel, as this NCSL event organiser makes clear:

> Central location in London with good transport links. I have used them before and the staff are very professional and the venue space is ideal.
>> (Event organiser, Leadership Development Workshop, February 2007)

Hotels and conference centres usually offer good access and parking, which may be perceived to be high-priority requirements in supporting participants' decisions to attend, by minimising the stress of attending the day.

Other venues

The NCSL has introduced at several of its events the notion of what it terms networking cafés. These have been developed from work on café communities by Brown with Isaacs (2005) in their publication *The World Café: Shaping Our Futures through Conversations That Matter*. They adopted a café-like layout using white paper as tablecloths, which double as space to write ideas on and can then be used to collate ideas from all the groups. Advice is given to potential café organisers as to how to set up a café, with particular attention paid to its physical expression: 'Consider how your invitation and physical set-up contribute to creating a welcoming atmosphere. . . . When people feel comfortable to be themselves, they do their most creative thinking, speaking and listening' (World Café Community 2002: 2). This idea has also been developed by the NCSL at many of its networked learning communities' (NLCs) day conferences as 'learning conversation' or 'knowledge' cafés. Groups from each NLC are invited to host these, with a view to chatting informally around coffee tables about their experiences.

> There's going to be about ten or twelve knowledge cafés or knowledge exchanges . . . I think there's going to be coffee and it's very informal. There will be about ten or fifteen minutes for each one, and then . . . a bell won't go, but there'll be some kind of thing that says 'move on' and you move to another table.
>> (Kate, NLC co-leader, interview, May 2004)

In addition, we have evidence that other, perhaps more unusual, locations have been used for events.

> I think also in terms of key places, and this is an awful thing to say, but my house. We have the senior management team meet formally once a year at my house and then we might meet intermittently informally. But we meet because my house is big, it is near school, so we feel safe; if [we] take all the senior staff out we can get here very quickly if we need to in an emergency. . . . So for the school leadership away day we have aims and agenda, then we go out for dinner in the evening. We start early and finish early enough and we go out and have dinner. We also buy in a consultant who comes to my house and helps us get through the agenda and helps keep on task. We do that once a year. I have done it over the last three years.

So I suppose that it's quite a special case – it is a productive place, we don't have the interruptions that we would have if we were here [in school].

(Alexandra, headteacher, Gingko Primary School,
LHTL final interview)

Those who use and create spaces for events that are part of educational networks outline a range of issues. Yet the way this is articulated is relatively basic. The architect Fisher (2004) bemoans what he terms a lack of spatial literacy when talking about educational contexts. Although he cites many quantitative studies of the impact of educational architecture, he highlights a lack of qualitative work drawing on the perceptions of the practitioners and their students using educational-related spaces. We argue that researchers need to clarify the use of terms if we are to be able to attribute significance to what educational practitioners tell us about their use of space in relation to networks.

Space or place?

A review by Hubbard *et al.* (2004) charts an ongoing debate about the relationship between two terms that are often used interchangeably (e.g. by Solomon *et al.* 2006), namely 'space' and 'place'. Tuan's (1977: 6) explanation is a helpful starting point: 'the ideas space and place require each other for definition . . . what begins as undifferentiated space becomes place as we get to know it better and endow it with value'. Drawing on the work of Harvey (1985), the term *place* is reserved for those locations which have specific meanings for users, as opposed to *space*, which is these same locations and venues when they have no significance for those who have occupied or are occupying them. Harvey refers to space–place as a general–particular dialectic. Places can be described because, having social meaning, their particularities as distinctive and unique can be outlined. This description will need to show how they interconnect and are interdependent on other places, through the activities of those for whom they have meaning. In a general sense, all places therefore occupy space. Space is a general category and places are particular spaces. The respondents in the LHTL project cited professional areas, such as staffrooms and classrooms, in which relationships develop and knowledge exchange is facilitated, along with locations in which they might meet colleagues from other schools, such as at a teacher development centre. This view of space and place sees the two as distinct. However, Massey (1994) suggests that there is a continuum from yet-to-be-defined spaces to intimately associated places. She talks about there being a balancing between defensive and enclosing (negative) views of space, through to progressive and outward-looking (positive) views of place. Spaces (and places) have a degree of spatiality reflecting their degree of relatedness, to which she attributes value.[8] By conflating the ideas of Massey and Harvey, *spaces* can be viewed as 'bad', non-meaningful or non-places (a term used by Castells [2000a] and Augé [1995]), while *places* are 'good', meaning-rich and key. Castells (2000a), for example, cited shopping malls, hotels and airports as generic, delocalised spaces or non-places. We have seen, from the discussion of the use of hotels and generic conference venues earlier in this chapter, how they might provide a relaxing and encouraging location that, if badged and tailored, has the potential to provide meaningful, if ephemeral, learning environments. Crang (2002), too, has reinterpreted hotels as being potentially highly meaningful and emotionally charged places to their users. For such users the spaces offered by a hotel might therefore be reconceptualised as 'place'.

We show in particular how applying more specific terminology can expose how the same location can have multiple meanings to different users, and enable us to explore the visibility and neutrality of locations.

Multiple perceptions of space and places

Given that places have social meanings, we expect people to have personal and therefore differing views of the same space, because of their different experiences of it. There are therefore multiple interpretations of space (Harvey 1990; Rose 1996). We explore these interpretations of spaces within UK schools, using the research of McGregor (2003, 2004) and some of our work with beginning teachers. First we consider competing areas for teachers to meet between classes, the staffroom or a departmental room, and then consider the use of space within the staffroom.

The socio-spatial use of school departments versus staffrooms

McGregor (2004) revealed the significance of departmental locations in schools (e.g. the science preparation room). She collected data from maps drawn to represent the spaces in schools by members of staff, integrated with data from surveys and interviews. Staff were able to articulate how schools had reacted in spatial ways to reflect changes in school ethos. For example, staff in one UK comprehensive school (Kingbourn School) reported that initially the implications of trying to develop a whole-school ethos in which cross-curricular relationships were prioritised were shown through staff being discouraged from staying within departments when not teaching. Instead, the staff were encouraged to work and interact in cross-curricular research groups aimed at building whole-school collegiality. The staffroom was therefore remodelled to include both break and work areas in which they were encouraged to spend time and work. The intention was to make these areas meaningful places and times for teachers, bringing them together from across the building. Teachers in the school reported that, ironically, one of the outcomes from working groups was the consensus to develop *departmental* collaborative cultures to enhance teacher learning. The change in culture in fact led to more informal departmental social interaction, within departmental locations, rather than interdepartmental collaboration. The impact of the change in culture outlined at Kingbourn School was recognised by the school's leadership and, having created work spaces in the staffroom, they then developed departmental work spaces to facilitate the new emphasis on departmental 'community' building:

> We gradually eased up a little and developed, not social areas for staff, but work areas for staff where they could be social, where they didn't have to come across here [the staffroom] at break time or lunchtime and work.
>
> (Bursar, Kingbourn School; quoted in McGregor 2003: 361)

This school's experiences reflect the work of Lima (2007) on the advantages of departments being attached, yet separate from the school as a whole – what he terms being loosely coupled. Both cross-curricular and the distinctive departmental relations in a school are valued. Lima (ibid.) recommends that the social networks of departments (i.e. the internal network), and their relationship with the wider inter-school network, be mapped to consider the potential for effective spread of school improvement initiatives. The leadership in schools like Kingbourn then have to work with their staff on the use spaces for work and rest between teaching periods.

A study of seventeen beginning science teachers in comprehensive schools in East Anglia (England) investigated teacher perceptions of workplaces in terms of support (Fox and Wilson 2009; Fox et al. 2010[9]). It revealed how interpersonal tensions within departments had implications for the use of space in the school. One student teacher's mentor (i.e. the person from the school working with the trainee) did not use the departmental staffroom (the 'prep' room), therefore not valuing it as a work and social space in the same way as other science staff:

> My mentor doesn't really come up to the prep[aration] room much except to gather resources, and yet you can see that [it] is the place where people gather. He has his classroom, which is also his form room,[10] and he spends his time pretty much all the time there. . . . I tend to be in the [science] prep room when I am off duty and, in my study periods, that is where I would go. I go to his [teaching] room . . . in the morning and don't tend to see him during the day unless he is in the lessons, but then I do tend to see the technicians, who are in the [prep room] a lot, and the other teachers when they are not teaching.
>
> (Harry, student teacher, school M, second-term interview)

The mentor's perceptions of particular places in the school, in using some rooms rather than others, had implications for this student concerning where to spend his time. Rather than following the behaviour of the mentor and staying near the room in which he taught, this student teacher found that his mentor's room and the science preparation room were both meaningful places to him. He explained that being in the science preparation room gave him opportunities to develop relationships with staff in a way that he might not have done if his mentor had also been there. A student in another school identified a similar difference in opinion as to where to spend time as a science teacher. She noted that the departmental room was avoided by some staff and she developed relationships with some science staff in other areas of the school:

> I didn't find [name of teacher] for a long time as he has his own office . . . he is a chemist [like me] . . . but he doesn't go into the science area, he sticks to the main staffroom. . . . [Also, another supply teacher] says she doesn't teach science here any more because of the tensions in the science staffroom.
>
> (Dawn, student teacher, school C, second-term interview)

This student teacher again tried to balance her time in the departmental area and the main staffroom, from which she developed several cross-curricular relationships, as well as relationships with her fellow science colleagues. It is evident that network links within a school will be manifest differently depending on the meaning attributed to where they are made. Indeed, it may be that the place frames the kinds of relationships made in different spaces in a school.

Given the quotation from Massey (1994) in the first section of the chapter, we would interpret the above research as being culturally specific. For example, schools in the Far East have staffrooms that are more like work rooms than places for relaxation. Indeed, it is likely that even in other subject or sector cultures within UK institutions the observations recorded here could be different.

Perceptions of the socio-spatial use of staffrooms

How areas such as departmental or school staffrooms are perceived affects the potential to encourage particular models of use. In a study of different workplaces in Australia, Solomon *et al.* (2006) detected an ambivalence in naming such spaces as meaningful places for learning. While some of the trade teachers in their study were happy to regard lunchtime in the tearoom as a place and time for informal learning, others were resistant to this, and Solomon and her colleagues comment on this: 'It appeared that the teacher regarded the naming of the lunchroom as a learning space as transgressive. He could admit that learning occurred, but to formally acknowledge it as a learning space was to intrude into a protected environment' (ibid.: 9). These teachers were resistant to the term 'learning' being applied by the researchers to their use of these places and times. This shows different perceptions of what is taking place in such areas, regardless of the intentions and interpretations of others. This private and protected notion of a staffroom as a *back space* (Tuan 1977; and see also McGregor 2000, 2003) allows teachers to talk and interact in such a way that they

> can recover their autonomy which is often compromised in the frontal contexts of the classroom. Resistance and protection of personal and professional identity may be played out through sharing anecdotes and joking as teachers relax together. . . . The staffroom is thus also a 'front region' for individuals wishing to impress their peers or mentors by playing out performances internal to the organisation and cultures of the school.
>
> (McGregor 2000: 7)

McGregor redefines areas in some schools as 'front spaces' in terms of their importance for inter-teacher relationships. However, this is not a generic definition, and in other schools the staffroom was not perceived as such a key place. The title of McGregor's paper (2000), 'The staffroom is the most underused room in the school', is a quotation from one member of staff about one of the schools in her study, illustrating the lack of meaning attached to the room. Paechter (2004) and McGregor (2003) both identified different sub-groups of teachers within staffrooms where some departmental groups were not represented, these staff choosing to use departmental areas or individual classrooms. We have seen how science staff and student teachers have to make practical decisions on their use of departmental and other school space, but student teachers also have a further dilemma: having an identity as a student teacher set within a department, but also often being one of a number of students located across a school. In Fox *et al.*'s (2010) study of student science teachers, all schools had a professional tutor allocated to liaise with the students and to organise a regular programme of cross-curricular professional studies sessions. In some schools this central leadership resulted in student teachers having rich cross-school networks.

When asked about how this had developed, the mentor of student science teacher Frank explained that the significance of spatial organisation within the staffroom had been critical:

> I think that it might be down to the fact that there is a dedicated area for them in the staffroom, and the professional tutor puts on tea, coffee and muffins for them. I think that there is a strong incentive on their part to be there and therefore they are networking when they are there. If there wasn't that space and things weren't being laid on, then I think they would be looking elsewhere and they might be far more in the prep[aration] room and in the department. . . . I don't know whether in fact it was an intentional action by the professional tutor as I think this arose because staff were complaining that they could not get a cup of tea at break times as there are a large number of staff to get through, and we have had up to twenty-plus trainees, and so to add these to the coffee queue people can get a bit irate. So she came up with the idea that they could create an area and lay some things on and that eased things for [our teaching] staff. I think that the unintentional outcome of that is that they meet quite regularly as a group.
>
> (Mentor of student teacher Frank, school E, first-term interview)[11]

As with off-site professional development spaces at events, etc., these within-school examples show how the perceptions of spaces as being meaningful places are influenced by individuals' perceptions, whether they be the leadership who assign the spaces or the staff who use them. Who is present, when and what interaction results are all related to the place. There are implications for schools that want to encourage relationships as well as for researchers who want to understand them.

The visibility of places

The earlier discussion of 'back spaces' and 'in-between spaces' suggests that there are likely to be a range of such spaces both within schools (on which the earlier discussion focused) and at events outside. This gives another dimension to the 'informality' in teacher learning, which we associated with networking. Solomon *et al.* (2006) reflected that the very banality of what respondents spoke about, which almost excluded these data from any analysis, gave it its importance. The following quotation from a deputy headteacher reveals the pressures on her to use time and space productively and 'formally':

> Informal meetings tend to be sparky, fun, there's a personal, emotional element in them, they are a release from what you think you ought to be doing. They feel a bit illicit. . . . They feel a bit naughty. I should be in a meeting now or I should be doing paperwork but I'm not. I'm having a giggle with [name of teacher] about a lesson that I've just taught. They feel a bit silly talking about teaching and learning but in a very anecdotal, silly, informal way. But out of that often comes 'oh, could I come and see that lesson next week?' or maybe 'we should revise that scheme of work and build this into it'.
>
> (Angela, deputy headteacher, Redwood High School, LHTL final interview)

Because of their everyday nature and the reluctance either to recognise spaces as being for learning (as in the case of the trade teachers reported by Solomon and her colleagues) or to admit to 'informal' interactions as above, it is important to recognise such times and places. Solomon *et al.* (ibid.: 7) categorise these in-between spaces:[12]

- overlap periods (e.g. refreshment breaks);
- actual spaces, usually labelled as either work or not (e.g. classroom or staffroom);
- talking spaces (e.g. the car on the way to work).

Angela, in the quotation above, indicates the overlap periods between 'work' and 'play', which may be defined by time. Actual spaces we have already discussed in terms of how staffrooms and science preparation rooms were used. Opportunistic 'catching' of people in the corridor merges the first two categories in terms of time and space. The talking spaces can be regular (journeys to school or cigarette breaks outside) or intermittent (journeys to meetings or events outside school). These hybrid spaces need to be recognised and investigated for their potential for teacher learning. We have already noted that the business world recognises meaningful places. For example, the Business Network International (Misner and Morgan 2000) and the Women's Business Network (2003) advocate using a range of venues for networking. Misner *et al.*, in their populist book *Truth or Delusion?*, advocate that '[t]here is no place that's inappropriate for networking' (2006: 84). All spaces should be considered as meaningful work*places*. The United Kingdom's Campaign for Learning (Lucas 1997) reported that a wide range of sites, which Lucas terms 'spaces for learning', should be valued. These equate with social sites in which informal and formal learning can take place through networking with others (see Table 8.1). Those sites represented on network maps by respondents during the LHTL project as places for networking are indicated in bold. Solomon *et al.* (2006) noted that local cafés were among the unexpected off-site meaningful places revealed by their research. The LHTL respondents referred to restaurants, pubs and cafés as places where leaders might meet up to have partly social but partly work-based meetings. The co-leaders of an 'assessment for learning' NLC network in an LA (who included advisers and teachers) met first in a particular pub and then, after changes in co-leadership, in a café or restaurant:

> Sally [the other co-leader] and I seem to hold our planning meetings in the pub. . . . We meet at least every two weeks, I would say. And sometimes Johnny [the LA critical friend to network] joins us. . . . We have a couple of hours where we sit and we just thrash out ideas. It's quite relaxing as well in that sort of environment.
>
> (Kate, school co-ordinator, LHTL final interview)

> We still meet socially, though – the original group of Kate, Wendy, Johnny and I. I know this sounds naff but we call ourselves the Champagne for Learning group and are actually meeting for dinner tonight as it happens.
>
> (Sally, former NLC co-leader and now headteacher, interview, January 2009)

Thus, the informality of this affiliation network has been established through its place and time of meeting. (We will put this in context in the Pluto case study in Chapter 9.)

Table 8.1 Spaces for learning

Obvious	Less obvious	Surprising
Pre-school groups	Businesses	Old people's homes
Nurseries	Community centres	Homeless shelters
Schools	Sports centres	Sheltered housing
Colleges	Arts centres	Refuges
Universities	Museums and attractions	Prisons
Adult learners' centres	Health centres	Shopping malls/supermarkets
Homes	Post offices	Hospitals
Libraries	Cities	Churches
Television	Towns	Surgeries
	Villages	Trains and stations
	The internet	Football stadia
	Nature reserves	Bookshops
	The outdoors	**Pubs**
	Newspapers	**Hotels**
		Restaurants and cafés
		Private houses

Source: Adapted from Lucas (1997: 5).

Note: Pubs ('public houses' – bars), hotels, restaurants, cafés and private houses, when used for professional purposes, have been added to the list.

Within organisations, these informal and hybrid (personal and professional) places might be around photocopiers, smoking areas, water coolers or even on the way to and from these places:

> There's informal lunchtime meetings, at the photocopier of course. Those things happen. I had a meeting yesterday with a deputy head from another school in [our LA] . . . we hadn't set an agenda, we just kind of wanted to . . . talk about the things that we do and if there were any areas that are black, let's just kick it about a bit. It was fantastic; we spent about fifty minutes just talking about odd jobs and what we do and our history and how we got where we were now, and then for the final forty minutes we started actually focusing in on areas as to where we thought we might be able to work together. That was just brilliant; it was one of the best meetings I ever had.
>
> (Angela, deputy headteacher, Redwood High School, LHTL final interview)

> We have found that I'll have been doing a bit of photocopying and found [one of my team] is sitting at his desk or is coming in to photocopy after me and then we will maybe say, 'Has anybody got time for a cup of tea?' and we will just sit down, the two of us, where we are – at the photocopier or at somebody's desk.
>
> (Eileen Laws, LA adviser, LHTL final interview)

The hybrid space, 'talking spaces' (Solomon *et al.* 2006), are between-time, transitionary places, examples of which are key times and places for learning:

> There is one PGCE student within school who lives near me so I give [her] a lift into school every morning . . . when we did the role-play I did that because she is [teaching] history so I had talked to her about that.
>
> (Dawn, student teacher, second-term interview)

> [My colleague in the department] doesn't drive so I've been giving him lifts into work for seven years now, which is quite a long time. We're similar sort of ages, similar sort of stages in our careers in some respects, although very different people, and got very different career aspirations. . . . Sometimes it's quite useful, talking about the future in teaching whatever it happens to be, for example training teachers. He mentors [trainee teachers] too. We just bounce ideas off on how that's going.
>
> (Philip, middle leader, initial interview)[13]

The significance of this time was also noted when unavailable, for example in this extract from a student teacher who felt somewhat excluded:

> A whole load of them car-share and are city based, and I suppose they get time to chat together each day. I am the separate one. I guess they don't feel the same need to speak to other students each day.
>
> (Harry, student teacher, second-term interview)

There is a great variety of these 'in-between' places, depending upon the type of the educational institution, its physical layout and the local traditions of use of space and time. They represent a rich vein to research informal learning through the interactions that occur in them. If meaning is ascribed by the people who use them, rather than being designated by any external labelling, then it is important that users' perceptions are taken into account.

Neutrality

Building on the work of Nespor (1994), Solomon *et al.* (2006) recognise in their discussion of hybrid spaces that they are not neutral spaces where professional identities and hierarchies are erased, but rather places that exhibit some expression of power relations among staff. The trade teachers reluctant to attribute learning to their lunchroom might be trying to protect their attempts to talk in a way that would not be possible in more formal interactions and spaces. Solomon and colleagues explain that 'in-betweenness' is something users might seek to protect. Gilchrist (2004) draws parallels between networking practices as an ecological necessity for biodiversity, arguing that instead of thinking of places as being good or bad, social diversity and contradictory views should be encouraged to guarantee an enriched society. She develops this by suggesting that neutral spaces need to be provided for social inter-action: 'For diversity to flourish, communities need neutral community spaces, which are neither private nor public' (ibid.: 93).

Schuler (1996) argues for the provision of what he terms 'third places'. These are described as having a playful, convivial atmosphere, where conversation is the main activity. Such places should be accessible and accommodating to different people, where they feel themselves to be neither guests nor hosts but, rather, users who engage with others as they choose. This would allow users to interact according to their own agendas and respond spontaneously to the opportunities afforded for interaction. Gilchrist and Schuler talk of looking for neutrality in the interactions that take place in these sites. Such neutrality might also facilitate equality of exchange or interaction.

Neutrality was in the minds of NLC meeting organisers interviewed in the LHTL project, when they were deciding where to host meetings. While it would have been easier, practically, to host meetings in the co-leaders' own schools, they were conscious of how this might affect the engagement of other schools, as the LA co-ordinator indicated:

> We were conscious that we've got to be careful here because people may see those schools [where meetings are arranged] as being the ones with all the answers, so we've returned it back to here [the teachers' centre] to try and create more of a neutral base for it. But the other danger we have is that some people also associate this building with 'this is the place where I come and I receive input'.
>
> (Johnny Stanton, LA co-ordinator, LHTL final interview)

Even using the teachers' centre could bias the expectations, and therefore the behaviours of participants attending, because of previous experiences. Hybrid spaces away from the immediate workplace can be reconceptualised by those using them to break down within-work barriers that reflect workplace hierarchies. Using pubs and cafés as meeting places enables interactions to take place in a non-hierarchical way. Hotels, too, in the way that they give a feeling of being on holiday rather than being at work, can encourage relaxation of normal barriers to relationships. Users might feel empowered to interact with one another if they see hotels as neutral sites where no one is on their home territory. Planning the use of spaces might need to be a communal activity on the part of all those who meet. Schuler (1996) argues that all intended participants should have shared ownership of the decisions that surround an event and that all advertising and promotion of the event should be inclusive. The potential for achieving such neutrality and any benefits warrants further research.

By way of a summary of some of the ideas on space and time dealt with in this chapter, we tabulate the key terms, ideas and the authors upon whom we have drawn (Table 8.2, overleaf).

Conceptualising space-time trajectories

We have noted a number of times the problem with network analyses that are inevitably limited by the static view that they give of interactions and the associated processes. This is particularly relevant when we view networks from the point of view of teacher learning. Wenger (1998) sees people as being on learning trajectories, participating more or less with others as part of communities of practice. At any one time, and in any particular place, learning is contextually situated, and hence interactions are given meaning by what a person brings to them, in terms of their history of participation, and where they are heading. These trajectories are the formation of identity, and what an individual seeks to be will determine how they frame their interactions. The events considered earlier in the chapter, and the examples of the formal and informal processes

Table 8.2 Key terms and ideas relating to space and place

Key term	Author	Key ideas
Space	Harvey (1985)	Generic locations in which places are situated
Back and front spaces	Tuan (1977) McGregor (2000)	Spaces distinguished in terms of their visibility and public access
In-between or hybrid space	Solomon *et al.* (2006)	Sites of social (personal) and professional interaction that are between usual sites of work
Place	Massey (1994)	Location which has become meaningful to users and who interact positively with it
	Harvey (1985)	Unique conjunction of social and physical that distinguish one locality from another, which can be viewed as similar within a common economic framework
Neutral place	Gilchrist (2004)	A neutral location, which is considered/ judged to be neither private nor public
Third place	Schuler (1996)	An alternative social location, in which users are equally perceived as neither hosts nor guests
Non-place	Castells (2000a) Augé (1995)	Indeterminate locations in which time and space are collapsed and could be anywhere

Note: Not all authors recognise the 'space–place' distinction.

operating within them, are discrete times and places set within a longer learning trajectory for each participating individual. The event set within the learning trajectory of each individual, we termed an 'event within the life' (Fox and McCormick 2009: 203). This creates possibilities for there to be trajectories (or lives) nested within the event itself. These ideas are represented in Figure 8.5. Wenger reminds us that these events within lives need to be studied with reference to both prior concerns and impact post-event. This was done for two school leaders who were followed from one month prior to, to three months after, the events under focus (Fox and McCormick 2009). This allowed us to collect reflections on the impacts (or not) of events with respect to any (or all) of four dimensions: knowledge and understanding, personal networks, identity and role (see Figure 8.5). We are conscious that further work needs to be done to expand the scale of such a study to put the evidence from these two leaders' experiences into a wider perspective, but it provides a useful starting point.

The tentative findings on each of the dimensions in Figure 8.5 were fourfold. First, when asked about their learning from the event, participants often made reference to the strategies they used to retain knowledge, for example their use of event materials. Respondents revealed dissatisfaction with their strategies, raising fundamental issues about the reification of new knowledge and understanding (e.g. in notes), particularly in relation to the impact of an event in the workplace. New understandings had to be articulated and made conscious, as Festner (2006) recognised.

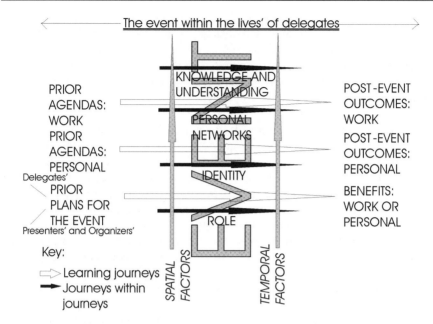

Figure 8.5 An emerging model of the role of events within professional lives.

Source: Adapted from Fox and McCormick (2009: 203).

Second, evidence of changes to personal networks was by far the most common finding. Respondents mentioned that networking with colleagues informally, and having a chance to interact with presenters during formal sessions, were worthwhile activities at events. Two headteachers who had come as part of a collaborative, yet geographically dispersed, group valued the range of contacts:

> Headteacher 1:
> There are colleagues who we have previously met and previously worked with . . . [and] those that we haven't. Because you have developed a network of people with whom you can establish contact today and keep that contact going. And also other delegates that we haven't come across before, who happen to be in the same session and asked a question that was reasonably interesting to follow up afterwards . . .

> Headteacher 2:
> And I think that's why it's really useful to have a delegate list so you can see where people are from and what their perspectives are.
> (Research Associates event; quoted in Fox and McCormick 2009: 209)

There were contrasting views expressed about preferences for either coming alone or with colleagues, because of the different impacts on meeting new people rather than developing existing relationships.

Third, in relation to changes in identity, it was noted that such changes can occur both during the event and in the longer term. This is more difficult to research, and our evidence in relation to school leaders indicates cases of multiple agendas, in particular between personal and work-related identities – a source of tension. The following reflection, made two weeks after an event, alludes to discomfort associated with boundaries between personal and professional identity. An activity at the event (referred to as a 'course') required participants to share with another delegate something personal:

> I said to [one delegate], 'my granddaughter' and she said, 'mine too'. I know that it sounds silly but actually that was quite a good example of me entering into my personal side a bit, because I'd never have said that before, but I felt that the course gave me permission. . . . It took something like that [event], to hear inspiring words . . . people really delved into their personal there. So actually it was interesting that the things that sustain you are the things from your personal life and it made me realise all the more, I mean I've always thought that you know, but . . . I think you have to have come from a background where you had a certain amount of input; whether it's love, caring, whatever, I just feel that you have to have something to give to others.
>
> (Headteacher, Leadership Development Workshop, interview post-event)

This headteacher found that those whom she took to personally during these interactions were those with whom she then wanted to discuss professional issues.

Fourth, we collected evidence in terms of changes in perception of role. A delegate's school role influenced the experience of an event, as this deputy head noted:

> The speakers really didn't do it for me . . . I didn't relate to their experiences, and this was funny because [my headteacher] particularly liked the first one, because he related to that. It was about the first day in as the new headteacher, and I haven't done that.
>
> (Deputy headteacher, Leadership Development Workshop, interview during event; quoted in Fox and McCormick 2009: 211)

He went on to say that, while the event was still relevant, he could not bring direct experience to some aspects of what was covered. However, by the end of the event he had started to see himself as an aspiring headteacher. In this particular case an impact of attending the event was a development of his identity, related to his role.

Space and time in understanding networking activity

This chapter presents novel and exploratory work into ways of applying notions of space and time to gain a richer understanding of their impact on teacher learning through networking activity. The language of spatiality clarifies the language and concepts to create analytic categories for viewing spaces. It is possible to gather evidence that a location is a valued and meaningful place for interactions. Searching for and identifying such places, whether through mapping exercises or through interviews, allows the informal hidden places to be revealed and their value recognised. This may overturn notions that such activity is not as valid or as respectable as other, more formal activity, such as meetings or briefings. Some authors in this area go further and challenge those charged with facilitating and supporting networking to consider ways of confronting power relations in spaces. They offer the potential of locations to become neutral places in which networking can facilitate interactions on a more egalitarian basis – a common aim in professional learning communities and the teacher networks examined in Chapter 1. It is, however, appropriate to offer a note of caution. Solomon *et al.* (2006) reported the resistance of their respondents to seeing their non-work places as sites for learning. Any attempt to research this could be seen as a threat to respondents' rights to separate work and relaxation in the working day. Of more concern would be the use of research information about places as a means to change the way these places are used without the agreement of all concerned. Even where the researcher has no specific agenda to change the use of space, any reporting, even in anonymised case studies, could reveal perceptions that ordinary teachers in a school would prefer their leadership not to know.[14]

In terms of considering the temporal nature of networking activity, more research is clearly needed. This can be conducted through following individuals in their experience of events, or by looking at the entire social activity during particular events (see Fox and McCormick [2009] for details). Some of the ideas in this chapter will be evident in the case studies in Chapter 9.

Chapter 9

Case studies

This chapter has two case studies situated within one local authority (Pluto), which had several sub-networks within a networked learning community (NLC). The first case study within this NLC is effectively three nested studies illustrating: leadership of a sub-network of the NLC, which focused on assessment for learning (AfL); co-ordination of a school's AfL development; and the development of an individual, Sally, through these two roles. The second case study, of a school within this sub-network, focuses in particular on the different network activities of the headteacher and the LHTL school co-ordinator. These studies give us a view of an NLC 'from the top' and 'from the bottom'.

Sally and the Pluto AfL networked learning community

Background

This case study is about a National College for School Leadership (NCSL) networked learning community in what we have called the Pluto local authority (LA), within which four schools were part of the LHTL project. The authority-wide NLC was set up in 2002 at the same time as the fieldwork for the LHTL project began. This is a study of a sub-network within the LA that, at its largest, involved thirty schools and focused on sharing and supporting the development of AfL practices. We focus on a key participant, Sally, between 2002 and 2006, together with reflections in 2009. Sally joined the LA as a deputy headteacher in Hawthorn High School, which was part of both the AfL network and the LHTL project. This account is based on evidence drawn from a number of LHTL respondents, in addition to Sally herself.

In 2002, Pluto LA applied to the NCSL to form an authority-wide NLC comprising a number of sub-networks, each working on developing and sharing practice on a particular theme. Each sub-network was co-led by two representatives from schools signed up to that network, in conjunction with a critical friend allocated from the LA's advisory staff and, where possible, a link to a higher education institution (HEI). In 2002, Johnny Stanton, the deputy director of the LA, represented the relationships between schools, LA staff and external institutions in a network map (see Figure 9.1).

Central to this representation is an area marked 'LEA learning' (associated with 'Wendy'), which Johnny described as being supported by three toolkits:

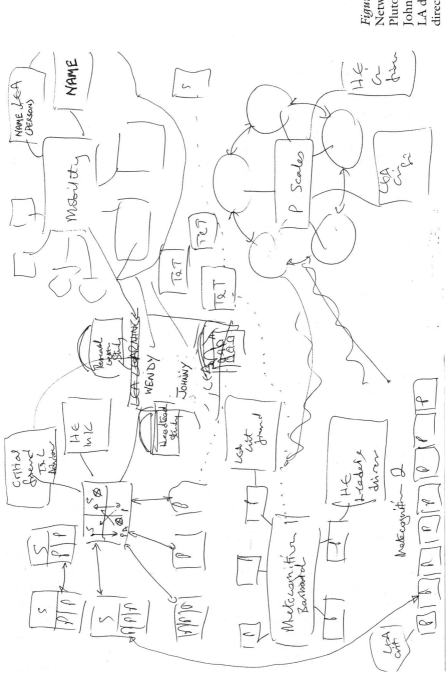

Figure 9.1
Network map of Pluto NLC by Johnny Stanton, LA deputy director.

1   'headteacher study', a steering group of headteachers across the LA;
2   'research lesson study', a programme of teachers researching their lessons in pairs, developed by Johnny in conjunction with the NCSL;
3   the Teacher Development Centre (represented diagrammatically below 'LEA learning'), housing the advisers and development activity.

The deputy director together with a senior adviser, Wendy Dix, co-led this network activity from within the LA.

The AfL sub-network is represented in the top left-hand corner of Figure 9.1 and was to become the largest in the LA. A large number of LA schools expressed an interest in joining the LHTL project and it was decided to use the AfL network to act as a mechanism to spread the impact of the work of the four selected schools. These four 'project' schools (indicated at the core of the AfL sub-network on Figure 9.1) were two secondary schools (Hawthorn High and Redwood High) and two primary (Deodar and Juniper). The co-leaders of the AfL sub-network were drawn from these schools. At the outset they were Brian (headteacher, Hawthorn High) and Kate (middle leader, Juniper Primary), working with Roger Newland (LA adviser) as 'critical friend and teaching and learning adviser'. Sally explains her understanding of the rationale for the selection of the schools as relating to perceptions that they were already central to a web of inter-school relationships:

> I think the reason that those four schools became LHTL research schools was because they were already linked in a number of ways. The two secondaries were both Specialist and Leading Edge schools,[1] and that makes them a family of schools, so our networks were already going on there. In that family of schools are [primary] schools that both feed into us, so we had cross-phase connections, which is why we'd been meeting on transition issues. . . . I remember [the researcher] coming in and making us draw these maps, and there were links all over the place.

> (Sally, NLC co-leader, presentation to
> LHTL teachers' conference, March 2005)

Sally was appointed in the autumn of 2002 to work alongside two other deputy heads, including Callum, who at that time was the LHTL school co-ordinator. In 2003, Callum left the school, and responsibility for developing AfL was reallocated to Sally. She acted as both school co-ordinator and co-leader of the AfL sub-network:

> I was asked to take over as the AfL project co-ordinator in the school and the reason for that was because I'm the deputy headteacher here with responsibility for Key Stage 3 and the head felt that the work that I was doing under the Key Stage 3 strategy and the work with transition [primary to secondary] dovetailed quite well with the AfL work. At the same time, he asked me to take on the role of co-leader of the network in the borough [LA]. . . . I already work with Kate, who's the other co-leader . . . on transition and we've worked together on a bridging project that we've designed.

> (Sally, NLC co-leader, interview, June 2003)

Up until this point, Sally had been working alongside other class teachers in one of six departments actively developing AfL practices within the school. Her map of the school's network, drawn in April 2003 as she took over both inward- (project co-ordination) and outward-looking (sub-network co-leadership) roles for AfL development, represents both internal and external links (Figure 9.2). The NLC is not indicated as an entity; rather, her links are to specific people, groups and organisations.

Sally and the AfL network's development

Co-leadership

Sally became a co-leader of the AfL sub-network while the network was still evolving. No advice was available on how best to proceed, and Sally, Kate and their adviser, Roger Newland, turned to one another:

> We actually began with, I suppose if you went to KwikFit[2] they'd call it a mission statement. It was really our own view of what we wanted to achieve. I think the important thing at the heart of this was always the risk taking, the fact that it wasn't something that we felt was going to be prescriptive. We were hoping that teachers were going to go away and take risks, try things out and that would enable us to help the process of sharing things that worked and that didn't work.
>
> (Kate, NLC co-leader, presentation to
> LHTL teachers' conference, March 2005)

Kate reported that Sally joining the team was significant for the direction and pace of change in the AfL network:

> I would add Sally now to the AfL network [on my map] as she wasn't a co-leader when I first met you.[3] That relationship has been probably . . . the most significant change in the network. [That link with Sally] is incredibly strong. It's almost like a case that, as soon as we worked as a team, the whole structure of the network changed. The whole impetus of the network changed.
>
> (Kate, NLC co-leader, interview, March 2004)

Reflecting on why this team with Sally became so successful, Kate pointed to an alignment of beliefs and a commitment that led to their friendship – a personal element in their network links. The relationship with Roger also became a strong one. As we shall show later, these relationships become enduring.

> We've got a particular quality of relationship. We've just been incredibly lucky, in that we've got three people (myself, Sally and Roger) who are all prepared to go beyond what we would normally do. So it's their time, commitment and personality. We laugh all the time, which helps. . . . It's about people who are committed to change, I think.
>
> (Kate, NLC co-leader, interview, March 2004)

What I'm particularly struck by is there's something in the quality of the relationships, something about the enthusiasm of the people involved that makes

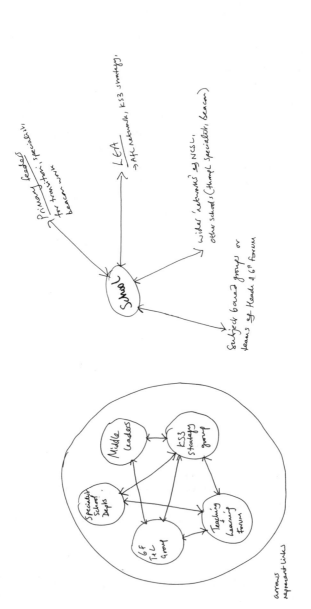

← → way communication works

Primary feeder, specialist,
for transition, beacon work

LEA
→ AFL networks, KS3 strategy.

Wider 'networks' eg NCSL,
other schools (through specialist, beacon)

Subject based groups or
teams eg Heads of 6th Forum

School

this is within HHS — If I
had drawn a bigger circle these
I would have fitted it in. I'm saying
these are networks in & out of the school

arrows
represent links

Specialist
School
Depts

Middle
Leaders

KS3
Strategy
group

6F
TcL
group

Teaching
+
Learning
Forum

Figure 9.2
Sally's initial network map of
Hawthorn High School.

me and others want to respond. . . . I was struck by the fact that when I got the pupil conference video and DVD that Hawthorn High school IT department had made, I actually wanted to go and look at it at home and then spent an hour and a bit on the computer typing up my thoughts. . . . It was an egg of an idea that Sally and Kate developed fantastically so I had a passion and interest in it anyway, but also it's something to do with the quality of the relationships with the other co-leaders and us pushing each other.

(Roger, LA adviser, interview, April 2004)

All three engaged in negotiating mutual goals and ways to proceed:

When I arrived, Johnny asked me to be the critical friend to the Assessment for Learning network and I have ended up being able to move away from that to be more like a co-leader. . . . With Kate and Sally it's just been so easy to work with them and it's hard to know where an idea started or ended, really.

(Roger, LA adviser, interview, April 2004)

Roger was relatively new to Pluto LA and indicated that he was not aware of the entirety of the NLC. A year later, when he came to review his map of the authority (Figure 9.3), Sally and Kate were key figures added.

Social spaces were important to help develop the productive relationships. Their professional time was squeezed because of formal commitments, but they were prepared to give over what would otherwise be social time in the evenings to 'thrash out ideas'. In the case of the co-leadership team, they chose a particular public house ('pub', i.e. a bar) to be a regular venue:

There are only two deputies here and so our jobs are fairly kind of hectic at the minute. Because Kate is a primary teacher, she can't get time off during the day when I might be able to, and, because we have become friends, we have found it easier to go the pub. We do our work there in the evenings.

(Sally, NLC co-leader, interview, February 2004)

We meet at least every two weeks and sometimes Roger joins us. . . . We have a couple of hours where we sit and we just thrash out ideas. It's quite relaxing as well, isn't it, in that sort of environment?

(Kate, NLC co-leader, interview, March 2004)

Sharing practice

Roger, Kate and Sally chose an approach that aimed for equality of leadership – a view that potentially anyone and everyone should contribute to the work of the AfL sub-network:

We needed to decide how to act as people that lead a network. We were very, very conscious of this as we wanted to do some sort of input but without making it become an issue of dependency, where people felt if they came along to a meeting we were going to tell them things. It's something that we constantly battled with,

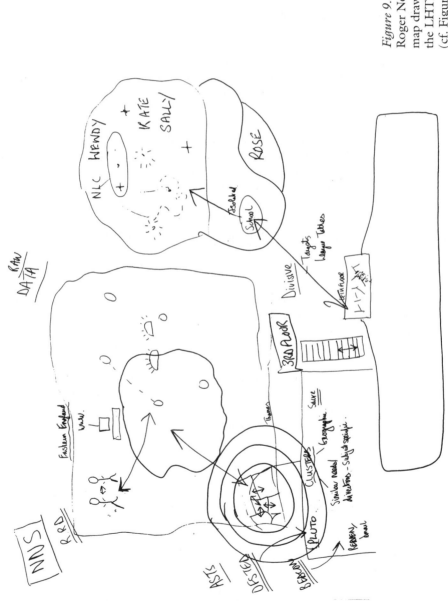

Figure 9.3
Roger Newland's amended map drawn three years into the LHTL project (cf. Figure 4.6).

getting that balance right. You do want to have things that are new and that give people information and talk about ideas but, on the other hand, you want this sense of shared ownership; that everybody takes responsibility for ideas and for learning.

> (Kate, NLC co-leader, presentation to
> LHTL teachers' conference, March 2005)

Because Sally and Kate were in LHTL project schools, they found that they were able to share their own school-generated developments with other schools. However, the equality of sharing envisioned by the co-leadership team did not always present itself. The project schools, having the practice to share initially, appeared to raise barriers to other schools offering examples:

> One of the things that we're struggling with in terms of networking – I think it's partly our problem, it's partly their problem in school – is that we should all be taking it in turns in terms of what we share. Perhaps this is partly due to there being a history where schools turn up to events and they get input and they go away, rather than they come along as equal stakeholders. It may be partly to do with structures, as one of the difficulties is, as soon as you've got leaders, it's almost like the rest of the group kind of look to you to feed them. . . . Partly you have got some history in terms of status, so some of our schools, for instance Hawthorn and Redwood schools, are also Leading Edge schools, they're very successful schools, excellent schools, but there is actually a flipside to that in that some other schools may actually see them as 'Oh my goodness, it's Hawthorn school again.'

> (Roger, LA adviser, interview, April 2004)

The co-leaders concluded that the network did rely on input for inspiration, but doing this through leading by example at network meetings had led to dependence. To help identify where practice was being developed, the co-leaders explored how to get other teachers into each other's schools, mirroring what they had done in their co-leadership roles. Sally adapted a programme of lesson observations to illustrate AfL practice, which she was aware happened elsewhere in the LA:

> Sally [had suggested lesson observations]. There is a programme in our authority, which she has been part of, where people go and watch each other's lessons and it is about best practice and there is a really glossy leaflet about lessons you can go and watch. . . . We decided not to go the whole way with photos and everything because we are not saying that we are setting this out yet as best practice. No one will have been in to look at these teachers that are volunteering. We are really wary that we are not holding this up as best practice but that we are sharing practice.

> (Kate, NLC co-leader, interview, October 2003)

Bidding for, and winning, funding for the following year was needed to enable cover for teachers as they went out to other schools across the LA. Volunteers were found to offer lessons to be observed and teachers took up these invitations to visit. Activity, if not the details of impact, were reported.

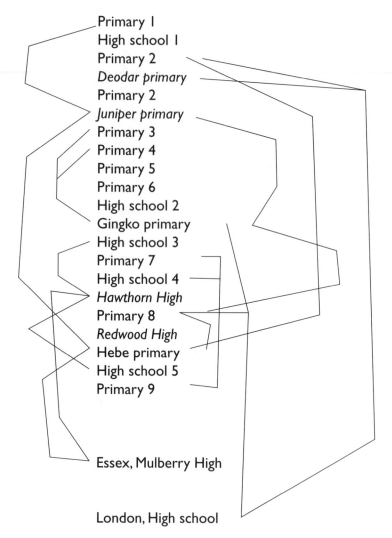

Primary 1
High school 1
Primary 2
Deodar primary
Primary 2
Juniper primary
Primary 3
Primary 4
Primary 5
Primary 6
High school 2
Gingko primary
High school 3
Primary 7
High school 4
Hawthorn High
Primary 8
Redwood High
Hebe primary
High school 5
Primary 9

Essex, Mulberry High

London, High school

Figure 9.4   A representation of inter-school networking among twenty of the AfL
        network schools in 2005.

Note: LHTL project schools in Pluto are indicated in italics and other schools are named with
the agreed pseudonyms.

> [In the last network co-ordinators' meeting] we did a feedback slot on what had
> been going on as it has been very, very active over the last term. There has been
> a programme of observations; which have tended to be primary–primary and
> secondary–secondary.
>
> (Sally, NLC co-leader, interview, February 2004)

In addition to facilitating teacher visits, the co-leaders also obtained funding for
teachers, other than themselves, to go out to external courses, events and conferences.

As before, the co-leaders were encouraging networking in a way that mirrored their own opportunities. This they reviewed at the end of the project as being highly beneficial:

> We were able to fund people to attend other conferences and courses as well. They would come back and feed back to us. I think it was the quality of these that really made the difference, having contact with people that teachers felt were at the forefront of AfL issues.
>
> (Kate, NLC co-leader, presentation to
> LHTL teachers' conference, March 2005)

By facilitating internal and external link opportunities, the co-leaders were trying to build capacity for networking that would allow others to be exposed to inspiration. We were able to summarise, in discussion with Kate and Sally, the degree to which school-to-school interaction had occurred between 2003 and 2005 as a result of the observation programme and other networking activity (see Figure 9.4[4]).

Network sustainability

The core of the co-leadership team changed in April 2004, when Kate left the LA. Sally's response to this expresses the nature of the personal relationship that had developed but looked forward to how the co-leadership team might continue:

> On a personal note I am devastated [that Kate is leaving] because we work really well together and I think that is one of the reasons why we have been so successful and so productive. Tim is taking over, who is a primary headteacher, so the primary links will still be there. I think the thing is in place now, we have a very good action plan, we know where we are going with the network. . . . Obviously we have got to keep on working together. It will be quite good that Tim is a headteacher as he won't have so many of the problems like getting out of a classroom like Kate did. He seems very committed and very 'up for it', so it will be good, I think.
>
> (Sally, NLC co-leader, interview, February 2004)

Five months later, Sally reported that a constructive, but not as intense, relationship had developed with Tim. As co-leaders they continued to meet socially (although less often), choosing a café rather than a pub to meet, but Tim's position as a head had changed things:

> Because the other co-leader is a headteacher, we are less active with other schools . . . now. Once Tim took over, he's a headteacher with all that comes with that, and we've met far less than Kate and I used to. . . . We now have little time to do anything with those in the network that are not active.
>
> (Sally, school co-ordinator, Hawthorn High School,
> LHTL interview, July 2004)

The period 2004–6 coincided with challenges for Tim in his school, and an increase in Sally's in-school responsibilities. Both left the co-leadership roles in 2006:

I then decided to leave, after five years in the post of co-leader, in about July 2006. This can mostly be put down to personalities . . . I guess partly just then I didn't want to invest in starting with someone else at that point. I was getting more roles in school myself as I geared up to go for the headship. . . . I may also have sensed that this was to be a time of change and that it was a good time to leave. That was probably due to my continuing strong relationships with Roger and Wendy in the local authority, and in fact now Roger has left too; it feels very different.

(Sally, former NLC co-leader, reflective interview, January 2009)

Despite the formal ending of funding from the NCSL in 2006, the network did continue in operation. Sally personally withdrew but, for her, what was sustained was a set of relationships with the initial team of Kate, Sally, Wendy and Roger. Even in 2009 they met socially, which Sally thought beneficial to her, as she indicated in the quotation in Chapter 8 where she explains that they met for dinner as the 'Champagne for Learning' group (p. 182). Sally reported that they talked about a whole host of professional issues that were of mutual interest, sharing their awareness of developments in the authority (through Wendy and Roger) and in other authorities (Kate). The earlier reallocation of the formal NLC administration from the teachers' centre to Hawthorn High School also had an impact on Sally's ability to keep in touch with network activity:

Wendy Dix has now got an office in our school. It keeps us at the centre of it, you know. So I mean, yesterday, I just popped up, spent an hour with her and the network administrator up there, talking about the conference and giving them some help.

(Sally, NLC co-leader, interview, May 2004)

AfL in Hawthorn High: Sally's impact

Status of school

Sally's earlier comments on the specialist school status of Hawthorn High coloured her view of the direction of sharing. As we indicated earlier, she felt that, on balance, the school was the originator of much of what was distributed across the network. This was in part because of her role as co-leader and in part because of the school's specialist and LHTL project status:

To be honest, our role in the network tends to be as a giver more than a taker, so we tend to go and do a lot of stuff or people come and watch our lessons. I can't remember sending a teacher out to watch a lesson in another school, for example.

(Sally, school co-ordinator, Hawthorn High School,
LHTL interview, July 2004)

I had been into another secondary school [in the LA] and given them copies of all our material and they were very grateful. . . . I went in with [the LA adviser] Wendy and did a session on AfL before half-term [holiday] to a group of middle leaders.

(Sally, NLC co-leader, interview, October 2003)

If you're going to work collaboratively, you can't be in competition. . . . Competition is still a big part of it [in our authority] and it's unequal because you've got some very good schools and you've also got schools in special measures.[5] Some schools, and we are one of them, probably feel like they're always giving, and that can be quite frustrating.

(Sally, school co-ordinator, Hawthorn High School, LHTL interview, July 2004)

Despite the frustrations, she also noted tangible benefits *to* Hawthorn School staff from interacting with others. Going to other schools made staff feel professionally recognised for their good practice. This appeared to the school leaders to be inspiring teachers to be more confident in volunteering for such work and motivated them to take on new initiatives. Visiting other schools also appeared to encourage staff to remain open-minded about ways to develop practice:

Exposure to outside schools is tremendous. It works two ways both on teacher self-confidence and also teacher self-awareness. It is always valuable to gain stimulation of working with people who are having similar experiences to you but will be seeing them slightly differently. You don't get the danger of everyone becoming institutionalised, where staff feel that theirs is the only way to do it.

(Brian, headteacher, Hawthorn High School, LHTL interview, April 2003)

Sharing practice

There was a range of ways of disseminating the work they had developed within the school: individual staff going out to other schools and staff being invited in to 'special' days. The resources generated were then shared through network project co-ordinator meetings:

We have a rather nice leaflet on questioning which we are just about to produce and I will be giving that out across the network. . . . The history department have produced it and gave a nice presentation to us at school about it so I said, 'Could you put it together into a leaflet?', and they have. There are lots of departments across the school using it . . . I will be [presenting it in a staff meeting]. There is a meeting devoted to AfL coming up.

(Sally, NLC co-leader, interview, October 2003)

Sally talked about how their work was also being noticed and promoted by others beyond school. This was partly due to Sally's own contacts with academics from the LHTL project, partly through Brian, as former headteacher, and partly through LA links:

I co-wrote an article with [one of the LHTL academics] for the TLRP [Teaching and Learning Research Programme] about the AfL work in Hawthorn High. . . . We've also been interviewed for *Teacher* magazine.

(Sally, NLC co-leader, interview, May 2004)

I think [the DfES visits and publicity] generates a real feel-good factor, and I think it acknowledges and celebrates the work that we're doing. I think it also flies the flag for me for AfL more than networking, I suppose, although the two things are linked.

(Sally, NLC co-leader, interview, May 2004)

During the project, Sally made a network-to-network link (infrequent among LHTL schools) through making a personal connection with a deputy headteacher, Ben, in an LHTL school in an NLC in another LA. This offered a longer-distance opportunity to share materials and proved of mutual benefit to both schools. The other school, Mulberry High, was noted to have also developed AfL work as a result of being in the LHTL project, but with different outcomes. Sally relates how this professional relationship with Ben began and then developed:

> I met Ben first at a LHTL co-ordinators' meeting and we got on quite well. . . . He said he knew one of our heads of department. . . . And then we found we were both involved in the research project with Johnny Stanton. . . . We have been emailing each other and are probably just about at the same place in terms of AfL but we have done things very differently. In our school, it feels very much that we have focused on AfL, but there they have fitted into the 'thinking and learning' agenda and done some quite creative things. They have brought it into their initial teacher training as they are a training school,[6] so I am quite interested in that because it feels like it has gone beyond classroom practice to a whole-school approach. I think ours is whole-school but still focused more at the classroom level. . . . I have arranged to go down and visit his school, and when the Pluto network conference came around, we decided we wanted a workshop on spreading AfL across the school, so invited him over.

(Sally, NLC co-leader, interview, February 2004)

It was the possibility for mutual benefit that inspired Sally to take a day out to visit Ben's school, and this was reciprocated. After Sally and Ben had reflected on what they could learn from the directions in which each school had taken AfL development (over a period of about a year), it appears that this relationship was no longer actively sustained.

Facilitating sources of inspiration for staff

As was noted earlier, Hawthorn High was keen to receive and use external sources of expertise as inspiration. Sally reported how direct links between the whole staff and academics, made possible through the LHTL project, greatly enhanced the way staff took on the AfL work. Sally, as a leader of AfL development in the school, explained how she changed her perception of the outcomes of this project from 'changing classroom procedures' to developing staff to make 'principled changes'.

> The whole-staff development thing that's come with the development aspect of the learning to learn project I think has been quite important. It's probably not how I saw the project in the beginning. I saw it as very much as kids learning, which would be about teachers possibly changing or refining their practice. Although that is therefore about staff learning, that wasn't explicit to me at the beginning.

(Sally, school co-ordinator, Hawthorn High School,
LHTL interview, July 2004)

With this came a new awareness of the need for internal staff collaboration – that is, strong link development within the school, to share practice. As a result of her network co-leader experiences, Sally began to realise that the observing of lessons in other people's classrooms, advocated by her and her co-leader throughout 2003 and 2004, was not taking place within the school:

> At the moment we do observations for performance management and we do lots of observations because of being in the network but we don't do it in our own school. You could teach a lesson in a classroom next to me and that practice would probably not escape [from the classroom] unless it was someone from another school. . . . What I'm suggesting next year is that everybody has to do two observations and just share ideas and practice. It's internal networking yet . . . our wealth of good practice we are probably better at sharing it externally than we are in the school.
>
> (Sally, school co-ordinator, Hawthorn High School,
> LHTL interview, July 2004)

While we have little evidence as to how they went about such internal network development, Sally's review of her network map between 2003 and 2004 (Figure 9.5) indicated changes to the school's working practices as a result of AfL involvement. New working groups had been set up, others changed membership and whole-school in-service materials had been developed from the former Teaching and Learning group. There were also fewer strong, external links made by staff.

The sustainability of AfL

The impact of being a co-leader of the AfL network made Sally feel central to LA activity. She reported how this happened informally, often through strong personal links with her headteacher (Brian) and with the LA's deputy director (Johnny). By 2004, Sally's relationship with Johnny was direct, as a result of her work on projects led by him:

> Our communication is a bit how people used to say, 'Oh, there's a bit of networking going on', meaning it was slightly dodgy, but we're so embroiled in it with each other now. Johnny will just phone up and say, 'There's this', or 'There's that', or 'Can we come and do this?' Or Brian will forward things to me from somewhere else and say, 'Do you want to go?' and it just happens.
>
> (Sally, school co-ordinator, Hawthorn High School,
> LHTL interview, July 2004)

Despite the funding for the LHTL project and the NLC finishing in 2006, the AfL network and AfL development work has been sustained by Pluto LA. Hawthorn High did not feel itself to be an active member of this network, either as contributor or as beneficiary, which Sally related to her personal withdrawal from the sub-network when she became the headteacher. Sally appointed Abigail, an advanced skills teacher (AST), as network co-ordinator, and a new assistant head whom she decided she wanted to take the lead for AfL within the school. Questions still remained for Sally when we interviewed her in 2009:

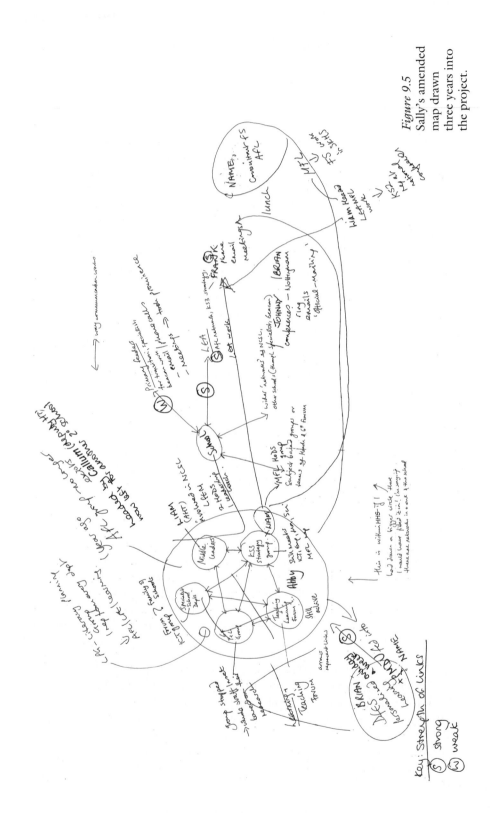

Figure 9.5
Sally's amended
map drawn
three years into
the project.

It seems to me that AfL stopped still when I stopped being the co-leader without wanting to sound big-headed about it. The AST found it difficult, because of her status to make the case in school, although she was working effectively at the micro-level with teachers. We have a new assistant head and he has now been given responsibility for AfL. What is interesting there is that he is not an expert but I feel that this is important to the school and therefore he needs to become familiar with it and hopefully be able to take a lead on it. But I have been giving all the presentations to new staff, etc., as I can explain where it has come from, what we have done and the principles behind it.

(Sally, former NLC co-leader, reflective interview, January 2009)

In conclusion

Over the period 2002–9, Sally changed in role professionally from a deputy head through to the headteacher of Hawthorn High School. Her co-leadership of the LA's AfL network and LHTL school co-ordination between 2003 and 2006, as a deputy head, enabled her to build relationships and helped support further AfL networking as well as acting as input to her development work in school. She, as part of a strong network co-leadership team, built capacity through giving networking opportunities to others. As a result of 'learning how to network' externally, Sally then tried to mirror some of these practices in school – for example, enabling teachers to observe one another.

Some of the meaningful relationships that Sally made were beyond school, such as with Ben and indeed Kate – Ben through LHTL project meetings and Kate originally through transition work. The strongest relationships in Sally's personal network developed over the time she co-led the AfL network and have been enduring. The sustainability of these relationships has been ascribed to the personal dimension of valuing and respecting one another as well as shared values and commitment to these values.

Juniper Primary School

Introduction

Juniper Primary School is a two-class entry for students aged 3–11 in an outer-city LA with approximately 450 children on roll. Its students are relatively disadvantaged and a large number of them have special educational needs. The data for this study were the maps and interviews of Barbara, the headteacher, and Kate, the assessment coordinator, who acted as the LHTL school co-ordinator. Kate also co-led the AfL sub-network of the Pluto NLC with Sally (the subject of the previous study).

Internal networks

Both Barbara and Kate indicated that they had shared perspectives on the maps of the school networks (Figures 9.6 and 9.7). Both showed the school with a large number of face-to-face links as opposed to paper-based or electronic links, for both internal and external communication. The maps also showed that the school was thought to

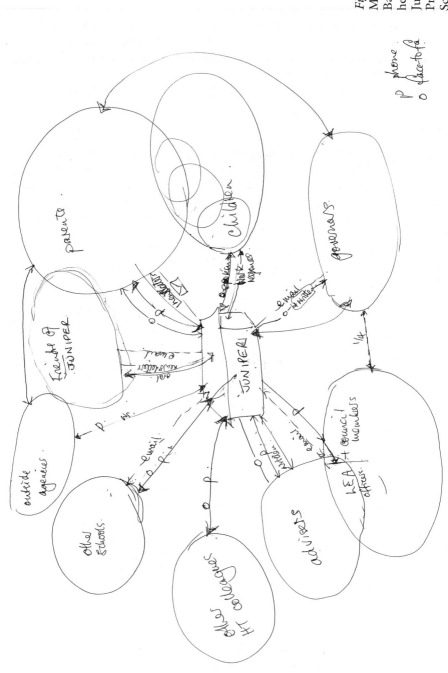

P phone
O face-to-fa

Figure 9.6
Map by
Barbara,
headteacher,
Juniper
Primary
School.

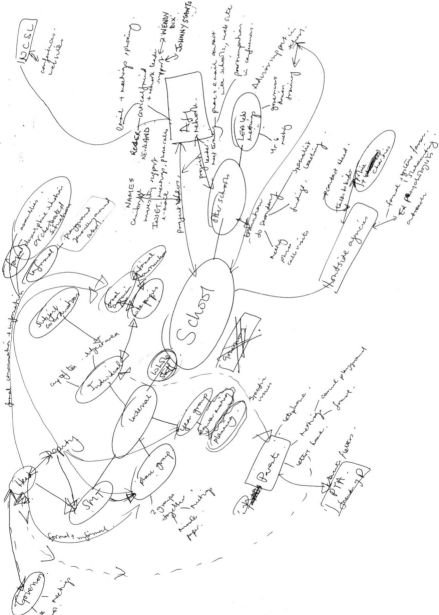

Figure 9.7
Map by Kate, school
co-ordinator, Juniper
Primary School.

LIVERPOOL JOHN MOORES UNIVERSITY
LEARNING SERVICES

be a 'well-connected' community of teachers and learners. Barbara's map has the school at the centre with links to parents, governors, children, teachers, the LA and a number of other agencies, and she commented that she had 'unpacked' the parts of the 'meaningful space', as she termed it, at the same time as she was 'thinking of the staff as a whole'. With a third of her links being internal, Barbara had more than the average for headteachers across the LA as a whole (see Fox *et al.* 2007). Barbara deliberately maintained links in an effort to provide opportunities for interaction:

> [t]he informal level of the head and deputy . . . communicating with children for example in the playground . . . just generally around the school.
>
> (Kate, school co-ordinator, Juniper)

> I have been into every single class and spent some time. It is something I aim to do but don't always manage to do each term, is to get into see people even if it is only for a short time.
>
> (Barbara, headteacher, Juniper)

An informal approach to maintaining links was common in the school, for example the 'open door' policy to parents:

> That could be done by telephone, we phone them up and discuss things, meetings, letters home, and then within meetings is that kind of casual playground . . . meeting.
>
> (Kate, school co-ordinator, Juniper)

Barbara's relationships with parents and governors, shown in Figure 9.6, indicate directionality:

> The school has networks with governors . . . I should probably have drawn that differently, but they actually link in to some of those who are from the parents. The arrow is both ways . . . and in fact they are both two-headed arrows because they come both ways . . . the governors and the parents are particularly useful in helping the school keep its ear to the ground.
>
> (Barbara, headteacher, Juniper)

Social events for local community groups and a welcoming environment for those needing second-language support included not only parents but those outside this group. Barbara and Kate also highlighted the importance of children as network participants in the school; note that both locate them centrally on their maps. Kate reported that the strongest links were 'between myself and the pupils I taught' (year 2 interview).

Both Barbara and Kate spoke of how they felt they should be working collectively with respect to professional learning, as Kate indicates here:

> I think as a collective body, we're all responsible for each other's professional development in a way, aren't we? We kind of all feed into it and, especially for my role, I've been very responsible for their professional development.
>
> (Kate, school co-ordinator, Juniper, LHTL year 1 interview)

This notion of a community of classroom practitioners was also extended to teaching assistants, who were included in all in-service training.

External networks

External links on both maps (Figures 9.6 and 9.7) were to educational consultants, higher education institutions, the LA, the NCSL and support agencies, and support for students with English as an additional language and those with special educational needs. Once in post as co-ordinator, Kate began to act as a 'bridge' between the school and two different groups of external people and their resources. First, she bridged to those involved in the AfL network, both in other schools and in the LA, when acting as co-leader of the AfL network:

> I have picked up some things from other schools, which have been really interesting and have fed into some of the things we've done, and vice versa. We've been able to share a lot.
>
> (Kate, school co-ordinator, Juniper, LHTL year 1 interview)

She also bridged to those involved in the LHTL project outside of the school, providing evidence of how her weak, yet highly valued, links with those on the project team were used to inspire her colleagues:

> One thing . . . that kicked it off, [our project critical friend] came and did the initial thing [an initial input lecture and workshop activities] right back in April, and I think that really impacted well, because it was like somebody different, from the outside world. And he had such vigour for everything and such enthusiasm that I think it really . . . translated quite well to everybody.
>
> (Kate, school co-ordinator, Juniper, LHTL year 1 interview)

This then allowed the school to be one of the first to share ideas of novel practice with others in the AfL network:

> So we've presented stuff about the 'success criteria' . . . and shown some of the practice that we've done and . . . things that have worked . . . or that haven't worked. We did the same with 'feedback'.
>
> (Kate, school co-ordinator, Juniper, LHTL year 1 interview)

For areas that they had not developed first, other schools in the network were exploited:

> We invited one school [that does] lots of work on questioning and they came along and talked about questioning, and presented some of the ideas they've used for that, and I think it was a good way of giving people ideas.
>
> (Kate, school co-ordinator, Juniper, LHTL year 1 interview)

Kate described the teachers' centre or events organised by the NCSL as 'venues [where] people felt they were leaving their own environment' (year 2 interview). Despite the close proximity of the LA teachers' centre, and its potential to make informal links with teachers from other schools and LA advisers, it was perceived as 'a depressing place . . . not the best place . . . [not] a very conducive place', and one where people attending formal meetings tended not to linger (Kate, year 2 interview). More conducive was a local pub, a neutral venue 'where we sit and just thrash out ideas' as 'it's quite relaxing . . . in that sort of environment' (Kate, year 2 interview).

Different networks, different perspectives?

Barbara described a group she was affiliated with: the 'Head Teachers' Forum'. While this was a formal group, it enabled a non-specific community for headteachers to discuss a range of issues and concerns that the existing professional association network precluded:

> [W]e have worked at times in sort of pulling the headteachers together. . . . It was called the 'curriculum area group' . . . actually it isn't the right word to use, 'curriculum', we used to call it 'cluster group', but the 'Head Teachers' Forum' to sort of separate it from the professional kind of interest . . . it is a fairly formal network . . . the NAHT [National Association of Head Teachers] group was retained for professional matters and we formulated the Forum for curriculum and managerial issues.
>
> (Barbara, headteacher, Juniper)

Interestingly, they referred to one another on the map by *role*, whereas in their interviews they referred to each other by *name*. Kate is described by Barbara as a broker: as a bridge, but also a maker of new bridges, linking the school externally to LA, regional and national networks different from those to which Barbara was linked. As the school's representative within the NLC, she had a formal role involving meetings, email exchanges and special events. She was also the 'face' of this external network, brokering information and reporting on and supporting the introduction of new practices across the LA and beyond.

We converted the maps of both Barbara and Kate to enable them to be compared (while being conscious of the issues about this we raised in Chapter 4). Figures 9.8 and 9.9 show these idealised representations, which reveal more clearly the comparative richness of description of sections of the maps. This was particularly evident in Kate's representation of her links with the AfL sub-network of the NLC, which shows the range of links that her role involved (Figure 9.9). Barbara's map (Figure 9.8) was less dense, with fewer links and some different representations of the relationships in this 'component' of the map.

Kate saw her role in the AfL NLC as one of mediating between school and the network. She pointed to the role of NLC network co-ordinator meetings and other events as a way of establishing links with other schools. Barbara's account is different in that although she supports the school's AfL practice development, she acknowledges that it is Kate who is 'going beyond' and 'opening up' links external to the school. Kate is not just executing delegated tasks managed by Barbara; she was given free rein to develop external networks, establish and maintain new links – that is, to build her

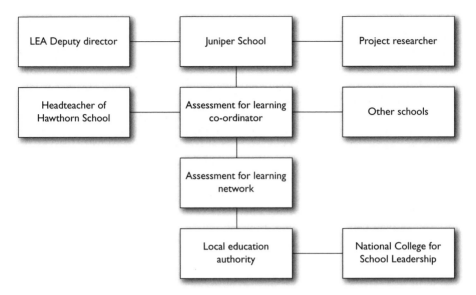

Figure 9.8 Simplified representations of the AfL network in the map by Barbara, headteacher, Juniper Primary School.

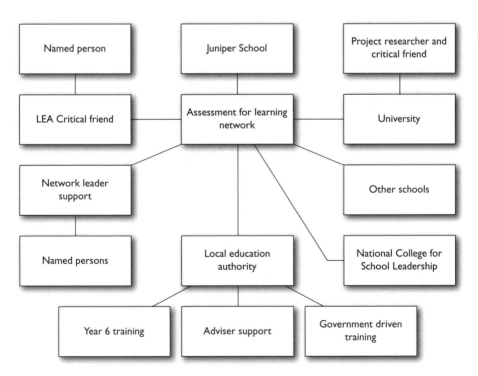

Figure 9.9 Simplified representations of the AfL network in the map by Kate, school co-ordinator, Juniper Primary School.

intensional network. Because of this, Kate has a greater range of AfL resources and expertise available to her personally, and for the school, than Barbara. From Barbara's perspective, Kate acts as a broker, reaching out to AfL practice in the wider network than that which she as a headteacher can access. The school is thus not a single 'node' in a network, but a setting in which individuals with different external contacts take various network roles by virtue of these contacts.

There are components of the maps where the situation of the network roles of Barbara and Kate are reversed. For example, in the relationship of the school and its governors: Figures 9.10 and 9.11 show the simplified components of Barbara's and Kate's maps with the *paths* (sequences of links) between school and governors represented in full and with arrows as drawn by them.

To Barbara, the maintenance of two-way links between school, governors and parents is generally a more important aspect of her school network, describing her role in terms of maintaining communication. Although Kate is a member of the school senior management team, she sees her interactions with the governors as mediated or

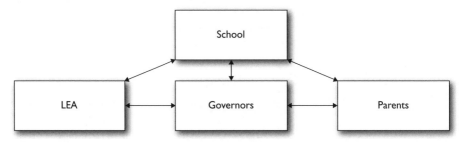

Figure 9.10 Representations of the relationship between school and governors by Barbara, headteacher, Juniper Primary School.

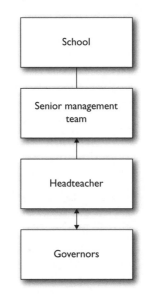

Figure 9.11
Representations of the relationship between school and governors by Kate, school co-ordinator, Juniper Primary School.

brokered by Barbara. Put crudely, if one of the activities Kate 'does' is AfL, then the one Barbara 'does' is manage relationships with the governors.

Strength, weakness and value of links

Barbara talked differently about her 'open door' relationship with the governors and parents as compared with how she talked about those she had with visiting speakers or occasional consultants. She did not always value the frequent communications with the LA, in part caused by the raft of national initiatives needing a response. Kate also reflected:

> It's not frequency, it's more . . . almost like value . . . the quality of the link, I think. . . . You can have a strong link with somebody that you don't have a quality relationship with. I think it's probably just maybe the role . . . there's also an element within yourself of satisfaction, isn't there? Which links you find the most satisfying . . . so obviously within that as well is my perception of how I think the link is.
>
> (Kate, school co-ordinator, Juniper)

Kate described how her close working relationships with Sally, the other co-leader of the AfL, and with others within the sub-network were not only strong but also of high value because they were 'effective':

> [W]e've just been incredibly lucky . . . in that we've got . . . the three people that are . . . all prepared to go beyond what we would normally do. . . . It's about people who are committed to change, I think, so committed to change that they're actually prepared to give up their own time to do it and to follow up. I mean to see something that's good and think there is a kind of duty for it to be shared and to know that the only way that's going to happen is by you working harder and accepting that, really.
>
> (Kate, school co-ordinator, Juniper, LHTL year 2 interview)

Both Barbara and Kate also identified 'weak' links of high value, for example with visits by outside experts. There were also organisations with which they had low-value links, because they had relatively little impact on school-level practice.

Multiple network roles

Kate participated in networks in a variety of ways. As a broker, she provided short cuts to potentially high-value people and resources beyond the school. She also strengthened weak links that had the potential to be of high value because they offered opportunities for professional development or improved classroom practice. Kate is also involved in knowledge construction activities with strong, high-value, 'effective' links with an impact on classroom practice. Each link has different foci and consequences; for example, increasing the value of weak links focuses on her role in building network capacity, whereas in relation to strong links she is just one of the actors in network activity. Kate recognised the role of Barbara's support for this:

[Barbara is] the sort of person who has a lot of trust in her staff so she allowed me to develop ideas, but then obviously I took them back to her and she sort of discussed them with me. And she was obviously the person that, because . . . overseeing the leadership of the school, she drove things forward as well . . . so in terms of the sort of AfL activity within the school, Barbara's commitment to it was totally vital.

(Kate, school co-ordinator, Juniper, LHTL year 2 interview)

Chapter 10

Electronic networks and teacher learning

At the start of the 'Learning How to Learn' project in 2001 there were great hopes for the role of electronic networks in supporting teacher learning, and in particular the learning within and across schools. These networks were seen as a critical enabler of teacher learning and the development of practice across the educational sector. Indeed, as we have indicated, several of our initial research questions focused specifically on the role of technology and what forms would enable the creation and sharing of knowledge. At the time we began our research (2001), there was increasing interest in collaborative environments and virtual learning spaces, but the subsequent upsurge in 'social' software or 'Web 2.0' was still some way off (O'Reilly being credited with the use of the term in 2005). This chapter explores the role of electronic networks in relation to our respondents' experiences of supporting and participating in networks (drawing again on the mapping task and other sources of data about their use of network technologies). It also explores how the continuing rise in popularity in electronic network tools, including 'social' software, might be theorised and how it might contribute to teacher networks and learning.

There is a complex but significant relationship between network theories in general and the development of electronic networks. Not only have the developers of electronic networks drawn on network theories and social network analysis (SNA) in order to design, analyse and theorise their activities, so too have network theorists drawn on the emergence of online networks, immersive environments (e.g. Second Life)[1] and other linked data in order to explore and exemplify network theories. This is exemplified by work such as the analysis by Watts (1999) of the Internet Movie Database, Barabási's work on the nature and 'dimensions' of the internet (2003), and the recent work of Contractor (2009), who has studied massively multiplayer environments such as World of Warcraft[2] and has employed 'confirmatory network analysis' to explore complex social relationships and information sharing. Contractor himself (2005) suggests that we have begun to see how network theories (specifically SNA) and the design of electronic infrastructures coexist and inform each other's development. This is clearly an interesting development and confirms Burt's observation (2000) about the important role played by 'experimental' settings – in this case, online environments and 'closed worlds' in which network concepts can be elaborated and hypotheses tested. At the same time, there is a risk that what emerges from such a close symbiosis is the establishment of normative practices and assumed analytical frameworks. These have the potential to ignore or understate the differences between the offline social networks and online environments and encourage the use of SNA concepts to *define* preferred forms of online interaction, with key metrics being used to ascertain whether a network is, or is not, 'successful' or 'effective'.

Electronic networks in respondents' schools

As described in Chapter 2, considerable optimism about the potential of electronic networks to disseminate 'best practice', support professional development and raise standards in schools, had informed investment in electronic collaboration environments and websites, and in developing the infrastructure of the virtual education action zones (VEAZs). As a precursor to the mapping task, we undertook a series of surveys, 'audits' (structured questionnaires) and interviews to establish what the technological 'baseline' might be in participating schools (Carmichael and Procter 2006). This was designed to establish how typical participating schools were when compared to the national picture (in terms of number of computers in schools, pupil–computer ratios, levels of staffing, availability of internet connections and so on). At the same time, it enabled us to explore how easy it would be to engage at least some project schools in electronic rather than face-to-face development activities and the dissemination of project resources using electronic networks. What emerged, however, rapidly dissuaded us from employing this as a 'mode of engagement' within the project, and also informed our subsequent framing and analysis of the mapping task.

As we have reported elsewhere, we discovered that the use of classroom ICT was well established across the schools involved in the project around 2002, and that these were, for the most part, well equipped with networked computers (in some case, very well equipped compared to national patterns [Carmichael and Procter 2006: 175]). But teachers' use of electronic resources, communication and collaboration tools to support their own learning was very limited. While individual teachers had, in many cases, identified useful sources of curriculum schemes, lesson plans and outlines, websites and other teaching resources, their engagement with ideas about classroom practice was much more limited, and teacher-to-teacher collaboration was limited to sharing web links to useful resources. School websites were for the most part concerned with the public representation of the school. Managed learning environments, where these existed, were largely concerned with online storage of schemes of work, homework resources and practice examination activities for learners (or their parents) to access from outside school.

There were some variations in access to computers in schools: interestingly, the concentration of computers in 'suites' for class use was identified by teachers, particularly in secondary schools, as a barrier to development of their own capabilities. The majority of teachers in both primary and secondary schools (60 per cent of 269 teachers, across fifteen schools, with no significant difference across school sectors) reported that they carried out the bulk of their computer-based professional work at home. While this may well have contributed to improved use of ICT in classrooms, engaging with professional development activities was not common – in or out of school. Only around one-fifth of teachers reported ever using online materials concerned with 'teaching techniques' as compared with about four-fifths who used the internet to find 'lesson resources'; and online collaboration tools were used very infrequently compared other applications (ibid.: 170–1).

The survey data also revealed how teachers tended to look beyond their local school networks for online resources, advice and expertise. While teachers in a small number of schools reported drawing on their colleagues' resources through some kind of shared online storage, external providers such as the local authority (LA), commercial organisations or government agencies were more likely sources of teaching and learning resources. Among secondary teachers, subject associations such as the Historical Association or the Association for Science Education were valued sources of information, resources and the interpretation of government policy (ibid.: 172). One outcome of the introduction of a national curriculum and national standards was that there was replication of resources across LAs and schools, and there was clearly a degree of information sharing between teachers as to which LA had 'the best' downloadable schemes of work, lesson plans, worksheets and other resources – even if it was not one's 'local' provider.

As was noted earlier, within schools, electronic communications were much less important than meetings, informal face-to-face communications and traditional media such as notice boards and weekly 'briefing' documents distributed to teachers' 'pigeonholes' (Table 6.1). Even when schools had implemented email lists or newsletters to staff, these were characteristically also printed out and distributed at staff meetings or displayed on notice boards. As one respondent from a primary school reported, while in her school other modes of communication were important, it was 'word of mouth [that] links it all together'.

Electronic networks and the mapping task

Against this background, the representation of electronic resources and modes of communication through the mapping task is significant. Rather than a 'layered' network of the kind suggested by Castells (2000a), in which a relatively unified electronic network underpins other activities, what we see are specific electronic elements emerging in a heterogeneous network – much as our survey respondents reported largely traditional modes of communication occasionally supplemented (and, more rarely, replaced) by electronic tools, resources and environments.

If we revisit the themes of previous chapters – 'nodes' (Chapter 5), 'links and relationships' (Chapter 6) and 'network traffic' (Chapter 7) – it is instructive to explore when, where and to what effect electronic elements 'surface' (or in some 'intrude') into individual respondents' representations of their networks. In some cases, these are described in positive terms, technology offering clear advantages, while in other cases their role is more ambivalent or contested.

Nodes

We have discussed the critical role of brokers and the processes of brokerage, and several of our respondents who characterised themselves as brokers explained how they made use of electronic networking in order to support specific brokerage processes. LA respondents described how they used electronic communication, often alongside other communication modes, in order to facilitate as yet emergent school-to-school networking. One adviser, reflecting on a network of seven schools with which she worked, of which 'three or four' would 'send email backwards and forwards', described how

[w]e are tending now to make more and more of our communication to schools electronic, although that at the moment has its own problems . . . we are finding some things we think schools have received have not necessarily been received, so . . . I would also follow through with paper copy, letters, simply because I know that is the way that they tend to access things.

(Una Hills, LA co-ordinator)

Once again in this example the need to accompany electronic communication with other modes is reiterated – this time, from a specific LA perspective.

Institutional websites represented as 'nodes' within respondent maps offered a way of engaging with the 'public face' of the organisation through the web, with email less appropriate for those without an understanding of the internal structure of the organisation. The role of the website is clearly important, then, acting as a public-facing gatekeeper, or even as a 'map' of the internal network structure of the unfamiliar 'territory' of an organisation with which respondents might be engaging for the first time. In this respect the organisational website represents not only a means of communication (by which token they then might be considered to be 'links') but also representations (or 'inscriptions' in actor-network theory [ANT] terms). Websites which appeared on maps, and which were discussed in accompanying interviews, included (in addition to the school, LA and subject association websites mentioned earlier) specific other schools and LAs, specialist associations, and websites set up by providers of consultancy and training. There was awareness that common national priorities and strategies were reflected (as they had been in the survey) by useful knowledge about other schools and LAs that were using websites in interesting or effective ways:

I mean, for example in [another LA not involved in the project], all their material to do with assessment for learning, thinking skills, everything's on their website. So if you ring them up, they always say, 'Just go to the website and look under . . . '

(Kevin Vine, LA co-ordinator)

This can be understood at (at least) three levels:

1 as a useful 'node' (albeit external to the school or authority reporting it in this case) to which a link has been established, and that link has been shared;
2 as a representation of a *valuable* source of information, providing corroboration with one's own practice and potentially new resources and ideas;
3 as a representation of effective networking and knowledge-sharing practice.

Within one LA participating in the project, web 'presence' was very explicitly couched in these broader terms. The website was being built as an organising and framing device for a strategy to which all schools within the authority were expected to engage. This was the authority described in Chapter 4 and subsequently, where a particular network structure was envisaged, with advisory staff and school contacts locating themselves within this. The same broad structure was used as a feature of the website, allowing teachers and other visitors to the website to 'navigate'. The conceptual underpinnings of the network were enacted in the ways in which the data were stored and described and the website interface was designed. In an interesting reversal of Castells' (2000a) assertion that managerial structures of the 'network society' grow around electronic infrastructure (and perhaps demonstrating Contractor's [2005] view that network theory and online infrastructures are developing symbiotically), here an organisational 'vision' was becoming realised in the form of a networked electronic resource.

At the same time, certain types of 'nodes' are poorly represented. While government agencies, the LA and the LHTL project itself were represented not only as sources of information, advice and expertise, 'expertise' itself (rather than policy, curriculum guidelines and examples of best practice) was, for the most part, represented in our respondents' maps as face-to-face encounters. Many respondents described how the visit to their school by a well-known individual had influenced practice and stimulated discussion (Chapters 6 and 8). School leaders also talked about how they encouraged staff to go to events at which they would not only meet other teachers with whom to establish contact, but hear about research projects or innovations in aspects of curriculum development, learner support or school leadership and transformation.

Links

When respondents talked about links, they specifically mentioned network technologies and their benefits and potential benefits, as well as the barriers to their adoption and problems they had faced in using them and encouraging others to do so. Here we found the greatest enthusiasm and optimism about incipient network technologies, tempered by the greatest frustrations as infrastructures, incompatible systems and lack of experience failed to realise the promised benefits for classroom practice and teacher learning.

The most common mode of electronic communication was email, the affordances of which ranged from the very obvious to the less obvious and rather more context-specific. If we remember that in the early part of this century most teachers (other than members of senior management) had little access to telephones during the day, the value of email as a 'near-synchronous' technology, which generates an 'audit trail', makes it a powerful tool for communication both within and beyond school:

> We use emails in particular to communicate with our schools [within the LA] although if it's a quick answer to be gained, obviously the telephone is used, but we often use email.
>
> (Nancy Iver, VEAZ co-ordinator)

> Email is a great way of recording informal conversations and actually ensures they elicit a response sometimes, because I find that with telephone systems you can have barriers put in your way and you can also forget what was said in the conversation. I was engaged in emailing a service contract that we have here. I have had no joy through the traditional ringing of them so I am informing them by email and I want a response from it.
>
> (Sam, headteacher, Alder Primary School)

What was evident in these kinds of descriptions was that email was replicating or supplementing traditional means of communication. But there was recognition on the part of respondents that it had the potential to offer more than this in terms of 'reach':

> [I]t's not connected with anything yet, but it's in place, if not being used. But of course within that email link would be a link to [other schools] and a link internally to things like staffrooms and notice boards. So I suppose it would be possible for me to put an email message onto every staff notice board.
>
> (Bill, headteacher, Walnut County Primary School)

Or, more interestingly, as a means of establishing sustainable school-to-school and teacher–teacher links:

> What we want to try and do is actually get those schools talking to each other more electronically. . . . What I would like to do at that meeting is to set that up . . . that would begin email communication, so that they keep in closer contact with each other.
>
> (Una Hills, LA co-ordinator)

Another area respondents talked about (although, perhaps significantly, it was not well represented on actual maps) was school-to-school videoconferencing. The terms in which this was described were different from those used for email. This was something distinctively different where network technology had the potential not to replicate or support, but to transform:

> [I am] just starting up a web-streaming teacher innovation [that] allows the school to create its own virtual television station via the web, which then allows communication between schools.
>
> (Bryn Yardley, VEAZ co-ordinator)

> We've got various strategic plans to develop that in terms of making more use of email conference groups and other things on that side of it and in relation to the children, videoconferencing as well for linking up . . . particularly in some of the smaller and larger schools so that there can be a sharing of professional expertise and opportunities to access areas of teaching and learning that may not be available within their own schools.
>
> (Frank Martin, LA adviser)

> [O]nce we start getting into videoconferencing, I think that . . . I mean these sort of things coming together, these are Open College Network, Networked [Learning] Community and being a partnership and so forth, I think there's some kind of happy coincidence with all these things merging . . . we can have phone traffic, voice-mail traffic and video traffic and email traffic going down the tube.
>
> (Nick, headteacher, Beech School)

What is particularly striking about these comments, and contrasts with those made about email, websites or other technologies, is that as well as the general claim to support 'communication between schools' there is explicit reference to teacher learning (in the second quotation) and to sources of professional development and opportunities for collaboration (in the last one). At the time we conducted our interviews, however, this optimism was tinged with frustration as attempts to realise this vision of video-enabled teaching and learning for both pupils and teachers had been frustrated by low bandwidth, incompatible systems and poor levels of training and support.

Traffic

In Chapter 7 it was argued that there was a range of answers to the question 'what travels' in networks, some involving artefacts being transferred (as in the case of websites disseminating teaching materials) and some more complex relationships between people, artefacts, concepts and technologies.

We see this again thrown into high relief in the context of electronic networks, where what emerged from the survey, maps and interviews was a range of practice. In some cases this was enabled by 'one-to-many' dissemination through websites, in others through email and email lists and instant messaging. Sometimes it was broadcast to a wide audience of indeterminate size, and sometimes carefully brokered by directing specific network traffic to particular individuals or groups. Across all of these potential settings, a range can be distinguished:

- Electronic networks being used to share references to resources, sources and other network elements (including people). This might be a useful website address, or an email address, or a link to specific documents to download.
- Electronic networks being used to transfer actual digital objects such as documents, images, videos or presentations – generally as email attachments, but potentially by republishing them on websites or discussion boards. Unlike the first example, this type of sharing has the potential to alter or edit the content or format, or to aggregate it with other digital resources.
- Electronic networks being used to transfer links or objects that enact, represent or illustrate specific practices, and so are offered in a learning context. This context might be provided by accompanying structured metadata,[3] less structured information such as a narrative (by way of a commentary or reflection), or by an accompanying discussion.
- Closely linked and probably overlapping with the last example is engagement in online discussion about practice, potentially illustrated by examples drawn from the teacher's own experience, or from other sources (as above). In this type of sustained interaction, the network is supporting, perhaps intermittently, or for a short period only, what Leach (1997) has described as a 'community of discourse'.
- Finally, there is a model of electronic networks as being so well integrated into a discursive practice that they are an intrinsic part of it, using electronic networking tools as an element of the learning environment in which teachers engage in collaborative learning and development.

This range of scenarios excludes specialised cases such as computer-based learning or simulations, which, although they can have networked elements, were not evident in any of the settings in which the project worked. What is evident from our analysis is that, while the earlier members of this list were reasonably well represented, those further down the list were few and far between in the accounts provided by our respondents. Indeed, the latter two scenarios were more evident in plans than in practice. At one end of the scale we have a conscious recognition that what is being done is limited in scope, with electronic networks being used as sources:

One thing we use websites for all the time . . . that's for resourcing the school . . . that is, accessing information . . . it isn't interactive.

(Kate, co-ordinator, Juniper Primary School)

At the other end of the scale is the optimistic vision of how videoconferencing will potentially transform practice not only in classroom practice but also in teacher learning. It is tempting to ascribe the lack of these more expansive practices to the failings of web technologies *c*.2002; however, our respondents pointed to more systemic challenges.

Electronic networking: work, change and learning

For the majority of teachers, then, many of the more complex practices of electronic networking (and networking as a social practice, for that matter) were not seen as important or legitimate 'work', let alone 'knowledge-construction' activities. What our respondents reported is a situation in which using electronic networks to access learning resources within and beyond schools is broadly supported and encouraged. But the more sustained online activity required to establish and maintain person-to-person links, or to engage in sustained discourse around online resources, in what might be seen as 'person-to-resource-to-person' links, is harder to achieve. To move beyond the 'community of discourse' *about* practice to networked discourse being *within* practice seems even more elusive (to use the distinction from Lave and Wenger [1991]).

In addition, there remain significant material obstacles to learning to use technologies and to accessing them. For many teachers, access to broadband-connected computers with the option of printing, using messaging services and other person-to-person networking applications is an after-hours activity. It is conducted in the home using computers that are also in demand for business, leisure, homework and (ironically) the social networking by other family members. This was acknowledged, but also seen by some respondents as an unacceptable intrusion – represented in their maps but not a welcome addition to their professional responsibilities:

I use email at home because I don't have time at school.

(Kate, co-ordinator, Juniper Primary School)

[W]hen are we meant to have a life? You know you can't spend all your time feeding into websites and accessing information off websites; you'd never do anything else but you would sit in a dark room with a computer all the time.

(Nell, co-ordinator, Oak Infant School)

This is reflected in differences in the nature of links made by headteachers and school co-ordinators within the project (Chapter 6). The school co-ordinators reported greater use of electronic communication than the headteachers (Table 6.2), which may reflect their lack of access to telephones and time to meet during school hours, and thus a greater reliance on asynchronous modes such as email. For the headteachers, email was sometimes redundant and inferior to other communication, despite their having access to office computers and videophones. The personal touch allowed by a telephone call in person was seen as being more effective in many contexts:

> If I've got a complaint (from a parent) I'll tend to want to phone them up because an email doesn't necessarily carry what I want.
>
> (Donald, headteacher, Hebe Church of England School)

For the school co-ordinators, like other teachers without this option, electronic modes of communication were essential as they allowed them 'out-of-hours' participation in networks to which they might otherwise have been denied access, but, as we have seen, at a cost in terms of personal time commitment.

There are exceptions to this broad picture: active online networks linking groups of teachers exist, and their enthusiastic engagement has been extensively documented. But participants in these networks often have specific reasons for participation. These may be:

- a concern with problematic practice (geography teachers sharing fieldwork exercises; history teachers searching and discussing 'primary sources' suitable for classroom use; others concerned with the 'moderation' of coursework);
- a response to isolation within school (e.g. co-ordinators of special educational needs connecting with others in role-equivalent posts in other schools);
- the requirements of accredited courses involving participation in structured online collaboration (such as the online activities initiated by the National College for School Leadership and the UK Open University).

It is important to remember that the mapping data, and those emerging from the survey, were collected in a 'Web 1.0' world when levels of broadband connection remained low (less than 1 per cent of homes in the United Kingdom had ADSL or cable broadband in 2001). At that time a series of initiatives to provide narrowband network infrastructure to schools, basic ICT training for teachers, and subsidised 'computers for teachers' schemes had only just been implemented (Cabinet Office 2001). Against this background the establishment of school-managed learning environments, LA 'web portals' and videoconferencing facilities was still relatively novel, and engagement with the LHTL project's own website represented a significant 'first step' for many teachers involved in the project. We also asked school co-ordinators (including many of the respondents in the mapping exercise) to keep online diaries on the project website (Carmichael et al. 2005). In retrospect, this was an ambitious undertaking, given the lack of familiarity at the time with 'blogging' technologies.

So, when respondents identified the online environments, websites or collaboration tools as elements of their network maps, this was a significant indication of the real or potential importance they attached to them – and perhaps an assertion of the fact that online aspects of networking should, indeed, be legitimised and supported. It was notable that among the most enthusiastic advocates of the use of electronic sources were senior members of staff whom we interviewed in their offices, within which they had access to computers (as a legitimate work accessory). In the case of the VEAZ respondents, there were also videophones with which they could maintain inter-school connections.

School and network leaders also felt it was their responsibility to promote the use of technologies; as facilitators of change, modelling new social practices was, in some cases, accompanied by gentle (or not-so-gentle) coercion which they achieved by responding only to emails, or making important information *only* available by online means:

> We do not email agendas, we don't post reports, what we do is make them available as a download from the website and, say, send . . . an email saying it's available on the website.
>
> (Richard Mann, VEAZ co-ordinator)

Despite the inclusive rhetoric of networks and networking, the development of electronic networking in particular represents a significant change-management process, with issues emerging around differential levels of engagement and commitment. There is a fine line to be trodden between encouragement and coercion; the legitimating of networking activities and the provision of time to learn and time to experiment with new technologies; and a recognition that innovations have to be integrated with existing social practices rather than replacing them. As two such managers of change commented,

> They are noticing that the face-to-face links aren't as strong and they're not happy about it.
>
> (Bill, headteacher, Walnut County Primary School)

> People have to see each other, they have to be able to communicate face to face. So it's supporting those relationships rather than replacing them.
>
> (Bryn Yardley, VEAZ co-ordinator)

This also needs to be set against the more general issue of the independence of teachers from each other and hence the difficulty of collaborating and sharing as part of their everyday activity (Little 1990; and see Chapter 7).

Whether in the context of website design, email use or videoconferencing, what we see particularly clearly in the case of electronic networks are dual strands of discourse and development around networks. Networks are not only a source of information about practices; networking itself is a new set *of* practices which themselves need to be explored at individual, school and authority level. The exemplary website established by another LA represents a source of expertise not only about *assessment* practice but also about *electronic networking* practice.

Networks, communities and the concept of 'online'

The maps and accounts of our respondents provide an interesting and rather unusual perspective on electronic networks. Since Rheingold's (2000) seminal *The Virtual Community*, the dominant view is that 'online' represents a particular kind of new environment within which new practices are developed, distinctive identities and relationships established, and new forms of learning takes place. This view has been reinforced by ever-richer 'online environments' including virtual learning environments, online communities and, most recently, immersive environments such as Second Life. Also by research approaches that have taken this notion of online-as-geographical space as their point of departure, leading to a whole field of 'online research' distinct from fields such as simulation, human–computer interaction or computer-supported collaborative work. We have contributed to methodological debates by exploring and questioning the implications of framing online interactions in terms of 'community' or 'network' (Thorpe *et al.* 2007). The dominant view of the 'online', however, aligns with a view that the patterns of interaction that are observed in such environments are reflections of 'community', either in the broad sense (Smith and Kollock 1999) or in the distinctive sense of 'communities of practice' (Wenger *et al.* 2009).

There is a tendency to try to deliberately construct online environments as self-contained 'spaces' either modelled on some kind of conceptual framework providing new opportunities for interaction, or reflecting an existing organisational structure. We can see this in the web-based collaboration environments established by LHTL project schools and authorities. In one LA a website with associated discussion boards and other resources was set up to reflect priorities (including 'assessment for learning') across the authority as a whole, in an attempt to encourage sharing of practice across schools. In a large secondary school, in contrast, there was a strong similarity between the existing school structure and the design of the managed learning environment, which reflected faculties and departments, curriculum subjects and school year groups. That said, attempts to constrain and 'containerise' online environments are often undermined by participants, who creatively appropriate technological features and often assert new norms of practice and discourse. Wilson *et al.* (2007) describe how the provision of an initially quite constrained and 'managed' online collaboration environment for groups of teachers involved in participatory research projects was rapidly undermined by participants asserting the kinds of collaborative practice in which they wanted to engage, leading to the co-design of a more flexible online space to support their school-based practice.[4]

The VEAZs were interesting examples in this respect. As wholly new organisational forms with emerging agendas, they had websites and online collaboration environments, but no clear model on which to base these. Even here, though, conventional organisational frameworks (sector, curriculum areas, policy priority) reasserted themselves to some extent: in the VEAZ, which was geographically dispersed (and particularly interested in videoconferencing), 'pairing' of teachers in similar or analogous roles emerged as an organising device, mainly driven by the expectation of school-to-school video links.

Recent work in higher education settings, where online collaboration environments have been enthusiastically adopted, suggests that establishing 'offline' practices and relationships is indeed a good predictor of successful 'online' activities. Stefanone and Gay (2008), for example, argue that existing social network structures established through face-to-face activities have a significant influence on emergent communication patterns in online environments. This suggests that existing relationships have a strong influence (and are more significant than other factors, including prior technology use) on subsequent computer-mediated communication. But this account still recognises a distinctive online 'space' into which 'offline' practices and relationships are imported. Our data suggested that a more complex relationship between the two exists.

The maps drawn by our respondents differ from those generated by looking *solely* at electronic communications, as in Thorpe *et al.* (2007), who looked at hotseat interaction;[5] or the work of Ahuja and Carley (1999) in their study of email inter-actions, referred to earlier. The networks that respondents drew, as we explained, differed widely in form and content and, as was explored in Chapter 4 and sub-sequently, represented widely heterogeneous network elements, including human and non-human actants, organisations, concepts, websites and technologies (digital and otherwise). Had we constrained the mapping task to ask only about electronic modes of communication, very different maps would have emerged; for most of our respondents, electronic technologies featured in their networks, but as we have seen, their adoption and application were highly dependent on many factors: prior experience, funding, school and home factors, bandwidth, or technologies that were too old, or too new, or too different from each other. The mapping task becomes significant in this respect because it is not a study of online networks, but rather locates networking technologies alongside other modes of communication, activities and potential contributory factors to teacher learning.

This analysis leads us to an interesting position whereby networks and networking may be best understood by doing away with the distinction between the online and the offline. This is not only supported by the widely heterogeneous maps of our respondents; for it is possible to reanalyse accounts like those of Stefanone and Gay (2008) not as comparisons of the 'online' and 'offline', but rather in terms of engagement with different modes of communication within the same heterogeneous network. By treating electronic tools, services, communication media and resources as part of such a network, we may be better placed to make sense of the accounts of network participants. Person-to-person communication technologies such as email can be considered alongside other means of sharing information. Websites, as we have seen, can be thought of as a particular kind of representation of organisations, people and practices. The process of engaging teachers with electronic resources can be understood in terms of brokerage across a network rather than participation in an online community. Technologies such as internet access can be seen as part of the social capital available to teachers, not simply the means by which they access it.

Chapter 11

Implications

Introduction

This chapter will look back over the book to pick out what the implications are for the development of an understanding of educational networks, and how they should be investigated further. This will include what they mean for schools and for researchers. We will start by looking back to the initial ideas of teacher networks in Chapter 1 (as represented by the work of Lieberman and others; e.g. Lieberman and Miller [2008a]) and the more elaborate ones from Hargreaves (2003a), to see how thinking has developed.

Where we started

Chapter 1 argued for attention to be paid to both the 'net' and the 'work' in 'network'! If there is to be anything significant in using the word 'network', it should be distinguished from 'community'. We have journeyed through a number of theories and approaches to networks in trying to understand what kinds of distinctions might exist. The attempt has not been to make a clear distinction so much as to ensure that we develop and understand what networks can contribute to the work of creating and sharing practice in schools, and indeed other educational institutions. Equally, drawing on network ideas from other domains, such as the software development world, can seduce us into thinking that we can see parallels in education (as we commented about Hargreaves [2003a]). In such situations the metaphor appears to be taken too far, or at least so far that it becomes thin, with no analytic purchase.

Metaphor versus concept was a recurring theme in the use of network ideas and, unlike Wellman (1988), we do not feel that the maturity of the network field is such as to enable researchers to move from metaphor to concept. Not least is the issue of qualitative versus quantitative approaches in the use of network ideas. For example, social contagion can be conceptualised in social network analysis (SNA) terms, but there is no basis for assuming that the 'exposure' model is at all helpful as applied to the sharing of classroom practice. There is little evidence about how teachers change their practice and the role of the different people with whom they relate in that change. The need for teacher learning to be central (our argument) complicates the mechanisms involved beyond mere 'exposure'.

The message from much of the book is the need to understand SNA, its assumptions and concepts, so that ideas can be developed for educational issues such as the creation and sharing of practice. However, there is an alternative world of detailed qualitative work such as actor-network theory (ANT), and also apparently non-network worlds such as activity theory (AT). We shall come back to these. In Chapter 2 we drew attention to the work of Mitchell (1974), reviewing thinking about networks after twenty years of work on the concept in anthropology. He was taking stock at an early stage in the development of empirical and theoretical work, and yet there were many studies on which to draw. In education there are a more limited number of studies. Some of those studies in relation to professional learning communities (PLCs), as we have argued, take us away from studying the unique insights that network theories could give. Others following the SNA tradition have contributed much, but they represent only the quantitative strand of research. Consequently, we should be modest in what we aim to achieve at this stage and to seek clarity and diversity in our views, rather than certainty and movement on a united front.

First, though, we turn to the implications for professional educators and then to those for researchers.

Implications for schools

A number of times in the book we have suggested what might be done by way of developing networking thinking among schools. There are two strands to the possibilities:

- First, we argue that those in schools, particularly leaders, need to be aware of the networks with which staff and others in school are associated.
- Second, opportunities need to be given for staff to develop networks and networking, particularly in relationship to learning about new practices both within the school and from outside, along with enabling them to share new practices with other schools.

This approach does not see a wholesale system of schools networked together in the way envisaged by Hargreaves (2003a). There is no obvious way that this could be 'engineered' that did not result in a burden on schools. There can be no doubt that the lines of development of PLCs and teacher networks, both built round collaboration with universities, along with action research collaborations, will contribute to the development of new practice. Scalability remains an issue (and one that we raised in Chapter 1), as McLaughlin *et al.* (2008: 203) recognised in their view of the future of networking practitioner research. Whatever its future, such collaborative work has to turn to other mechanisms to involve, and be shared with, the majority of teachers who are not involved but who could benefit from the work of such communities. This is the area where we see schools could put more emphasis as a form of professional development – that is, seeing the nurturing of networks and network activity as an agenda for such development.

In the first strand of work identified above is the need for schools to become aware of the importance of informal and personal networks in the development of their practice. We have suggested mapping in some way, for example using the visualisation exercise presented and explored in this book. There are tools available to do this within a school (James *et al.* 2006a) and literature that advocates its use (Fox 2008). These maps can be drawn by individuals and used as the basis for discussions in professional development activities to see what resources and range of new practice are available, perhaps to a department or to those teachers who deal with a particular age group of students. We do not envisage this being a data collection exercise for the school senior management team, not least because they would be faced with the same kind of analysis problems as those we have discussed in this book. Alternatively, there are SNA approaches, for example as advocated by Daly (2008): for educational leaders to complete a wholesale SNA of their school or district to collect more systematic information and help them plan for change (he cites an intervention study in one school district in the United States). This would reveal in detail the network structure and locate various individuals and groups within the structure.

Whichever method is used, the network ideas we have dealt with, including the role of well-connected people, the exercise of brokerage across structural holes, and the existence of intensional and affiliation networks, can be discussed among teachers – our second strand of possibilities. This might be usefully separated into discussions of internal and external networks, not because they are distinct but because they raise different issues. The separation is also helpful because they have to complement each other in the way argued by Burt, for strongly bound, closed groups needing to be fed by weak links to other networks. (Our case studies indicate the need for school leaders to nurture and retain those who have such connections.) The endeavour is not only to see how the school can use these network processes and connections, but that teachers might understand their potential and their legitimacy as ways of improving practice. Although ideas of social contagion as advocated by SNA cannot be used, how teachers learn about and come to use different practices can be discussed as a process. Teachers' improved understanding of this can be used by researchers to integrate with ideas from other kinds of studies.

The ideas of space and time are more complex, and the lack of spatial literacy within the field of education and education research has been noted as hindering progress in this area (Fisher 2004). Within the school the use of space for informal contact of staff can be an area for planning by school leadership as well as discussion by teachers in professional development activities. Attendance at events outside the school, particularly where they offer opportunities for informal contacts, needs systematic support: to prepare staff before they go, to give strategies to use at the event and to enable reflection, sharing and other follow-up on return. Although many schools will have reporting procedures for formal elements (e.g. courses and other professional development activity), there is less likely to be advice and support for the other informal (networking) parts of events.

However, all of these suggestions, including the use of space, raise ethical issues. We have noted that intrusion into places and times that staff see as 'non-work' is likely to be resisted (Solomon *et al.* 2006). Tuan's (1977) 'back spaces' might need to remain, just so that they retain their value as locations to interact meaningfully. They also have the right to some time and place that is 'their own'. There are perhaps even more ethical issues related to the mapping of teachers' personal networks, especially if this is through SNA. Although the kind of revelations made by Lima (2007, 2008) in the context of a school could be helpful for more productive collaboration within the school, it is not evident that this can be done in a way that would not expose teachers or *cause* conflict (Achinstein 2002).[1] There are no obvious ways to deal with these issues, but it is important to do so in a cautious and sensitive manner. It is these ethical issues that led us to suggest teachers collectively discussing maps (in small groups), to reduce the impact of possible 'surveillance' by school management. In SNA approaches it is less easy to avoid this surveillance. The suggestion in Chapter 5 (p. 90) to carry out a kind of SNA study of the relationships of the 'learning to learn' committee in Beech School to help Ken, the LHTL school co-ordinator, clarify how it could informally influence others in the school, is something that is much less threatening.

These implications for schools are premised on a policy environment that will support network activity. We have in mind here not a networked learning community (NLC) type initiative (nor, in England, what has followed); rather, creating a climate that values teacher learning. Indeed, a view of continuing professional development (CPD) that focuses on *learning*, not just through the formal activities that usually occur, but by considering the teachers' *workplace* learning. There is a large literature on this in workplaces other than educational institutions, and the approaches there should be developed with regard to teachers' learning. But we are going further. We want workplace learning to extend to including the ideas on networks we have discussed: to consider the networks that exist, can be developed, and used. Where governments like to control the educational system centrally, they need to see the school as the focus of this activity. Setting up networks throughout a system is not in our view realistic, as there will be too much energy expended in the organisational infrastructure, as was evident in the UK networked learning communities. Governments need to support teacher learning, and perhaps to switch from talking of CPD, to talking of learning. In England, and other parts of the United Kingdom, there has been support for school-based CPD, as we indicated in Chapter 1. However, recent evidence on the state of this in schools is mixed, and particularly unhelpful for teachers learning from one another:

> [M]ost teachers' approaches to CPD tend not to be collaborative, nor clearly contextualised in classroom practice. . . . [T]his might suggest an absence of systematic school support for collaborative, research-informed approaches to CPD in both primary and secondary.
>
> (Pedder *et al.* 2008: 7)

The reason appears to be within the schools: Pedder *et al.* (ibid.: 9) refer to a 'widespread absence of a strategic approach to CPD in schools'. The answer to this is not just to advocate more collaboration of the kind engendered by PLCs (more than a quarter of a century of activity in the United Kingdom gives us the picture above), but to supplement what collaborative activity exists with that which builds on teacher and school networks. Our call is to widen the view of what counts as teacher learning and to capitalise both on those who are committed to creating knowledge and those who just want to share it. Policy makers need to support this aim by enlarging their view and building capacity within schools. Part of the building of capacity will be what higher education institutions can do to support not only collaborative activity (as advocated by McLaughlin *et al.* [2008], Lieberman and Miller [2008a] and others) but networking. We hope our considerations will enable them to do this, although there is a need for more research to underpin this work.

Implications for research

Looking back

Our journey, both personally and in the book, has been one of revelation of first the disappointments that early educational thinking was either too ambitious or not ambitious enough. Too ambitious in that networks were seen as the way to go and were bestowed with a myriad of concepts that turned out to be metaphors supported by little evidence to show they were productive. Not ambitious enough in that they did not help us to understand the uniqueness of what network thinking could bring to bear. The request from Little (2005b: 278) we quoted in Chapter 1 was for researchers to open up the processes within schools and to understand what happens when they move from 'one institutional space to another'. Our starting point in the LHTL project was the latter, but our work in this book reveals that similar thinking on this problem is needed just as much within the school, to understand the internal networks and how they might link to external ones. SNA seemed to offer a way of dealing with these issues but it makes assumptions and uses measures that, while relevant to the educational processes we have sought to understand, do not adequately account for the emerging picture that our data revealed.

SNA has an important tradition of ego-centric views of networks, but we argued that these should not simply assume these views are a way of sampling 'known' networks, even if they are only theoretical rather than substantive entities. In practice it turns out that even when it is seen as sampling a theoretical network, such as 'society' or 'community', selections are made on the basis of pragmatic limitations. Assuming a bounded network, as in an NLC, does not then justify limiting the empirical scope to only those within it, as might be done in SNA. Rather, we argue that there are many networks, some very personal, representing teachers' and their colleagues' various identities. We considered this idea of identity as a way of framing learning in Chapter 3, recognising that it can account for social and individual aspects of learning. But it was also expanded in the views of spatial and temporal dimensions of networks (Chapter 8).

Although internal school networks are in theory bounded, and hence open to the classic whole-network studies of SNA, it is clear that quantitative studies must be combined with qualitative ones to enable the 'realities' and meanings attached to such networks to be understood. At a simple level the arguments in Chapters 4–6 indicate that the quantitative representations of SNA do not do justice to how teachers and others can represent their networks, or to their relationships, and what they include on their maps. Simple ideas of 'strength of a relationship' are often reduced to a few elements and with assumptions about meaning and value that are limited, or not necessarily those of the respondents. Most quantitative SNA studies have a qualitative element, but we wonder if they are only for illustration of the quantitative data. The qualitative alternative is less obvious and seldom found. Few 'network' ethnographies of the school exist, and where they do (e.g. Nespor 1997), they also draw on actor-network theory (ANT). This is for later.

Nevertheless, SNA has provided us with important ideas of relevance. For example, evidence from much of the educational literature assumes that brokers and experts are often a feature of agents external to schools, yet SNA leads us to consider brokerage in a different way. In particular, it encouraged us to look inside the school for brokers, and our evidence reveals that those internal to schools are indeed important, and in situations where schools no longer rely on local authorities for support, schools may be the best source of such agents. In that sense we agree with Lieberman and her various colleagues on the importance of raising the profile of teachers as a source for the development of their own professional knowledge. The role of brokers should, in particular, be seen in relation to the bridging function argued for in Chapter 5.

Notwithstanding the importance of particular network roles, it is necessary to see network activity as more than the morphology of the network structure. In other words, actors do not just take their significance from network position, but from what they do. A focus on processes is in our view central to any investigation of networks. In the context of the creation and sharing of practice, these processes need to be seen as transactions or transformations. Research needs to make more effort towards investigating the means of creation and sharing, with an emphasis on sharing. Understanding 'creation' processes seems to be an area in itself and, though it is related to network thinking, is not in our view enlightened by such thinking; collecting a group from across schools to work collectively on classroom practices is logistically more difficult, but it becomes more of a *network* issue when they share their outcomes with their colleagues not involved in the creation process. The focus on transactions or transformations is premised on a view of creation and sharing as a form of teacher learning – although when this is interpreted along the lines Wenger (1998) takes (e.g. identity development), we do not believe that it relies exclusively on communities of practice. We have already considered 'networks of practice' and Engeström's (2007) metaphor of 'mycorrhizae' as an alternative. We would also argue that taking a network approach enables us to explore a whole new dimension of 'informal learning' (the argument in Chapter 6). Whether Engeström's more general view on activity theory (as the basis for expansive learning) is of relevance, we shall deal with when we consider theoretical issues.

We would argue also that network processes have spatial and temporal dimensions, which could be seen as the context for network processes (taking 'context' to mean what Lave [1996] argued for). Unlike those who see an impact of information technologies on the way to think about networks (e.g. Castells 2000a; Wellman 2001), we are convinced that in networks of knowledge 'flows' about classroom practice, the physical and temporal are important. Even where the physical is there to create socio-emotional support and hence has dimensions other than knowledge, all points in the network nevertheless occur somewhere. The evidence in Chapter 10 in particular indicates not only the relative lack of impact of individual-to-individual communication of classroom practice through electronic means, but that there remains an importance in creating 'physical' analogies in the electronic world. ('Tapped in' comes to mind.[2]) One of the interesting developments in spatial and temporal considerations in networks is in sites of informal learning, and there is an important role for investigating such sites outside the conventional 'workplace', which for teachers is of course the school.

Finally, our discussion of electronic networks still reveals a similar situation we faced when we started the LHTL research: although much is promised, we still await the transformations that such networks promise to contribute to the type of development of professional practice with which we have been concerned. The new elements of web tools and environments have not so far delivered this transformation. As we indicated in Chapter 10, it may be that it is only where 'marginality' of a teaching group is relevant that there is sufficient of an imperative to bring such networks more centrally to professional exchange. It is evident that teaching as 'production' will not benefit in the way commercial companies have with regard to knowledge creation and sharing, something we will return to when we consider again 'mycorrhizae' as a form.

All of this indicates to us the start of the journey of research in understanding educational networks, with a myriad of different areas of work for those who want to think in terms of networks. It is not, however, a critique of those who focus on communities (or indeed any other from of structure); it is simply a call to look both inside and outside of them from the perspective of a network where relationships can be varied in their forms and value. Any attempt to look 'with different eyes' needs a set of tools, and moving away from the well-honed ones from SNA pushes us into some uncertain territory.

Methodological implications

Moving beyond SNA brings significant methodological challenges, some of which we examined in Chapter 4. There we rehearsed the familiar qualitative challenges: a lack of operationalisation of concepts, dealing adequately with bias and the lack of statistical generalisation. The latter was best shown in the efforts in Chapter 5 to count nodes across maps and make inferences about the meaning of the numbers. Even at its simplest level, being able to say primary schools have more relationships with those in close proximity to the school and secondary schools more geographically widely spread ones is not unimportant, but in terms of our data can be said only very tentatively. Chapter 4 also indicated that the maps themselves presented problems in understanding the context within which teachers responded, or indeed the extent to which their own network metaphors (and ours) might have influenced their representations. Visualisation in itself might prefigure particular metaphors, though the wide variation was an important antidote to our taking up any particular set of representations.

SNA, on the other hand, while able to overcome many of these problems, is dominated by particular views of networks, as we have indicated. Nevertheless, we would support the development of more SNA work both within and across schools (as Lima [2007], Daly *et al.* [2009] and others encourage). Our comments above would lead us to add the caveat of not relying on SNA as the main representation of educational networks. We have already indicated the importance of qualitative additions, but we go further and ask for deeply qualitative studies. As we indicate below, just what such studies would look like is unclear, even if ANT is taken as a guide, but we will discuss this further. Our LHTL and subsequent research was unable to examine the connections between the creation and sharing processes and *network* processes (for example, there is no evidence that social contagion actually occurs with respect to school practices), and it is these processes that need to be the focus. SNA assumes the nature of the process (e.g. in the features of relationships it asks respondents to rate or identify) and then seeks to say something about morphology with respect to the actors' relationships. We ask that this is turned inside out and take the process involved as requiring investigation. Chapter 7 gave some hints of this in terms of following through the processes involved in the practice being developed in one classroom or school site and being shared and transformed into practice in another site. This is not just a matter of understanding sharing, for, as Little (2002) pointed out, representations of practice by professionals even in the act of creation of new practice (or at least the investigation of existing practice) have been a neglected research topic. Such issues of representation are also at work in the reification of practice that is an inevitable part of any sharing, whether it is within a close-knit group in a school (a community) or between schools.

The implication of the above discussion is that the unit of analysis is associated with *practice*, which is not straightforward. Should we be studying individuals (or groups or schools) and their involvement in creation and sharing (sampling *individuals* and not the practices in question)? Or should the focus be on the practices themselves with an attempt to trace their 'development' (i.e. how they are created and shared)? There are obvious problems in the latter even in a situation such as in the LHTL project, where there was an identifiable practice or set of associated practices (e.g. questioning techniques, and feedback on student work). If it is to be done 'live', as it were, then how are the sites for its creation and sharing chosen? Where there is a specific effort to develop practices, based on advice and examples from elsewhere, what gives the indication of when the practice 'appears', and how is it sampled? In some senses the LHTL project assumed that potentially in any of the forty schools sampled it could happen. But when we came to choose 'target teachers' to study as individuals, we were advised by the school co-ordinator, and she often picked those teachers who were most likely to do something, and something that was good. Can a researcher scan the school horizon looking for practice emerging? Even then, it might emerge but go nowhere, or at least be invisible in its traces. If we focus on individuals who are active in developing practice as the unit of analysis, we will equally be unsure that practice sharing will take place. One possibility is to do a retrospective study where identifiable development and sharing has occurred (or at least been reported to have occurred). The answers to some of these questions will not, however, result in elegant research designs.

But, by way of an exploration of what some of these issues might mean, we reconceive the LHTL project not as a three-level study but as a *network* study. In fact, this would have to be a number of studies, which may or may not be linked (funding and school overload issues determine this); but they should be conceived of as a group of studies:

1   SNA studies within and between a limited group of schools. These could be schools that are in a defined network or partnership (as we saw in Chapter 9). These studies will explore similar work to Daly *et al.* (2009) and others, but with a more specific emphasis on some particular classroom practice such as AfL.

2   A case study of a school to trace networks across the school using qualitative methods that explore how practice is, or could, be shared; to do effectively a qualitative version of Lima (2007, 2008). (This is likely to be a weak approach and suffer from some of the problems that we encountered; it is difficult to be sure of finding any specific traces.) This could also be done with a number of teachers (e.g. a department) being the unit of the case study rather than a whole school. This could be accompanied by a parallel SNA study if conducted in some way that did not interact with the case study.

3   The same approach as the previous one but focused on a specific initiative such as assessment for learning (AfL) that is or had been developed in the school. The

details of the methods will depend upon whether this is 'live' development (i.e. there are 'events' that can be attended) or one reconstructed after some or all of the processes have taken place. Any degree of reconstruction will probably result in less specificity of traces (as LHTL suffered). Who is sampled will depend upon the progress of the initiative, rather than ahead of time deciding on 'target' teachers (as in LHTL). The focus here is on transactions, and those involved. (This study will involve both creation and sharing within the school.)

4   The approach in (3) would be developed to look across schools and to 'follow' the development or 'movement' of a practice from one school to another. (This might be a variation of Lawrence's study (2009), though the methods might not be the same.)

5   The pilot work by Fox and McCormick (2009) needs to be developed both in scale of work (and nested within some of the approaches (3) and (4)), and in the form of analysis both of the 'event within life' and a 'life within an event' (discussed in the penultimate section of Chapter 8 [pp. 185–8]).

In the suggestions in (2)–(4), no specific qualitative approaches have been assumed, and below we discuss ANT and AT as 'competing' approaches. These are of course not simple 'methodological' choices, as ANT, for example, rejects preordained substantive assumptions about the processes involved (Monteiro 2000), but we will further examine the work of Miettinen (1999), who argues for AT rather than ANT. Given the problem of tracing outside influences on teachers (certainly so in LHTL), we would question whether ANT studies can actually be done in an educational context.

Theoretical implications

In this subsection we look at some of the 'alternatives' to the main considerations we have given to network theories. Our basic stance is to recognise the usefulness of SNA as an approach to networks, but to pick up some of its results and leave behind its quantitative and mathematical methods. In part, this was to do with the way networks are represented: as whole networks that seek to reveal a structure (Chapter 4 arguments), as a unitary set of nodes (usually human actors; Chapter 5), as unitary set of relationships with limited sets of dimensions (e.g. strength; Chapter 6), and seeing information as 'flowing' rather than knowledge being transacted (Chapter 7). Yet we have found the ideas of brokers, and intensional and affiliation networks, in particular, useful ways of thinking about knowledge creation and sharing in education. Social contagion seems less suited to this as it is not clear that the underlying theory is indeed helpful to a process that we see not as diffusion, but as learning, where creating meaning is the prime activity. Indeed, theoretical ideas that derive from the educational literature (of which learning is the most important) compete, as it were, with network theories to explain the responses that teachers and headteachers made to our investigations. This reiterates the point we made in Chapter 2, echoing Mitchell (1974), about the need to rely not on network theories but on substantive theories about the phenomena being studied. The challenge is how to use these insights while still being able to use qualitative data. For us this represents, at least at this stage of our understanding, the best way to approach the nature of the networks with which teachers and schools engage. Quantitative studies, as our discussion above indicates, are needed, but without parallel qualitative approaches that construct case studies of networks and networking, an understanding of networks is likely to remain too narrow.

There are of course other ways of investigating networks that do not take a quantitative approach, and in particular we have discussed that of ANT, as a possible one to take.

Actor-network theory

In Chapter 2 we discussed this alternative and examined some of its basic ideas, but noted, as many others have (e.g. Miettinen 1999), that it is more a methodological than a substantive theory. Although a discussion of ANT may seem more methodologically appropriate to those discussed in the previous section, the way it conceives of networks nevertheless also gives it important *theoretical* imperatives. Chapter 4 indicated the recognition of the heterogeneity of networks that ANT emphasises and, in particular, the role of non-human as well as human actants. More important is the centrality of change in ANT that, for example, will only reveal parts of the network that have been 'black-boxed' in ANT terms – their role, nature, function and importance submerged and unchallenged until circumstances made them evident and brought them into sharper focus (see p. 75). However, we considered the critics of ANT, concerned that choices of which actors to study (they are potentially unlimited) result in only those with 'loud voices' being heard. The fact that actors must do something reveals a further important element of their defining characteristic, discussed in Chapter 5, leading to the importance of mediators in interactions. Chapter 6 took up the activity of transformation by mediators and related it to the making of meaning from objects that can result, in our terms, in learning and hence new practice. ANT offers the prospect of investigating this process, which was our concern in Chapter 7. Tracing associations offers a way of investigating the processes involved when practice in one classroom finds its way, in a different form, to another classroom, whether that be within a single school or between several. Those in education, like Little (2004), argue for the kinds of detail that ANT offers, but from the slightly less exotic field of ethnography.

Our final discussion of a role for ANT was on issues of space and time in Chapter 8. Latour (2005: 194) discusses what he calls 'articulators' and 'localizers': 'the transported presence of places into other ones'. This is part of the general discussion of the role of non-social agencies that make the social viable. His example is the way in which the physical construction of a lecture theatre does not determine the actions of the lecturers and students, but it has a role, and it becomes a 'place' (in the Chapter 8 sense) through the drawings, specifications and materials that make it up. Latour seeks to avoid moving away from the local to some view of its 'context' or 'structure' – that is, taking a more global view. He wants the ANT investigator rather to ask how the local is generated and hence is concerned to trace the site of production of local interactions. Place is important in this. There is an interesting theoretical difference between this stance, which is in part methodological,[3] and that of the literature we considered in Chapter 8 (stemming in part from geographical studies). In contrast to ANT, authors such as Massey (1994, 2005) bring substantive theories to bear to understand space and time, and we have used them to try to understand events, and the places within which they occur. Solomon *et al.* (2006) use socio-cultural theory to explore space in parallel ways, but they draw on Nespor (1994), who in turn uses socio-cultural ideas such as identity and trajectories, which we have also drawn on, but not in identical ways. Nespor (ibid.: 12) is concerned that the communities of practice, as discussed by Lave and Wenger (1991), 'are treated as bounded, localized settings' unconnected to other times and places.[4] He turns to ANT ideas to enable the mobilisation of a distributed and spatialised network, where the linkages are not fixed and static, but ongoing. This is in part a way of seeing the many (and for him, competing) identities that are evident, which we discussed in Chapter 3 (drawing on Tonso [2007] and Hughes [2008]). Of equal interest is Nespor's variation on Latour's topology metaphor, where he does not accept complete fluidity in the landscape of the network that Latour wants to keep flat. Nespor acknowledges that there are issues such as class and gender that mean that 'it would be a mistake to emphasize the fluidity of the world without noting that it flows at times in very deeply worn channels' (1994: 15). He thus uses ANT language to produce a conception of knowledge construction that allows for the existence of worn landscapes as well as flows. This is not a simple reinstatement of theory over methodology, as Nespor (ibid.: 2) says at an earlier point:

> [T]heories are ways of talking about worlds that can be moved about and used in different situations for different purposes. Theory does not subsume or explain 'empirical' work, it's simply a way of moving it, or as Latour . . . suggests, of connecting different networks of knowledge work.

It is therefore difficult to reconcile these contrasting views of Latour's purely methodological view of ANT and Nespor's use of ANT, at least in his use of the geographic metaphor of territory.

But even as a methodology it has conceptual problems, which we will come to shortly when we consider AT. For the uninitiated – that is, those, like us, who have not participated in an 'ANT study' – the accounts of ANT by Latour and others do not provide easy guides to action. For example, Latour (2005) seems more preoccupied with refuting the traditional approach of sociology and its use of the 'social' (as indicated in Chapter 2). The result is that in the second part of his account, dedicated to indicating 'how to render associations traceable again' (ibid.: 157), there is much made of how to avoid the assumptions and inclinations of traditional sociologists to, as indicated above (note 3), 'jump' to contexts as explanations for local interactions. At one point he acknowledges that 'ANT's lessons will be only negative because clearing the way is what we are after so that the social could be deployed enough to be assembled again' (ibid.: 200) (Latour then goes on in this instant to say five things that face-to-face interactions cannot be). Thus, critics see problems, for example, in selecting what actors to investigate when there is '[n]o theoretically relevant elements of the network [that] can be discerned in advance' (Miettinen 1999: 181). When the alternative is complete description, Miettinen thinks that '[i]f the object of the research is an innovation process, the task seem hopeless' (ibid.).[5]

We are conscious that we have ignored a central feature of ANT, namely power. As Law (1992: 6) puts it, 'actor-network theory is all about power – power as a (concealed or misrepresented) effect, rather than power as a set of causes'. Such considerations cannot be ignored, but we are not clear how it fits into the knowledge creation and sharing process – not because we believe it is absent, but because we are unclear how it operates. Creating meaning and identity in a network is to deal with issues of power, but we do not yet have the means of dealing with this in terms of teacher learning. We await some ANT studies that can uncover this in networks of knowledge creation and sharing.[6] Although we have acknowledged that in tracing the associations of knowledge creation and sharing among teachers and schools, ANT seems to offer an important approach, it is not obvious to us just what such a study would be like (nor are we aware of one that has taken place). All the more reason for someone to try to carry out such investigations.

Activity theory

Notwithstanding that ANT can be seen primarily as a methodology, there exists a conceptual issue at its core, according to Miettinen (1999). An underlying issue for him, taking a cultural-historical theory of activity (note 14 to Chapter 3), is the concept of mediated action: a human agent is related to an object through the mediation of cultural means or artefacts. (It is through such mediation that meaning is made in the terms we discussed in Chapter 3.) Miettinen (ibid.: 182) argues that because of ANT's equal treatment of human and non-human elements in a network, it ignores the 'role of human cognition, intentionality, and learning in the innovation processes',[7] something we would also be concerned about. For example, Latour would reject the notion of 'reification' as one means by which mediation takes place (Miettinen 1999: 178). Miettinen then goes on to argue that AT enables mediation to be taken into account while placing this in the context of an activity system (made up of 'rules', 'division of labour' and 'community', along with the actor, object and artefact). It is thus possible to represent individuals and groups of teachers (in a school) as subjects (actors) in an activity system, and to link these in a network of activity systems. From this we have a completely different approach to networks, which can link to ideas on learning and which maintains the concern for human and non-human elements. We feel that this kind of analysis takes us beyond the scope of the book, but it nevertheless opens up another, and perhaps fruitful, line of inquiry.[8]

The idea of artefacts as mediating human action ('subjects' in an activity system) creates an issue of the status of such artefacts and how they affect the agency of human actors. Mediation does not mean 'control' by the artefacts. Thus, in electronic networks the way the software displays discussion forums has a huge impact. An example is the studies we did for the NCSL on Talk2learn, which showed that what was read by participants was a feature of the display order of messages (and the fact that the default was to show the messages in their entirety, rather than, say, the first line, or even who sent the message and how it was threaded).[9] There are similar issues in the Open University (UK) use of Moodle forums,[10] where the order of discussion threads is always the one with the newest message at the top (rather than the order of creation of the discussions, say). Interaction can in these circumstances be 'governed' by the technology as it frames how and what discussions to enter into, as well as being the medium of the interaction (e.g. through typing messages or speaking in a video- or audio-based system[11]). Whether or not this mediation argument generalises to other artefacts is less clear; Little's (2002) ideas on conceptual and representational artefacts of how teachers represent classroom practice to each other are decided and controlled by teachers themselves (rather than by software designers).

As we indicated in Chapter 7, where we questioned what happened when teachers find something useful on a website, investigating the associations involved and how teachers' agency is exhibited in 'learning' is a rich vein of research.

Looking to the future

Throughout the book, we have been concerned with the two forms of 'community' and 'network' and have considered briefly other forms such as 'mycorrhizae' and activity systems. We indicated in Chapter 3 that we would return to consider these in the light of our discussions. The idea of mycorrhizae is an easier one to put to one side, not because it is not intriguing and full of potential, but because at this stage in its development we have little to go on. More importantly, the premise of Engeström (2007), in proposing it, was a modern form of production reflecting contemporary companies and the like. However, we argued in Chapter 7 that there was no reason to presume that the 'production' of teaching is in any way as interdependent as modern-day industries and that the role of knowledge with regard to new practices would likewise not necessarily be the same. Similarly, when we considered Castells' ideas in Chapter 2, we were sceptical about the role of electronic networks in this regard. The analysis in Chapter 10 indicates that our view has not fundamentally changed. Even with the newest developments of Web 2.0 and the increase in use of social networking by teachers, the nature of teaching as a form of 'production' does not lend itself well to a role for ICT in knowledge creation and sharing in relation to practice. If teaching and learning were indeed transformed by ICT, as we have long been promised, then this might change its potential for teacher learning. The message of Chapter 10 was, however, 'we are not there yet'. If we look to the UK government initiatives, such as the e-learning strategy (DfES 2005a) and the Building Schools for the Future programme,[12] with the possibilities of transforming both the use of ICT and educational establishments, we find little discussion of pedagogy, though some hopes of ICT's impact. The 'transforming learning' ideas for ICT include the following:

> We have to address three critical problems in the provision of e-learning: the quantity and range of resources available to teachers and learners; the quality and degree of innovation of those resources; and the embedding of e-learning and ICT across the curriculum.
>
> (ibid.: 27)

This vision seems to still see schools and classrooms looking much the same, though there is a recognition that 'our teaching institutions ought to be advancing beyond the traditional formats that are still so prevalent' (ibid.: 26). The policy document acknowledges the need for research to develop more innovative pedagogical methods, and ways to deliver them more effectively through e-learning, but that is for the future. Talking of the next generation of e-learning:

> The focus should be on design flexibility for teachers and engaging activity for learners. Flexible learning design packages would enable teachers in all sectors to build their own individual and collaborative learning activities around digital resources. This would help them engage in designing and discussing new kinds

of pedagogy, which is essential if we are to succeed in innovating and transforming teaching and learning.

(ibid.: 28)

When these kinds of developments take place, there may be some possibility of the 'interdependence' of teachers in their everyday working that Little (1990) called for (Chapter 7), through a new form of 'production'. But we may still be asking in another decade, 'Are we there yet?'

This still leaves us with thinking about community and networks and their relationship. The evidence from Chapter 7 is that when we examine the research on the fine grain of knowledge creation, there is still much to understand about the processes involved. There is also evidence from SNA that the relationships among teachers that exist within schools, and perhaps even in such knowledge production communities, are not necessarily sufficient to enable sharing within the community. Sharing beyond the group certainly is problematic. Although we acknowledge that the analysis of knowledge creation through the concept of 'community' is sound (despite the many criticisms of 'communities of practice' we considered), our view is that this still needs to be complemented by network ideas of the kind we have discussed. The case for this in relation to sharing outside the community is irrefutable, in our view. The network ideas we have in mind in both cases are those of SNA, with its quantitative approaches, and of the qualitative approaches of institutional case study and ANT. These latter approaches are neither straightforward nor exemplified in the case of educational networks, and, to reiterate an earlier point, at this stage of our understanding and state of research about such networks we advocate a multi-method approach. With this we accept that there will be parallel and perhaps not always communicative lines of development; as Knox *et al.* (2006: 114) argue, 'network ideas are remarkably poorly networked among themselves'. We can only hope that developments in both research and understanding in the future do try to emulate the very form the research is intent on investigating.

Notes

Preface

1 In fact Hakkarainen and his colleagues were concerned with education – the education of students in schools – to enable them to carry out the networking that was of so much concern to commercial innovation.

1 Educational policy and technological contexts

1 For an early account of these approaches in relation to ideas on education and development, see McCormick and James (1988: 30–41).

2 This approach did not reflect the understanding of work-based learning that currently exists, and which draws upon a wide range of working environments (e.g. Billett 2006).

3 The reference to networks was largely to networks as a form of organised links among schools. We will return to this specific evidence on networks in Chapter 2.

4 There are other networks (e.g. the Pennsylvania Action Research Network), but CARN is one of the original ones and, as we argue, such networks are characterised more by their focus on action research than by their focus on their networking.

5 Action research need not necessarily only involve a teacher researching in her own classroom, and can involve outsiders. In addition it has now taken on a particular cycle of research and action. See Somekh and Zeichner (2009) for a recent account of this field. They trace the origins of ideas on action research, including those of Lawrence Stenhouse and John Elliott.

6 This network has a website, www.did.stu.mmu.ac.uk/carnnew (accessed 11 November 2009).

7 This is not universally true in the case of such action research. For example, Posch and Mair (1997) give an account of teacher networking and knowledge building, although their focus on social networks is on personal relations that lead to trust as part of community, rather than for the spread of innovation. Interestingly, they do note that when teachers visit other's classrooms to observe innovations, the developments that flow from this should not be seen as dissemination, as the ideas are transformed, something we will come back to in Chapter 7.

8 We are indebted to Bridget Somekh for directing us to recent information on CARN.

9 Weak links are those that do not involve close relationships. They will be the subject of later explanations.

10 In an account of the National Writing Project, Lieberman and Wood (2004: 66) refer to networks as 'loose and flexible organisational forms'.

11 In the United Kingdom there was also a strong accountability element, missing from the account by Stoll *et al.* (2006); see Day and Sachs (2004) and McCormick and James (1988).

12 Bolam *et al.* (2005) is the report of a study for the Department for Education and Skills (responsible for education in England), and a section of it was published as Stoll *et al.* (2006).

13 Online at: www.innovation-unit.co.uk (accessed 16 September 2009). The research project's website, 'Creating and sustaining effective professional learning communities', had not been

updated since 2006 at the time of writing (online at: www.eplc.info; accessed 18 September 2009).

14 Their use of Granovetter (1973) is quite the opposite of Lieberman and Grolnick (1996).

15 An earlier report (Lieberman and Wood 2004) cited 167 sites. The figures cited at other times are 100 (Lieberman and Wood 2003b), 175 (Lieberman and Wood 2003a) and 195 (Lieberman and Miller 2008a).

16 He also includes 'managerial capital' to support knowledge creation and utilisation.

17 This is the government agency responsible for supporting the use of ICT in schools (online at: www.becta.org.uk; accessed 20 May 2009).

18 A site selling a range of products including books, electronic equipment, movies, groceries, etc. (online at: www.amazon.com; accessed 20 May 2009).

19 A site reviewing a range of products (online at: www.epinions.com; accessed 20 May 2009).

20 Some of these can be specifically structured for such knowledge creation, for example Knowledge Forum software, which can be used to create workspaces designed to enable knowledge building (online at: www.knowledgeforum.com; accessed 20 May 2009); or Fle3, a computer-supported collaborative learning environment (online at: http://fle3.uiah.fi; accessed 20 May 2009).

21 This site originally allowed individuals to share files of music that they had recorded by any means. However, it was forced by the courts in the United States to withdraw this facility and it now sells music in a variety of ways: www.napster.ca (accessed 20 May 2009). A history of this can be found on Wikipedia: http://en.wikipedia.org/wiki/Napster (accessed 20 May 2009).

22 Doubt is also cast on his views by McLaughlin *et al.*, who, in their view of the way forward, describe Hargreaves' approach as a 'maximal view of networks' (2008: 214), concluding that 'there is no evidence of networks of schools having the capacity or the desire to work on co-ordinated research projects' (ibid.).

23 http://sam11.moe.gov.sg/tn (accessed 21 May 2009).

24 This is now called the National College for Leadership of Schools and Children's Services (online at: www.nationalcollege.org.uk; accessed 6 December 2009).

25 David Jackson, one of the authors of this article, was the NLC Programme Director within the NCSL.

26 This idea is taken from Church *et al.* (2002) and was featured in a review of networked learning communities carried out by the English National Foundation for Educational Research (Kerr *et al.* 2003: 13). We shall discuss this review later in the chapter.

27 There is some semblance here to knotworks (Engeström *et al.* 1999), but these derive from an activity theory analysis rather than a network theory, and in any case do not necessarily have strong links.

28 Despite this, Hadfield (2005: 183) still sees PLCs as having the most influence on the NLC programme.

29 For example: Lieberman (1999), reprinted in an NLC publication (NCSL 2005) for the NLCs; Lieberman and Stoll both contributed to a seminar for the NLC Group: *International Perspectives in Networked Learning* (NCSL undated).

30 An earlier reference in the review to electronic networking was not favourable.

31 The response rate in terms of teachers is 38 per cent (assuming 5 teachers in each of the 662 schools in the population), with 57 per cent of schools being represented. However, little information is given about the sample in terms of how it represented such factors as types of schools or size of networks.

32 Their analysis resembles that of Stoll *et al.* (2006) on PLCs in relation to knowledge creation as making implicit knowledge explicit, reinforcing the similarity of their approaches, though one talks of communities and the other networks.

33 The original NCSL paper (Little 2005a) was later published as Little (2005b), from which we quote. The passage in the original paper has a slightly different start, but the thrust of the quotation here is the same as that of the original.

34 However, we should not underrate the contribution they have made, and the NLC publications on the NCSL website are very extensive, with a publications directory being available online at: www.nationalcollege.org.uk/docinfo?id=31342&filename=learning-networks-publications-directory.pdf (accessed 15 March 2010).

35 This strategy brought together the national literacy and numeracy strategies; details can be found online at: http://nationalstrategies.standards.dcsf.gov.uk/primary (accessed 19 September 2009).

36 This would give an average of 3.5 schools per network, against a minimum of 5 and a recommended average of 6. There are some 20,000 primary schools in England.

37 The final one on visits would be a 'sharing' activity if it was something for all teachers, but our evidence of observing an NLC revealed large 'cover' costs to release teachers and to set up an administrative system for a visits programme. There is no evidence of this being sustainable without external funding.

38 The website no longer has a specific set of pages on networks; rather, they are found in a variety of areas related to PLCs and the like. However, many of the Primary Strategy Learning Networks documents are still available on the DCSF website (online at: www.dcsf.gov.uk/index.htm; accessed 21 September 2009) if one uses 'primary strategy learning networks' in the search engine.

39 One could be forgiven for being sceptical of educational fashion when the DEMOS collection on networks (McCarthy *et al.* 2004) is compared with a later collection on collaboration (Parker and Gallagher 2007), both of which involved the NCSL and David Jackson. In the first, the power of networks is argued for (and it contains Hargreaves' [2004] critique of Lieberman and Wood [2004], discussed earlier), and in the second, NLCs are an example of collaboration in action. This reinforces for us the shift in emphasis (see also Glatter 2003: 'Collaboration, collaboration, collaboration').

40 By the time the proposal for the research was accepted for funding by the research council, Hargreaves had left the team because of a move out of the university sector.

2 Theorising networks

1 As indicated in Chapter 1, David Hargreaves had moved to another post, as did Geoff Southworth. We have already considered some of Hargreaves' ideas on networks in Chapter 1; Southworth originally led the network-level research in LHTL with a focus on electronic networks, but has also written on the school as a learning organisation, with teachers working collaboratively to create knowledge. In this work he makes a brief reference to the power of internal and external networks (Southworth 2000).

2 These were networks set up across schools in more than one local authority, sometimes geographically distant, with enhanced ICT in schools to enable them to work together. They existed in the early part of the century, but are no longer extant.

3 The dominant model for the analysis of electronic discussion networks was that based on communities of practice (Lave and Wenger 1991), rather than network theories, a model we have questioned (Thorpe *et al.* 2007).

4 Church *et al.* (2002) was the source for much of the literature on networks discussed in Chapter 1, and they set out to define networks as a form of structure that is organised and co-ordinated.

5 The literature on SNA uses 'ties' and 'links' interchangeably, and we follow this convention.

6 Graph theory is the mathematical study of the arrangement of points and lines, used in SNA to probe the underlying deep structures.

7 Wellman *et al.* (1988) examine three views of community as lost, saved or liberated. More recently, Clark (2007) examines the different views of community and what a network approach offers by way of understanding. We acknowledge that the concept of 'community' is contested.

8 There is an extensive collection of work on SNA in four volumes, edited by Scott (2002).

9 Granovetter revisited this work in 1983, presenting empirical evidence to substantiate his earlier claims about the importance of both weak and strong ties.

10 Clark (2007) gives a range of Milgram's experiments and the results (all with disappointing returns), noting the empirical weakness of this work. Watts (2003) recounts the work of a researcher who tried, unsuccessfully, to find out whether any of these experiments were ever statistically good enough to justify the claim Milgram made.

11 A different kind of study using Microsoft Messenger avoided the problems of these kinds of experiments. For the purposes of their experiment, two people were considered to be

acquaintances if they had sent one another a text message. The researchers looked at the minimum chain lengths it would take to connect 180 billion different pairs of users in the database. They found that the average length was 6.6 steps and that 78 per cent of the pairs could be connected in seven hops or fewer. (Reported by Peter Whoriskey, *Washington Post* staff writer, 2 August 2008: 'Instant-Messagers really are about six degrees from Kevin Bacon. Big Microsoft study supports small world theory'; online at: www.washingtonpost.com/wp-dyn/content/article/2008/08/01/AR2008080103718.html.) Watts *et al.* (2002) have proposed a model of social structures that offers an explanation for what Milgram (1967) found – what Watts *et al.* (2002) describe as 'searchability'.

12 There is an interestingly different language between the two authors in discussing the theoretical network worlds of the mathematics and the real networks to which they apply them. Watts (2003: 16) describes how his book has two stories, one the science of networks, and the other about real-world phenomena that the science of networks attempts to understand. He sees a networked way of thinking about the real world, rather than treating networks as objects of study. Barabási (2003) vacillates between the two, and at times actually says that the science 'governs' the real world: 'Network evolution is governed by the subtle yet unforgiving law of preferential attachment. Guided by it, we unconsciously add links at a higher rate to those nodes that are already heavily linked' (ibid.: 86); 'By uncovering the mechanisms that govern network evolution we have grasped the universality of the arsenal of tools nature uses to create the complex world around us' (ibid.: 107).

13 This is a further extension of the links of structure and agency that underlie the structural and transactional perspectives of Mitchell (1974).

14 Watts (2004) reviews the contributions to sociology of what he calls the 'new' science of networks; in fact, he shows how many of the developments reflect earlier findings in social sciences, but that the new science offers methodological advances from mathematics and physics.

15 Latour (2005: 87) talks of the 'ether of society', recalling the nineteenth-century invention of a substance (a medium) in physics to explain the propagation of light waves. This 'ether' is like using an idea such as 'social force' as an explanation for interactions, rather than looking at what produces it through the associations among actors.

16 This design involved studying forty schools at three levels: classrooms, schools and networks. At each of these levels the sampling decisions were necessarily different (James *et al.* 2006b).

17 Note that these knots are different from those used by Church *et al.* (2002), discussed in Chapter 1.

18 The reason Valente gives for this was that the adoption of the new drug was not meeting much resistance. He does not consider whether this was because, for example, it required a minimal change in doctors' practices or whether it was to do with overwhelming research evidence of the drug's effectiveness.

19 This brings to mind the distinction between etic networks in anthropology, where the study of indigenous values of a particular society is done in its own terms, as opposed to emic networks, where broader theoretical models are applied across a number of societies.

20 He was discussing such things as the early telegraphy operators, whose minds and hands were linked through the keys and wires they used, and more recently Stephen Hawking, of whom Otis asks, 'where is he when communicating through a computer and voice box?' (2001: 221).

21 She also noted that SNA's use of formalised mathematics occurred to such an extent that this analysis became more important than the empirical data upon which it was supposed to be working.

22 In *Education Epidemic* he refers to schools themselves choosing to innovate (Hargreaves 2003a: 38), though for 'front-line innovation', leading-edge schools are supported by government (ibid.: 39) and hence presumably selected by it. Interestingly, guidance material from a professional development group talks of 'showcase schools' as hubs for 'satellite schools' in the network (Akoh and Gutherson 2007).

23 The starting point of this review was a search of WorldCat, British and Australian Education Indexes, ERIC, and the ProQuest dissertation and thesis databases.

24 There is a study of the relations within the educational research community in Finland, where the extent of communication, collaboration and citation was investigated for professors

(Palonen and Lehtinen 2001). It revealed that there is limited communication and collaboration across universities, but more within particular institutions, and that some professors were in fact very isolated from their colleagues.

25 All of these, apart from Hite *et al.* (2006) are PhD and EdD theses from University of Pennsylvania, indicating that SNA is a particular interest there. There is other work, not cited here but reviewed by Daly *et al.* (2009) and Baker-Doyle (2008b).

26 There are a number of higher-degree theses that similarly explore the nature of collaboration and the 'community environment' in schools: Slater (1991) looked at collegiality and related this to school performance; Purinton (2005) also looks at collegiality and relates it to the need to give good teachers a prominent role in departments; Waetjen (2005) and Vodicka (2007) examine trust, the former looking at departments and the lack of cohesion often found within them, the latter at the trust in the school principal and how connected teachers felt.

27 Apart from four of the studies we have cited, little work had been done using an SNA approach prior to the establishment of the NLCs. However, it is somewhat surprising that the twenty-five years of experience of PLCs had not produced any such work until after twenty years.

28 These are teams of teachers within a school dealing with a particular student age group (parallel to subject departments in secondary schools).

29 Alan Daly is editing a book on social networks, drawing on international studies, which will add significantly to the understanding of the SNA as applied to education (Daly forthcoming).

3 Teacher learning

1 Part of this debate was played out in *Educational Researcher*, with articles by Anderson *et al.* (1996, 1998) on the cognitive side and Greeno (1997), among others, on the situated. They produced a joint article with some kind of agreement on the two perspectives in Anderson *et al.* (2000).

2 See Rogoff (1990) for an account of how Piaget and Vygotsky differ in their consideration of the social dimension.

3 They are isolated in the classrooms from other teachers, though clearly there are intense social activities with students.

4 Schemes of work thus mediate the world of the classroom.

5 In fact Lieberman and Miller (2008b: 16) do deal with the three criteria, but they are not applied analytically to the specific example (Moir and Hanson 2008) they include in their book on PLCs. This is not to deny that at least some of the criteria are evident, but they are taken as self-evident rather than to be established in the research. In their discussion of networks as communities of practice, Veugelers and O'Hair (2005b: 213–14) imply joint enterprise, referring to 'groups who share common concerns', but again the criteria of a community of practice are not dealt with directly, despite the claim that 'all the networks in the book describe how they try to develop such communities of practice'. In one example in the book (Veugelers and O'Hair 2005a) concerning PLCs, there is a reference to communities of practice, but it is assumed that the teachers involved do indeed constitute such a community (O'Hair *et al.* 2005: 78).

6 This is an important idea in relation to our discussion of networks, and at the end of the chapter we will return to consider communities and networks.

7 This concept of a 'bridge' is not the same as that discussed in relation to networks (Chapter 2), where the bridge is a relationship (in social network analysis). It is not straightforward in the various network theories because, if we consider actor-network theory, the object could be the non-human actor in associations that exist.

8 Fox (forthcoming) is working on how teachers develop a leadership identity in addition to that of a classroom teacher. Here we are interested in something perhaps more subtle: teachers remaining classroom teachers, just better ones, with a new conception of what it means to practise in the classroom.

9 Even the brief discussion above indicates that more experienced teachers learn. We will later explore the ways in which this learning relates to other discussions of knowledge creation in the literature.

10 In fact one of her co-editors (Jewson 2007) does argue for the use of network analysis, giving a brief account of SNA concepts (e.g. bridges, centrality, clusters and density) as well as a brief account of actor-network theory, but unfortunately does not develop this by providing empirical or illustrative material in workplace learning, or by a detailed analysis of communities of practice verses networks (apart from acknowledging Wenger's [1998] distinction of the two, to which we will return).

11 In investigating the learning of two teachers in a secondary school, Hodkinson and Hodkinson (2004) acknowledge that the idea of a community of practice explored by Lave and Wenger (1991) is appropriate for this situation, though they extended it using Bourdieu's concepts of habitus, cultural capital and field.

12 This work on the third metaphor was being carried in the writing of Hakkarainen *et al.* (2004), which was entirely concerned with innovative knowledge communities, and it contains a chapter covering the ideas of the third metaphor.

13 In fact Paavola *et al.* (2004) refer to a number of Engeström's publications, but this is typical.

14 This is a cultural-historical approach that has many features in common with a socio-cultural approach. For example, the basic part of the triangle in an activity system represents the mediation of the subject and the object by tools and artefacts – a basic tenet of socio-cultural theory. However, Engeström and Miettinen (1999) give an account of the relationship of activity theory (AT) and socio-cultural theory that shows how AT adds an understanding of the context for this mediation, including their reservations about learning in communities of practice as argued for by Lave and Wenger (1991).

15 Details can be found online at: www.knowledgeforum.com (accessed 30 May 2009).

16 Expansive learning is presented as a series of actions that form an expansive cycle: questioning accepted practice, analysing the situation, modelling new solutions, examining the model, implementing the new model, reflection on the process and consolidating new practice.

17 Even within this area there is a difference between taking a 'design' approach to new products and taking a 'product development' approach (Murphy and McCormick 1997).

18 Although the LHTL project investigated individual teachers' classroom practice through observation and interview, the sample for this was different from that used to investigate the school network data (see Chapter 4).

19 We think her approach suffers from the same problems as the general 'what works' research; see the following for critiques: Hammersley (2001); Berliner (2002); Cobb *et al.* (2003).

20 Knight (2002: 441) does this despite exploring an example where the managers of the companies involved were taken as proxies for the organisations, as she explored the nature of the network formed and the learning that could result.

4 Mapping networks

1 Note that on a number of maps, respondents used the term 'L2L', 'learning to learn' or 'learn to learn', which was a shorthand familiar in schools and is therefore how we initially presented assessment for learning. Later we were more careful in using the term 'learning how to learn' (LHTL). See Black *et al.* (2006) for the theoretical explanation for this term.

2 These co-ordinators are usually responsible for co-ordinating work with children who have special educational needs.

3 This is a multipurpose centre that is used as a resource centre and place to hold professional development events, usually run by a local authority.

5 Network nodes: entities or relationships?

1 The full details of this mapping exercise, including suitable reservations about the data and their interpretation, are given in Fox *et al.* (2007). The relative numbers of particular nodes given in the account that follows in this chapter need to be treated with caution, given the limitations of the sample. However, the observations made on the relative proportions are an interesting start for further investigation.

2 The different age groups in England are split into 'key stages': Key Stage 1, ages 5–7; Key Stage 2, ages 7–11; Key Stage 3, ages 11–14; Key Stage 4, ages 14–16.

3 Latour's ideas on this are related to that of actors as intermediaries or mediators (see Chapter 2).

4 Websites as nodes were categorised by us as 'organisations', and we dealt with the link to them as a mode of communication (see Chapter 6). In a later study of beginning teachers we asked 'whom or what', and respondents did show non-human entities, including resources and websites (Fox and Wilson 2009).

5 SNA analysts would say the ties in the network are too sparse to reveal any measures of equivalence (Berkowitz 1988: 489).

6 An alternative is to ask the members of the NLC central team to list all those with whom they connect, and then see what network they produce collectively. Some combination of a predefined and respondent-generated list can be used.

7 This illustration is taken from Wasserman and Faust (1994: 171). Details of the definition and calculation of each of the measures of centrality covered here are given in their text.

8 The actual value is 0.2, but the calculation here and for Figure 5.4c requires a little mathematics (see Wasserman and Faust 1994). This is also true for the next measure of centrality, 'closeness'.

9 The distinction between these two can be seen in terms of Castells' (2000a) layers: the internet is the hardware level, layer 1, and the 'www' is the information layer 2, i.e. the interconnections of web pages.

10 Burt does not explain in what sense these are levels, but they bear a striking resemblance to Bloom's (1956) taxonomy of educational objectives.

11 Gladwell (2002) sees being 'well connected' as an individual attribute, and this is typical of networking approaches in business (e.g. Misner and Morgan 2000).

12 There were a large number of articles related to brokering students, for example, to help them manage their learning in the 'Train to Gain' programme to enable them to enter the workplace (Fletcher 2007).

13 A teacher within the school who takes overall responsibility for the development of the use of ICT in teaching.

14 This is a point Little (1990) makes, and we examine it in Chapter 7. (Of course teachers may share information through schemes of work, and share student assessment information to enable them to know the prior understanding, etc. of their students.)

15 For example, Hakkarainen *et al.* (2004) focus on expertise within organisations and, although they do consider the role of external networks, their focus is on internal ones. Chapter 2 reviewed the SNA work in education, and this indicated that most of it focused within schools (apart from Daly and Finnigan [forthcoming a] and Daly *et al.* [2009]). It is also important to note we are not concerned with the novice–expert distinction in the PM as, in a sense, all the teachers we are concerned with are 'experts'.

16 Such a person was responsible for the inspection service in education, including schools (see www.ofsted.gov.uk; accessed 11 August 2009).

17 Shirley Clarke regularly gives talks to schools or at conferences of teachers and was cited by our respondents. She is a national figure in assessment for learning (online at: www.shirleyclarke-education.org; accessed 11 August 2009).

18 Bill Rogers is an international speaker dealing mainly with behaviour management issues in schools (see www.billrogers.com.au; accessed 11 August 2009).

19 Dylan Wiliam was a member of the LHTL research team and, along with Paul Black, well known internationally for work on assessment for learning (see references).

20 Teachers designated as having advanced classroom skills, whose role is to work with other teachers, including those in other schools. Their success with regard to working in other schools appeared to be mixed in the middle of this decade (Cooper 2008).

21 Fielding *et al.* (2005) do discuss individuals and roles (e.g. ASTs), though largely in terms of how 'originators' (the experts) and partners in collaboration (those 'receiving' the expertise) view themselves.

22 Some of the LHTL project staff are internationally and nationally known, and they made specific inputs to schools as part of the project, but we have excluded them from this discussion. We do, however, deal with them later in their role as critical friends.

23 This scheme involves young people in challenging activities, such as helping people or the community, getting fitter, developing skills, going on an expedition and taking part in a residential activity (see www.dofe.org; accessed 11 August 2009).

24 Becta is a government agency responsible for ICT in schools in England (see www.becta.org.uk; accessed 11 August 2009), and DfES was an earlier abbreviation for the ministry department responsible for schools (currently the Department for Children, Schools and Families; see www.dcsf.gov.uk/index.htm; accessed 11 August 2009).

25 This sexist term is used for the person who is responsible for maintaining a website: http://en.wikipedia.org/wiki/Webmaster (accessed 20 November 2009).

26 This is a charity set up to support schools that have specialist status (in a curriculum area for example). Online at: www.ssatrust.org.uk/Pages/home.aspx (accessed 6 December 2009).

27 Sue Swaffield (2008) has written more generally about critical friendship in another context.

28 The OECD is the Organisation for Economic Co-operation and Development (online at: www.oecd.org/home/0,2987,en_2649_201185_1_1_1_1_1,00.html; accessed 12 August 2009).

6 Network links: interactions or transactions?

1 If person A indicates that she has a relationship with B, then this is one direction, and if B also indicates one for A, then the relationship is reciprocal (see Figure 2.2). However, in some studies reciprocity is assumed and if one person indicates the relationship, then the other is also given it in the data representation. For example, Palonen and Lehtinen (2001) did this, assuming that their academic subjects might have forgotten a relationship.

2 Other researchers applied micro-political perspectives to understanding how teachers learn through collaboration with one another, i.e. in terms of developing the PLCs discussed in Chapter 1. This was not a dimension we looked for in the LHTL data (Achinstein 2002; Little 1990).

3 The LHTL data were collected at a time in the United Kingdom when primary school teachers were in their classrooms all the time, with no planning and preparation time common for secondary school teachers. Since September 2005, all teachers have had rights to this out-of-class time.

4 This study was part of that reported in Fox *et al.* (2010), although the diary data have yet to be analysed.

5 As noted earlier, reciprocity exists when two individuals each say that they seek advice from, or consult with, each other. A measure of ego-centric reciprocity for an individual is the ratio of the number of reciprocal relationships and the total number of ties for that individual.

6 In Chapter 4 we noted that 'advice size' could be non-reciprocal; those seen by others as providers of knowledge did not see themselves in this way.

7 Their measure of trust of colleagues is based on an instrument developed by Hoy and Megan (2003) and available online at: http://mxtsch.people.wm.edu/research_tools.php (accessed 22 October 2009). There are eight items asking such questions as 'Do teachers in your school look out for each other? . . . can depend on each other? . . . trust each other? . . . are open with each other?' The instrument is well trialled and developed, with robust factor analysis statistics and concurrent validity against other measures (e.g. self-estrangement and teacher efficacy), but the measure is inevitably a general one, devoid of context. Whether this is relevant to the creation and sharing of practice is unclear. (The factor related to 'trust in colleagues' correlates with those of trust in their principal and clients [parents and students], and hence can be seen as a general school atmosphere measure rather than a specific one.) For example, Hakkarainen *et al.* (2004), in discussing commercial knowledge creation, show the importance of relationships developed through activities such as the sauna, are important in building up general trust for creation and sharing. The Hoy and Megan instrument has no questions related to creation and sharing, and it is not reflected in their definition of trust. The Dutch translation of the questionnaire by Moorlenaar and her colleagues includes six items that asks teachers to answer for themselves (rather than their school): for example, 'I can depend on my co-workers.' Although their factor analysis carried out on these items also reveals a single factor with satisfactory correlations and reliability, they rely on the Hoy and Megan (2003) study for other kinds of validity that may not relate to sharing of classroom practice, for example. The measure of innovation is based on instruments by Bryk *et al.* (1999) and Consortium on Chicago School Research (2004). The items are: 'How many

teachers in your school are willing to take risks to make this school a better place? . . . are eager to try new ideas? . . . have a "can do" attitude? . . . are encouraged to "stretch and grow"? . . . are continually learning and seeking new ideas?' (online at: http://ccsr.uchicago.edu/surveymeasures2007/innv.html; accessed 22 October 2009). Bryk *et al.* (1999) use an assessment item analysis technique to establish validity and reliability, again without any concurrent validity check, particularly with regard to a specific innovation or change. These are inevitable 'limitations' in otherwise excellent and rigorous studies that point only to the need for more detailed case-study work.

8 This is now called the Qualifications and Curriculum Development Agency, the government agency in England responsible for curriculum and examinations (online at: www.qcda.gov.uk; accessed 20 October 2009).

9 This is a professional organisation to which LA advisers often belong, along with academics and other education-based professionals.

10 At the time, Michael Barber was in the Prime Minister's Office with a responsibility for education.

11 An exploration of a sample of LHTL project schools, including this one, and their attitude and responses to government policies is dealt with by Swaffield and MacBeath (2006).

12 SATs are Statutory Assessment Tests, which are part of a national testing programme for all schools in England.

13 This is an assessment level in the national assessment programme.

14 As noted in Chapter 5, these Beacon schools give a lead to local schools and are similar to the Leading Edge schools discussed in Chapter 1.

15 The debate by Hoekstra *et al.* (2007) draws on Eraut (2004) and is concerned to distinguish a wide range of formal and informal learning activities, which are not necessarily about relationships (or even 'associations'), and we think that a discussion of this would be a distraction at this point. Ideas on what *learning* takes place are of importance and we will consider these in Chapters 7 and 8.

16 Although this appears to be like a 'knotwork' (Engeström *et al.* 1999), such a group can be set up with people who have no prior connection (see Nardi *et al.* 2000).

7 Network traffic: creation and sharing

1 Fielding and his colleagues were in fact more exercised by what constituted 'good' practice and, like others (e.g. Hargreaves [2003a], who was concerned with 'best' practice), wanted to consider what was worth transferring.

2 Underlying AfL is the principle of learner autonomy, and hence we argue that it is fundamentally about teaching students how to learn (Black *et al.* 2006).

3 These are reproduced in James *et al.* (2006a) as part of 'tools for schools' and are also on the LHTL website (www.learntolearn.ac.uk; accessed 11 September 2009), which also has associated slide presentations. The 'tools' are also accompanied by some extracts of schools' experience in using them.

4 This is where students are given *comments* focusing on what they should do to improve, rather than *grades*, for most of their classroom or home work.

5 An example of another use of traffic lights can be seen on the Teaching and Learning Research Programme website at: www.tlrp.org/pub/videopip.html (accessed 2 December 2009). See the clip 'Assessment should support learning'.

6 This work followed their review of the literature in which they laid out the case for the use of formative assessment strategies, which LHTL built upon, where they said, '[T]eachers cannot be expected quickly to abandon habitual roles and methods for a limited experiment' (Black and Wiliam 1998a: 20).

7 Wenger would qualify this explanation of what is happening, as he argues that 'it is not possible to make everything explicit and thus get rid of the tacit' (1998: 67). It may be that this is as much personal knowledge, which needs to be shared, some of which could be explicit.

8 In their collection on professional learning communities, Stoll and Louis (2007a) include a chapter that examines the role of artefacts in structuring these communities (Halverson

2007). Halverson gives a topology of such artefacts and examines the different role of artefacts in different stages of the development of a community. Some of these are objects (e.g. student assessments), some activities (e.g. a breakfast club where teachers discussed classroom strategies) and some were both objects and processes (e.g. a school improvement plan and associated activities). The details of how they enable the development of practice are not, however, given in this account.

9 'Headlamp', or Leadership and Management Programme for New Headteachers, was a programme set up in 1995, and subsequently replaced by the Headteacher Induction Programme, part of the National College of School Leadership programmes (see www.ofsted. gov.uk/Ofsted-home/Forms-and-guidance/Browse-all-by/Other/General/Headlamp-Training-for-newly-appointed-headteachers; accessed 14 September 2009).

10 It will be evident later that some outside education refer to 'knowledge of practice' (Allee 2003).

11 Gray (2000) notes that in the very first institute in 1974, a pair of teachers brought a video of their own classroom (they taught as a team).

12 Teachers College, Columbia University, has materials on conducting these; online at: www.tc.edu/lessonstudy/tools.html (accessed 24 October 2009).

13 He did not study the processes by which teachers found out what mentor schools had to offer.

14 This study was part of an EdD qualification that has now been completed (Lawrence 2009). The later round of interviews confirmed those in the first round, upon which Lawrence (2007) was based. No doubt there will be subsequent publications.

15 As was explained in Chapter 2, when individuals indicate whom they seek advice from, collaborate with, etc., a matrix is constructed (as in Figure 2.2b). For any one node it is possible to see how many links are made with others (are 'sent') and how many other nodes (people) link with the node in question (received ties).

16 The 20 per cent figure matched the results of the staff questionnaire that identified a group of teachers who reported that their practice promoted pupil autonomy, which represents those who encapsulate the 'spirit' of AfL (James *et al.* 2007: 180).

17 The quotation marks around 'high organisation based on ideas' was taken from an earlier quotation in the article from Dewey (1966: 28–9).

18 Note that the term 'communities of learners' as used by Brown is not the same as that used by Wenger (1998), though there may be some similarities in terms of a subject community and its discourse(s).

19 Susan Stodolsky and Pamela Grossman together and separately have published much on subject differences (e.g. Stodolsky and Grossman 1995; Grossman and Schoenfeld 2005) and the need to take these into account in reforming education.

20 There is an extensive literature on organisational learning, which has been applied to schools, but this often does not adopt a very profound view of 'learning' (however, see Boreham and Morgan 2004). We do not feel that exploring organisational learning would help us in the general argument.

21 The literature on change also is substantial and separate, though there is an overlap in terminology (but less so conceptually). For example, SNA terms such as 'adoption' and 'diffusion' are also used in the change literature, but it also extends to other ideas such as 'implementation' and 'embedding'. Our consideration of the latter here is only partial, but is intended to indicate there is a substantive layer of complexity associated with the school level, which represents a substantive theory that SNA ignores.

22 There is a related set of issues around the conditions in a school to enable collaborative inquiry work to create AfL practice within a school (see Chapter 3), but we feel that this would complicate the discussion unnecessarily and turn the focus away from sharing. See Pedder (2006) for an account of the relationships of classroom practice, teacher learning, and school management practices and systems.

23 Subsequent to analysis, the role of personal networks revealed that it would have been useful to have sampled differently. This is considered further in Chapter 11.

24 In the language of those who construct repositories, this description is the *metadata* associated with the object.

8 Networks in context: spatial and temporal issues

1 We also noted the idea of a 'third space' by Lieberman and Wood (2003a) in Chapter 1, but this seems to be, as it were, a conceptual space that gives teachers the room to explore their knowledge. However, they do acknowledge that it exists between local and remote, between the school and the university, and enables both inside and outside knowledge to be explored. The summer institutes are the physical location where this takes place, though they are not concerned with its physicality (but the extended time it represents clearly is important).

2 The LHTL data here draw on LA and school co-ordinator interviews that were part of the 'school-level' investigation and some case-study follow-up interviews. These data and some from other specifically identified studies are used in this chapter.

3 Wenger graphically illustrates this in a video interview (originally for the University of Southern Denmark) in which he describes the 'situation' in situated learning as being not an isolated instant but something with a history, and indeed a trajectory continuing after the situation (online at the Knowledge Lab: www.knowledgetv.dk/video.php?mov=37; accessed 2 November 2009.)

4 The full report is available from the authors (Fox and McCormick 2008).

5 Not state funded – that is, it is a private school.

6 Online at: www.conferences-uk.org.uk/Nottingham.asp?venue=NCSL%20Learning%20and %20Conference%20Centre (accessed 2 November 2009).

7 Online at: www.etcvenues.co.uk (accessed 2 November 2009).

8 Massey (1994: 155) also refers to Castells' (2000a) notion of 'space of flows', concluding that places are not static, but 'places are processes, too'.

9 This work was funded by the Gatsby Charitable Foundation as part of its support for teacher retention.

10 It is normal practice in secondary schools in England for teachers to be responsible for a class (a form), and they register students in the morning, and also take some periods of social and pastoral activities with them. This class has a particular classroom base, called the 'form room'.

11 This quotation is not taken from Fox *et al.* (2010), but was part of the data collected as part of the study.

12 Solomon *et al.* (2006) do not distinguish between 'space' and 'place' in the way we use the terms.

13 This quote is taken from Alison Fox's current PhD study (see Fox forthcoming).

14 Stenhouse (1982) noted that such case studies are not anonymous to those within the institution who know research was conducted and who can therefore identify most of the people and places involved.

9 Case studies

1 We have previously referred to the Specialist Schools and Academies Trust. The Leading Edge Partnership Programme was established in 2003 to encourage schools to work in partnership to solve some of the most intractable problems in education. Leading Edge schools are likely to also be Specialist Schools. Online at: www.ledge.org.uk (accessed 6 December 2009).

2 This is a well-known chain of car exhaust system and tyre fitting services.

3 'You' refers to the researcher responsible for carrying out the mapping exercise with her.

4 Note that we have no indication of how many and how significant the connections were between the schools, or how they were enacted.

5 These schools have had serious concerns raised in a formal inspection and they are subject to close scrutiny to ensure that agreed improvements are made.

6 Such schools are a base for training teachers and have been granted a special status for this training and that of the supporting mentors of trainees in schools; see www.standards.dcsf. gov.uk/trainingschools/what_are/?version=1 (accessed 16 November 2009).

10 Electronic networks and teacher learning

1 This is a virtual world, online at: http://secondlife.com/whatis/?sourceid=0909-sergoog-en-intl-wisl-en&gclid=CL2ng8KWup4CFZQA4wodcERCmg (accessed 3 December 2009).
2 This is a game in a mythical world involving battles and other adventures. Online at: https://eu.battle.net/account/creation/wow/signup/index.xml?gclid=CN-0vYugup4CFZ1h4wodGTDLmA (accessed 3 December 2009).
3 This is literally 'data about data', which in this case might include what practice is illustrated and the age group of students involved.
4 This is the kind of interaction between online and offline practices that Wenger *et al.* (2009) document.
5 This is where one person will answer questions (be in the 'hot seat') and create some kind of limited discussion.

11 Implications

1 Lima in fact was not suggesting that SNA be done in this way, in the way Daly (2008) did.
2 This is an online workplace for educational professionals: http://tappedin.org/tappedin (accessed 30 November 2009).
3 In the second part of his book, Latour (2005) seeks to render associations traceable, and part of this endeavour is to create a flat topology to prevent the investigator from retreating from a close look at interactions to a 'context' to make sense of these interactions. He introduces the idea of various 'clamps' for such jumps (ibid.: 174).
4 Much as did the critiques considered in Chapter 3. It would be interesting to see whether Nespor would view Wenger's (1998) later idea of 'imagination' (Chapter 3) as a way of overcoming this, or whether the non-physical and spatial nature of this would rule it out.
5 We have already noted (from Chapter 5) Miettinen's worry about 'loud voices'.
6 Fenwick and Edwards (2010) have recently completed an account of ANT as applied to education.
7 This equal treatment of both kinds of actants is also behind Miettinen's other two criticisms, considered earlier, of the impossibility of choosing which actors to study and attending to the loud voices.
8 Miettinen is part of the group working with Engeström, and hence his ideas on mycorrhizae can be incorporated into this view.
9 This was commissioned by the National College for School Leadership: *For the Provision of Evaluation and Impact Study – Talk2Learn Tender Reference: ITT051.* The reports were not public documents.
10 Moodle is a virtual learning environment, one element of which provides discussion forums: http://moodle.org/ (accessed 30 November 2009).
11 For example, Elluminate is a tutorial system that gives audio communication along with a shared whiteboard and associated tools: www.elluminate.com (accessed 30 November 2009).
12 General details can be found at: www.teachernet.gov.uk/management/resourcesfinance andbuilding/bsf/aboutbsf/educationvision (accessed 5 December 2009). Documents for schools can be found online at: www.teachernet.gov.uk/docbank/index.cfm?id=7991 (accessed 5 December 2009).

References

Achinstein, B. (2002) 'Conflict amid community: the micropolitics of teacher collaboration', *Teachers College Record*, 104(3): 421–55.

Adams, J.E. (2000) *Taking Charge of Curriculum: Teacher Networks and Curriculum Implementation*, New York: Teachers College Press.

Ahuja, M.K. and Carley, R.M. (1999) 'Network structure in virtual organizations', *Organization Science*, 10(6): 741–57.

Akoh, J. and Gutherson, P. (2007) *Setting Up Supplementary School Hubs and Networks: A Reflective Handbook*, London: CfBT Education Trust. Online, available at: www.cfbt.com/evidenceforeducation/pdf/91083_Hubs&Networks_Handbook.pdf (accessed 30 September 2009).

Allee, V. (2003) *The Future of Knowledge: Increasing Prosperity through Value Networks*, Burlington, MA: Elsevier Science.

Amsterdamska, O. (1990) '"Surely, you must be joking, Monsieur Latour!"' *Science, Technology and Human Values*, 15: 495–500.

Anderson, J.R., Reder, L.M. and Simon, H.A. (1996) 'Situated learning and education', *Educational Researcher*, 25(4): 5–11.

Anderson, J.R., Reder, L.M. and Simon, H.A. (1998) 'Situative versus cognitive perspectives: form versus substance', *Educational Researcher*, 26(1): 18–21.

Anderson, J.R., Greeno, J.G., Reder, L.M. and Simon, H.A. (2000) 'Perspectives on learning, thinking, and activity', *Educational Researcher*, 29(4): 11–13.

Assessment Reform Group [ARG] (2002) *Assessment for Learning: 10 Principles*, Cambridge: University of Cambridge School of Education.

Aston, S.M. (1997) 'A study of the impact of social networks and teacher beliefs on educational change', unpublished thesis, Oklahoma State University.

Augé, M. (1995) *Non-places: Introduction to an Anthropology of Supermodernity*, London: Verso.

Baker-Doyle, K. (2008a) 'Social network analysis in research on teacher networks: uncovering informal support networks and networking characteristics of teachers', paper presented to the annual meeting of the American Educational Research Association, New York, 24–8 March.

Baker-Doyle, K. (2008b) 'Circles of support: new urban teachers' social support networks', unpublished thesis, University of Pennsylvania.

Barabási, A.-L. (2003) *Linked: How Everything Is Connected to Everything Else and What It Means for Business, Science and Everyday Life*, New York: Plume.

Bereiter, C. (2002) *Education and Mind in the Knowledge Age*, Hillsdale, NJ: Lawrence Erlbaum.

Bereiter, C. and Scardamalia, M. (1993) *Surpassing Ourselves: An Inquiry into the Nature and Implications of Expertise*, La Salle, IL: Open Court.

Berkowitz, S.D. (1988) 'Afterword: toward a formal structural sociology', in B. Wellman and S.D. Berkowitz (eds) *Social Structures: A Network Approach* (pp. 477–97), Cambridge: Cambridge University Press.

Berliner, D.C. (2002) 'Educational research: the hardest science of all', *Educational Researcher*, 31(8): 18–20.

Bidwell, C.E. (2001) 'Analyzing schools as organizations: long-term permanence and short-term change', *Sociology of Education* (extra issue), 74: 100–14.

Billett, S. (2006) 'Constituting the workplace curriculum', *Journal of Curriculum Studies*, 38(1): 31–48.

Black, P. and Wiliam, D. (1998a) 'Assessment and classroom learning', *Assessment in Education*, 5(1): 5–75.

Black, P. and Wiliam, D. (1998b) *Inside the Black Box: Raising Standards through Classroom Assessment*, London: School of Education, King's College London. (Reprinted in *Phi Delta Kappan*, 80(2): 139–48.)

Black, P., Harrison, C., Lee, C., Marshall, B. and Wiliam, D. (2002) *Working inside the Black Box: Assessment for Learning in the Classroom*, London: NFER Nelson.

Black, P., Harrison, C., Lee, C., Marshall, B. and Wiliam, D. (2003) *Assessment for Learning: Putting It into Practice*, Maidenhead, UK: Open University Press.

Black, P., McCormick, R., James, M. and Pedder, D. (2006) 'Assessment for learning and learning how to learn: a theoretical inquiry', *Research Papers in Education*, 21(2): 119–32.

Blasé, J. (1987) 'Political interactions among teachers: sociocultural context in the schools', *Urban Education*, 22(3): 286–310.

Blasé, J. (1991) *The Politics of Life in Schools: Power, Conflict and Cooperation*, London: Sage.

Bloom, B.S. (1956) *Taxonomy of Educational Objectives: The Classification of Educational Goals*, Handbook I: *Cognitive Domain*, London: Longman.

Bolam, R. and McMahon, A. (2004) 'Literature, definitions and models: towards a conceptual map', in C. Day and J. Sachs (eds) *International Handbook on the CPD of Teachers* (pp. 33–63), Maidenhead, UK: Open University Press.

Bolam, R. and Weindling, D. (2006) *Synthesis of Research and Evaluation Projects Concerned with Capacity-Building through Teachers' Professional Development*, London: General Teaching Council for England.

Bolam, R., McMahon, A., Stoll, L., Thomas, S. and Wallace, M. (2005) *Creating and Sustaining Effective Professional Learning Communities*, Bristol: University of Bristol. Online, available at: www.eplc.info/ (accessed 17 September 2009).

Boreham, N. and Morgan, C. (2004) 'A sociocultural analysis of organisational learning', *Oxford Review of Education*, 30(3): 307–25.

Borko, H. (2004) 'Professional development and teacher learning: mapping the terrain', *Educational Researcher*, 33(8): 3–15.

Bourdieu, P. (1990) *The Logic of Practice*, Cambridge: Polity Press.

Bredo, E. (1997) 'The social construction of learning', in G.D. Phye (ed.) *Handbook of Academic Learning: Construction of Knowledge* (pp. 3–45), San Diego, CA: Academic Press.

Brown, A.L. (1997) 'Transforming schools into communities of thinking and learning about serious matters', *American Psychologist*, 52(4): 399–413.

Brown, A.L. and Campione, J.C. (1996) 'Psychological theory and the design of innovative earning environments: on procedures, principles, and systems', in L. Schauble and R. Glaser (eds) *Innovations in Learning: New Environments for Education* (pp. 289–325), Mahwah, NJ: Lawrence Erlbaum.

Brown, J. with Isaacs, D. (2005) *The World Café: Shaping Our Futures through Conversations That Matter*, Cambridge, MA: Pegasus.

Brown, J.S. and Duguid, P. (2000) *The Social Life of Information*, Boston: Harvard Business School Press.

Brown, J.S. and Duguid, P. (2002) 'Organizing knowledge', in S. Little, P. Quintas and T. Ray (eds) *Managing Knowledge: An Essential Reader* (pp. 19–40), London: The Open University in association with Sage.

Bryk, A., Camburn, E. and Louis, K.S. (1999) 'Professional community in Chicago elementary schools: facilitating factors and organizational consequences', *Educational Administration Quarterly*, 35(5): 751–81.

Buchberger, F., Hudson, B., El Gamal, A. and Laanpere, M. (2003) *Analysis of success factors in network building (Phase 1)*, ERNIST Networking study, December. Online, available at: http://community.eun.org/content.cfm?area=601&sa=3797&oid=24806&ov=24806 (accessed 19 May 2009; password protected).

Burt, R.S. (1982) *Towards a Structural Theory of Action: Network Models of Social Structure, Perception, and Action*, New York: Academic Press.

Burt, R.S. (1992) *Structural Holes: The Social Structure of Competition*, Cambridge, MA: Harvard University Press.

Burt, R.S. (2000) 'The network structure of social capital', in R.I. Sutton and B.M. Staw (eds) *Research in Organizational Behavior* (pp. 345–423), San Diego, CA: Elsevier.

Burt, R.S. (2001) 'Structural holes v. network closure as social capital', in N. Lin, K. Cook and R.S. Burt (eds) *Social Capital: Theory and Research* (pp. 31–56), New York: Aldine de Gruyter.

Burt, R.S. (2005) *Brokerage and Closure: An Introduction to Social Capital*, Oxford: Oxford University Press.

Cabinet Office (2001) *UK Online Annual Report 2001*, London: Office of the E-Envoy. Online, available at: http://archive.cabinetoffice.gov.uk/e-envoy/reports-anrep2001-downloads/ $file/annrep2.pdf (accessed 1 December 2009).

Callon, M. (1986) 'Some elements of a sociology of translation: domestication of the scallops and the fishermen of St Brieuc Bay', in J. Law (ed.) *Power, Action and Belief* (pp. 196–223), London: Routledge.

Carmichael, P. and Procter, R. (2005) *Metadata, Networks and Creative Professionalism*, Learning How to Learn Project working paper, Cambridge: Faculty of Education, University of Cambridge.

Carmichael, P. and Procter, R. (2006) 'Are we there yet? Teachers, schools and electronic networks', *The Curriculum Journal*, 17(2): 167–86.

Carmichael, P., Procter, R. and James, M. (2005) 'Using electronic tools to support a large development and research project: a case study' (Thematic Session on 'Managing Large Projects'), paper presented at Teaching and Learning Research Programme annual conference, University of Warwick, November. Online, available at: www.tlrp.org/dspace/handle/ 123456789/436.

Carmichael, P., Procter, R. and Laterza, V. (2007) 'Research design, roles and relationships in the Virtual Research Environment for Education project', paper presented at British Educational Research Association Conference, London, September.

Carmichael, P., Fox, A., McCormick, R., Procter, R. and Honour, L. (2006) 'Teachers' professional networks in and out of school', *Research Papers in Education*, 21(2): 217–34.

Castells, M. (1999) 'Flows, networks, and identities: a critical theory of the informational society', in M. Castells, R. Flecha, P. Freire, H.A. Giroux, D. Macedo and P. Willis (eds) *Critical Education in the New Information Age*, Lanham, MD: Rowman & Littlefield.

Castells, M. (2000a) *The Rise of the Network Society*, vol. 1: *The Information Age: Economy, Society and Culture*, 2nd edition, Oxford: Blackwell.

Castells, M. (2000b) 'Materials for an exploratory theory of the network society', *British Journal of Sociology*, 51(1): 5–24.

Child, J. (2001) 'Trust – the fundamental bond in global collaboration', *Organizational Dynamics*, 29(4): 274–88.

Church, M., Bitel, M., Armstrong, K., Fernando, P., Gould, H., Joss, S., Marwaha-Diedrich, M., De la Torre, A.-L. and Vouhe, C. (2002) *Participation, Relationships and Dynamic Change: New Thinking on Evaluating the Work of International Networks*, London: University College London.

Clark, A. (2007) *Understanding Community: A Review of Networks, Ties and Contacts*, NCRM Working Paper Series 9/07, Southampton: ESRC National Centre for Research Methods. Online, available at: http://eprints.ncrm.ac.uk/469/ (accessed 7 May 2009).

Cobb, P., Confrey, J., diSessa, A., Lehrer, R. and Schauble, L. (2003) 'Design experiments in educational research', *Educational Researcher*, 32(1): 9–13.

Cole, R. (2008) 'The distributed leadership experiment: first year impacts on school culture, teacher networks, and student achievement', unpublished thesis, University of Pennsylvania.

Collins, H.M. and Yearley, S. (1992) 'Epistemological chicken', in A. Pickering (ed.) *Science as Practice and Culture* (pp. 301–26), Chicago: University of Chicago Press.

Consortium on Chicago School Research (2004) *Public Use Dataset: 2001 Survey of Students and Teachers: User's Manual*, Chicago: Consortium on Chicago School Research.

Contractor, N. (2005) 'The role of social network analysis in enabling cyberinfrastructure and the role of cyberinfrastructure in enabling social network analysis', White Paper prepared for the National Science Foundation Workshop on Cyberinfrastructure for the Social Sciences, Airlie House, Warrington, VA. Online, available at: http://nosh.northwestern.edu/manuscripts/noshCI.pdf (password protected).

Contractor, N. (2009) 'The emergence of multidimensional networks', *Journal of Computer-Mediated Communication*, 14(3): 743–7.

Cooper, D. (2008) 'Crossing the borders: the challenge of advanced skills teachers' outreach work in other schools', unpublished thesis, The Open University.

Cordingley, P. *et al.* [CPD Review Group] (2005a) *The Impact of Collaborative CPD on Classroom Teaching and Learning. Review: What Do Teacher Impact Data Tell Us about Collaborative CPD?*, London: EPPI-Centre.

Cordingley, P. *et al.* [CPD Review Group] (2005b) *The Impact of Collaborative Continuing Professional Development (CPD) on Classroom Teaching and Learning. Review: How Do Collaborative and Sustained CPD and Sustained but Not Collaborative CPD Affect Teaching and Learning?*, London: EPPI-Centre.

Crang, M. (2002) 'Between places: producing hubs, flows and networks', *Environment and Planning A*, 34(4): 569–74.

Daly, A.J. (2008) 'Unleashing the power in professional networks', *Leadership in Focus*, 9: 2–5.

Daly, A.J. (ed.) (forthcoming) *The Ties of Change: Social Network Theory and Application in Education*, Cambridge, MA: Harvard University Press.

Daly, A.J. and Finnigan, K.S. (forthcoming a) 'A bridge between two worlds: understanding network structure to understand change strategy', *Journal of Educational Change*. DOI 10.1007/s10833-009-9102-5.

Daly, A.J. and Finnigan, K.S. (forthcoming b) 'The ebb and flow of social network ties between district leaders under high stakes', *American Educational Research Journal*.

Daly, A.J., Moolenaar, N.M., Bolivar, J.M. and Burke, P. (2009) 'Getting by with a little help from my friends: reform goes to school', paper presented to the Annual Meeting of the American Research Association, San Diego, 13–17 April.

Day, C. and Sachs, J. (2004) 'Professionalism, performativity and empowerment', in C. Day and J. Sachs (eds) *International Handbook on the CPD of Teachers* (pp. 3–32), Maidenhead, UK: Open University Press.

Department for Education and Employment [DfEE] (2000) *Professional Development: Support for Teaching and Learning*, London: DfEE.

Department for Education and Employment [DfEE] (2004) *Five Year Strategy* (Cm 6272), London: DfEE.

Department for Education and Skills [DfES] (2004) *Primary Strategy Learning Networks: Groups of Schools Working Together to Improve Children's Learning – An Introduction*, London: DfES.

Department for Education and Skills [DfES] (2005a) *Harnessing Technology: Transforming Learning and Children's Services*, London: DfES.

Department for Education and Skills [DfES] (2005b) *Primary Strategy Learning Networks: Planning Materials*, London: DfES. Online, available at: http://publications.teachernet.gov. uk/default.aspx?PageFunction=productdetails&PageMode=publications&ProductId=DfES+ 1169-2005G& (accessed 19 September 2009).

Dewey, J. (1966) *Experience and Education*, London: Collier Books.

Diani, M. (2003) 'Introduction: social movements, contentious actions and social networks', in M. Diani and D. McAdam (eds) *Social Movements and Networks: Relational Approaches to Collective Action* (pp. 1–18), Oxford: Oxford University Press.

Dyer-Witheford, N. (1999) *Cyber-Marx: Cycles and Circuits of Struggle in High Technology Capitalism*, Chicago: University of Illinois Press.

Earl, L. and Katz, S. (2005) *Learning from Networked Learning Communities: Phase 2 – Key Features and Inevitable Tensions*, Toronto: Aporia Consulting.

Earl, L., Katz, S., Elgie, S., Jaafer, S.B. and Foster, L. (2006) *How Networked Learning Communities Work*, vol. 1: *The Report*, Toronto: Aporia Consulting.

Edwards, A. (2005) 'Let's get beyond community and practice: the many meanings of learning by participating', *The Curriculum Journal*, 16(1): 49–65.

Emirbayer, M. and Goodwin, G. (1994) 'Network analysis, culture, and the problem of agency', *American Journal of Sociology*, 99(6): 1411–54.

Engeström, Y. (1999) 'Innovative learning in work teams: analyzing cycles of knowledge creation in practice', in Y. Engeström, R. Miettinen and R.-L. Punamäki (eds) *Perspectives on Activity Theory* (pp. 377–404), Cambridge: Cambridge University Press.

Engeström, Y. (2001) 'Expansive learning at work: toward an activity theoretical reconceptualization', *Journal of Education and Work*, 14(1): 133–56.

Engeström, Y. (2007) 'From communities of practice to mycorrhizae', in J. Hughes, N. Jewson and L. Unwin (eds) *Communities of Practice: Critical Perspectives* (pp. 41–54), London: Routledge.

Engeström, Y. and Miettinen, R. (1999) 'Introduction', in Y. Engeström, R. Miettinen and R.-L. Punamäki (eds) *Perspectives on Activity Theory* (pp. 1–16), Cambridge: Cambridge University Press.

Engeström, Y., Engeström, R. and Vähäaho, T. (1999) 'When the center does not hold: the importance of knotworking', in S. Chaklin, M. Hedagaard and U.J. Jensen (eds) *Activity Theory and Social Practice: Cultural-Historical Approaches* (pp. 345–74), Aarhus: Aarhus University Press.

Engeström, Y., Engeström, R. and Suntio, A. (2002) 'Can a school community learn to master its own future? An activity-theoretical study of expansive learning among middle school teachers', in G. Wells and G. Claxton (eds) *Learning for Life in the 21st Century* (pp. 211–24), Oxford: Blackwell.

Engeström, Y., Kerosuo, H. and Kajamaa, A. (2007) 'Beyond discontinuity: expansive organizational learning remembered', *Management Learning*, 38(3): 319–36.

Eraut, M. (2004) 'Informal learning in the workplace', *Studies in Continuing Education*, 26(2): 247–73.

Erickson, B.H. (1988) 'The relational basis of attitudes', in B. Wellman and S.D. Berkowitz (eds) *Social Structures: A Network Approach* (pp. 99–121), Cambridge: Cambridge University Press.

Faust, K. (2005) 'Using correspondence analysis for joint displays of affiliation networks', in B. Wellman and S.D. Berkowitz (eds) *Social Structures: A Network Approach* (pp. 117–47), Cambridge: Cambridge University Press.

Fenwick, T. and Edwards, R. (2010) *Actor-Network Theory in Education*, London: Routledge.

Fernandez, C. (2002) 'Learning from Japanese approaches to professional development: the case of lesson study', *Journal of Teacher Education*, 53(5): 393–405.

Festner, D. (2006) 'The effectiveness of training in occupational health and safety: considerations about "effectiveness" and the design of a study', paper presented to the annual conference of the American Educational Research Association, San Francisco, 7–11 April.

Fielding, M., Bragg, S., Craig, J., Cunningham, I., Eraut, M., Gillinson, D., Horne, M., Robinson, C. and Thorp, J. (2005) *Factors Influencing the Transfer of Good Practice*, London: Department for Education and Skills.

Fisher, K. (2004) 'Revoicing classrooms: a spatial manifesto', *Forum*, 46(1): 36–8.

Flap, H.D., Snijders, T.A.B., Völker, B. and Van der Gaag, M.P.J. (2003) 'Measurement instruments for social capital of individuals', *Social Survey on the Networks of the Dutch Project*. Online, available at: www.xs4all.nl/~gaag/work/SSND.pdf (accessed 11 November 2009).

Fletcher, M. (2007) 'Do the brokers know best?', *Adults Learning*, 19(1): 16–18.

Fox, A. (2008) 'Personal networks: the professional development potential', *Professional Development Today*, 11(2): 46–51.

Fox, A. (forthcoming) 'Exploring biographical approaches to understanding learning as identity: cases of emergent school leaders', in B. Merrill and E. Bourgeois (eds) *Learning to Change? The Role of Identity and Learning Careers in Adult Education*, Frankfurt am Main: Peter Lang.

Fox, A. and McCormick, R. (2008) *Mapping Professional Knowledge Creation and Sharing in Teachers and School Leaders from Events to Impacts: Developing a Methodological Framework. A Report to the Teaching and Learning Research Programme and the National College for School Leadership*, Cambridge and Milton Keynes: Faculty of Education, University of Cambridge and the Centre for Research in Education and Educational Technology, The Open University.

Fox, A. and McCormick, R. (2009) 'Events and professional learning: studying educational practitioners', *Journal of Workplace Learning*, 21(3): 198–218.

Fox, A. and Wilson, E. (2009) '"Support our networking and help us belong!" Listening to beginning secondary school science teachers', *Teachers and Teaching: Theory and Practice*, 15(6): 701–18.

Fox, A., Deaney, R. and Wilson, E. (2010) 'Examining beginning teachers' perceptions of workplace support', *Journal of Workplace Learning*, 22(4): 212–27.

Fox, A., McCormick, R., Procter, R. and Carmichael, P. (2007) 'The design and use of a mapping tool as a baseline means of identifying an organisation's active networks', *International Journal of Research and Method in Education*, 30(2): 127–47.

Fraser, R. (2008) 'Demystifying teacher leadership in comprehensive high schools', unpublished thesis, University of Pennsylvania.

Freeman, L.C. (2000) 'Visualising social networks', *Journal of Social Structure*, 1. Online, available at: http://social.cs.uiuc.edu/class/cs598kgk/papers/freeman.pdf (accessed 9 July 2009).

Fuller, A. (2007) 'Critiquing theories of learning and communities of practice', in J. Hughes, N. Jewson and L. Unwin (eds) *Communities of Practice: Critical Perspectives* (pp. 17–29), London: Routledge.

Fuller, A., Hodkinson, H., Hodkinson, P. and Unwin, L. (2005) 'Learning as peripheral participation in communities of practice: a reassessment of key concepts in workplace learning', *British Educational Research Journal*, 31(1): 49–68.

Gilchrist, A. (2004) *The Well-Connected Community*, Bristol: Policy Press.

Gladwell, M. (2002) *The Tipping Point: How Little Things Can Make a Big Difference*, New York: Little, Brown and Company.

Glatter, R. (2003) 'Collaboration, collaboration, collaboration: the origins and implication of a policy', *Management in Education*, 17(5): 16–20.

Gloor, P., Laubacher, R. *et al.* (2004) *Temporal Visualization and Analysis of Social Networks*, Pittsburgh, PA: North American Association for Computational Social and Organizational Science, Carnegie-Mellon University.

Goodall, J., Day, C., Lindsey, G., Muijis, D. and Harris, A. (2005) *Evaluating Impact of Continuing Professional Development*, London: Department for Education and Skills.

Goodyear, P. (2001) *Effective Networked Learning in Higher Education: Notes and Guidelines*,

Networked Learning in Higher Education Project (JCALT), Lancaster, UK: Lancaster University. Online, available at: http://csalt.lancs.ac.uk/jisc/guidelines_final.doc (accessed 19 May 2009).

Granovetter, M. (1973) 'The strength of weak ties', *American Journal of Sociology*, 78: 1360–80.

Granovetter, M. (1983) 'The strength of weak ties: a network theory revisited', *Sociological Theory*, 1: 201–33.

Gray, J. (2000) *Teachers at the Centre: A Memoir of the Early Years of the National Writing Project*, Berkeley, CA: National Writing Project Corporation.

Greeno, J.G. (1997) 'On claims that answer the wrong question', *Educational Researcher*, 26(1): 5–17.

Grossman, P.L. and Schoenfeld, A. with Lee, C.D. (2005) 'Teaching subject matter', in L. Darling-Hammond, J. Bransford, P. LePage, K. Hammerness and H. Duffy (eds) *Preparing Teachers for a Changing World: What Teachers Should Learn and Be Able to Do* (pp. 201–31), San Francisco: Jossey-Bass.

Hadfield, M. (2005) 'From networking to school networks to "networked" learning: the challenge for the Networked Learning Communities', in W. Veugelers and M.J. O'Hair (eds) *Network Learning for Educational Change* (pp. 172–91), Maidenhead, UK: Open University Press.

Hakkarainen, K., Palonen, T., Paavola, S. and Lehtinen, E. (2004) *Communities of Networked Expertise: Professional and Educational Perspectives*, Amsterdam: Elsevier.

Halverson, R. (2007) 'How leaders use artifacts to structure professional community in schools', in L. Stoll and K.S. Louis (eds) *Professional Learning Communities: Divergence, Depth and Dilemmas* (pp. 91–105), Maidenhead, UK: Open University Press/McGraw-Hill Education.

Hammersley, M. (2001) 'On "systematic" reviews of research literatures: a "narrative" response to Evans and Benefield', *British Educational Research Journal*, 27(5): 543–54.

Hammersley, M. (2008) *Questioning Qualitative Inquiry: Critical Essays*, London: Sage.

Hancock, G. (2008) 'School leadership: a study investigating how emergent formal school leaders understand and collaborate with informal leaders to develop a better understanding of the terrain they are entering', unpublished thesis, University of Pennsylvania.

Hannon, V. (2005) 'Networks for a purpose: decisions facing school leaders', *Nexus*, Summer: 2–4.

Hardt, M. and Negri, A. (2000) *Empire*, Cambridge, MA: Harvard University Press.

Hargreaves, A. (2007) 'Sustainable professional learning communities', in L. Stoll and K.S. Louis (eds) *Professional Learning Communities: Divergence, Depth and Dilemmas* (pp. 181–95), Maidenhead, UK: Open University Press/McGraw-Hill Education.

Hargreaves, D.H. (1994) 'The new professionalism: the synthesis of professional and institutional development', *Teaching and Teacher Education*, 10(4): 423–38.

Hargreaves, D.H. (1996) 'Teaching as a research-based profession: possibilities and prospects', Teacher Training Agency Annual Lecture, London: Teacher Training Agency.

Hargreaves, D.H. (1999) 'The knowledge-creating school', *British Journal of Educational Studies*, 47(2): 122–44.

Hargreaves, D.H. (2001) 'A capital theory of school effectiveness and improvement', *British Educational Research Journal*, 27(4): 487–503.

Hargreaves, D.H (2003a) *Education Epidemic: Transforming Secondary Schools through Innovation Networks*, London: DEMOS.

Hargreaves, D.H. (2003b) *Working Laterally: How Innovation Networks Make an Education Epidemic*, London: DEMOS.

Hargreaves, D.H. (2004) 'Networks, knowledge and innovation: reflections on teacher learning', in H. McCarthy, P. Miller and P. Skidmore (eds) *Network Logic: Who Governs in an Interconnected World?* (pp. 78–88), London: DEMOS.

Hartnell, Y.E. (2006) 'Teachers' roles and professional learning in communities of practice supported by technology in schools', *Journal of Technology and Teacher Education*, 14(3): 461–80.

Harvey, D. (1985) *The Urbanization of Capital*, Oxford: Blackwell.

Harvey, D. (1990) 'Between space and time: reflections on the geographical imagination', *Annals of the Association of American Geographers*, 80: 418–34.

Hite, J.M., Hite, S.J., Jacob, W.J., Rew, W.J., Mugimu, C.B. and Nsubuga, Y.K. (2006) 'Building bridges for resource acquisition: network relationships among headteachers in Ugandan private secondary schools', *International Journal of Educational Development*, 26: 495–512.

Hodkinson, P. and Hodkinson, H. (2004) 'The significance of individuals' dispositions in workplace learning: a case study of two teachers', *Journal of Education and Work*, 17(2): 167–82.

Hoekstra, A.-M., Beijard, D., Brekelmans, D. and Korthagen, F. (2007) 'Experienced teachers' informal learning from classroom teaching', *Teachers and Teaching: Theory and Practice*, 13(2): 189–206.

Hogden, J. and Marshall, B. (2005) 'Assessment for learning in English and mathematics: a comparison', *The Curriculum Journal*, 16(2): 153–76.

Hoy, W.K. and Megan, T.-M. (2003) 'The conceptualisation and measurement of faculty trust in schools: the Omnibus T-Scale', in W.K. Hoy and C.G. Miskel (eds) *Studies in Leading and Organizing Schools* (pp. 181–208), Greenwich, CT: Information Age.

Hubbard, P., Kitchin, R. and Valentine, G. (eds) (2004) *Key Thinkers on Space and Place*, London: Sage.

Huberman, M. (1992) 'Teacher development and instructional mastery', in A. Hargreaves and M.G. Fullan (eds) *Understanding Teacher Development* (pp. 122–42), London and New York: Cassell/Teachers College Press.

Hughes, J., Jewson, N. and Unwin, L. (2007) *Communities of Practice: Critical Perspectives*, London: Routledge.

Hughes, J.E. (2008) 'A sociocultural investigation into teaching and learning in postgraduate accountancy', unpublished thesis, The Open University.

Huisman, M. and Snijders, T.A.B. (2003) 'Statistical analysis of longitudinal network data with changing composition', *Sociological Methods and Research*, 32(2): 253–87.

Jackson, D. and Temperley, J. (2006) 'From professional learning community to networked learning community', paper presented at International Congress for School Effectiveness and Improvement (ICSEI) Conference, Fort Lauderdale, FL, 3–6 January.

Jackson, D. and Temperley, J. (2007) 'From professional learning community to networked learning community', in L. Stoll and K.S. Louis (eds) *Professional Learning Communities: Divergence, Depth and Dilemmas* (pp. 45–62), Maidenhead, UK: Open University Press/McGraw-Hill Education.

Jacobs, N. and McFarlane, A. (2005) 'Conferences as learning communities: some early lessons in using "back-channel" technologies at an academic conference – distributed intelligence or divided attention?', *Journal of Computer Assisted Learning*, 21: 317–29.

James, M., Black, P., Carmichael, P., Conner, C., Dudley, P., Fox, A., Frost, D., Honour, L., MacBeath, J., McCormick, R., Marshall, B., Pedder, D., Procter, R., Swaffield, S. and Wiliam, D. (2006a) *Learning How to Learn: Tools for Schools*, London: Routledge.

James, M., Black, P., McCormick, R. and Pedder, D. (2006b) 'Learning how to learn, in classrooms, schools and networks: aims, design and analysis', *Research Papers in Education*, 21(2): 101–18.

James, M., McCormick, R., Black, P., Carmichael, P., Drummond, M.-J., Fox, A., MacBeath, J., Marshall, B., Pedder, D., Procter, R., Swaffield, S., Swann, J. and Wiliam, D. (2007) *Improving Learning How to Learn: Classrooms, Schools and Networks*, London: Routledge.

Jewson, N. (2007) 'Cultivating network analysis: rethinking the concept of "community" within communities of practice', in J. Hughes, N. Jewson and L. Unwin (eds) *Communities of Practice: Critical Perspectives* (pp. 68–82), London: Routledge.

Jones, A. and Moreland, J. (2005) 'The importance of pedagogical content knowledge in assessment for learning practices: a case-study of a whole-school approach', *The Curriculum Journal*, 16(2): 193–206.

Jones, C. (2004) 'Networks and learning: communities, practices and the metaphor of networks', *ALT-J*, 12(1): 81–93.

Jones, C., Ferreday, D. and Hodgson, V. (2006) 'Networked learning, a relational approach – weak and strong ties', paper presented at the symposium on Relations in Networks and Networked Learning at the conference Networked Learning 2006, Lancaster: Lancaster University, 10–12 April. Online, available at: www.networkedlearningconference.org.uk/past/nlc2006/abstracts/pdfs/01Jones.pdf (accessed 7 October 2009).

Katz, L. (1953) 'A new status index derived from sociometric analysis', *Psychometrika*, 18: 39–43.

Kerr, D., Aiston, S., White, K., Holland, M. and Grayson, H. (2003) *Review of Networked Learning Communities*, Maidenhead, UK: National Foundation for Educational Research.

Kilpatrick, S. (1998) 'Promoting learning networks for small business: how can group learning facilitate change?', *CRLRA Discussion Paper Series*, Launceston, Tasmania: Centre for Research and Learning in Regional Australia.

Knight, L. (2002) 'Network learning: exploring learning by interorganizational networks', *Human Relations*, 55(4): 427–54.

Knox, H., Savage, M. and Harvey, P. (2006) 'Social networks and the study of relations: networks as method, metaphor and form', *Economy and Society*, 35(1): 113–40.

Kossinets, G. and Watts, D.J. (2006) 'Empirical analysis of an evolving social network', *Science*, 311: 88–90.

Krackhardt, D. (1996) 'Social networks and the liability of newness for managers', in C.L. Cooper and D.M. Rousseau (eds) *Trends in Organizational Behavior*, vol. 3 (pp. 159–73), London: John Wiley.

Küppers, G. (2002) 'Complexity, self-organisation and innovation networks: a new theoretical approach', in A. Pyka and G. Küppers (eds) *Innovation Networks: Theory and Practice* (pp. 22–52), Cheltenham, UK: Edward Elgar.

Küppers, G. and Pyka, A. (2002) 'The self-organisation of innovation networks: introductory remarks', in A. Pyka and G. Küppers (eds) *Innovation Networks: Theory and Practice* (pp. 3–21), Cheltenham, UK: Edward Elgar.

Lanzara, G.F. (1999) 'Between transient constructs and persistent structures: designing systems in action', *Journal of Strategic Information Systems*, 8: 331–49.

Larsen, J., Urry, J. and Axhausen, K. (2006) *Mobilities, Networks, Geographies*, Aldershot, UK: Ashgate.

Latour, B. (1999) 'On recalling ANT', in J. Law and J. Hassard (eds) *Actor Network Theory and After* (pp. 15–25), Oxford: Blackwell/The Sociological Review.

Latour, B. (2005) *Reassembling the Social: An Introduction to Actor-Network-Theory*, Oxford: Oxford University Press.

Lave, J. (1996) 'The practice of learning', in S. Chaiklin and J. Lave (eds) *Understanding Practice: Perspectives on Activity and Context* (pp. 3–32), Cambridge: Cambridge University Press.

Lave, J. and Wenger, E. (1991) *Situated Learning: Legitimate Peripheral Participation*, Cambridge: Cambridge University Press.

Law, J. (1992) *Notes on the Theory of the Actor Network: Ordering, Strategy and Heterogeneity*. Online, available at: http://web.archive.org/web/20040214135427/http%3A//www.comp.lancs.ac.uk/sociology/soc054jl.html (accessed 1 July 2009).

Law, J. (2004) *After Method: Mess in Social Science Research*, London: Routledge.

Law, J. and Mol, A. (2002) *Complexities: Social Studies of Knowledge Practices*, Durham, NC: Duke University Press.

Lawless, K.A. and Pellegrino, J.W. (2007) 'Professional development in integrating technology into teaching and learning: knowns, unknowns, and ways to pursue better questions and answers', *Review of Educational Research*, 77(4): 575–614.

Lawrence, P. (2007) *The Strength of Weak School Ties: The Importance of 'Weak' Relationships in Sharing Good Practice between Schools*, Research Associate report, Nottingham: National College for School Leadership. Summary online, available at: www.nationalcollege.org.uk/docinfo?id=17429&filename=the-strength-of-weak-school-ties-summary.pdf (accessed 14 September 2009).

Lawrence, P. (2009) 'A study of practice transfer in a collaborative school improvement project', unpublished thesis, University of Nottingham.

Leach, J. (1997) 'English teachers "on-line": developing a new community of discourse', *English in Education*, 31(2): 63–72.

Levy, D.A. and Nail, P.R. (1993) 'Contagion: a theoretical and empirical review and reconceptualization', *Genetic, Social and General Psychology Monographs*, 119(2): 235–85.

Lieberman, A. (2000) 'Networks as learning communities: shaping the future of teacher development', *Journal of Teacher Education*, 51: 221–7.

Lieberman, A. (2007) 'Professional learning communities: a reflection', in L. Stoll and K.S. Louis (eds) *Professional Learning Communities: Divergence, Depth and Dilemmas* (pp. 199–203), Maidenhead, UK: Open University Press/McGraw-Hill Education.

Lieberman, A. and Grolnick, M. (1996) 'Networks and reform in American education', *Teachers College Record*, 98(1): 7–45.

Lieberman, A. and Miller, L. (eds) (2008a) *Teachers in Professional Communities: Improving Teaching and Learning*, New York: Teachers College Press.

Lieberman, A. and Miller, L. (2008b) 'Context and commitments', in A. Lieberman and L. Miller (eds) *Teachers in Professional Communities: Improving Teaching and Learning* (pp. 7–17), New York: Teachers College Press.

Lieberman, A. and Miller, L. (2008c) 'Developing capacities', in A. Lieberman and L. Miller (eds) *Teachers in Professional Communities: Improving Teaching and Learning* (pp. 18–28), New York: Teachers College Press.

Lieberman, A. and Miller, L. (2008d) 'Balancing content and process: facing challenges', in A. Lieberman and L. Miller (eds) *Teachers in Professional Communities: Improving Teaching and Learning* (pp. 29–38), New York: Teachers College Press.

Lieberman, A. and Wood, D. (2003a) *Inside the National Writing Project: Connecting Network Learning and Classroom Teaching*, New York: Teachers College Press.

Lieberman, A. and Wood, D. (2003b) 'Sustaining the professional development of teachers: learning in networks', in B. Davies and J. West-Burnham (eds) *Handbook of Educational Leadership and Management* (pp. 478–90), Harlow, UK: Pearson Education.

Lieberman, A. and Wood, D. (2004) 'Untangling the threads: networks, community and teacher learning in the National Writing Project', in H. McCarthy, P. Miller and P. Skidmore (eds) *Network Logic: Who Governs in an Interconnected World?* (pp. 65–75), London: DEMOS.

Lima, J.Á. de (2001) 'Forgetting about friendship: using conflict in teacher communities as a catalyst for school change', *Journal of Educational Change*, 2(2): 97–122.

Lima, J.Á. de (2003) 'Trained for isolation: the impact of departmental cultures on student teachers views and practices of collaboration', *Journal of Education for Teaching*, 29(3): 197–218.

Lima, J.Á. de (2004) 'Social networks in teaching', in F. Hernandez and I.F. Goodson (eds) *Social Geographies of Educational Change* (pp. 29–46), Dordrecht: Kluwer Academic Publishers.

Lima, J.Á. de (2007) 'Teachers' professional development in departmentalised, loosely coupled organisations: lessons for school improvement from a case study of two curriculum departments', *School Effectiveness and School Improvement*, 18(3): 273–301.

Lima, J.Á. de (2008) 'Departmental networks and distributed leadership in schools', *School Leadership and Management*, 28(2): 159–87.

Lin, N. (2001) 'Building a network theory of social capital', in N. Lin, K. Cook and R.S. Burt (eds) *Social Capital: Theory and Research* (pp. 3–29), New York: Aldine de Gruyter.

Little, J.W. (1987) 'Teachers as colleagues', in V. Richardson-Koehler (ed.) *Educators' Handbook: A Research Perspective* (pp. 491–518), New York: Longman.

Little, J.W. (1990) 'The persistence of privacy: autonomy and initiative in teachers' professional relations', *Teachers College Record*, 91(4): 509–36.

Little, J.W. (2002) 'Locating learning in teachers' communities of practice: opening up problems of analysis in records of everyday work', *Teaching and Teacher Education*, 18: 917–46.

Little, J.W. (2003) 'Inside teacher community: representations of classroom practice,' *Teachers College Record*, 105(6): 913–45.

Little, J.W. (2004) '"Looking at student work" in the United States: a case of competing impulses in professional development', in C. Day and J. Sachs (eds) *International Handbook on the CPD of Teachers* (pp. 94–118), Maidenhead, UK: Open University Press.

Little, J.W. (2005a) 'Nodes and nets: investigating resources for professional learning in schools and networks', working paper prepared for the National College for School Leadership (NCSL), Nottingham: NCSL.

Little, J.W. (2005b) 'Professional learning and school-network ties: prospects for school improvement', *Journal of Educational Change*, 6: 277–84.

Lucas, B. (1997) 'The campaign's view of the range of learning environments', *Journal of the UK Campaign for Learning*, 6: 1–11.

McCarthy, H., Miller, P. and Skidmore, P. (eds) (2004) *Network Logic: Who Governs in an Interconnected World?*, London: DEMOS.

McCormick, R. and Carmichael, P. (2005) 'Theorising and researching teacher learning across schools', paper presented at the TLRP Seminar Series Knowledge and Skills for Learning to Learn, University of Newcastle, 15 March.

McCormick, R. and James, M. (1988) *Curriculum Evaluation in Schools*, 2nd edition, London: Croom Helm.

McCormick, R., Carmichael, P., Fox, A., Hughes, R. and Thorpe, M. (2006) *Online Evaluation and Impact Study ITT 055*, a report by the Centre for Education and Educational Technology, The Open University, Nottingham: National College for School Leadership.

McCormick, R., Banks, F., Morgan, B., Opfer, D., Pedder, D., Storey, A. and Wolfenden, F. (2008) *Literature Review Report: Schools and Continuing Professional Development (CPD) in England – State of the Nation Research Project (T34718)*, a report commissioned by the Training and Development Agency for Schools, Cambridge and Milton Keynes: Cambridge University/Open University. Online, available at: www.tda.gov.uk/upload/resources/pdf/c/cpd_statenation_report_literature.pdf (accessed 17 September 2009).

Mace, D.H.P. (2008) 'Learning from practice/learning in practice: using multimedia to support teacher development', in A. Lieberman and L. Miller (eds) *Teachers in Professional Communities: Improving Teaching and Learning* (pp. 51–60), New York: Teachers College Press.

McGregor, J. (2000) '"The staffroom is the most underused room in the school": a study exploring the influence of space and gender in teacher workplace cultures', paper presented at the British Educational Research Association annual conference, Cardiff University, 7–10 September. Online, available at: http://brs.leeds.ac.uk/cgi-bin/brs_engine?*ID=13&*DB=BEID&*DD=Document:%201%3CBR%3E&*TH=BEIT&*TX=Y&*HI=N&*UZ=000113130[DOCN]&*QH1=~~%27MCGREGOR%27[AUTH]&*QC=1&*QD=1 (accessed 5 December 2009).

McGregor, J. (2003) 'Spatiality and teacher workplace cultures: the department as nexus', in R. Edwards and R. Usher (eds) *Space, Curriculum, and Learning* (pp. 44–58), Greenwich, CT: Information Age Publishing.

McGregor, J. (2004) 'Spatiality and teacher workplace cultures', unpublished thesis, The Open University, Milton Keynes, UK.

McLaughlin, C., Black-Hawkins, K. and McIntyre, D. with Townsend, A. (2008) *Networking Practitioner Research*, London: Routledge.

Marsden, P. (1998) 'Memetics of social contagion: two sides of the same coin?', *Journal of Memetics: Evolutionary Models of Information Transmission*, 2(2): 68–86. Online only, at: http://web.ebscohost.com.libezproxy.open.ac.uk/ehost/detail?vid=4&hid=12&sid=5240f0 8b-f323-4a74-9a80-ff2be151d033%40sessionmgr11&bdata=JnNpdGU9ZWhvc3QtbGl 2ZSZzY29wZT1zaXRl#db=bth&AN=2304696 (accessed 23 November 2009).

Marsden, P.V. (2005) 'Recent developments in network measurement', in P.J. Carrington, J. Scott and S. Wasserman (eds) *Models and Methods in Social Network Analysis* (pp. 8–30), Cambridge: Cambridge University Press.

Marshall, B. (2004) 'Goals or horizons – the conundrum of progression in English: or a possible way of understanding formative assessment in English', *The Curriculum Journal*, 15(2): 101–13.

Marshall, B. and Drummond, M.-J. (2006) 'How teachers engage with assessment for learning: lessons from the classroom', *Research Papers in Education*, 21(2): 133–49.

Massey, D. (1984) 'Introduction: geography matters', in D. Massey and J. Allen (eds) *Geography matters! A Reader*, Cambridge: Cambridge University Press in association with The Open University.

Massey, D. (1994) *Space, Place and Gender*, Cambridge: Polity Press.

Massey, D. (2005) *For Space*, London: Sage.

Mavers, D., Somekh, B. and Restorick, J. (2002) 'Interpreting the externalised images of pupils' conceptions of ICT: methods for the analysis of concept maps', *Computers and Education*, 38(1/3): 187–207.

Miettinen, R. (1998) 'Object construction and networks in research work: the case of research on cellulose-degrading enzymes', *Social Studies of Science*, 38: 423–63.

Miettinen, R. (1999) 'The riddle of things: activity theory and actor-network theory as approaches to studying innovations', *Mind, Culture, and Activity*, 6(3): 170–95.

Milgram, S. (1967) 'The small world problem', *Physiology Today*, 2: 60–7.

Miller, P.M. (2007) 'Examining boundary-spanning leadership in university–school–community partnerships', *Journal of School Public Relations*, 28(2): 189–211.

Mintrop, H. (2004) 'Fostering constructivist communities of learners in the amalgamated multi-discipline of social studies', *Journal of Curriculum Studies*, 36(2): 141–58.

Misner, I. and Morgan, D. (2000) *Masters of Networking: Building Relationships for Your Pocketbook and Soul*, Marietta, GA: Bard Press.

Misner, I., Macedonio, M., and Garrison, M. (2006) *Truth or Delusion? Busting Networking's Biggest Myths*, Nashville, TN: Nelson Business.

Mitchell, J.C. (1974) 'Social networks', *Annual Review of Anthropology*, 3: 279–99.

Moir, E. and Hanson, S. (2008) 'The New Teacher Center Forum: developing a community of practice', in A. Lieberman and L. Miller (eds) *Teachers in Professional Communities: Improving Teaching and Learning* (pp. 61–72), New York: Teachers College Press.

Monteiro, E. (2000) 'Actor-network theory and information infrastructure', in C.U. Ciborra (ed.) *From Control to Drift: The Dynamics of Corporate Information Structures* (pp. 71–83), Oxford: Oxford University Press.

Moolenaar, N.M., Daly, A.J. and Sleegers, P.J.C. (forthcoming) 'Ties with potential: social network structure and innovation in Dutch schools', *Teachers College Record*.

Moolenaar, N.M., Karsten, S., Sleegers, P.J.C. and Zijlstra, B.J.H. (2009) 'A social capital perspective on professional learning communities: linking social networks and trust', paper presented at the Annual Meeting of the American Educational Research Association (AERA), San Diego, CA, 13–17 April.

Moore, E. (2009) 'Assessing the changes: an investigation into the middle leader leading change – the implementation of formative assessment', unpublished thesis, The Open University.

Morales, R. and Carmichael, P. (2007) 'Mapping academic collaboration networks: perspectives from the first year of the Reusable Learning Objects CETL', *Journal of Universal Computer Science*, 13(7): 1033–41. Online, available at: www.jucs.org/jucs_13_7/mapping_academic_ collaboration_networks (accessed 11 November 2009).

Moreno, J.L. (1932) *Application of the Group Method to Classification*, New York: National Committee on Prisons and Prison Labor.

Morgan, G. (1997) *Images of Organization*, Thousand Oaks, CA: Sage.

Murphy, P. and McCormick, R. (1997) 'Problem solving in science and technology education', *Research in Science Education*, 27(3): 461–81.

Nardi, B., Whittaker, S. and Schwarz, H. (2000) 'It's not what you know, it's who you know: work in the information age', *First Monday*, 5(5). Online, available at: http://firstmonday. org/htbin/cgiwrap/bin/ojs/index.php/fm/article/view/741/650 (accessed 29 April 2009).

National College for School Leadership [NCSL] (2005) 'Networks (by Ann Lieberman)', Reprinted from *Journal of Staff Development*, 20(3), 1999. Nottingham: NCSL.

National College for School Leadership [NCSL] (undated) *International Perspectives in Networked Learning*, Nottingham: NCSL.

Negri, A. (2007) *Reflections on Empire*, Cambridge: Polity Press.

Negri, A. (2008) *Empire and Beyond*, Cambridge: Polity Press.

Nespor, J. (1994) *Knowledge in Motion: Space, Time and Curriculum in Undergraduate Physics and Management*, London: Falmer Press.

Nespor, J. (1997) *Tangled Up in School: Politics, Space, Bodies, and Signs in the Educational Process*, Hillsdale, NJ: Lawrence Erlbaum.

Networked Learning Group/Centre for the Use of Research Evidence in Education [NLG/CUREE] (2005) *Systematic Research Review: The Impact of Networks on Pupils, Practitioners, Organisations and the Communities They Serve*, Nottingham: National College for School Leadership.

Nielson, K. (1997) 'Musical apprenticeship: trajectories of participation at the Academy of Music', *Journal of Nordic Educational Research*, 17(3): 160–8.

Nonaka, I. and Takeuchi, H. (1995) *The Knowledge-Creating Company*, Oxford: Oxford University Press.

Novak, J.D. and Gowin, D.B. (1984) *Learning How to Learn*, New York: Cambridge University Press.

O'Hair, M.J., Reitzug, U.C., Cate, J., Averso, R., Atkinson, L., Gentry, D., Garn, G. and Jean-Marie, G. (2005) 'Networking for professional learning communities: school–university–community partnerships enhance student achievement', in W. Veugelers and M.J. O'Hair (eds) *Network Learning for Educational Change* (pp. 72–97), Maidenhead, UK: Open University Press.

O'Reilly, T. (2005) 'What is Web 2.0? Design patterns and business models for the next generation of software'. Online, available at: http://oreilly.com/web2/archive/what-is-web-20.html (accessed 1 December 2009).

O'Rourke, S.L. (1999) 'The identification of opinion leadership within the elementary school', unpublished thesis, University of Pittsburgh.

Otis, L. (2001) *Networking: Communicating with Bodies and Machines in the Nineteenth Century*, Ann Arbor: University of Michigan Press.

Paavola, S., Lipponen, L. and Hakkarainen, K. (2004) 'Models of innovative knowledge communities and three metaphors of learning', *Review of Educational Research*, 74(4): 557–76.

Paechter, C. (2004) 'Power relations and staffroom spaces', *Forum*, 46(1): 33–5.

Palmer, L. (2008) 'Connections: a study of leadership and influence', unpublished thesis, University of Pennsylvania.

Palonen, T. and Lehtinen, E. (2001) 'Exploring invisible scientific communities: studying networking relations within an educational research community. A Finnish case', *Higher Education*, 42: 493–513.

Palonen, T., Hakkarainen, K., Talvitie, J. and Lehtinen, E. (2004) 'Network ties, cognitive centrality, and team interaction within a telecommunication company', in H. Gruber, E. Boshuizen and R. Bromme (eds) *Professional Development: Gaps and Transitions on the Way from Novice to Expert* (pp. 273–94), Dordrecht: Kluwer Academic Press.

Parker, A. (1977) 'Networks for innovation and problem solving and their use for improving education: a comparative overview', unpublished manuscript, School Capacity for Problem Solving Group, National Institute of Education, Washington, DC.

Parker, S. and Gallagher, N. (2007) *The Collaborative State: How Working Together Can Transform Public Services*, London: DEMOS.

Passy, F. (2003) 'Social networks matter. But how?', in M. Diani and D. McAdam (eds) *Social Movements and Networks: Relational Approaches to Collective Action* (pp. 21–48), Oxford: Oxford University Press.

Pedder, D. (2006) 'Organizational conditions that foster successful classroom promotion of Learning How to Learn', *Research Papers in Education*, 21(2): 171–200.

Pedder, D., Storey, A. and Opfer, D. (2008) *Synthesis Report: Schools and Continuing Professional Development (CPD) in England – State of the Nation Research Project (T34718)*, a report commissioned by the Training and Development Agency for Schools, Cambridge/Milton Keynes: Cambridge University/Open University. Online, available at: www.tda.gov.uk/ upload/resources/pdf/c/cpd_stateofthenation_report.pdf (accessed 16 September 2009).

Pitts, V.M. and Spillane, J.P. (2009) 'Using social network methods to study school leadership', *International Journal of Research and Method in Education*, 32(2): 185–207.

Pixley, C. (2008). 'A social network analysis of the role negotiations of instructional technology resource teachers', unpublished PhD thesis, George Mason University, Fairfax, VA.

Posch, P. and Mair, M.G. (1997) 'Dynamic networking and community collaboration: the cultural scope of educational action research', in S. Hollingsworth (ed.) *International Action Research: A Casebook for Educational Reform* (pp. 261–74), London: Falmer Press.

Purinton, T.R.-F. (2005). 'Ties that illuminate: A social network analysis of high school teacher collegiality', unpublished thesis, University of Southern California, Los Angeles.

Putnam, R.T. and Borko, H. (2000) 'What do views of knowledge and thinking have to say about research on teacher learning?', *Educational Researcher*, 29(1): 4–15.

Pyka, A. and Küppers, G. (2002) *Innovation Networks: Theory and Practice*, Cheltenham, UK: Edward Elgar.

Rheingold, H. (2000) *The Virtual Community: Homesteading on the Electronic Frontier*, Cambridge, MA: MIT Press. Online, available at: www.rheingold.com/vc/book (accessed 3 December 2009). First published 1993.

Rico, S.A. and Shulman, J.H. (2004) 'Invertebrates and organ systems: science instruction and "Fostering a Community of Learners"', *Journal of Curriculum Studies*, 36(2): 159–81.

Riles, A. (2000) *The Network Inside Out*, Ann Arbor: University of Michigan Press.

Rogoff, B. (1990) *Apprenticeship in Thinking: Cognitive Development in a Social Context*, New York: Oxford University Press.

Rose, G. (1996) 'As if the mirrors had bled: masculine dwelling, masculinist theory and feminist masquerade', in N. Duncan (ed.) *Bodyspace* (pp. 56–74), London: Routledge.

Rudduck, J., Berry, M., Brown, N. and Frost, D. (2000) 'Schools learning from other schools: co-operation in a climate of competition', *Research Papers in Education*, 15(3): 259–74.

Ryberg, T. and Larson, M.C. (2006) 'Networked identities: understanding different types of social organisation and movements between strong and weak ties in networked environments', paper presented at the symposium on Relations in Networks and Networked Learning at the conference Networked Learning 2006, Lancaster: Lancaster University, 10–12 April. Online, available at: www.networkedlearningconference.org.uk/past/nlc2006/abstracts/pdfs/01 Ryberg.pdf (accessed 7 October 2009).

Sack, R. (1980) *Conceptions of Space and Social Thought*, London: Macmillan.

Salleh, H. (2006) 'Action research in Singapore education: constraints and sustainability', *Educational Action Research*, 14(4): 513–23.

Schuler, D. (1996) *New Community Networks: Wired for Change*, San Francisco: Addison-Wesley.

Scott, J. (2002) *Social Networks: Critical Concepts in Sociology*, 4 vols, London: Routledge.

Sfard, A. (1998) 'On two metaphors for learning and the dangers of choosing just one', *Educational Researcher*, 27(2): 4–13.

Sfard, A. (2006) 'Participationist discourse on mathematics learning', in J. Maasz and W. Schloeglmann (eds) *New Mathematics Research and Practice* (pp. 153–70), Rotterdam: Sense Publishers.

Sherin, M.G., Mendez, E.P. and Louis, D.A. (2004) 'A discipline apart: the challenges of "Fostering a Community of Learners" in a mathematics classroom', *Journal of Curriculum Studies*, 36(2): 207–32.

Skilbeck, M. (1976) *School-Based Curriculum Development* (Unit 26, E203 Curriculum Design and Development), Milton Keynes: The Open University.

Slater, M.R. (1991) 'Leadership, social networks, and school performance', unpublished thesis, University of California, Santa Barbara.

Smith, M. and Kollock, P. (1999) *Communities in Cyberspace*, London: Routledge.

Snijders, T.A.B. (1996) 'Teacher's corner: what to do with the upward bias in R2: a comment on Huberty', *Journal of Educational and Behavioral Statistics*, 21(3): 283–7.

Solomon, N., Boud, D. and Rooney, D. (2006) 'The in-between: exposing everyday learning at work', *International Journal of Lifelong Education*, 25(1): 3–13.

Somekh, B. (2009) 'The Collaborative Action Research Network: 30 years of agency in developing educational action research', keynote lecture presented at the CARN Conference, Valladolid, October 2007 (to be published in *Educational Action Research* in 2010).

Somekh, B. and Zeichner, K. (2009) 'Action research for educational reform: remodelling action research theories and practices in local contexts', *Educational Action Research*, 17(1): 5–21.

Southworth, G. (2000) 'How primary schools learn', *Research Papers in Education*, 15(3): 275–91.

Stefanone, M. and Gay, G. (2008) 'Structural reproduction of social networks in computer-mediated communication forums', *Behaviour and Information Technology*, 27(2): 97–106.

Stenhouse, L. (1975) *An Introduction to Curriculum Research and Development*, London: Heinemann.

Stenhouse, L. (1982) 'The conduct, analysis and reporting of case study in educational research and evaluation', in R. McCormick, J. Bynner, P. Clift, M. James and C. Morrow Brown (eds) *Calling Education to Account* (pp. 261–73), London: Heinemann Educational in association with The Open University.

Stodolsky, S.S. (1988) *The Subject Matters: Classroom Activity in Math and Social Studies*, Chicago: University of Chicago Press.

Stodolsky, S.S. and Grossman, P.L. (1995) 'The impact of subject matter on curricular activity: an analysis of five academic subjects', *American Educational Research Journal*, 32(2): 227–49.

Stoll, L. and Louis, K.S. (eds) (2007a) *Professional Learning Communities: Divergence, Depth and Dilemmas*, Maidenhead, UK: Open University Press/McGraw-Hill Education.

Stoll, L. and Louis, K.S. (2007b) 'Professional learning communities: elaborating new approaches', in L. Stoll and K.S. Louis (eds) *Professional Learning Communities: Divergence, Depth and Dilemmas* (pp. 1–13), Maidenhead, UK: Open University Press/McGraw-Hill Education.

Stoll, L., Bolam, R., McMahon, A., Wallace, M. and Thomas, S. (2006) 'Professional learning communities: a review of the literature', *Journal of Educational Change*, 7: 221–58.

Stoll, L., Robertson, J. Butler-Kisber, L., Sklar, S. and Whittingham, T. (2007) 'Beyond borders: can international networks deepen professional learning community?', in L. Stoll and K.S. Louis (eds) *Professional Learning Communities: Divergence, Depth and Dilemmas* (pp. 63–76), Maidenhead, UK: Open University Press/McGraw-Hill Education.

Suchman, L., Blomberg, J., Orr, J.E. and Trigg, R. (1999) 'Reconstructing technologies as social practice', *American Behavioral Scientist*, 43(3): 392–408.

Swaffield, S. (2007) 'Light touch critical friendship', *Improving Schools*, 10(3): 205–19.

Swaffield, S. (2008) 'Critical friendship, dialogue and learning, in the context of Leadership for Learning', *School Leadership and Management*, 28(4): 323–36.

Swaffield, S. and MacBeath, J. (2006) 'Embedding Learning How to Learn in school policy: the challenge for leadership', *Research Papers in Education*, 21(2): 201–16.

Tate, R.C. (1998) 'A study of the value of technical assistance networks as a factor in the diffusion of technological innovations in schools', unpublished thesis, Georgia State University, Atlanta.

Teacher Training Agency [TTA] (2005) *The Teacher Training Agency's Role in the Future of Continuing Professional Development: Response to the Secretary of State*, London: TTA.

Thorpe, M. and Kubiak, C. (2005) 'Working at community boundaries: a micro-analysis of the activist's role in participatory learning networks', *Studies in the Education of Adults*, 37(2): 151–65.

Thorpe, M., McCormick, R., Carmichael, P. and Kubiak, C. (2007) 'Talk in virtual contexts: reflecting on participation and online learning models', *Pedagogy, Culture and Society*, 15(3): 349–66.

Timperley, H. (2008) *Teacher Professional Learning and Development*, Educational Practices series 18, Brussels: International Academy of Education.

Tonso, K.L. (2007) *On the Outskirts of Engineering: Learning Identity, Gender, and Power via Engineering Practice*, Rotterdam: Sense Publishers.

Tripp, D. (2004) 'Teachers' networks: a new approach to the professional development of teachers in Singapore', in C. Day and J. Sachs (eds) *International Handbook on the CPD of Teachers* (pp. 191–214), Maidenhead, UK: Open University Press.

Tuan, Y.-F. (1977) *Space and Place: The Perspective of Experience*, London: Edward Arnold.

Tynjälä, P. (2008) 'Perspectives into learning at the workplace', *Educational Research Review*, 3(2): 130–54.

Valente, T.W. (1995) *Network Models of the Diffusion of Innovations*, Cresskill, NJ: Hampton Press.

Valente, T.W. (2005) 'Network models and methods for studying the diffusion of innovations', in P.J. Carrington, J. Scott and S. Wasserman (eds) *Models and Methods in Social Network Analysis* (pp. 98–116), Cambridge: Cambridge University Press.

Van der Gaag, M.P.J. and Snijders, T.A.B. (2003) 'A comparison of measures for individual social capital', paper presented at the conference 'Creation and returns of Social Capital', Amsterdam, 30–31 October. Online, available at: www.xs4all.nl/~gaag/work/comparison_paper.pdf (accessed 11 November 2009).

Veugelers, W. and O'Hair, M.J. (eds) (2005a) *Network Learning for Educational Change*, Maidenhead, UK: Open University Press.

Veugelers, W. and O'Hair, M.J. (2005b) 'Networking for learning and change', in W. Veugelers and M.J. O'Hair (eds) *Network Learning for Educational Change* (pp. 211–21), Maidenhead, UK: Open University Press.

Veugelers, W. and Zijlstra, H. (2005) 'Keeping school networks fluid: networks in dialogue with educational change', in W. Veugelers and M.J. O'Hair (eds) *Network Learning for Educational Change* (pp. 33–51), Maidenhead, UK: Open University Press.

Vodicka, D. (2007) 'Social capital in schools: teacher trust for school principals and the social networks of teachers', unpublished thesis, Pepperdine University.

Waetjen, D.C. (2005) 'The circle of influence: how trust networks influence professional practice in high schools', unpublished thesis, University of Southern California, Los Angeles.

Warfield, C. (2009) 'A social network analysis of distributed leadership in schools', unpublished thesis, University of Pennsylvania.

Wasserman, S. and Faust, K. (1994) *Social Network Analysis: Methods and Applications*, Cambridge: Cambridge University Press.

Watts, D.J. (1999) *Small Worlds: The Dynamics of Networks between Order and Randomness*, Princeton, NJ: Princeton University Press.

Watts, D.J. (2003) *Six Degrees: The Science of a Connected Age*, New York: W.W. Norton.

Watts, D.J. (2004) 'The "new" science of networks', *Annual Review of Sociology*, 30: 243–70.

Watts, D.J., Dodds, P.S. and Newman, M.E.J. (2002) 'Identity and search in social networks', *Science*, 296: 1302–5.

Wellman, B. (1988) 'Structural analysis: from method and metaphor to theory and substance', in B. Wellman and S.D. Berkowitz (eds) *Social Structures: A Network Approach* (pp. 19–61), Cambridge: Cambridge University Press.

Wellman, B. (2001) 'Physical place and cyberplace: the rise of personalized networking', *International Journal of Urban and Regional Research*, 25(2): 227–52.

Wellman, B. and Berkowitz, S.D. (1988a) 'Introduction: studying social structures', in B. Wellman and S.D. Berkowitz (eds) *Social Structures: A Network Approach* (pp. 1–14), Cambridge: Cambridge University Press.

Wellman, B. and Berkowitz, S.D. (eds) (1988b) *Social Structures: A Network Approach*, Cambridge: Cambridge University Press.

Wellman, B., Carrington, P.J. and Hall, A. (1988) 'Networks as personal communities', in B. Wellman and S.D. Berkowitz (eds) *Social Structures: A Network Approach* (pp. 130–84), Cambridge: Cambridge University Press.

Wenger, E. (1998) *Communities of Practice: Learning, Meaning, and Identity*, Cambridge: Cambridge University Press.

Wenger, E., White, N. and Smith, J.D. (2009) *Digital Habitats: Stewarding Technology for Communities*, Portland, OR: CPsquare.

Whitcomb, J.A. (2004) 'Dilemmas of design and predicaments of practice: adapting the "Fostering a Community of Learners" model in secondary school English language arts classrooms', *Journal of Curriculum Studies*, 36(2): 183–206.

White, H. (1992) *Identity and Control*, Princeton, NJ: Princeton University Press.

Whittle, A. and Spicer, A. (2008) 'Is actor network theory critique?', *Organization Studies*, 29(4): 611–29.

Whyte, W.F. (1943) *Street Corner Society: The Social Structure of an Italian Slum*, Chicago: University of Chicago Press.

Wilson, A., Rimpilainen, S., Skinner, D., Cassidy, C., Christie, D., Coutts, N. and Sinclair, C. (2007) 'Using a virtual research environment to support new models of collaborative and participative research in Scottish education', *Technology, Pedagogy and Education*, 16(3): 289–304.

Wilson, S.M. and Berne, J. (1999) 'Teacher learning and the acquisition of professional knowledge: an examination of research on contemporary professional development', in A. Iran-Nejad and P.D. Pearson (eds) *Review of Research in Education*, 24 (pp. 173–209), Washington, DC: American Educational Research Association.

Women's Business Network (2003) *The Blue Book: A Network Co-ordinator's Guide*. Online, available at: www.equal-works.co.uk/resources/contentfiles/888.pdf (accessed 9 November 2006).

World Café Community (2002) *The World Café presents ... Café to Go*, Whole Systems Associates. Online, available at: http://lmscontent.nscl.org.uk/ECM/documents/36/World%20Cafe%20presents%20Cafe%20to%20go.pdf (accessed 2 November 2009).

Author index

Subject index